Trauma
and
Substance
Abuse

Trauma
and
Substance
Abuse

*Causes, Consequences,
and Treatment of
Comorbid Disorders*

Edited by
PAIGE OUIMETTE AND
PAMELA J. BROWN

American Psychological Association
Washington, DC

First Printing October 2002
Second Printing January 2006

Published by
American Psychological Association
750 First Street, NE
Washington, DC 20002
www.apa.org

To order
APA Order Department
P.O. Box 92984
Washington, DC 20090-2984
Tel: (800) 374-2721
Direct: (202) 336-5510
Fax: (202) 336-5502
TDD/TTY: (202) 336-6123
Online: www.apa.org/books/
Email: order@apa.org

In the U.K., Europe, Aftica, and the Middle East, copies may be ordered from
American Psychological Association
3 Henrietta Street
Covent Garden, London
WC2E 8LU England

Typeset in Goudy by World Composition Services, Inc., Sterling, VA

Printer: United Book Press, Inc., Baltimore, MD
Cover Designer: Naylor Design, Washington, DC
Technical/Production Editor: Jennifer L. Zale

The opinions and statements published are the responsibility of the authors, and such opinions and statements do not necessarily represent the policies of the American Psychological Association.

Library of Congress Cataloging-in-Publication Data
Trauma and substance abuse : causes, consequences, and treatment of comorbid disorders / edited by Paige Ouimette and Pamela J. Brown
    p. cm.
Includes bibliographical references and index.
  ISBN 1-55798-938-9
  1. Post-traumatic stress disorder—Patients—Rehabilitation. 2. Substance abuse—Patients—Rehabilitation. 3. Comorbidity. 4. Psychiatry. I. Ouimette, Paige. II. Brown, Pamela J.
  RC489.C63 T72 2003
  616.85′21—dc21   2002008422

British Library Cataloguing-in-Publication Data
A CIP record is available from the British Library.

Printed in the United States of America

CONTENTS

CONTRIBUTORS

Cynthia L. Battle, PhD, Department of Psychiatry and Human Behavior, Brown University and Butler Hospital, Providence, RI

Andreas R. Bollinger, PhD, VA Boston Healthcare System and Boston University School of Medicine, Boston

Kathleen T. Brady, MD, PhD, Department of Psychiatry and Behavioral Sciences, Medical University of South Carolina, Charleston

Pamela J. Brown, PhD, private practice, New Bedford, MA, and Department of Psychiatry and Human Behavior, Brown University, Providence, RI

Howard D. Chilcoat, ScD, Department of Mental Hygiene, Johns Hopkins Bloomberg School of Public Health, Baltimore

Scott F. Coffey, PhD, Department of Psychiatry, State University of New York at Buffalo

Patricia J. Conrod, PhD, Department of Psychology, University of British Columbia, Vancouver, British Columbia, Canada

Bonnie S. Dansky, PhD, CB Technologies, Inc., Exton, PA

Rose M. Giaconia, PhD, Graduate School of Social Work, Simmons College, Boston

Marysol Gutierrez, BA, Butler Hospital, Providence, RI

Christopher W. Kahler, PhD, Center for Alcohol and Addiction Studies, Brown University, Providence, RI

David Lisak, PhD, Department of Psychology, University of Massachusetts–Boston

Donald Meichenbaum, PhD, Department of Psychology, Waterloo University, Waterloo, Ontario, Canada

Christian Menard, MHS, PhD candidate, Department of Mental Hygiene, Johns Hopkins Bloomberg School of Public Health, Baltimore

Paul M. Miller, PhD, Department of Psychiatry and Human Behavior, Brown Medical School, Providence, RI

Rudolf H. Moos, PhD, Center for Health Care Evaluation, VA Palo Alto Health Care System, Menlo Park, CA, and Department of Psychiatry, Stanford University School of Medicine, Stanford, CA

Lisa M. Najavits, PhD, Department of Psychiatry, Harvard Medical School, Boston, and Trauma Research Program, McLean Hospital, Belmont, MA

Paige Ouimette, PhD, Department of Psychology, Washington State University, Pullman

Angela D. Paradis, BA, Graduate School of Social Work, Simmons College, Boston

Jennifer P. Read, PhD, Center for Alcohol and Addiction Studies, Brown University, Providence, RI

Helen Z. Reinherz, ScD, Graduate School of Social Work, Simmons College, Boston

Josef I. Ruzek, PhD, Education and Clinical Laboratory Division, National Center for Post-Traumatic Stress Disorder, VA Palo Alto Health Care System, Menlo Park, CA

Erica Sharkansky, PhD, Boston VA Medical Center and Women's Health Sciences Division, National Center for Post-Traumatic Stress Disorder, Boston

Cecilia K. Stashwick, BA, Graduate School of Social Work, Simmons College, Boston

Sherry H. Stewart, PhD, Department of Psychology, Dalhousie University, Halifax, Nova Scotia, Canada

Celia Winsor, BS, The Providence Center and Rhode Island Department of Corrections Women's Facility, Cranston

Caron Zlotnick, PhD, Department of Psychiatry and Human Behavior, Brown University and Butler Hospital, Providence, RI

FOREWORD

As the adage goes, one of the tasks of science is to "carve nature at its joints." In the area of developmental psychopathology, this translates into the need to identify distinct mental disorders and to ascertain how they may co-occur. Such co-occurrence of mental disorders, or *comorbidity*, refers to the presence of independent psychiatric disorders. These disorders may be present during the same period of time (concurrent comorbidity), or they may occur during one's life (lifetime comorbidity), thus taking the forms of simultaneous or sequential disorders, respectively. Such comorbidity of mental disorders has been found to be more the rule than the exception, especially in the case of posttraumatic stress disorder (PTSD) and substance use disorder (SUD).

The contributors to this edited volume highlight the critical need of attending to the issue of comorbid PTSD and SUDs. They note the high incidence of comorbidity of PTSD and SUD. Moreover, patients who evidence comorbid disorders of PTSD and SUDs have more severe levels of psychopathology, with greater symptomatology for each disorder; more life stressors (e.g., more medical problems, higher unemployment, higher arrest records); higher health care utilization; less effective coping strategies; and poorer response to treatment than do patients with either PTSD or SUD alone. They are also more likely to experience additional comorbid affective disorders (panic disorders, major depressive disorders), personality disorders, and a record of antisocial and violent behaviors.

Even though the prevalence and incidence and the impact of the comorbid disorders of PTSD and SUD are high, clinicians often fail to systematically assess for SUDs, exposure to trauma, and PTSD. Few patients with PTSD and SUDs receive any type of psychiatric treatment. This is especially troubling when one considers that new innovative integrative treatments now exist that have led to promising results. The recent work discussed in detail in this volume provides a hopeful clarion call for clinicians to systematically assess for comorbid disorders and to implement and evaluate treatment programs.

This valued book is more than a call to action; it is a model on how to study comorbid disorders. I believe that the study of how various comorbid disorders interact and function will help explicate the mechanisms underlying psychopathology. The authors critically evaluate how cross-sectional, life-span prospective, correlational (i.e., studies of the gradient of effects between the severity of two disorders of PTSD and SUDs) studies and differential treatment studies can explicate the complex relationships among the gender of the patients, the nature of the victimization, and the polysubstance abuse. Such research will help investigators to test various models, such as self-medication, high-risk, and susceptibility hypotheses.

The authors highlight the value of adopting a life-span perspective tracking the developmental relationships between comorbid disorders of PTSD and SUDs. Such analyses will go a long way in explicating the pathways and mechanisms of various forms of psychopathology. Kudos to those who conduct such studies, such as the authors of this important book. They will help us to "carve nature at its joints."

—Donald Meichenbaum

Trauma
and
Substance
Abuse

INTRODUCTION

PAMELA J. BROWN AND PAIGE OUIMETTE

Posttraumatic stress disorder (PTSD) is an anxiety disorder the hallmark of which is the development of a pattern of characteristic symptoms following exposure to a traumatic event (e.g., combat, sexual assault, natural disaster, urban violence). The experience of such an event (referred to as a *Criterion A event*) is the first of several diagnostic criteria for PTSD specified by the fourth edition of the *Diagnostic and Statistical Manual for Mental Disorders* (American Psychiatric Association, 1994). Remaining diagnostic criteria specify that such a traumatic event is then followed by a constellation of symptoms, including persistent re-experiencing of the event (Criterion B), avoidance and numbing (Criterion C), and increased physiological arousal (Criterion D). In addition, to receive a diagnosis of PTSD, symptoms must persist for more than 1 month (Criterion E) and must cause clinically significant distress or impairment in functioning (Criterion F).

Substance abuse and dependence disorders (SUDs) refers to a cluster of cognitive, behavioral, and physiological symptoms and maladaptive patterns of substance use that result in recurrent and negative consequences for the individual or for others around him or her or in clinical impairment (American Psychiatric Association, 1994). Symptoms of substance abuse focus on the individual's social, work, or personal role functioning and on harmful consequences. Diagnostic criteria for substance dependence include physical (i.e., tolerance, withdrawal) and psychosocial (e.g., increased time spent using or obtaining the substance; impaired social, occupational, or recreational functioning) symptoms and address an individual's control of and involvement with the substance.

A body of two complementary research literatures has been growing that documents the frequent co-occurrence of these disorders in both community and clinical samples (for reviews, see Brown & Wolfe, 1994; Najavits, Weiss, & Shaw, 1997; Ouimette, Brown, & Najavits, 1998; Stewart, 1996). The suffering associated with SUD–PTSD comorbidity is alarming. These individuals have more psychological and medical comorbidity, including HIV, and poorer functioning, including unemployment and homelessness (Brown, Stout, & Mueller, 1999; Najavits, Weiss, & Shaw, 1999; Ouimette, Ahrens, Moos, & Finney, 1997; Triffleman, Marmar, Delucchi, & Ronfeldt, 1995). Patients with this dual diagnosis comply less with treatment (e.g., Brady, Killeen, Saladin, Dansky, & Becker, 1994) and respond less favorably to treatment (e.g., Ouimette, Ahrens, Moos, & Finney, 1998). It is not surprising that these patients can be a costly burden to the treatment system.

Efforts to evaluate and synthesize the burgeoning literature on comorbid addiction and PTSD problems have been hampered by the schism between the two fields. PTSD and substance use researchers have traditionally worked in mutually exclusive programs and organizations, have received funding from separate government agencies, and have disseminated their findings in different specialized journals and conferences. The failure to cross-disseminate findings may help explain research evidence that addiction treatment providers do not regularly screen for PTSD and do not make appropriate treatment referrals (e.g., Brown, Stout, & Gannon-Rowley, 1998). This book aims to bridge the schism between the addiction and PTSD fields by including contributions and collaborations from experts in both areas.

Part I of this book focuses on the epidemiology and etiology of SUD–PTSD comorbidity. In the first chapter, Howard D. Chilcoat and Christian Menard present an overview of SUD–PTSD epidemiological investigations and potential causal relationships. To help place these findings in context, they provide readers with a brief primer on general concepts, advantages, and limitations associated with epidemiological research. In chapter 2, Sherry H. Stewart and Patricia J. Conrod critique an array of methodologically varied psychosocial research studies that shed light on possible mechanisms underlying causal relations (i.e., functional relations) between SUDs and PTSD. In a complimentary and separate chapter (chapter 3), Conrod and Stewart examine laboratory-based experimental studies that investigate biological and cognitive mechanisms underlying SUD–PTSD comorbidity. David Lisak and Paul M. Miller in chapter 4 elucidate the synergistic associations between the perpetration of violence and childhood trauma, PTSD, and substance abuse. They present a composite case study modeling the causal chain of relationships that begins with childhood abuse and ends in violence.

The topics of assessment and treatment of comorbid SUD–PTSD are covered in Part II of the book. In the first chapter of this section, Paige Ouimette, Rudolf H. Moos, and Pamela J. Brown review empirical research on the course and treatment of SUD–PTSD comorbidity and, on the basis of their review, extrapolate a set of initial working practice guidelines for clinicians treating patients with this dual diagnosis.

In chapter 6, Jennifer P. Read, Andreas R. Bollinger, and Erica Shark-ansky provide a highly practical, detailed guide to the assessment of comorbid

SUD–PTSD and review a variety of measures for interested researchers and practitioners. Recognition of the dialectical interplay of addiction problems and PTSD has led to the evolution of treatments designed to treat both disorders. Hence, two chapters in this book are devoted to describing treatments specifically designed for patients suffering from both SUDs and PTSD. In chapter 7, Scott F. Coffey, Bonnie S. Dansky, and Kathleen T. Brady describe exposure-based treatments, and in chapter 8 Lisa M. Najavits provides an overview of her cognitive–behavioral treatment, Seeking Safety.

In the past few years, findings from several naturalistic, prospective studies of treatment-seeking individuals with SUD–PTSD comorbidity have been reported (e.g., Ouimette, Finney, & Moos, 1999) that offer some insights into the interrelationship of the two disorders and suggest particular treatment options. In chapter 9, Pamela J. Brown, Jennifer P. Read, and Christopher W. Kahler provide a sample of one such study, conducted by Brown and her colleagues, that examined how changes in substance use affect PTSD status and vice versa and that highlights the pivotal role of coping skills in both SUD and PTSD outcomes.

In Part III of the book, attention is given to SUD–PTSD comorbidity among special populations. Given that the substance use–PTSD connection was first recognized in male combatants of the Vietnam war, this section begins with chapter 10, by Josef I. Ruzek, which is devoted to the relevant research among veterans of military service across a variety of military deployments. In chapter 11, Cynthia L. Battle, Caron Zlotnick, Lisa M. Najavits, Marysol Gutierrez, and Celia Winsor summarize empirical findings on SUD–PTSD comorbidity among incarcerated women, a growing population in which these disorders are more than twice as high as rates among women in the general community. Battle and her colleagues describe characteristics of this population; connections among women's victimization, substance use, and criminality; and existing treatments and challenges in addressing these complex, interconnected problems.

In contrast to the burgeoning research with adult populations on the prevalence, course, and impact of SUD–PTSD comorbidity, relatively little research has been conducted with adolescents. In chapter 12, Rose M. Giaconia, Helen Z. Reinherz, Angela D. Paradis, and Cecilia K. Stashwick target this understudied group and review existing comorbidity studies with an eye toward outlining needed research avenues.

We thank the authors for their quality chapters and timely contributions. Their chapters collectively provide a comprehensive inventory of research on SUD–PTSD comorbidity and, whenever possible, offer treatment recommendations and suggestions for future research. We hope that this book, a presentation of this body of work under one cover, will serve as a resource for clinicians, researchers, and students to develop an updated perspective on the causes, consequences, and treatment of SUD–PTSD comorbidity.

I

EPIDEMIOLOGY AND
ETIOLOGICAL ISSUES

1

EPIDEMIOLOGICAL INVESTIGATIONS: COMORBIDITY OF POSTTRAUMATIC STRESS DISORDER AND SUBSTANCE USE DISORDER

HOWARD D. CHILCOAT AND CHRISTIAN MENARD

In this chapter we use an epidemiological perspective to examine the comorbidity between posttraumatic stress disorder (PTSD) and substance use disorders (SUDs). Our primary goal is to present epidemiological evidence of the association between these disorders and potential causal relationships between them. To place these findings in context, we begin the chapter by discussing the unique advantages, as well as the limitations, of epidemiological investigations of the comorbidity between these two disorders. We also present basic epidemiological concepts to guide readers who are less familiar with research in this field. Finally, we address gaps in the epidemiological literature and propose future directions for research in this area.

ADVANTAGES OF EPIDEMIOLOGICAL RESEARCH

Epidemiology involves the study of patterns of disease occurrence in human populations as well as the factors that influence these patterns (Lilienfeld & Stolley, 1994). In the case of SUD–PTSD comorbidity, this typically involves selecting a sample from a defined population, measuring PTSD and substance use outcomes in sampled individuals, and then testing the association between PTSD and SUDs. The populations to be studied can be defined in a variety of ways. For example, in the National Comorbidity Survey (NCS; Kessler, Sonnega, Bromet, Hughes, & Nelson, 1995) a multistage sample that was designed to be representative of the entire U.S. population ages 15–54 years was selected. Populations are typically more narrowly defined. In the Epidemiologic Catchment Area Study (ECA;

Helzer, Robins, & McEvoy, 1987), respondents were sampled from five sites across the country: New Haven, CT; Baltimore, MD; Durham, NC; Los Angeles, CA; and St. Louis, MO. In their study of the comorbidity of PTSD and SUDs, Cottler, Compton, Mager, Spitznagel, and Janca (1992) restricted their analysis to the St. Louis sample, because information about PTSD was not collected at the other sites. Breslau et al. (Breslau, Davis, & Andreski, 1995; Breslau, Davis, Andreski, & Peterson, 1991) focused on a sample of young adults (ages 21–30 years) randomly selected from the enrollment list of a major health maintenance organization in southeast Michigan. Other researchers (e.g., Kulka et al., 1990; McFall, Mackay, & Donovan, 1992) have used samples selected from the Vietnam veteran population.

A hallmark of epidemiological studies is that they allow inferences to be made about specific populations. To make such inferences, and to reduce the potential for bias, it is critical that the study sample be representative of the defined population. This is accomplished by drawing a sample from the population, using a variety of sampling schemes (e.g., simple random sample, stratified random sample, complex multistage sample), and then maximizing the response rates from the selected sample. Response rates for some of the major epidemiological studies of PTSD and SUDs range around 80% (e.g., ECA: 67% of original target population [Helzer et al., 1987]; NCS: 82.4% [Kessler et al., 1995]; Detroit study of young adults: 83.9% [Breslau et al., 1991]). Failure to attain a sufficient response rate increases the likelihood that the individuals who participate in the study are different in some way from the targeted population, thereby increasing the potential for bias.

The reduced risk of self-selection is one of the key advantages of epidemiological studies over clinical studies that sample treatment-seeking individuals. The potential for bias in clinical samples is an important consideration, which Berkson (1946) demonstrated mathematically. This selection bias can occur when exposure to a risk factor is associated with whether an individual enters a hospital or other setting to obtain treatment for a disorder. Studies of comorbidity are especially vulnerable to this type of bias, because the presence of a comorbid disorder could increase the likelihood that an individual with another disorder might seek treatment. For example, an individual who has PTSD and then develops an SUD might be more likely to seek treatment for PTSD relative to someone with PTSD that is of comparable severity and who does not have an SUD. In this case, a comparison of the prevalence of SUDs among individuals seeking treatment for PTSD to the prevalence among those in a control group who have not sought psychiatric treatment could lead to inflated estimates of the association between PTSD and SUDs.

Despite the possibility of selection bias, studies in which treatment samples are used can yield fruitful results. For example, knowledge about the prevalence of PTSD in individuals seeking treatment for SUDs is essential for developing services needed to provide effective addiction treatment. Similarly, evidence that a large number of people who seek treatment for PTSD have a comorbid SUD would suggest a need for drug treatment services and that clinicians who treat PTSD patients should take a careful substance use history and offer treatment when appropriate. However, clinical studies cannot provide valid estimates of the prevalence of disorders and comorbidity in the general population. Epidemiological studies can provide such evidence, which is of great importance given that only a small percentage of patients who experience PTSD seek treatment (Kessler et al., 1995).

There are a number of reasons for using epidemiological studies to assess the comorbidity between PTSD and SUDs. As stated previously, quantitative estimates of the comorbidity between these disorders can provide important information about the need for services in a population. Furthermore, epidemiological studies can provide clues about causal pathways between PTSD and SUDs.

TYPES OF STUDIES

In general, epidemiologists are forced to rely on observational studies in their efforts to estimate and to understand the comorbidity between PTSD and SUDs. For obvious ethical reasons it is not possible to conduct experimental studies to assess this comorbidity. Although experimental studies are not feasible, the fact that PTSD requires, by definition, exposure to a traumatic event, provides opportunities to study natural experiments, such as when a population is exposed to the same traumatic event. Examples of this include natural disaster (McMillen, North, & Smith, 2000), combat or war atrocities (Kulka et al., 1990), and other tragic events, such as fires (Maes et al., 1998) or bombing (North et al., 1999).

An overview of several epidemiological studies of SUD–PTSD comorbidity is presented in Table 1.1. In the following discussion, we have organized these studies into three categories: (a) cross-sectional, (b) prospective, and (c) natural experiments. We recognize that these categories might overlap. For example, prospective studies often have a cross-sectional component (e.g., Breslau et al., 1991). Each of these study types has unique advantages and disadvantages that must be considered when evaluating study findings.

Cross-Sectional Studies

In cross-sectional studies, a random sample is selected from a specified population at one point in time (Lilienfeld & Stolley, 1994). Information

TABLE 1.1

Summary of Epidemiological Studies of Substance Use Disorder
(SUD)–Posttraumatic Stress Disorder (PTSD) Comorbidity

Citation	Sample description	Findings
Community-based samples		
Cottler et al. (1992); Helzer et al. (1987)	Epidemiologic Catchment Area: men and women ($N = 2,663$)	RO = 2.63 Average age of first substance use predated average age of PTSD onset
Kessler et al. (1995)	National Comorbidity Survey: men and women ages 15–54 years ($N = 5,877$)	RO for alcohol A/D, men = 2.06 RO for drug A/D, men = 2.97 RO for alcohol A/D, women = 2.48 RO for drug A/D, women = 4.46 Comorbid cases of SUD and PTSD in which PTSD was the primary disorder: 52.7%–65.3% in men and 65.1%–84.3% in women
Giaconia et al. (1995, 2000)	Men and women age 18 years ($N = 384$)	RO for alcohol dependence = 4.25 RO for drug dependence = 8.80 Comorbid cases of SUD and PTSD in which PTSD was the primary disorder: 66.7% for drugs and 45.5% for alcohol
Chilcoat & Breslau (1998a, 1998b)	Men and women ages 21–30 years (baseline; $N = 1,007$)	RO for any SUD = 3.0 Relative risk of SUD in PTSD+ vs. PTSD– at baseline = 4.4 Relative hazards of prescribed drug A/D in PTSD+ vs. PTSD– = 13.0 No difference in the odds of trauma for PTSD in SUD+ vs. SUD– at baseline
Kilpatrick et al. (2000)	Males and females ages 12–17 years ($N = 4,023$)	RO for alcohol A/D = 3.98 RO for marijuana A/D = 6.17 RO for drug A/D = 8.68 Average age of victimization less than average age of substance onset

(continued)

on exposure to traumatic events, PTSD symptoms linked to specific events, substance use, and problems related to use (e.g., *Diagnostic and Statistical Manual of Mental Disorders* [4th ed.; *DSM–IV*; American Psychiatric Association, 1994] symptoms of abuse or dependence, as well as risk factors and respondent characteristics) are collected at the same time. Structured diagnostic interviews (e.g., the Diagnostic Interview Schedule [DIS]; Robins, Helzer, Cottler, & Golding, 1989), or checklists (PTSD checklist; Najavits,

TABLE 1.1
(Continued)

Citation	Sample description	Findings
Combat-exposed samples		
McFall et al. (1992)	Vietnam vets, combat exposed or not exposed; men (N = 259)	Combat-exposed men with PTSD experienced more severe substance problems than those without PTSD; re-experiencing and avoidance/numbing more strongly associated with drug abuse; physiological arousal associated with alcohol abuse
Reifman & Windle (1996)	Combat-exposed Vietnam veterans; men (N = 2,400)	Combat exposure significantly related to recent drug use, controlling for Army drug use and demographic factors
Boscarino (1995)	Vietnam veterans, combat exposed or not exposed; men (N = 4,462)	Combat exposure was not associated with alcohol or drug abuse
Disaster studies		
North et al. (1999)	Victims of Oklahoma City bombing; men and women ages 18 years and older (N = 182)	Occurrence of PTSD linked to bombing in relation to preexisting SUD: alcohol, 37.5%; drugs, 41.5%; no prior disorder, 27.0%

Note. Odds ratios presented are adjusted for covariates that differ across studies. RO = relative odds of SUD in individuals with versus without PTSD (PTSD+/PTSD–). A/D = abuse/dependence.

Weiss, Reif, et al., 1998) measure exposure to traumatic events, PTSD symptoms, and alcohol/drug use symptoms. Cross-sectional studies can measure symptoms that are present at the time of the interview and can use retrospective reports of events and symptoms, covering the respondent's lifetime.

On the basis of current measures and retrospective reports, cross-sectional studies provide estimates of the prevalence of exposure to traumatic events, PTSD, and SUDs, as well as the associations between them. *Prevalence* is defined as the proportion of the population with "disease" (or specified outcome) in a specified period of time (Lilienfeld & Stolley, 1994). In epidemiological studies of psychiatric disorders, commonly used estimates of prevalence include lifetime, past-year, and past-month prevalence. With a simple random sample, lifetime prevalence of traumatic exposure is estimated by the number of respondents who ever were exposed to a traumatic event divided by the total number of respondents in the sample. For example,

Breslau et al. (1991) found that 394 individuals out of 1,007 respondents reported that they had been exposed to a traumatic event at some point in their lifetime, yielding a lifetime prevalence of 39.1% (394 ÷ 1,007). Similarly, past-year prevalence is estimated by the proportion of respondents who were exposed to a traumatic event in the year prior to the interview. Prevalence estimates are extremely useful for understanding the extent of disease and the need for services in a population.

Despite their usefulness, prevalence estimates should be considered with caution. These estimates can vary considerably across studies because of factors such as the use of different instruments to measure disorders and case definitions, which have varied over time with the transition from *DSM–III* (American Psychiatric Association, 1980) to *DSM–III–R* (American Psychiatric Association, 1987) to *DSM–IV* (American Psychiatric Association, 1994). For example, the ECA and NCS have yielded remarkably different estimates of the prevalence of several major mental disorders, which could not be accounted for by differences in sample characteristics (Regier et al., 1998). Chilcoat and Breslau (1999) tested the level of agreement of measures of SUDs using the DIS and the University of Michigan Composite International Diagnostic Interview (UM–CIDI; Kessler et al., 1994), which were used in the ECA and NCS studies, respectively. Respondents were administered the SUD sections of both instruments in the same assessment session. The DIS tended to produce higher estimates of past-year prevalence of alcohol and marijuana disorders than the UM–CIDI, and agreement between the instruments, assessed using the kappa statistic (Fleiss, 1981) was modest at best. Because no "gold standard" exists for diagnosing psychiatric disorders, it is necessary to rely on self-reports of psychiatric symptomatology. It appears that different instruments used to elicit these responses might have different thresholds for defining a respondent as a case, which is then reflected in the prevalence estimates. Although prevalence estimates vary by diagnostic instrument used to assess psychiatric disorders, measures of association appear to be more robust. For example, Chilcoat and Breslau (1999) found that the magnitude of associations with risk factors and comorbid psychiatric disorders were nearly identical regardless of whether the DIS or UM–CIDI measures of SUDs were used.

Changes in diagnostic criteria also can have an impact on prevalence estimates. For example, the stressor criterion (Criterion A) broadened considerably in the transition from *DSM–III–R* (American Psychiatric Association, 1987) to *DSM–IV* (American Psychiatric Association, 1994). Using *DSM–IV* criteria, Breslau et al. (1998) found nearly universal exposure (prevalence = 89.6%) to a qualifying traumatic event, yielding prevalence estimates that were considerably higher than those found in studies based on *DSM–III–R* criteria (Breslau et al., 1991, 1995).

Estimates of Comorbidity

In cross-sectional studies, there are a number of ways to estimate the comorbidity between PTSD and SUDs. Depending on the research focus, it is possible to compare the prevalence of SUDs in respondents with versus without PTSD or, conversely, to compare the prevalence of PTSD by presence of SUDs. This strategy requires selecting one disorder as the outcome and the other as the predictor. An alternative approach, which does not require selecting one disorder over the other as the outcome or predictor, is to estimate *odds ratios* (ORs), or relative odds, which are used widely in epidemiological studies. To illustrate the use of ORs, we present data from an epidemiological study of young adults (Table 1.2; Chilcoat & Breslau, 1998a). As the name implies, an OR is simply a ratio of odds. Using Table 1.2 as an example, we first compare the odds of drug use disorders by PTSD status. The odds of SUDs in individuals with PTSD are 34/83; the corresponding odds estimate for those without PTSD is 106/784. The ratio of the odds is $(34/83) \div (106/784) = 3.03$. Therefore, the odds of drug use disorders are three times greater in individuals with versus without PTSD. To estimate the OR of PTSD by drug use disorder status, we estimate the odds of PTSD for individuals with drug use disorder (34/106) and for those without (83/784). The OR is $(34/106) \div (83/784) = 3.03$. Thus, the OR provides an estimate of comorbidity that is equivalent regardless of which disorder is selected as the outcome. Statistical models, such as logistic regression, can estimate adjusted ORs taking multiple variables into account and controlling for potential confounding of key relationships. *Confounding* occurs when the relationship between two variables is due to the presence of a third variable that relates to each but is not positioned along the causal pathway between them. For example, an observed association between PTSD and SUDs could be accounted for by conduct disorder, which has been linked to both of these disorders.

In the following section we present findings from cross-sectional studies, emphasizing findings from community-based samples. Epidemiological research on the comorbidity between PTSD and drug use disorders unfortu-

TABLE 1.2
Number of Respondents by Posttraumatic Stress Disorder
(PTSD) and Drug Abuse/Dependence (A/D) Status

	Drug A/D	
PTSD	Present	Absent
Present	34	83
Absent	106	784

Note. Based on Chilcoat and Breslau (1998a).

nately is relatively sparse. Few reports have focused explicitly on interrelationships between these disorders. Instead, this comorbidity often is examined in the context of the comorbidity of PTSD with several psychiatric disorders.

ECA Survey

The ECA (Helzer et al., 1987) included the first noninstitutionalized population survey of PTSD prevalence. Helzer et al. (1987) assessed the prevalence of PTSD among a sample of 2,943 participants in St. Louis, MO. The sample reflected the demographics of both rural and urban areas around St. Louis. The authors assessed PTSD using the DIS (Robins et al., 1989), a highly structured instrument that can be administered by trained lay interviewers. Diagnoses were based on criteria from *DSM–III* (American Psychiatric Association, 1980). They assessed respondents' trauma histories using the DIS's standard open-ended question, accepting responses that met *DSM–III* Criterion A, which stipulated that a qualifying event be "a psychologically traumatic event that is generally outside the range of usual human experience."

Helzer et al. (1987) estimated the lifetime prevalence of PTSD to be 0.5% among men and 1.3% among women, or 1% overall. Vietnam veterans who were wounded in combat experienced the highest prevalence of PTSD at 20%. Delayed onset of PTSD at least 6 months following traumatic exposure was reported only among Vietnam combat veterans and only among 16% of that group. About one third of respondents who experienced PTSD reported persistence over 3 or more years.

With respect to comorbidity, Helzer et al. (1987) reported the relative odds of experiencing a drug disorder among respondents with PTSD compared with those without PTSD to be 2.2 (5.0 among men and 1.4 among women). They reported the relative risk of experiencing alcoholism among respondents with PTSD compared with those without PTSD to be 1.6 (1.9 among men and 2.8 among women).

Cottler et al. (1992) conducted further analyses of PTSD and drug use comorbidity using the ECA data and found that substance users were more likely to report traumatic events than nonusers (OR = 1.83). ORs varied considerably across drug types. Polydrug and cocaine/opiate users were most likely to report a traumatic event (OR = 5.06, statistically significant); alcoholics were not significantly more likely than nonusers to report a trauma. Substance users were also significantly more likely to experience PTSD than nonusers (OR = 2.63). PTSD was most common among cocaine/opiate users (OR = 10.75). Among only those respondents who reported a trauma, cocaine/opiate users remained significantly more likely to experience PTSD than nonusers (OR = 3.62). Conversely, users of marijuana only were less likely than nonusers to experience PTSD (OR = 0.27), although the result was not statistically significant.

Cottler et al. (1992) reported that, on average, drug use significantly predated the development of PTSD. It deserves mention that they defined the onset of drug use as the age at first drug use rather than the age at which problems related to drug use developed. The onset of use can precede the development of problems by several years. As a result, there is a potential for bias in comparisons of age at onset of PTSD versus age at onset of drug use when age at first drug use is used rather than age at problem onset. When age, race, gender, history of antisocial personality disorder, depression, and substance use pattern were entered into logistic regression as independent variables, only female gender and cocaine/opiate use significantly predicted PTSD.

NCS

Kessler et al. (1995) collected data from a representative national, noninstitutionalized sample of 5,877 men and women between ages 15 and 54 years. They used *DSM–III–R* criteria. They assessed comorbid disorders using the UM–CIDI, which is a structured interview administered by trained lay interviewers. They assessed PTSD using the Revised DIS (Robins et al., 1989); however, the trauma history segment was modified. Rather than asking the two standard open-ended trauma history questions, the NCS researchers asked about each of 12 trauma types individually. In addition, participants were asked to respond by a number assigned to each trauma type, not by name, to minimize their discomfort and to increase responsivity. Psychological sequelae were assessed for the one trauma, when multiple traumas were reported, that the respondent nominated as most upsetting. This practice deviates from the Revised DIS, which stipulates that the interviewer assess up to three traumas. It was implemented as a time- and cost-saving option and because Kessler et al. (1995) reasoned that the most upsetting trauma would be most likely to produce PTSD. However, as Kessler et al. (1995) noted, this practice yielded lower bound estimates of lifetime prevalence of PTSD.

The NCS generated a lifetime PTSD prevalence estimate of 5.0% among men and 10.4% among women, or 7.8% overall. The NCS also yielded far higher estimates of lifetime prevalence of trauma exposure and of the risk of developing PTSD conditioned on trauma type than did the ECA. Lifetime prevalence of trauma exposure was estimated to be 60.7% among men and 51.2% among women. The majority of those who reported one trauma reported multiple traumas. Overall, the risk of developing PTSD conditioned on trauma exposure was estimated to be 8.1% among men and 20.4% among women. Again, the conditional risk of developing PTSD varied by trauma type. The highest conditional risk was associated with rape (65% among men and 45.9% among women). Trauma types that involved interpersonal violence, in general, demonstrated higher conditional risks of PTSD development than did other trauma types. Combat was most frequently associated with PTSD in men; sexual assault (rape or molestation) was most frequently associated with PTSD in women. PTSD proved more persistent in the NCS than in the ECA. The median time to remission was 36 months among treatment seekers and 64 months among those who did not seek treatment.

With respect to comorbidity, the vast majority of respondents (88% of men and 79% of women) who experienced PTSD experienced at least one comorbid disorder. Among both men and women, the relative odds of experiencing either an alcohol disorder or a drug disorder among those who experienced PTSD compared with those who did not were statistically significant. Among men, the OR for an alcohol disorder was 2.06, and the OR for a drug disorder was 2.97. Among women, the ORs for an alcohol disorder and a drug use disorder were 2.48 and 4.46, respectively.

Using date of disorder onset reports, Kessler et al. (1995) estimated upper and lower bounds for the proportion of comorbid PTSD and SUDs in which PTSD occurred first. Among men, the estimates ranged from 52.7% to 65.3%; among women, the estimates ranged from 65.1% to 84.3%. These results suggest that PTSD predates SUD in the majority of individuals who experience both PTSD and an SUD. The primacy of PTSD was further supported in later analyses conducted by Kessler (2000), who found that an increased risk of developing a secondary disorder existed, on average, only when individuals experienced an active disorder. The increased risk abated once PTSD entered remission.

Early Adulthood Research Project (Giaconia et al., 1995; 2000; chapter 12, this volume)

The preceding studies focused entirely or predominantly on adults. The Early Adulthood Research Project (EARP) focused exclusively on adolescents (Giaconia et al., 1995, 2000). Giaconia and her colleagues collected data from 384 eighteen-year-olds. These adolescents have been participants in an ongoing longitudinal study that began when they were 5 years of age. Although these data were collected in the context of a longitudinal study, information on PTSD and SUDs was collected only at the age-18 assessment; consequently, data on SUD–PTSD comorbidity are cross-sectional. The sample contained a largely homogeneous group with respect to ethnicity and socioeconomic status. The authors assessed PTSD and SUDs using the Revised DIS. They assessed trauma history using the standard open-ended question of the DIS. The interviewers collected data on up to three traumas.

Equal proportions of men and women (42.8% vs. 43.2%) in the sample had experienced at least one qualifying trauma. Only 2.1% of men had experienced PTSD, whereas 10.5% of women had experienced PTSD. These findings indicate that women's odds of experiencing PTSD were 5.59 times greater than the odds for men. In a qualitative sense, this gender difference mirrors those found in the ECA and the NCS; however, the magnitude of the gender difference appears far greater in this young sample. Overall, these figures translated into a 14.5% risk of developing PTSD conditioned on trauma exposure.

With respect to comorbidity, every association that was tested proved statistically significant. In a comparison of respondents who qualified for a lifetime PTSD diagnosis with those with no trauma exposure the ORs for lifetime alcohol dependence diagnosis and drug dependence were 4.25 and 8.80, respectively, and OR estimates for lifetime alcohol and drug dependence for those with trauma exposure (without PTSD) compared with those with no exposure were 2.30 and 4.62, respectively. OR estimates comparing individuals with lifetime PTSD with those with no trauma exposure were 3.23 for current (past-year) alcohol dependence and 14.14 for current drug dependence. Exposure to trauma in the past year signaled a twofold increase in odds of current alcohol dependence and an eightfold increase in odds of current drug dependence relative to no trauma exposure. There was no clear temporal sequence of PTSD and SUDs: 66.7% of respondents with comorbid PTSD and drug dependence and 45.5% of those with comorbid PTSD and alcohol dependence experienced PTSD onset prior to the onset of the SUD.

National Survey of Adolescents (Kilpatrick et al., 2000)

Kilpatrick et al. (2000) collected data from a national sample of 4,023 adolescents of both genders between ages 12 and 17 years, oversampling minority respondents. They assessed SUDs using a structured clinical interview designed by Kilpatrick and assessed PTSD using a modified version of an instrument designed for the National Women's Study (Resnick, Kilpatrick, Dansky, Saunders, & Best, 1993). Both instruments were designed to reflect *DSM–IV* criteria. Unlike the methods used in most epidemiological surveys, the National Women's Study method did not require respondents to link PTSD symptoms to a specific trauma. Victims were considered to be exposed to trauma and to meet Criterion A if they reported experiencing at least one sexual assault, physical assault, or indirect victimization event (Kilpatrick et al., 2000; Resnick et al., 1993). Kilpatrick et al. (2000) also collected data on age of onset of nonexperimental drug use, detailed sexual assault and physical assault history, detailed witnessed violence history, and familial (i.e., family-of-origin) alcohol and drug problems. They found that 7% of the sample met diagnostic criteria for an SUD, 47% reported a history of victimization, and 5% reported current PTSD. They analyzed alcohol abuse/dependence, marijuana abuse/dependence, and hard drug abuse/dependence in separate regression analyses. In each analysis, they regressed the SUD onto demographic variables, familial substance use, trauma history, and PTSD.

Alcohol abuse/dependence was associated with familial alcohol problems (OR = 2.13), physical assault history (OR = 1.71), sexual assault history (OR = 2.40), witnessed violence (OR = 2.73), and PTSD (OR = 1.56). Similar associations were found for marijuana abuse/dependence (familial drug problems, OR = 2.11; physical assault history, OR = 1.76; witnessed violence, OR = 4.58; and PTSD, OR = 2.86) and for hard drug abuse/dependence (familial alcohol problems, OR = 2.57; familial drug problems OR = 2.54; physical assault history, OR = 3.28; sexual assault history, OR = 2.56; witnessed violence, OR = 4.15; and PTSD, OR = 2.41).

Kilpatrick et al. (2000) did not present findings regarding the order of onset of comorbid SUD and PTSD, although they did examine onset of substance use in relation to victimization status. In a comparison of the average age of nonexperimental alcohol use, ages of onset for victimized and nonvictimized adolescents were 14.4 and 15.1 years, respectively, a difference that approached statistical significance. Corresponding ages of onset of nonexperimental marijuana use among victimized and nonvictimized adolescents were 13.4 and 14.8 years, respectively, a statistically significant difference. Kilpatrick et al. (2000) were unable to make a similar comparison for hard drug use, because 28 of the 29 hard drug users in their sample reported victimization. Among the hard-drug-using group, the average age of nonexperimental onset was 13.1 years. Although these differences, alone, do not indicate whether substance use increases the risk of victimization or whether victimization increases the risk of substance use, they do indirectly favor the latter hypothesis in light of the finding that the average age of victimization was 11.6 years.

The evidence of SUD–PTSD comorbidity from these cross-sectional studies is remarkably consistent. Although the magnitude of the association varies across studies, each indicates a significant level of comorbidity between PTSD and SUD. Thus, it appears that these disorders are likely to co-occur within individuals. Based on retrospective reports of age of onset of PTSD and SUD, most studies indicate that PTSD tends to precede the onset of SUD, although there are a considerable number of cases in which SUD comes first. Because cross-sectional studies measure both disorders at only one point in time, control of temporal sequencing of disorders, as well as of risk factors, is difficult. In addition, assessment of PTSD and SUD in the same interview session introduces the possibility of response bias, in which respondents differ in their thresholds for reporting symptoms or display a tendency to endorse symptoms. Such a bias would tend to inflate estimates of an association between these disorders. The use of prospective studies overcomes some of the limitations of cross-sectional studies and can fill some of the gaps in researchers' understanding of causal relationships between these disorders.

Prospective Studies

Prospective studies offer many advantages over cross-sectional studies. Most significantly, they allow investigators to gain a greater degree of control over the temporal sequencing of these disorders—a necessary, but not sufficient, condition for causality. Despite their distinct advantages, there is a dearth of prospective studies that have investigated the comorbidity between PTSD and SUD.

Although cross-sectional studies enable estimation of the prevalence of a disease, they provide little information about the risk of a disorder over a specific period of time. Prospective studies, on the other hand, provide direct estimates of risk, because they can measure the incidence of a disease. *Incidence* is defined as the number of new cases of disease in a specified time period divided by the number of individuals at risk for the disease. Epidemiological studies typically set out to compare the incidence of disease in individuals exposed versus not exposed to a specified risk factor. The ratio of the incidence of disease, known as the *relative risk*, in the exposed versus not-exposed groups provides a measure of the effect of the exposure. Most important, because exposure is measured prior to the incidence of disease, the temporal sequence of exposure and disease is known.

In the only longitudinal analysis of data from a community-based sample, Chilcoat and Breslau (1998a) conducted a 5-year longitudinal study of PTSD using a sample drawn from a health maintenance organization in southeast Michigan. Of the 1,007 participants who completed assessment at baseline when they were between ages 21 and 30 years, 955 (95%) completed follow-up assessments 3 and 5 years later. These data were used to investigate causal pathways between PTSD and drug abuse/dependence.

Chilcoat and Breslau (1998a) sought to investigate three predominant hypotheses that had been proposed to explain the consistent findings around PTSD and substance use comorbidity (Brown & Wolfe, 1994). In brief, the three hypotheses were:

1. *Self-medication hypothesis:* Individuals with PTSD use psycho-active substances in an attempt to control painful symptoms (Brown & Wolfe, 1994; Khantzian, 1985; Stewart, 1996).
2. *High-risk hypothesis:* Drug use is a high-risk behavior that increases individuals' risk of exposure to trauma.
3. *Susceptibility hypothesis:* Drug users become more susceptible to PTSD following trauma exposure.

The authors recognized the possibility that no direct relationship exists between PTSD and SUDs and that the association appears because both conditions derive from a third, common factor (e.g., conduct disorder, genetics, common psychosocial or neurological deficit).

The sample of respondents at risk for the incidence of SUD consisted of those with no history of drug abuse/dependence at the time of the baseline interview. One hundred ten respondents had a history of drug abuse/dependence at baseline, leaving 845 at risk for onset of drug abuse/dependence during the 5-year follow-up interval. As shown in Table 1.3, preexisting PTSD signals an increased risk of drug abuse/dependence. The incidence of drug abuse/dependence was four times higher for respondents with versus without a history of PTSD (adjusted relative odds = 4.4; 95% confidence interval [CI] = 1.6–12.0).

Regardless of their exposure to traumatic events at baseline, all respondents were at risk for a traumatic event during the 5-year follow-up interval. Incidence of exposure to traumatic events in this interval was nearly identical for those with (n = 110) and without (n = 845) a history of drug abuse/dependence at baseline (25.5% vs. 24.7%, respectively).

The final stage of the prospective analysis compared the risk of PTSD by history of drug abuse/dependence. Because PTSD can occur only in individuals who have been exposed to a traumatic event, this analysis was limited to the 237 respondents who reported a traumatic event in the 5-year follow-up interval. Preexisting SUD (n = 28) signaled a slight, but not statistically significant, increase in risk of PTSD, relative to those without SUD (n = 207; 14.3% vs. 10.5%, respectively). Adjusted for age, sex, race, and education, there was no significant difference in risk (adjusted relative odds = 1.7; 95% CI = 0.52–5.6), although the small number of respondents with drug abuse/dependence at baseline who were exposed to a traumatic event during the follow-up interval (n = 28) limited the precision of this estimate. The association remained unchanged after adjustment for history of alcohol abuse/dependence.

TABLE 1.3

Incidence of Drug Abuse/Dependence (A/D) in 5-Year Follow-Up Interval by History of Posttraumatic Stress Disorder (PTSD) at Baseline

PTSD	n	Incidence of drug A/D (%)	Relative odds (95% CI)[a]
Present	70	8.6	4.4 (1.6–12.0)
Absent	775	2.2	1.0

Note. CI = confidence interval. From "Investigations of Causal Pathways Between PTSD and Drug Use Disorders" by H. D. Chilcoat and N. Breslau, 1998a, Addictive Behaviors, 23, p. 832. Copyright 1998 by Elsevier Science. Reprinted by permission.
[a]Adjusted for age, sex, race, and education.

Overall, these findings provide the greatest support for the self-medication hypothesis. There was a fourfold increase in the risk of SUD for respondents with a history of PTSD compared with those without PTSD. On the other hand, failure of drug abuse/dependence to signal increased risk of traumatic events or PTSD provided little evidence in favor of the high-risk or vulnerability hypotheses.

Despite the advantages of the prospective approach in Chilcoat and Breslau's (1998a) study, some important limitations deserve mention. First, because the analysis was based on a sample of 21- to 30-year-olds followed for a 5-year interval, the findings cannot be generalized beyond the period of young adulthood. This is an important consideration, especially in light of the strong empirical evidence that much of the incidence of drug abuse/dependence occurs prior to young adulthood (Warner, Kessler, Hughes, Anthony, & Nelson, 1995). Second, to gain control over the temporal sequencing, it was necessary to fix respondents' risk factors on the basis of their status at baseline; changes from baseline status during the follow-up interval were not addressed. For example, in the analysis comparing risk of drug abuse/dependence, respondents' baseline PTSD status was fixed on the basis of their lifetime history of PTSD at the baseline interview. Some of the respondents with a negative history of PTSD could have had an onset of PTSD during the follow-up period. Such a change from baseline status would not be accounted for in this analysis. To effectively address these limitations, it would be necessary to begin collecting prospective data, starting at a very young age and at very regular intervals (e.g., monthly). However ideal it may be, collecting data in childhood and at regular intervals over a long period of time can be prohibitively expensive. An alternative strategy would be to combine retrospective reports at baseline with data gathered prospectively at follow-up and use a survival analytic strategy to study events occurring across the life span.

In a *survival analysis* the time to an event is studied and can be applied to a variety of discrete outcomes that have a definite onset. In general, survival analysis enables the "survival" with respect to an outcome of interest to be compared across different groups. It offers two main advantages over conventional statistical approaches: it (a) accounts for censoring and (b) enables the inclusion of time-dependent covariates. *Censoring* occurs when follow-up of an observation ends before the occurrence of the outcome, either because of participant dropout or termination of the study. In survival analysis observations contribute information until the time that the event occurs or the time of censoring. Time-dependent covariates are an especially powerful feature of survival models because they take into account the variation in the timing of dependent and independent variables and because they enable the status of independent variables in a survival model to change over time. The use of time-dependent covariates permits the incorporation of covariate status changes during follow-up. In Figure 1.1 an example is depicted in which individuals can have different patterns of onset of PTSD and SUD over time. The first line depicts an observation in which a traumatic event occurs, followed by rapid onset of PTSD, with later onset of SUD. In a Cox proportional-hazards model in which drug abuse or dependence is defined as the outcome, this observation would initially contribute information as being negative for exposure to trauma and PTSD and then would contribute information as positive for each interval following exposure and subsequent PTSD. The second observation was negative for trauma and PTSD prior to the onset of SUD, at which time follow-up effectively ends in a survival analytic framework. The third observation switches from negative to positive for both trauma and PTSD until the end of follow-up, when it becomes censored.

Extending their prospective analyses, Chilcoat and Breslau (1998b) combined retrospective data collected at baseline and longitudinal data collected at the 3- and 5-year follow-ups, which provided a history of PTSD and drug abuse/dependence across each respondent's lifetime. Three sets of Cox proportional-hazards models estimated hazard ratios in which SUD, PTSD, and trauma exposure were treated as distinct outcomes. PTSD signaled increased risk of SUD: The relative hazard for developing drug abuse/dependence among individuals with PTSD compared with those not exposed to a traumatic event was 4.5 (95% CI = 2.6–7.6). On the other hand, respondents who were exposed to a traumatic event but did not develop PTSD had no increase in risk relative to those without traumatic exposure. Drug abuse/dependence signaled a slight increase of risk of subsequent PTSD (relative hazard = 1.6; 95% CI = 0.9–2.9) but no increase in risk of traumatic exposure (relative hazard = 1.0; 95% CI = 0.7–1.4). These results lend themselves to the same conclusions as the prospective analyses, which favored the self-medication hypothesis.

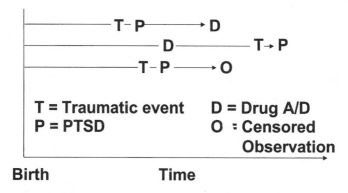

Figure 1.1. An illustration of traumatic events, posttraumatic stress disorder (PTSD), and drug abuse/dependence (A/D) as time-dependent covariates.

Building on these results, Chilcoat and Breslau (1998b) investigated the relationship between SUD and early conduct problems, depression, and PTSD, as well as the relationship between PTSD onset and SUD onset by drug type. Controlling for early conduct problems, which are a suspected shared etiological factor in the development of PTSD and SUD, they also found significant relationships between depression without previous PTSD (relative hazard = 2.9), PTSD without previous depression (relative hazard = 4.0), and PTSD with previous depression (relative hazard = 7.6). These results suggest that, at least among individuals ages 21 to 35 years, a relationship exists between PTSD and drug abuse/dependence onset that is independent of the effect of early conduct problems and depression.

In survival analyses of the relationship between PTSD and drug abuse/dependence by drug type, Chilcoat and Breslau (1998b) failed to find a significantly different hazard of developing marijuana or cocaine abuse/dependence among individuals with PTSD and those without PTSD. They also failed to find a significant association between trauma exposure and an increased hazard of SUD onset for any examined drug type. They did find a substantial and significant increased hazard of prescribed drug abuse/dependence among individuals with PTSD relative to those without PTSD (hazard ratio = 13.0). These results suggest that, among the population sampled, no ubiquitous relationship between PTSD and SUD exists.

The findings from these prospective studies, which used data from the same sample, provide support for the self-medication hypothesis over the susceptibility and high-risk hypotheses. Specifically, preexisting PTSD increased risk of abuse of or dependence on prescribed drugs but did not increase risk for more widely abused drugs, such as marijuana or cocaine. Although these studies have helped to shed light on the causal pathways from PTSD to SUDs, their limitations point to ways in which future studies can improve an understanding of these pathways. Assessment of PTSD and SUDs at regular intervals starting in early adolescence will enable less reliance on retrospective reports, thereby allowing even greater control over the temporal sequencing of these disorders. Also, prospectively gathered data on stages of drug use will provide further clues about the mechanism of SUD–PTSD comorbidity. Including information about multiple exposure to traumatic events and subsequent PTSD will strengthen future studies. Finally, these findings require replication in multiple samples representing a range of populations, including urban children exposed to high levels of violence and other traumatic events.

Disaster Studies

A number of studies have examined the consequences of trauma following a disaster, either natural or human-made. A disaster serves as a natural experiment, because a large number of people are exposed to the same traumatic event, and it is then possible to study how individuals differ in their response to that event. One such study was conducted by North et al. (1999) to assess psychiatric morbidity, including PTSD and SUDs, among survivors of the bombing of the Alfred P. Murrah Federal Building in Oklahoma City, OK, in April 1995. A total of 182 individuals were assessed using a version of the DIS within 4–8 months following the bombing. Of these, 62 (34.3%) developed PTSD in connection with the bombing. An examination of these data indicates that 7 out of 17 individuals (41.5%) who had a lifetime history of a drug use disorder prior to the bombing and 18 of 48 (37.5%) with predisaster alcohol use disorder developed PTSD in response to the bombing. The occurrence of PTSD was somewhat lower among those with no predisaster psychiatric disorder (28 out of 103 = 27%). These findings suggest that individuals with a predisaster SUD might have been more susceptible to PTSD following the bombing than those with no predisaster disorder. Further analysis, which controls for other comorbid disorders and possible confounders, will be necessary to shed more light on this question.

Disaster studies have the advantage of being able to hold the type of trauma constant and sample individuals with varying levels of exposure to a well-defined traumatic event. On the other hand, there are important limitations of these studies relative to prospective studies. Because it is not possible to predict when and where a disaster will occur, baseline measures of preexisting disorders cannot be obtained. For example, North et al. (1999) relied on retrospective reports of psychiatric symptoms preceding and following the bombing. It is difficult to ascertain the extent to which the retrospective reports of predisaster disorders are affected by the response to the trauma, which is a potential source of bias. Because of the lack of baseline measures (prior to the traumatic event), it is difficult to test whether exposure to a traumatic event or PTSD increases the risk of subsequent SUDs.

Studies of Combat Veterans

Studies of the consequences of exposure to combat can help shed light on the SUD–PTSD relationship in a manner similar to disaster studies. They offer unique opportunities to study the relationships among combat exposure, PTSD, and SUDs in population-based samples. Several studies of Vietnam veterans have provided evidence of comorbidity between PTSD and SUDs. McFall et al. (1992) compared 108 combat-exposed Vietnam veterans with 151 who had no combat exposure and found no between-groups difference in the severity of SUDs. However, they did find that veterans with PTSD had more severe drug problems. In a study of 2,490 Vietnam veterans with combat exposure and 1,972 without combat exposure,

Boscarino (1995) also found that combat exposure was not associated with alcohol or drug abuse. In contrast, Reifman and Windle (1996) found that level of combat exposure was significantly related to recent drug use. This discrepancy between Reifman and Windle's findings and those of Boscarino, which were based on data from the same sample, might be explained by the different outcome measures of drug use used in these studies. Reifman and Windle used recent illicit drug *use* controlling for Army drug use, whereas Boscarino used alcohol and drug *abuse*.

IMPLICATIONS AND DIRECTIONS FOR FUTURE RESEARCH

There are a number of ways in which future epidemiological studies can build on recent findings. Most important, there is a clear need for more prospective studies to investigate the comorbidity between PTSD and SUDs. Because adolescence is an important developmental period for the onset of both PTSD and SUDs, future longitudinal studies should begin follow-up assessments during this developmental stage. These studies should incorporate frequent and precise measures of traumatic events, PTSD, alcohol and drug use, and problems related to alcohol and drug use. Future longitudinal studies of adolescents, as well as adults, should include careful measures of stages of alcohol and drug use. With these data, it would be possible to test interrelationships and potential causal pathways among traumatic exposure, PTSD, and stages of substance use. For example, it would be important to know whether PTSD increases the likelihood of transition from substance use initiation to patterned substance use and development of substance-related problems.

Recent developments in biostatistical methods and epidemiological study design will help shed greater light on the comorbidity between PTSD and SUDs. Recent developments in longitudinal data analytic strategies, such as generalized estimating equations (Zeger & Liang, 1986), are now widely available. Survival analytic strategies, such as those used by Chilcoat and Breslau (1998a, 1998b), hold great promise for shedding light on causal pathways between these disorders. Recent developments in survival models, which model time to an event and recurrence of the event simultaneously (Wang & Chang, 1999), are also promising. As we discussed earlier in this chapter, prospective-study designs and their ability to control temporal sequencing are extremely useful for trying to untangle the complex relationships between PTSD and drug use. However, despite their advantages, very few prospective studies of this comorbidity have been carried out. There clearly is a need for additional longitudinal studies, particularly those that begin follow-up assessments in late childhood or early adolescence, prior to the incidence of PTSD and SUD.

Finally, we point out that many of the epidemiological data sets discussed in this chapter are available to the public. For example, data sets from the ECA study and the NCS are available on the World Wide Web for public use. The availability of such rich sources of data holds great opportunities for researchers with creative research questions to put their analytic skills to work in answering important questions about the relationships among trauma, PTSD, and substance use.

2

PSYCHOSOCIAL MODELS OF FUNCTIONAL ASSOCIATIONS BETWEEN POSTTRAUMATIC STRESS DISORDER AND SUBSTANCE USE DISORDER

SHERRY H. STEWART AND PATRICIA J. CONROD

Epidemiological studies have focused on establishing comorbidity of posttraumatic stress disorder (PTSD) and substance use disorders (SUDs) in clinical and nonclinical samples (see chapter 1, this volume). These studies have established a statistical relationship between the presence of these two disorders among victims of a wide variety of potentially traumatic events, including combat, sexual assault, and disaster (see review by Stewart, 1996). In other words, having PTSD increases the risk of having an SUD, and vice versa. However, comorbidity research has merely established that these two disorders are statistically related to one another; it has not established whether any functional relationships exist between the two disorders (Rachman, 1991). Other types of research methods must supplement traditional epidemiological investigations of comorbidity rates to determine whether one disorder is causally related to the other and to gain insight into the mechanisms underlying causal relations between these disorders (i.e., functional relations). In this chapter we review studies using psychosocial research methods that shed light on functional relations that may explain this common form of comorbidity. Studies in which laboratory-based experimental methods are used to investigate biological and cognitive mechanisms underlying SUD–PTSD comorbidity are reviewed in chapter 3.

We begin by reviewing some of the potential causal relations that have been suggested to underlie the high rates of comorbidity between PTSD and SUDs and some of the functional associations that might underlie such purported causal pathways (see also the review by Stewart, Pihl, Conrod,

& Dongier, 1998). First, PTSD could be causally related to SUD development. An example functional association that could be involved in this PTSD-to-SUD causal pathway is that alcohol or drugs (or both) may be abused by PTSD patients in attempts to control PTSD symptoms (i.e., self-medication; Khantzian, 1985), ultimately culminating in substance dependence. Second, an SUD could be causally related to PTSD development, following exposure to a traumatic event. An example functional relation that could account for this alternative causal pathway is PTSD being more likely to arise from trauma as a consequence of heightened physiological arousal from repeated alcohol/drug withdrawal. A third potential pathway is that an SUD could increase risk for development of PTSD by increasing the likelihood of exposure to certain types of trauma. For example, the lifestyle associated with drug abuse might place an individual at increased risk for exposure to violence (see Stewart & Israeli, 2002). Although this would involve an indirect causal relation between SUDs and PTSD, no functional relation between the two disorders would be indicated in this case. Finally, some third variable (e.g., poor coping skills) might be related to increased risk for development of both PTSD and SUDs following trauma exposure, contributing to high SUD–PTSD comorbidity but again suggesting no functional relation between these two forms of behavioral pathology.

Functional relations to explain SUD–PTSD comorbidity do not necessarily involve causality in terms of one disorder leading to the initial development of the other. Instead, or in addition, functional relations may pertain to symptom maintenance. For example, once comorbidity is established, PTSD symptoms could serve to maintain SUD symptoms again through the process of self-medication. Conversely, active substance misuse could maintain or prolong the PTSD symptoms (e.g., by interfering with habituation to the trauma). Another possibility is that both of these processes are operating in a vicious cycle (see Stewart, 1996). Specifically, continued PTSD symptoms could promote and maintain substance misuse through patients' attempts to control their aversive posttraumatic symptoms. Substance misuse in turn could maintain, prolong, or exacerbate PTSD symptoms, which in turn could serve to promote further substance misuse, and so on. This hypothetical vicious cycle between PTSD and SUD symptoms is illustrated in Figure 2.1. Note that the similar cyclical-interplay hypothesis has been previously invoked to explain comorbidity between alcohol use disorders and anxiety disorders other than PTSD (e.g., Kushner, Abrams, & Borchardt, 2000).

In this chapter we review studies that have used varying types of psychosocial research methodologies to investigate potential causal–maintenance relations, and underlying functional associations, between PTSD and SUD symptoms among victims of various types of trauma. Understanding these pathways and processes can help mental health professionals

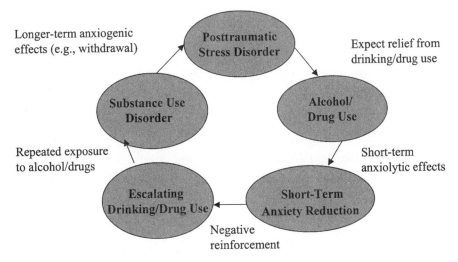

Figure 2.1. Illustration of the hypothetical vicious cycle involved in posttraumatic stress disorder–substance use disorder comorbidity maintenance.

tailor treatments more specifically to individuals afflicted with this form of dual diagnosis.

GRADIENT OF EFFECT

One criterion that has been suggested to help determine whether a causal relationship exists between PTSD and SUDs is to establish a *gradient of effect* (see review by Chilcoat & Breslau, 1998a). This criterion contends that if a causal relationship exists, the effect on the causal outcome should be greater as the level of exposure to a causal agent increases. If PTSD and SUDs are causally related, then as levels of symptoms of one disorder increase, so should levels of symptoms of the second disorder. In this section we review the results of correlational studies that have examined the degree to which this criterion is met with respect to the potential causal relationship between PTSD and SUDs.

McFall, Mackay, and Donovan (1992) examined possible functional relations between the various *Diagnostic and Statistical Manual of Mental Disorders* (3rd ed., rev.; *DSM–III–R*; American Psychiatric Association, 1987) PTSD symptom clusters and severity of alcohol use disorder symptoms in a clinical sample. Participants were 108 male war veterans presenting for SUD treatment. In this study, PTSD symptoms were divided conceptually into the three *DSM* clusters: (a) intrusions, (b) numbing/avoidance, and (c) arousal. Relations of these sets of PTSD symptoms with substance misuse were evaluated separately for alcohol versus other drugs. Levels of alcohol problems were significantly positively associated with levels of PTSD arousal and intrusions symptoms (particularly arousal symptoms), but not with avoidance/numbing symptoms. Levels of problems with drugs other than alcohol were significantly positively associated with PTSD avoidance/numbing and intrusion symptoms, but not with arousal symptoms. However, the fact that drugs other than alcohol were examined as a group in this study means that the results do not address whether problems with different types of drugs are differentially related to the various sets of PTSD symptoms.

Stewart, Conrod, Pihl, and Dongier (1999) examined potential functional relations between the various *DSM–IV* (American Psychiatric Association, 1994) PTSD symptoms and severity of alcohol and prescription drug use disorder symptoms in a sample of 295 female substance abusers recruited from the community. In this study, PTSD symptoms were divided into four empirically derived symptom clusters that closely approximated the *DSM–IV* organization: (a) intrusions, (b) numbing, (c) avoidance, and (d) arousal. Severity of alcohol disorder symptoms was correlated with severity of PTSD arousal symptoms. Severity of anxiolytic and analgesic dependence was correlated with severity of PTSD numbing and arousal symptoms, and analgesic dependence severity was additionally correlated with PTSD intrusion symptoms.

Across these two studies, a fairly consistent relation was obtained between PTSD arousal symptoms and level of SUD symptoms, at least in the cases of alcohol and prescription depressant drugs. These findings are compatible with notions of functional relations, suggesting that PTSD arousal symptoms motivate PTSD patients to abuse alcohol, prescription depressant drugs, or both, in an attempt to self-medicate their hyperaroused state. This self-medication could involve attempts to aid in sleep, reduce irritability, reduce concentration difficulties, reduce hypervigilance, or control excessive startle (cf. LaCoursiere, Godfrey, & Ruby, 1980; Stewart, 1997). These findings are also consistent with suggestions that the functional association instead might reflect chronic heavy use of alcohol or other drugs that ultimately exacerbates PTSD arousal symptoms over the longer term (see Kolb, 1985; LaCoursiere et al., 1980). For example, chronic alcohol abuse, alcohol withdrawal, or both, might lead to an intensification of certain PTSD arousal symptoms (e.g., heightened startle) over time (see review by Stewart et al., 1998). Finally, these findings are also consistent with the symptom redundancy position posited by Saladin, Brady, Dansky, and Kilpatrick (1995), who argued that symptoms of withdrawal from alcohol and drugs can mimic PTSD arousal symptoms, which might account for the correlations between PTSD arousal symptoms and levels of SUD symptoms in these gradient-of-effect studies. However, if substance withdrawal symptoms are often misinterpreted by patients as PTSD arousal symptoms, as Saladin et al. (1995) suggested, this misinterpretation could promote further heavy alcohol/drug use by patients in attempts to control these "PTSD arousal symptoms." Further research is needed to rule in or rule out the symptom redundancy position.

Taken together, these two studies also suggest that PTSD numbing symptoms appear associated with increased levels of SUD symptoms, at least in the case of drugs other than alcohol. This pattern is consonant with Krystal's (1984) suggestion that individuals suffering from PTSD develop a dread of emotion and strive to block emotional experiences through misuse of drugs. Stewart, Conrod, et al.'s (1999) findings suggest that prescription depressant drugs may be particularly likely to be used for this purpose, at least by female trauma victims. This pattern is also consistent with the suggestion that drug abuse may serve to maintain high levels of PTSD emotional numbing symptoms by preventing or delaying a working through of the traumatic experience (see Stewart, 1996).

Finally, the finding that PTSD intrusions scores were associated with increased prescription analgesic dependence corresponds with theoretical positions that have posited that PTSD patients may misuse substances to control or eliminate intrusive memories of the trauma (Krystal, 1984; La-Coursiere et al., 1980; Stewart, 1997). It may be that opioid analgesics are particularly rewarding in this respect (Stewart, Conrod, et al., 1999). This observed correlation is also consistent, however, with the position that opioid analgesics might serve as an agent in promoting expression of intrusive cognitive symptoms of PTSD (cf. Kolb, 1985).

The findings reviewed in this section show that a gradient of effect exists between PTSD symptoms and severity of SUD symptoms. The pattern of results is consistent with the position that a causal relation may exist between these two commonly comorbid disorders. We caution that these studies may underestimate the degree to which symptoms of the two disorders are related, because the correlational methods used cannot rule out the possibility that active alcohol/drug abuse may dampen or mask true levels of certain PTSD symptoms (see Stewart, 1996). Moreover, even if the observed relation is causal, the direction of causality remains unclear from the results of these correlational studies: PTSD could cause SUDs, or vice versa. We proceed to a discussion of methodologies that more specifically attempt to address the issue of direction of causation—namely, epidemiological studies of temporality.

TEMPORALITY

Another method that has been suggested to help in determining whether a causal relationship exists that might explain SUD–PTSD co-morbidity is to establish *temporality* (see review by Chilcoat & Breslau,

1998a). This criterion is based on the logic that a causal agent must temporally precede a causal effect. If SUDs cause PTSD (e.g., by increasing risk of exposure to traumatic events or by inducing a state in which PTSD is more likely to develop following trauma exposure), then the onset of the SUD must precede the development of the PTSD. Conversely, if PTSD causes SUDs (e.g., through self-medication), then the onset of PTSD must precede the development of the SUD. In this section we review studies that have examined the degree to which the temporality criterion is met with respect to the potential causal relationship between PTSD and SUDs.

Research on the temporal relations between PTSD and SUDs has generally involved two types of methodologies: (a) those using retrospective self-report methods versus (b) those using longitudinal, prospective methods. Studies that have retrospectively assessed the chronology of onset of PTSD versus SUDs in clinical or community samples generally suggest that the onset of SUDs follows the onset of PTSD symptoms. For example, Mellman, Randolph, Brawman-Mintzer, and Flores (1992) surveyed treatment-seeking Vietnam veterans at a Veterans Affairs hospital about the onset of their presenting symptoms. PTSD was the most common disorder to develop after combat exposure and was highly comorbid with other disorders, such as alcoholism. Moreover, veterans with PTSD and a comorbid disorder reported that the onset of the comorbid disorder generally followed the onset of PTSD symptoms. Similarly, Najavits, Weiss, and Shaw (1999) found that within a sample of PTSD patients with a comorbid SUD, 61% reported that the onset of the PTSD symptoms predated the onset of the SUD. In a large community-based epidemiological study, Kessler, Sonnega, Bromet, Hughes, and Nelson (1995) retrospectively examined the relative order of onset of PTSD versus SUDs among comorbid cases identified in the National Comorbidity Survey. They found that PTSD was the primary disorder (in the sense of having an earlier age at onset) more often than not with respect to comorbid SUDs. Among comorbid cases, the majority (i.e., 53%–65% of the men and 65%–84% of the women) developed the PTSD prior to the SUD.

Bremner, Southwick, Darnell, and Charney (1996) further examined the temporality issue by measuring the relative order of emergence of specific PTSD symptom clusters and related SUD symptoms. They interviewed 61 combat veterans with PTSD and learned that the onset of PTSD symptoms usually occurred close to the time of combat exposure, with arousal symptoms developing first and intrusion symptoms developing last. The onset of SUD symptoms typically occurred around the time of the initial emergence of PTSD symptoms, and the increase in SUD symptoms paralleled the increase in patients' PTSD symptoms following trauma exposure. This study appears to support the self-medication of arousal symptoms as an initial motivator for substance misuse in PTSD patients (Stewart et al., 1998).

However, the accuracy of retrospective self-report as a method of estimating the differential age of onset of comorbid disorders has been challenged. Studies have shown that when other sources of information are available (e.g., records, informants), individuals with comorbid addictive and nonaddictive disorders tend to be particularly inaccurate in estimating the chronology of onset of the two disorders (Atkinson, Slater, Patterson, Grant, & Garfin, 1991; Morrissey & Schuckit, 1978). For example, Stockwell and Bolderston (1987) demonstrated that when patients are asked to estimate the onset of their comorbid anxiety disorder they tend to specify the first symptom of nervousness experienced rather than the onset of the diagnosable disorder. Whether such findings apply to the specific issue of comorbid SUD–PTSD is unclear; however, they do suggest the need for designs that allow for the prospective assessment and evaluation of the temporal association between PTSD and SUDs.

Another issue that must be kept in mind when interpreting the results of temporality studies is how *time of onset* is defined. Are the researchers examining relative order of onset of first symptoms or of the full-blown disorder? The self-medication explanation of SUD–PTSD comorbidity contends that substances are used by patients to "medicate" for certain psychiatric symptoms (e.g., PTSD arousal or intrusion symptoms). It is possible that patients may begin self-medicating for sub-threshold symptoms of PTSD prior to the emergence of full-blown PTSD. In this case, the SUD would technically have an earlier onset, despite the fact that PTSD symptoms emerged first and motivated substance misuse. Longitudinal prospective studies tracking the emergence of symptoms of both disorders over time are necessary for clarification of this issue.

Longitudinal studies are now emerging in the SUD–PTSD comorbidity area that help clarify the direction and nature of the relationship between the two disorders. For example, Blanchard, Hickling, et al. (1996) assessed 132 motor vehicle accident victims shortly after their accident and again 1 year later. The presence of an alcohol disorder at the initial assessment predicted PTSD symptom maintenance at the 1-year follow-up, over and above initial PTSD symptom severity. This longitudinal finding is consistent with the idea that alcohol use disorders serve to maintain PTSD following trauma exposure (e.g., by interfering with the working through of traumatic events or preventing habituation to traumatic memories; Machell, 1993).

Acierno, Resnick, Kilpatrick, Saunders, and Best (2000) studied a national probability sample of 3,006 adult women in a three-wave longitudinal investigation to identify risk factors for rape and physical assault and associated PTSD. Demographic factors (age, socioeconomic status, ethnicity) and past history of victimization and psychopathology, including substance abuse, were assessed at baseline. Participants were then reassessed for history of victimization 2 years later. Using this design, the investigators were able to explore which past variables (assessed retrospectively) were associated with the development of PTSD and then which factors were associated with future victimization (assessed prospectively). In the first assessment wave, lifetime history of illicit substance use was not shown to be associated with the presence of a PTSD diagnosis among women who reported a past history of physical assault. Analyses of the 2-year prospective follow-up assessment data similarly showed no relationship between alcohol abuse and risk for a new rape or physical assault. However, exclusive alcohol abuse was associated with a current diagnosis of PTSD among participants who reported a past history of rape (cf. Blanchard, Hickling, et al., 1996). Unfortunately, PTSD was not assessed at the 2-year follow-up, so the effect of a preexisting SUD on the eventual development of PTSD after a new victimization could not be explored within the context of the authors' prospective design.

The results from the retrospective assessment wave of Acierno et al.'s (2000) study suggest that, despite popular belief, alcohol and drug abuse do not place an individual at greater risk for victimization, but they do increase the likelihood of being diagnosed with current PTSD. This latter finding could be explained in a number of ways. First, it is possible that alcohol abuse caused the development of PTSD following victimization, possibly by means of increased arousal due to repeated alcohol withdrawal. Second, alcohol abuse may have changed the course of the PTSD; for example, alcohol abuse may have prolonged the course of PTSD by interfering with the process of recovery from trauma, as described above for Blanchard, Hickling, et al.'s (1996) study. Alternatively, chronic or persistent PTSD symptoms may have caused alcohol abuse through a self-medication process. Unfortunately, the retrospective nature of this wave of Acierno et al.'s (2000) study does not allow clarification of these issues of causality and directionality. However, results from the prospective wave of this study do rule out the hypothesis that preexisting SUDs place individuals at risk for future traumatic exposure.

Chilcoat and Breslau (1998b) also conducted a longitudinal study with a randomly selected sample of 21- to 30-year-old adults ($N = 1,200$) by assessing them for addictive and nonaddictive psychopathology 3 and 5 years after initial assessment ($N = 955$). Consistent with Acierno et al.'s (2000) findings, they failed to show a relationship between SUDs (past or current) and risk for future victimization. Unlike the results of Acierno et al.'s retrospective assessment, Chilcoat and Breslau (1998b) showed that, within the subsample of participants who were newly victimized in the follow-up period, there was no relationship between preexisting SUD (i.e., diagnosed at baseline) and the eventual development of PTSD. Therefore, Acierno et al.'s finding of a relationship between past SUD and current PTSD diagnosis likely reflects an effect of SUD on the course of PTSD rather than a causal effect of SUD on PTSD development. In subsequent analyses, using Cox proportional-hazards ratios with time-dependent covariates, Chilcoat and Breslau (1998b) showed that a PTSD diagnosis at baseline predicted a greater likelihood of the eventual development of an SUD (hazard ratio = 4.5). This increased risk conferred by PTSD was particularly evident in the case of SUDs involving prescription drugs (e.g., benzodiazepines). In similar models that estimated the risk of PTSD due to SUD diagnoses, the hazard ratio was significantly smaller (1.6). Therefore, the results rather unequivocally indicate that PTSD is associated with an increased risk for the development of an SUD but provide less support for the possibility that SUDs are associated with an increased risk for the development of PTSD.

A recent prospective study that examined psychological adjustment in survivors of the Oklahoma City bombing (North et al., 1999) challenges the notion that there is a specific temporal relationship between PTSD and alcohol abuse, however. North et al. (1999) found that postdisaster alcohol use to cope with disaster characterized individuals with PTSD only if they presented with other psychiatric comorbidity. Individuals with PTSD alone did not report using alcohol to cope with the trauma. This study suggests the possibility that PTSD may lead to increased risk for an SUD only among vulnerable individuals (i.e., those with additional psychiatric comorbidity). The results of Chilcoat and Breslau's (1998b) study provide data relevant to this issue. They reported the results of an additional analysis on their national sample of 18- to 35-year-old women in which they explored the extent to which the relationship between PTSD and SUD could be accounted for by additional comorbidity with depression. They found that the risk for an SUD developing after the onset of depression was significantly higher in participants with comorbid PTSD than those with depression alone, suggesting a relationship between PTSD and SUDs that is independent of the relationship of depression to these two disorders. Given the inconclusive nature of the findings to date, further research is needed to determine the possible role of additional psychiatric comorbidity in accounting for or moderating the temporal relation between PTSD and increased risk for an SUD.

Taken together, these various studies suggest that, indeed, the temporality criterion of causality is met in the case of comorbid SUD–PTSD. Specifically, PTSD has been shown to develop before the SUD in the large majority of comorbid cases in retrospective studies, and PTSD has been shown to contribute to increased risk for SUDs in prospective studies. These temporal data are consistent with self-medication explanations for the etiology of comorbid SUD–PTSD. Specifically, PTSD patients may come to abuse alcohol and drugs in an attempt to self-medicate their aversive PTSD symptoms. However, although temporality is a necessary condition for causality, it cannot be used to confirm causal hypotheses (Chilcoat & Breslau, 1998a). In addition, more research is required to determine whether other comorbid psychiatric disorders account for or contribute to the temporal relation between PTSD and SUD development. Finally, it should be pointed out that the temporality criterion applies only to understanding the *onset* of comorbidity, not to understanding comorbidity *maintenance*. For example, even if self-medication for PTSD symptoms applies to the initiation of substance misuse among most trauma victims, the possibility of a vicious cycle between these two forms of behavioral pathology developing over the longer term should be considered (see Stewart, 1996).

Even though most studies support the notion that PTSD precedes SUD in the majority of cases, there do appear to be cases where the SUD is temporally primary. An interesting question is whether these two groups of comorbid patients differ in any important ways. To investigate this issue, Brady, Dansky, Sonne, and Saladin (1998) divided 33 adult patients with comorbid PTSD and cocaine dependence into two groups. In the *primary PTSD* group the PTSD developed before the onset of cocaine dependence. In the *primary cocaine* group the PTSD developed after cocaine dependence was established. Some potentially important differences between groups were indeed observed. In the primary-PTSD group the precipitating trauma was generally childhood abuse, whereas in the primary-cocaine group the trauma exposure was generally associated with using or obtaining cocaine. In the primary-PTSD group there were more women, as well as increased use of benzodiazepines and opiates (i.e., prescription depressant drugs). Thus, Brady et al.'s (1998) findings suggest that subgroups of comorbid patients for whom the PTSD is temporally primary or secondary to the SUD may differ in important ways, such as gender (see Ouimette, Kimerling, Shaw, & Moos, 2000; Stewart, Ouimette, & Brown, in press), the type of precipitating trauma, and use of prescription depressant drugs. Although more research is required on this issue, these preliminary findings suggest different treatment approaches for comorbid patients for whom the PTSD developed first than for those for whom the SUD developed first. The former group might benefit most from training in healthier methods of arousal management alternative to misuse of prescription depressants, whereas the latter might benefit most from strategies such as education about increased risk for victimization associated with a drug-abusing lifestyle.

PATIENT PERCEPTIONS OF FUNCTIONAL RELATIONS

Rachman (1991) recommended that, in addition to the simple determination of the co-occurrence of two disorders, attention should be given to comorbid patients' perceptions of the "psychological connectedness" of their two disorders. Brown, Stout, and Gannon-Rowley (1998) were the first to investigate this issue as it pertains to SUD–PTSD comorbidity. They examined perceptions of functional associations between PTSD and SUDs among 42 comorbid patients receiving treatment for an SUD. Consistent with the self-medication hypothesis, the large majority of comorbid patients reported feeling that their SUD symptoms worsen when their PTSD symptoms worsen (77%) and that their SUD symptoms improve when their PTSD symptoms improve (79%). Consistent with the substance-induced intensification of PTSD symptoms hypothesis, more than half the comorbid patients reported feeling that their PTSD symptoms worsen when their SUD symptoms worsen (51%) and that their PTSD symptoms improve when their SUD symptoms improve (52%). This pattern of findings regarding patient perceptions highlights the importance patients place on PTSD symptoms contributing to their SUDs. However, the results are also consistent with a vicious cycle being operative between symptoms of these two disorders, such that one disorder sustains the other (Stewart, 1996).

In another study conducted by Bremner et al. (1996), 61 combat veterans with PTSD were asked to report on their perceptions of the effects of specific drugs on their PTSD symptoms. Patients reported perceiving that alcohol, heroin, marijuana, and benzodiazepines tended to make PTSD symptoms better, whereas cocaine was perceived as making PTSD symptoms (particularly PTSD arousal symptoms) worse. This study suggests differences in patients' perceptions of the potential of depressant versus stimulant drugs to alleviate versus worsen PTSD symptoms. Given these perceptions, it would be interesting to examine the degree to which PTSD patients' drug outcome expectancies (i.e., beliefs about the consequences of drug use) contribute to their drug use behaviors (cf. Schafer & Brown, 1991). Because existing expectancy measures assess only general beliefs about drug-induced tension reduction, it might be useful for researchers to develop drug expectancy measures specific to PTSD symptoms for use in future work in this area (see Stewart et al., 1998).

SITUATIONAL SPECIFICITY

The self-medication hypothesis of SUD–PTSD comorbidity asserts that substances are used in an attempt to reduce or control the behavioral, affective, cognitive, or physiological symptoms (or some combination of these) of PTSD. In operant-conditioning terminology, individuals with PTSD are said to learn to drink or to use drugs for their *negatively reinforcing* effects (e.g., arousal reduction, dampening of intrusive memories; see Stewart, 1996, 1997). If, indeed, substance use serves a negatively reinforcing function among traumatized individuals with PTSD, the heavy drinking/

drug-taking behavior of those substance abusers with PTSD should be relatively *situation specific*—that is, their substance abuse should occur most commonly in contexts that have been associated in the past with a substance's tension-reducing effects (Stewart, Conrod, Samoluk, Pihl, & Dongier, 2000). In this section we review studies that have examined the situational-specificity hypothesis among samples of SUD patients.

Sharkansky, Brief, Peirce, Meehan, and Mannix (1999) administered measures of PTSD symptom severity and situation-specific drinking and drug taking to a sample of 86 veterans (84 men and 2 women) seeking treatment for an SUD. Frequency of drug taking and heavy drinking in specific situations were assessed with the Inventory of Drug Taking Situations (Annis, Turner, & Sklar, 1996) and the short form of the Inventory of Drinking Situations (Annis, Graham, & Davis, 1987; Stewart, Samoluk, Conrod, Pihl, & Dongier, 2000), respectively. These instruments assess past-year drug taking and heavy drinking, respectively, in the following eight situations: Unpleasant Emotions, Physical Discomfort, Pleasant Emotions, Testing Personal Control, Urges and Temptations, Conflict With Others, Social Pressure, and Pleasant Times With Others (cf. Marlatt & Gordon, 1985). Substance abusers with and without PTSD were compared in terms of their frequency of heavy drinking/drug taking in each type of situation. The findings were consistent with situational-specificity hypothesis predictions. Comorbid PTSD was associated with greater drinking/drug taking in situations involving Unpleasant Emotions, Physical Discomfort, and Conflict With Others but was unrelated to frequency of drinking/drug taking in situations involving Pleasant Emotions, Testing Personal Control, Urges and Temptations, Social Pressure, or Pleasant Times With Others.

These findings were recently replicated in a study conducted by Stewart, Conrod, et al. (2000) in which situation-specific heavy drinking by female substance abusers recruited from the community was assessed with the short form of the Inventory of Drinking Situations. Thus, the results of both Sharkansky et al. (1999) and Stewart, Conrod, et al. (2000) suggest that substance abusers with clinically significant levels of PTSD symptoms drink or take drugs more frequently, relative to other substance abusers, in potentially negatively reinforcing situations. Because Sharkansky et al.'s study was conducted largely with men, and Stewart, Conrod, et al.'s (2000) study was conducted entirely with women, we can conclude that support for the situational-specificity hypothesis is consistent across genders (see also review by Stewart et al., in press). This suggests that relapse prevention efforts (Marlatt & Gordon, 1985) in men and women with comorbid PTSD–SUDs should focus on these types of situations as involving a high potential for relapse in this population.

ROLE OF ANXIETY SENSITIVITY

Stewart, Conrod, et al.'s (2000) study of community-recruited SUD women also provides information on the role of *anxiety sensitivity*—fear of anxiety-related sensations (Peterson & Reiss, 1992)—in contributing to SUD–PTSD comorbidity among women. Anxiety sensitivity is a cognitive individual-difference variable that has been suggested as a risk factor for substance abuse (see literature review by Stewart, Samoluk, & MacDonald, 1999). Anxiety sensitivity levels are elevated in PTSD and are higher in PTSD than in all other anxiety disorders save panic disorder (Taylor, Koch, & McNally, 1992). It has been suggested that anxiety sensitivity may represent a premorbid vulnerability factor for the development of PTSD following exposure to a traumatic event, because people with high anxiety sensitivity should be more likely to develop conditioned fear reactions (e.g., increased startle) to trauma cues. In turn, the experience of anxiety-related PTSD symptoms may increase anxiety sensitivity levels (Taylor et al., 1992). Stewart, Conrod, et al. (2000) found that anxiety sensitivity mediated the observed associations between PTSD symptoms and situation-specific heavy drinking in negative contexts. In other words, substance abusers with more frequent PTSD symptoms drink heavily in certain negative situations (e.g., contexts involving physical discomfort) at least partly because they are highly fearful of anxiety sensations. These findings suggest that interventions for comorbid SUD–PTSD patients might benefit from a focus on techniques that have been demonstrated to be effective in treating anxiety sensitivity (see review by Otto & Reilly-Harrington, 1999).

PTSD SYMPTOMS AS MEDIATORS

The self-medication explanation of SUD–PTSD comorbidity implies a mediating role for PTSD symptoms. Specifically, trauma exposure is said to relate to increased rates of SUDs because trauma results in PTSD symptoms, which patients attempt to self-medicate through drinking and drug misuse. Epstein, Saunders, Kilpatrick, and Resnick (1998) empirically examined the potential mediating role of PTSD symptoms in explaining relations between childhood sexual abuse and alcohol problems in adulthood. Participants were a random nonclinical sample of close to 3,000 adult women who were interviewed about childhood sexual abuse history and lifetime PTSD and alcohol abuse symptoms. Childhood sexual abuse history was associated with a doubling of the number of alcohol abuse symptoms in adulthood. Alcohol abuse was greater in sexual abuse victims who developed PTSD than among those who did not. Path analysis demonstrated significant pathways connecting childhood sexual abuse to PTSD symptoms and PTSD symptoms to alcohol abuse. The association between childhood sexual abuse and adult alcohol abuse was completely mediated by PTSD symptoms. Epstein et al. suggested that PTSD may be an important variable affecting alcohol abuse patterns in women who were victims of sexual abuse in childhood. Future studies could use similar methods to investigate the potential mediating role of PTSD symptoms in explaining relations between exposure to other forms of trauma and SUDs and to determine whether PTSD symptom mediation extends to men as well as women.

FAMILY STUDIES

Family studies can also contribute to understanding the mechanisms involved in SUD–PTSD comorbidity by providing evidence for or against specific causal and functional models (see reviews by Kushner et al., 2000; Merikangas, Stevens, & Fenton, 1996). For example, if a common genetic mechanism were operative in accounting for SUD–PTSD comorbidity, then probands with pure PTSD should have family members at risk for pure PTSD, combined (comorbid) SUD–PTSD, and pure SUD (by means of cross-transmission). Similarly, probands with pure SUD should have family members at risk for pure SUD, combined SUD–PTSD, and pure (cross-transmitted) PTSD. In contrast, if PTSD causes SUDs, then familial transmission studies would reveal increased risk of both pure PTSD and combined SUD–PTSD (comorbid form) in the families of PTSD probands but no increased risk for pure SUDs in the families of such probands. The converse would be true if SUDs cause PTSD (i.e., increased risk of both pure SUD and combined SUD–PTSD in the families of SUD probands but no increased risk for pure PTSD in the families of such probands).

Studies dating back to the first half of the 20th century indicate an increased prevalence of anxiety-related psychopathology (PTSD and other anxiety disorders) and alcoholism in family members of combat-exposed probands with PTSD-like symptoms (see review by Connor & Davidson, 1997). These findings could be consistent with either the notion of a common genetic mechanism for PTSD and alcoholism or the possibility that PTSD causes alcoholism. However, most of these studies failed to examine and report whether the alcoholism in proband family members was pure or comorbid with PTSD. Moreover, many of these studies lacked an appropriate control group in which proband families were compared with families of trauma-exposed individuals who did not develop PTSD-like symptoms. Control groups that are appropriately matched for trauma exposure are essential in family studies of SUD–PTSD comorbidity, because trauma exposure has been linked with a family history of psychopathology, including SUDs (Breslau, Davis, Andreski, & Peterson, 1991).

A family study conducted by Davidson, Smith, and Kudler (1989) compared 108 combat-exposed male veterans with PTSD to 21 nonpsychiatric, 24 depressed, and 15 alcoholic male veteran controls. There was a twofold increased risk for PTSD, alcoholism, and other SUD diagnoses among family members of probands with PTSD and probands with alcoholism, relative to probands with depression or another psychiatric diagnosis. Because Davidson et al. (1989) did not report whether the SUDs and PTSD in family members were pure or comorbid, these findings cannot determine whether PTSD causes SUDs, SUDs cause PTSD, or whether the two disorders share a common genetic basis. Moreover, comparison groups were not necessarily matched for combat exposure with the PTSD veterans group. To control for this possible limitation, Davidson et al. (1989) performed a subsequent reanalysis of their data on only the PTSD and control cases who had been exposed to combat. Combat-exposed PTSD probands demonstrated greater familial morbidity of anxiety disorders only (and not SUDs) relative to a combat-exposed control group that was heterogeneous with respect to psychiatric diagnosis (including SUDs). Therefore, among trauma-exposed individuals, there did not seem to be an increased risk for SUDs in family members of individuals with PTSD, a finding that fails to support the notion of a common genetic basis for the two disorders. However, considering that the comparison group included patients with SUDs, and that the familial transmission of SUDs is widely documented, the comparison group used in this reanalysis might have resulted in an underestimation of relative risk of SUDs among family members of individuals with PTSD.

In another family study of veterans, Speed, Engdahl, Schwartz, and Eberly (1989) compared 31 World War II prisoners of war with PTSD to 31 World War II prisoners of war without PTSD. In this study, the experimental and control groups were matched for trauma exposure. Speed et al. did not find evidence for an association between PTSD status in the veteran probands and increased familial risk for alcoholism, which again fails to support the notion of a common genetic basis for the two disorders. Davidson, Tupler, Wilson, and Connor (1998) investigated whether rape survivors with PTSD exhibit increased rates of familial SUDs relative to rape survivors without PTSD, patients with major depression, patients with other anxiety disorders, or healthy controls. In contrast to Davidson et al.'s (1989) study, control groups in this study did not include patients with primary SUDs. There was no evidence from this investigation that alcoholism or other SUDs were more prevalent in families of probands with rape-related PTSD, once again failing to support a common genetic basis for PTSD and SUDs.

When family studies have included appropriate trauma-exposed control groups (including combat and civilian traumas), no evidence has been obtained for an increased prevalence of SUDs among family members of PTSD-positive individuals. The failure to find such a relationship rules out the possibility that a shared genetic effect between PTSD and SUDs can explain their co-occurrence. It is unfortunate that these studies have failed to examine whether comorbid PTSD and SUDs are more prevalent in families of PTSD probands, which is necessary to support the position that PTSD causes SUDs. Too few studies have yet examined rates of PTSD, SUD, and comorbid SUD–PTSD in family members of SUD-positive and control probands to draw any firm conclusions as to whether SUDs might cause PTSD.

A further limitation of the family studies we have discussed pertains to the nature of PTSD as compared with other psychiatric disorders. PTSD is the only psychiatric diagnosis that is dependent on the occurrence of a traumatic event (*DSM–IV*; American Psychiatric Association, 1994). Thus, when using family studies to understand the comorbidity of PTSD with SUDs, the interpretive principles outlined by Merikangas et al. (1996) might apply to families only in which there is multigenerational traumatic exposure. One such study, conducted by Yehuda, Schmeidler, Wainberg, Binder-Brynes, and Duvdevani (1998), explored the risk for PTSD among children of Holocaust survivors. Although they demonstrated a familial effect on PTSD risk within the context of trauma exposure, parental PTSD was not associated with increased risk for other forms of psychopathology, including SUDs, in the offspring. Thus, even in more narrow examinations of only families in which there is multigenerational trauma exposure, the evidence to date fails to support a common genetic basis for PTSD and SUDs. Yehuda et al. (1998) unfortunately did not examine the prevalence of comorbid SUD–PTSD in family members of PTSD-positive parents. Therefore, the extant familial–genetic literature is of limited utility in addressing the potential causal relationship between PTSD and SUDs.

To summarize, very few family studies have specifically investigated the cotransmission of PTSD and SUDs. In those that have, PTSD in probands is not associated with higher rates of SUDs in family members, providing no support for a common genetic mechanism accounting for SUD–PTSD comorbidity. Regarding the second set of hypotheses (i.e., that PTSD causes SUDs, or vice versa), there are no studies that have been adequately designed to test potential causal relations between PTSD and SUD in a family study design. To adequately test this hypothesis, it will be necessary for future research to explore trauma exposure among family members of PTSD and SUD (or comorbid) probands and to examine rates of not only the pure forms of each disorder in family members but also the comorbid form.

TREATMENT STUDIES

There are a number of ways in which treatment studies can be informative about the nature of the relationship between comorbid disorders (see review by Kushner et al., 2000). First, treatment studies can be helpful for exploring whether factors specific to each comorbid disorder may interfere with recovery from the other disorder. Second, treatment studies can also be helpful in exploring the proximal determinants of changes in symptoms. Specifically, treatment studies with multiple follow-up assessments can be informative about which factors are predictive of relapse to substance abuse or PTSD during the recovery phase. For example, is an exacerbation of PTSD symptoms temporally related to the onset or relapse to substance use or abuse? Such a pattern would be consistent with an explanation of comorbidity attributing a causal role to PTSD symptoms. Third, treatment studies allow for the examination of changes in symptom patterns within the context of a prospective experimental design. By studying the differential effects of interventions that target specific symptom clusters and the subsequent change in symptoms of both the targeted disorder and the comorbid disorder, one can make inferences about the functional relations between two disorders. For example, such a design might be helpful in determining whether treatments that are specifically designed to reduce PTSD symptoms are also effective in reducing SUD symptoms. If PTSD-focused treatments result in reduction of symptoms of both disorders, then it can be inferred that the presence of PTSD symptoms was involved in maintaining the SUD. Conversely, if SUD-focused treatments result in reduction of symptoms of both disorders, then it can be inferred that the presence of SUD symptoms was involved in maintaining the PTSD. Finally, comparisons of the relative effectiveness of therapies targeting symptoms of both comorbid disorders versus therapies that target the symptoms of only one disorder can be informative in testing the notion of the vicious cycle (Stewart, 1996). If both comorbid disorders serve to maintain each other, then combined therapies should produce superior outcomes relative to therapies that target only one of the comorbid disorders.

The first issue addressed in treatment studies is whether factors specific to each comorbid disorder might interfere with recovery from the other disorder. A number of studies have examined differential outcomes of SUD patients with and without PTSD on measures of change that reflect severity of substance abuse, psychiatric disturbance, and psychological maladjustment, which might shed light on whether and how PTSD maintains or exacerbates an SUD. For example, Brown, Recupero, and Stout (1995) studied male and female treatment-seeking SUD patients and found that those with PTSD reported a greater number of admissions to inpatient addiction programs throughout their lifetime, relative to patients without PTSD. This suggests that comorbid PTSD may cause an exacerbation of the SUD, contribute to more frequent SUD relapse following treatment, or both. In fact, Brown, Stout, and Mueller (1996) showed that SUD inpatients with comorbid PTSD diagnoses relapsed more quickly following SUD treatment than non-comorbid inpatients. Six months after discharge, although patients with PTSD did not differ from those without PTSD on overall relapse rates and percentage of days abstinent, PTSD comorbid patients relapsed faster, drank more on the occasions when they did drink, and reported more heavy drinking days at follow-up (Brown et al., 1996). Thus, comorbid PTSD appears to interfere with recovery from an SUD.

Together, the above findings also suggest that standard SUD treatment may not be as effective in reducing substance-related problems when they are comorbid with PTSD. This is consistent with the position that untreated PTSD perpetuates or exacerbates the SUD (or both). Brady, Killeen, Saladin, Dansky, and Becker (1994) demonstrated that SUD patients with comorbid PTSD evidenced difficulty complying with prescribed aftercare SUD treatment services compared with those without PTSD. This suggests that treatment noncompliance may be a potential mediating variable in explaining the effect of comorbid PTSD on poorer SUD treatment outcome. However, the above studies are somewhat limited by the fact that they lacked appropriate control groups (e.g., comparison with SUD patients comorbid for psychiatric disorders other than PTSD) and did not account for initial group differences in severity of addictive and nonaddictive psychopathology.

Ouimette, Ahrens, Moos, and Finney (1998) recently reported the results of a better controlled multisite treatment outcome study in which SUD patients were assessed immediately after participating in an SUD treatment program at 1 of 15 different Veterans Affairs programs. SUD patients with and without PTSD comorbidity (i.e., the *SUD only* and *SUD + PTSD* groups, respectively) were compared with SUD patients with another Axis I diagnosis (i.e., the *SUD + PSYCH* group) to explore the specific and nonspecific effects of PTSD comorbidity on SUD treatment outcome. All patients demonstrated change on most measures of SUD symptom severity after treatment. The SUD + PTSD patients reported more psychological distress at discharge compared with SUD-only and SUD + PSYCH patients even after controlling for baseline differences. There was an interaction between PTSD diagnosis and involvement with self-help during the index episode on most measures of outcome, with SUD + PTSD patients having a better outcome if they had been involved with self-help. These results suggest that treatment that targets SUD symptoms only is effective in reducing SUD symptoms among comorbid SUD–PTSD patients; however, such treatment is less effective in reducing nonaddictive psychological distress. At a 1-year follow-up, SUD + PTSD patients were more likely than the other groups to have been readmitted for inpatient/residential treatment during the follow-up (Ouimette, Ahrens, Moos, & Finney, 1997). Although PTSD symptoms were not specifically assessed, these findings may suggest that SUD-specific treatments possess poor efficacy in reducing PTSD symptoms and that untreated PTSD symptoms may place comorbid patients at increased risk for posttreatment relapse. Future studies should specifically measure short-term and longer term outcome of SUD-focused treatments in terms of reduction in both SUD and PTSD symptoms.

Treatment studies can also be useful in contributing to an understanding of functional relations by allowing exploration of the proximal determinants of changes in symptoms of either comorbid disorder. For example, Ouimette, Ahrens, et al. (1998) explored whether SUD patients with and without comorbid PTSD or other psychiatric disorders responded differentially to SUD treatment on measures that could be considered proximal determinants of relapse to substance abuse, such as coping styles, substance use expectancies, and perceived benefits of quitting. They found that the SUD + PTSD and the SUD + PSYCH patients did not show significant change on measures of positive substance use expectancies and positive expectancies for quitting, whereas the SUD-only patients improved on these measures. These findings suggest that although the three groups may not have differed in their ability to achieve abstinence from treatment, the comorbid SUD + PTSD and SUD + PSYCH groups demonstrated less change on motivation to maintain abstinence (e.g., they believed less in the benefits of quitting). Previous research has shown such motivational factors to be robust predictors of change in substance misuse behaviors (see review by Prochaska & DiClemente, 1986). In terms of coping strategies, SUD + PTSD and SUD + PSYCH patients reported greater use of cognitive avoidance and emotional discharge, and evidenced less change on such measures at treatment completion, than SUD-only patients. Thus, SUD patients with a comorbid psychiatric disorder who receive traditional SUD treatment may be less motivated to maintain abstinence because of maladaptive coping with negative affect. These potential psychological mediators of poor longer term outcome do not appear specific to SUD–PTSD comorbidity, however.

Ouimette, Finney, and Moos (1999) recently reported additional results of their treatment study over a 2-year follow-up period. All patient groups significantly reduced their substance use from posttreatment to 1-year follow-up and maintained these changes throughout the second year of follow-up. However, even after group differences in initial substance abuse severity were accounted for, the SUD + PTSD group evidenced more frequent and more severe substance use throughout the follow-up periods (i.e., drank more, evidenced more substance-related problems, and were less likely to be in remission). SUD + PTSD patients also evidenced less change on certain psychosocial outcome variables. For example, they did not show change on psychological symptoms, whereas SUD-only and SUD + PSYCH patients did report a decrease in psychological symptoms. The SUD + PTSD patient group also evidenced less improvement in terms of social supports, employment status, and arrest history at the 1-year follow-up relative to the other two patient groups. These results were maintained when all patients with an additional Axis I disorder were excluded from the SUD + PTSD group, indicating that the findings were specific to PTSD comorbidity.

Ouimette et al. (1999) also examined the potential mediational role of various psychological variables in explaining the relationship between a comorbid PTSD diagnosis and poorer substance-related outcomes. Problem solving, cognitive avoidance, and "emotional discharge" were all shown to be significant mediators of this relationship. Only emotional discharge remained a significant mediator when other psychiatric comorbidity was controlled. Therefore, there appears to be a pathway to SUD treatment resistance that is unique to PTSD comorbidity, which involves the tendency toward emotional discharge as a means of coping with emotional distress. *Emotional discharge* is a dimension of coping that reflects the extent to which an individual focuses on and vents his or her distress, rather than thinking about and implementing strategies for reducing or resolving the distress (Carver, Scheier, & Weintraub, 1989). The specificity of emotional discharge coping to PTSD comorbidity might be secondary to these patients experiencing more severe anxiety symptoms, such as hyperarousal. In the absence of more effective strategies for reducing or resolving distress, such symptoms in SUD–PTSD comorbid clients could lead both to elevated levels of venting of emotions and to poorer substance-related outcomes in SUD-focused treatment.

Ouimette et al.'s (1999) treatment study demonstrated that, over and above the contribution of other Axis I disorders, PTSD in combination with an SUD is associated with more severe psychological impairment. This increased psychological impairment is specifically related to rumination over, or venting of, negative emotion and to poorer psychosocial functioning. This increased psychiatric distress is also associated with a more severe pattern of substance abuse symptoms following treatment and with greater risk for drug abuse relapse. However, Ouimette et al. (1999) were not able to explore the direction of the relationships between these variables. For example, the findings do not resolve whether PTSD causes deficits in coping and these deficits in turn cause an exacerbation of SUD symptoms, or whether SUD symptoms cause deficits in coping which in turn exacerbate PTSD symptoms.

The third way in which treatment outcome studies can contribute to understanding functional relations is by demonstrating whether effective treatment of symptoms of one disorder is associated with reductions in symptoms of the comorbid disorder. Brown (2000) used this type of methodology in a treatment outcome study to shed some light on the direction of the relationship between PTSD and SUDs. She examined both PTSD and SUD 6-month treatment outcomes following traditional SUD treatment in a sample of 29 female SUD–PTSD comorbid patients. In particular, she assessed the value of specific addiction variables in predicting PTSD status (remitted or unremitted) at follow-up and, conversely, the value of specific PTSD variables in predicting SUD outcome (relapsed or not relapsed) at follow-up. By the 6-month follow-up, about one quarter of the initially comorbid patients were remitted from PTSD; approximately half had relapsed on alcohol, drugs, or both. Logistic regressions showed that baseline severity of PTSD intrusion symptoms was a significant predictor of SUD relapse at follow-up. No baseline SUD measure (e.g., baseline percentage of days abstinent) emerged as a significant predictor of PTSD remitted or unremitted status at follow-up. These findings suggest that high levels of PTSD symptoms, particularly intrusion symptoms, may increase risk for SUD relapse in comorbid patients undergoing traditional treatment for their SUD. On the basis of these results one might suggest that concurrent treatment targeting and effectively treating PTSD intrusion symptoms might result in improved longer term SUD outcomes for comorbid SUD–PTSD patients. Nonetheless, these findings require replication because of the small sample size of women involved.

Studies of the effects of PTSD treatment on SUD symptoms in comorbid patients could help determine the degree to which PTSD symptoms are exacerbating or maintaining the SUD. One reason for the relative absence of such research in the literature is that the majority of studies concerning treatment for PTSD have specifically excluded individuals with comorbid SUDs given recommendations that treatment of trauma-related issues be deferred until the SUD has been treated (e.g., Nace, 1988; Schnitt & Nocks, 1984). Such recommendations are based on the notion that treatment for PTSD (which involves cognitive exposure to traumatic events) would be too stressful and would lead to increased substance misuse (see chapter 7, this volume).

Ouimette, Moos, and Finney (2000) evaluated the association between PTSD treatment and the long-term course of SUDs in comorbid patients. Participants were male SUD–PTSD patients who completed 1- and 2-year posttreatment follow-ups. Patients were divided into one of three groups on the basis of their remission from substance abuse at the follow-ups: (a) stably remitted, (b) partially remitted, or (c) not remitted. These three groups were compared on mental health service use indexes (i.e., outpatient substance abuse, psychiatric, and PTSD services). PTSD treatment predicted SUD remission status over and above substance abuse treatment. Because PTSD treatment reduces substance abuse, the results of this study are consistent with the position that PTSD serves to maintain SUDs. However, future treatment outcome research should specifically evaluate both PTSD and SUD symptom outcomes to determine if reduction of PTSD symptoms by PTSD treatment is specifically mediating this improved SUD outcome in comorbid patients.

Although not truly a study of PTSD treatment, recent research by Deahl et al. (2000) provides some data relevant to the issue of the effects of PTSD-focused treatment on SUD symptoms. These authors studied the efficacy a secondary prevention strategy known as *psychological debriefing*, which involves providing trauma survivors with brief psychological interventions immediately or shortly after trauma exposure. Such debriefing is designed to help prevent the development of PTSD. A total of 106 British soldiers received an operational stress-training package prior to their deployment to the former Republic of Yugoslavia for United Nations peacekeeping duties. On their return, a randomly selected subgroup also received a postoperational psychological debriefing. Deahl et al. found low rates of PTSD overall (possibly related to the fact that all soldiers received stress training prior to deployment). Thus, it is not surprising that they did not find a significant effect of psychological debriefing on PTSD symptoms. However, the participants did evidence initially high rates of alcohol misuse, which diminished significantly in the debriefed group relative to the nondebriefed control group by the end of the follow-up. These findings suggest that the psychological debriefing around the management of posttraumatic stress may have prevented the development of more severe SUD symptoms. However, this conclusion must be qualified by several caveats. First, the reduction in alcohol misuse associated with debriefing was not accompanied by a reduction in PTSD symptoms (possibly because of a floor effect), which places in question a PTSD-treatment mediational account of the effectiveness of debriefing on SUD symptoms. Second, despite equivalent severity of trauma exposure across the experimental versus control groups, the nondebriefed group reported more distress in association with trauma exposure and more severe depression, anxiety, and PTSD symptoms at baseline. These initial differences were unfortunately not treated as covariates in the analyses of alcohol abuse at the follow-up; therefore, it is unclear whether their initially greater levels of psychopathology or posttraumatic distress caused a maintenance of alcohol-related problems in the nondebriefed control group, or whether the psychological debriefing caused a reduction in such problems in the experimental group. A further limitation is that soldiers' predeployment drinking histories were not assessed. Therefore, the conclusions that can be drawn from this preliminary study are limited. Further investigation is required before one can firmly conclude that PTSD-focused treatments lead to a reduction in substance-related problems.

The final way in which treatment studies can be informative about functional relations is in testing predictions made by theories that advocate the vicious cycle. Some have argued that once this hypothetical cycle between symptoms of the two disorders is established (e.g., in more chronic cases of SUD–PTSD comorbidity), treatment for only one disorder may not be sufficient for comorbid patients, regardless of which disorder was temporally or causally primary (e.g., Stewart, 1996). Advocates of such positions argue that symptoms of both disorders require attention in therapy for optimal treatment outcome and that combined treatments should confer greater advantages to comorbid clients than treatments designed to target the symptoms of one disorder only. Researchers are beginning to develop and investigate the effectiveness of combined therapy programs where both PTSD and SUD symptoms are targeted in comorbid clients. In the only study to date to compare such a combined approach with a single-therapy treatment, Abueg and Fairbank (1991) investigated the relative efficacy of a combined SUD–PTSD relapse prevention program ($N = 42$) as compared with a PTSD treatment program alone ($N = 42$) for comorbid SUD–PTSD patients. Combined treatment was associated with a greater likelihood of abstinence at 6-month follow-up and lighter drinking at the 9-month follow-up. However, groups did not differ on abstinence rates at 9 months. Harvey, Rawson, and Obert (1994), although they failed to compare their combined-treatment approach to a traditional single-treatment approach, found SUD–PTSD patients to respond equally well as SUD-only patients to an SUD treatment program that included group treatment addressing sexual assault and other trauma. These findings suggest that, consistent with the notion of a vicious cycle, a combined-treatment approach may override the well-documented tendency for SUD–PTSD patients to demonstrate poorer treatment outcome. However, Harvey et al. did not assess for initial group differences in psychiatric or substance abuse severity, include a control group, or report outcomes on several of the response dimensions (e.g., amount of consumption on drinking days) on which comorbid SUD–PTSD patients have shown poorer outcome in previous research.

Open trials of two new combined approaches to PTSD and SUD have recently been conducted. Although these new combined approaches have yet to be compared with therapies targeting only SUD symptoms or only PTSD symptoms (see chapter 7, this volume), their study still has implications for understanding functional relations. For example, Najavits, Weiss, Shaw, and Muenz (1998) examined the treatment outcome of 35 women with comorbid SUD–PTSD diagnoses who were provided with a new psychosocial treatment called "Seeking Safety" that targets simultaneously both PTSD and substance abuse issues. Patients showed significant improvement in a variety of areas, including psychopathology, substance-related attitudes, social adjustment, and family functioning. However, rate of completion of this program was very low: Only 14 of 35 patients who met eligibility criteria for the study completed treatment or attended at least 6 of 24 sessions. More recently, Brady, Dansky, Back, Foa, and Carroll (2001) reported on the preliminary results of their concurrent, integrated treatment for comorbid SUD–PTSD. This approach involves a combination of exposure therapy for PTSD and cognitive–behavioral therapy for SUD (see also chapter 7, this volume). Patients showed significant improvement in a variety of areas, including PTSD symptoms and depressive symptomatology. Moreover, the combined treatment appeared to be effective in treating substance abuse, in that cocaine use declined from baseline to end of treatment, and addiction severity scores declined. However, as in Najavits, Weiss, Shaw, and Muenz's (1998) study, dropout rates were again extremely high with Brady et al.'s (2001) combined treatment: Only 15 of 39 patients were classified as completers. Because there were no control groups included in these two studies, relative outcome and relative therapy dropout rates associated with these combined treatments cannot be established. Nonetheless, the high observed dropout rates suggest that combined-treatment programs that concurrently address comorbid disorders may not be feasible for assisting many SUD–PTSD patients, possibly because they place too many demands on the patient at one time. For patients who are able to tolerate these demands, however, combined treatments appear to have many potential benefits in terms of improvements in both comorbid disorders.

Several conclusions can be drawn from the extant treatment studies with dually diagnosed SUD–PTSD patients. First, SUD patients with comorbid PTSD appear to respond less favorably to SUD-focused treatment than do SUD patients without PTSD. Over and above initial group differences in symptom severity, SUD–PTSD patients appear to demonstrate more frequent and more severe substance use following SUD treatment. There is also some evidence for a greater risk for SUD relapse (or at least for faster relapse) following SUD-focused treatment among such dually diagnosed patients. These findings are consistent with the notion that PTSD interferes with recovery from an SUD. Second, treatment studies that have explored proximal determinants of changes in symptoms have yielded evidence suggesting that both PTSD-specific factors (e.g., emotional discharge coping, psychiatric distress) and nonspecific factors (e.g., fewer expected benefits of quitting) may influence the poorer substance abuse treatment outcome in comorbid SUD–PTSD patients. Third, studies of the differential effects of treatments targeting specific symptom clusters and subsequent change in symptoms of the targeted disorder and the comorbid disorder suggest the following conclusions. Traditional approaches to the treatment of SUDs do not appear to fully address the factors that maintain substance-related problems in comorbid SUD–PTSD patients. These findings provide little support for the position that PTSD symptoms are caused or maintained by substance abuse alone. In contrast, preliminary evidence suggests that PTSD-focused treatment is helpful in reducing SUD symptoms and that recovery from PTSD in comorbid patients is associated with reductions in SUD problems. This pattern suggests that SUD in the context of comorbid PTSD is exacerbated or at least maintained by the emotional distress associated with PTSD.

There is some evidence to suggest that combined treatments may prevent poorer outcome of SUD–PTSD patients relative to SUD-only patients. However, the overall effectiveness of current combined treatment programs may be limited because of high dropout rates that possibly are due to the increased demands placed on patients in these more intensive programs. The evidence presented in this chapter suggests that once comorbidity is established each disorder can serve to maintain the other with patients self-medicating for PTSD symptoms with substances but repeated substance withdrawal ultimately heightening PTSD symptoms. Given this vicious cycle, SUD–PTSD treatment does clearly need to address symptoms of both disorders. However, there may be less demanding methods for accomplishing this goal than with the intensive combined programs that have been developed to date. For example, a brief motivational coping skills intervention has been specifically developed and demonstrated to be effective for substance abusers high in fear of anxiety and PTSD symptoms (Conrod, Pihl, Stewart, & Dongier, 2000; Conrod, Stewart, et al., 2000). In this brief treatment, clients explore the functional relations between their PTSD symptoms and SUD behaviors (cf. Miller & Rollnick, 1992; see also recommendations by Coffey et al., chapter 7, this volume), and learn alternative methods of coping with their intrusive anxiety-related symptoms. We recommend that this brief integrated treatment be compared with more intensive combined therapy in terms of efficacy in reducing symptoms of both disorders and in terms of relative client dropout rates.

CONCLUSION

Epidemiologic studies have unequivocally established a high rate of co-occurrence between PTSD and SUDs. In the course of this chapter, we reviewed the literature on a large body of methodologically varied studies to examine the evidence for potential causal and functional relations to explain SUD–PTSD comorbidity. We were able to draw a number of conclusions regarding the nature of the relationship between these two disorders. First, correlational studies examining the gradient of effect between severity of the two disorders have indicated that, at least with respect to alcohol and prescription depressant drugs, severity of SUDs covary with severity of

PTSD symptoms, thus establishing one criterion for causality. Retrospective and prospective investigations that explore the temporal patterning of the onset of the two disorders also provide support for a causal link between them and further suggest that PTSD usually precedes the SUD. Moreover, one study revealed qualitative differences between dually diagnosed patient groups with primary PTSD relative to those with a primary SUD. In cases in which PTSD was the primary disorder, patients reported higher rates of prescription depressant drug use and misuse and different traumatic histories. Studies that have assessed patient perceptions of the factors that exacerbate or maintain their psychiatric symptoms suggest a self-medication process by which use of drugs with central nervous system depressant properties are reportedly used as a way to cope with physical or emotional discomfort or to avoid exacerbation of PTSD symptoms. Studies that attempt to identify factors that determine who develops an SUD in response to trauma point to two general mediating factors: (a) PTSD and (b) anxiety sensitivity. These studies suggest that trauma-exposed individuals who develop unmanageable anxiety symptoms (i.e., PTSD) and who catastrophize about the consequences of such symptoms (i.e., display high anxiety sensitivity) are particularly likely to cope with their PTSD symptoms by using drugs that have arousal- and anxiety-reducing properties.

Our review of the results of treatment studies with SUD–PTSD patients points to similar conclusions. Several studies that have examined the differential response of dually diagnosed versus SUD-only patients to traditional addiction treatment indicate poorer outcome on both drug-related and psychosocial variables for comorbid patients and particularly poor outcome for SUD–PTSD patients relative to other patient groups with an additional Axis I disorder. Studies that have attempted to identify factors implicated in the posttreatment recovery process suggest that deficits in specific coping strategies, namely, emotional discharge, account for the relatively poor response to SUD treatment by SUD–PTSD patients. We suggest that such deficits may actually reflect the effect of PTSD hyperarousal symptoms on coping. We argue that hyperarousal symptoms may be the specific feature of PTSD that renders certain PTSD patients particularly likely to resort to substance abuse and to prove additionally resistant to traditional SUD treatment. It is unfortunate that very few studies have been published that assess the effect of PTSD treatment on substance use behavior. Such studies would provide further evidence for a causal link between PTSD and SUD and would provide important additional information regarding the direction and nature of the relationship between the two disorders. Results of the few studies that have examined the efficacy of combined SUD–PTSD treatments for dually diagnosed patients suggest that those who complete such programs are able to achieve significant improvement on a variety of variables, including psychopathology. Nonetheless, high treatment dropout rates may be a particular problem with such intensive combined treatment strategies. We conclude by suggesting that alternative approaches to treatment of dually diagnosed SUD–PTSD patients explore the efficacy of providing brief motivational interventions for SUD in combination with PTSD treatment. There are available empirically supported brief-intervention strategies that target patients who use drugs for specific reinforcing effects, including management of anxiety and arousal. Future studies should explore the different combinations of SUD and PTSD treatments for dually diagnosed clients while paying particular attention to the issue of feasibility for this currently underserved clinical population.

3

EXPERIMENTAL STUDIES EXPLORING FUNCTIONAL RELATIONS BETWEEN POSTTRAUMATIC STRESS DISORDER AND SUBSTANCE USE DISORDER

PATRICIA J. CONROD AND SHERRY H. STEWART

In chapter 2, we reviewed the literature on a large body of methodologically varied studies to examine evidence supporting potential causal or other functional relations between posttraumatic stress disorder (PTSD) and substance use disorders (SUDs). We were able to draw a number of conclusions regarding the nature of the relationship between these two disorders. Studies that have examined covariation between PTSD and SUD symptoms with respect to severity, temporal patterning, patient perceptions of their relationship, and posttreatment mediators of change suggest two functional processes. First, PTSD and SUDs appear to be related through a self-medication process by which drugs with arousal- and anxiety-reducing properties (alcohol, benzodiazepines, and opioids) are used for the management of PTSD symptoms, particularly hyperarousal and intrusion symptoms. More specifically, these studies suggest that substance abuse and dependence are most likely in PTSD patients who have catastrophic interpretations of their anxiety symptoms (anxiety sensitivity), who believe that discontinuation of such use will result in a recurrence or exacerbation of their symptoms, or who lack adaptive coping strategies for managing emotional distress and arousal. Second, PTSD and SUDs may also be related through a cyclical pattern of substance abuse leading to brief PTSD symptom relief, followed by a gradual PTSD symptom exacerbation, possibly as a result of drug withdrawal. This longer term withdrawal-induced PTSD symptom enhancement may promote further substance abuse in the patients' continued attempts at self-medication (see chapter 2, this volume).

Despite the contribution of these previously reviewed studies to the understanding of the comorbidity between PTSD and SUD, their methodologies have generally relied on the use of self-report. Given the many potential biases inherent in patient self-report, alternative approaches to assessment can provide important validation of the findings discussed in chapter 2. Another approach to understanding SUD–PTSD comorbidity, alternative to patient self-report methods, is to examine this relationship in the laboratory using experimental methods. Direct examination of the effects of administration of alcohol and other drugs (e.g., Conrod, Pihl, & Vassileva, 1998; Stewart & Pihl, 1994) in conjunction with controlled investigations of the characteristics of patients with PTSD (e.g., McNally, 1997) can provide important information on the potential reinforcing effects of drugs for individuals suffering from PTSD. Through control over extraneous variables, these studies can allow for much stronger conclusions regarding causality. In this chapter we review relevant laboratory findings, present a model for understanding the mechanisms of action of drugs of abuse on PTSD symptoms, point out gaps in the literature to date, and make suggestions for future laboratory-based experimental research.

ELECTROPHYSIOLOGICAL STUDIES

In response to studies suggesting a possible genetic predisposition to PTSD (e.g., Davidson, Tupler, Wilson, & Connor, 1998; Yehuda, Schmeidler, Wainberg, Binder-Brynes, & Duvdevani, 1998), a number of researchers have begun to explore the biological mechanisms that might mediate such vulnerability. Results of laboratory-based biological research in PTSD have revealed several findings that may have implications for understanding SUD–PTSD comorbidity. For example, PTSD vulnerability has been associated with abnormalities in the P300 component of the event-related brain potential (Kounios et al., 1997; Metzger, Orr, Lasko, Berry, & Pitman, 1997; True & Pitman, 1999). This event-related brain potential component is thought to reflect efficiency of the nervous system in classifying novel stimuli (see review by Picton, 1992). P300 abnormalities are not unique to PTSD; they have been observed in alcoholics and in individuals at high genetic risk for alcoholism (e.g., Begleiter, Porjesz, Bihari, & Kissin, 1984), as well as in patients with depression, panic disorder, and schizophrenia (Roschke et al., 1996). This neurophysiological characteristic may represent a genetically mediated vulnerability factor for the development of PTSD following trauma exposure, possibly reflecting a vulnerability to psychopathology in general. True and Pitman (1999) offered the following two interpretations of the link between reduced P300 responding and increased PTSD symptoms. First, they suggested that reduced P300 may reflect a decreased ability to encode the traumatic event such that, when reminded of the event, individuals with P300 deficits have difficulty integrating intrusive memories into current awareness. Second, they alternatively speculated that P300 abnormalities may reflect impaired attentional processes such that, when intrusive memories arise, susceptible individuals are more distracted by such memories. With respect to understanding functional relations between PTSD and SUDs, alcohol has been shown to normalize abnormalities in the P300 responses of individuals with a genetic predisposition to alcoholism (Pollock et al., 1983). It is currently unclear whether the P300 deficits that characterize individuals at high risk for alcoholism are similar in nature to the P300 abnormalities observed in PTSD patients and, subsequently, whether alcohol normalizes the P300 deficits of PTSD patients. This is an area worthy of future research.

PSYCHOPHYSIOLOGICAL STUDIES

The *Diagnostic and Statistical Manual of Mental Disorders* (American Psychiatric Association, 1994) includes elevated startle as a diagnostic criterion for PTSD. Laboratory-based research has validated its inclusion by revealing that PTSD patients do indeed display exaggerated startle responses (e.g., Butler et al., 1990; Morgan, Grillon, Lubin, & Southwick, 1997). The *startle response* is an involuntary defensive reflex that occurs in response to the presentation of strong and abrupt stimulation (Davis, 1984; P. J. Lang, 1995). Moreover, fear-potentiated startle (i.e., enhanced startle responses due to the presence of a conditioned fear stimulus) is even further exaggerated in PTSD patients (Morgan, Grillon, Southwick, Davis, & Charney, 1995). There is also an extensive body of laboratory-based research with normal participants demonstrating that acute alcohol and benzodiazepine administration causes a dose-dependent reduction in startle reactivity, blocks fear-potentiated startle, or both (Grillon, Sinha, & O'Malley, 1994; Patrick, Berthot, & Moore, 1993; Stritzke, Patrick, & Lang, 1995). Whether the primary reinforcing effects of alcohol and benzodiazepines for PTSD patients involve dampening of their exaggerated startle is at present unknown. However, in order to link this mechanism to reinforcement it will be important to determine whether the experience of startle elicits greater craving for alcohol and sedative drugs in individuals with PTSD or whether elicitation of the startle response is associated with drug self-administration in a drug choice procedure (Johanson & de Wit, 1989).

A related body of research has shown that PTSD is associated with other physiological indexes of stress reactivity. In a follow-up study of 86 trauma survivors admitted to the emergency room for trauma-related injury, Shalev and Rogel-Fuchs (1993) assessed heart rate levels of these individuals on admission to the emergency room and then 1 week, 1 month, and 4 months later. Heart rate levels on admission and at the 1-week follow-up assessment differentiated participants who met criteria for PTSD at the 4-month follow-up period from those who did not. These results were maintained even while controlling for age, trauma severity, intensity of immediate subjective reaction to the trauma, and dissociation during the trauma. These findings suggest that heightened heart rate reactivity in the first few weeks after trauma may be a risk factor for the development of PTSD. In a related study, Shalev, Peri, Gelpin, Orr, and Pitman (1997) assessed physiologic arousal in response to traumatic memories and showed that individuals who developed PTSD after a civilian trauma demonstrated more physiologic reactivity (cardiac, electrodermal, and motoric) than those who did not develop PTSD. Similar differences between PTSD and non-PTSD trauma-exposed individuals were revealed in a study described by Shalev (1997) that examined heart rate, eyeblink, and skin conductance habituation responses to startling auditory stimuli. However, in Shalev's study, group differences emerged 1 month and 4 months after the trauma; group differences were not evident 1 week after the trauma. This series of studies suggests that individual differences in tonic arousal levels around the time of and just after the trauma are related to PTSD vulnerability, whereas autonomic reactivity to startling and threatening stimuli may simply reflect a physiologic correlate of PTSD.

With regard to implications for SUDs, alcohol and other sedative drugs (anxiolytics and opioids) have been shown to reduce physiologic arousal in response to startling and threatening stimuli (e.g., Davis, 1986; Davis, Falls, Campeau, & Munsoo, 1993; Hijzen, Houtzager, Joordens, Oliver, & Slanger, 1995; Patrick et al., 1993). No study has actually tested whether such drugs actually dampen physiologic arousal in PTSD patients. Nonetheless, this is a plausible notion considering that correlational gradient-of-effect studies (see chapter 2, this volume) suggest that PTSD arousal symptoms are strongly related to abuse of and dependence on alcohol as well as to dependence on prescription anxiolytics and prescription opioids. Moreover, Saladin, Brady, Dansky, and Kilpatrick (1995) reported that PTSD patients with a comorbid SUD demonstrate higher PTSD arousal symptoms compared to patients with pure PTSD. They also found that PTSD patients who were dependent on alcohol reported more arousal symptoms than did PTSD patients who were cocaine dependent. A recent series of alcohol-challenge studies showed that individuals high in anxiety sensitivity, a personality factor that appears to at least partially mediate the relationship between PTSD and SUDs (Stewart, Conrod, Samoluk, Pihl, & Dongier, 2000), are particularly sensitive to the dampening effects of alcohol on cognitive and psychophysiological measures of arousal and fear reactivity (Conrod et al., 1998; Stewart & Pihl, 1994). These studies suggest that arousal-dampening drugs might be used by PTSD patients to control hyperarousal symptoms.

This type of self-medication might be particularly likely among patients who are most susceptible to such symptoms.

NEUROPSYCHOLOGICAL AND NEUROIMAGING STUDIES

Studies on the neuropsychological functioning of survivors of both combat and sexual abuse forms of trauma suggest that PTSD susceptibility is associated with a number of impairments. These include lower global IQ, soft signs of neurological deficits in childhood (e.g., delay of walk, attention deficits, learning problems), and poor performance on memory and executive cognitive function tests of planning and abstraction skills (e.g., Gurvits et al., 2000; Yehuda, Keefe, Harvey, & Levengood, 1995). These differences are independent of group differences in alcohol dependence (e.g., Gurvits et al., 2000), but such deficits are also found in alcoholic patients and nonalcoholic children of alcoholics (see review by Pihl, Peterson, & Finn, 1990). Functional neuroimaging studies have similarly revealed abnormalities in brain structures that are involved in the regulation of executive cognitive functions, memory, and the startle response. For example, Shin et al. (1997) asked Vietnam veterans with and without PTSD to imagine themselves in combat. The results indicated that the PTSD group showed hyperactivity in the right amygdala and hypoactivity in the inferior frontal cortex. Other studies have documented structural abnormalities in the hippocampus as well (e.g., Gurvits et al., 1996). These brain structures have been shown to be integrally involved in the mediation of stress-induced sensitization of the startle response (Sananes & Davis, 1992), memory and executive cognitive function, and to be particularly susceptible to the effects of alcohol (Gray, 1982; A. R. Lang, Patrick, & Stritzke, 1999; Peterson, Finn, & Pihl, 1992). It has been suggested the pathophysiology of PTSD is primarily located in these brain areas (Rauch & Shin, 1997), and it is plausible that certain drugs of abuse also have their effects on PTSD symptoms by means of their interaction with these brain structures. The amygdala and the hippocampus are densely populated with GABA-ergic neurons, and the reinforcing effects of drugs of abuse that have been linked with PTSD symptoms in correlational studies (i.e., alcohol, benzodiazepines, and opioids; Stewart, Conrod, Pihl, & Dongier, 1999) are mediated directly or indirectly by GABA-ergic mechanisms (Gray, 1982).

NEUROENDOCRINE STUDIES

These findings of hypersensitive stress responding and neuropsychological deficits in PTSD patients may be related to findings of a relationship between dysregulation of the hypothalamic–pituitary–adrenal (HPA) axis and PTSD vulnerability (Yehuda, 1997a). Moreover, these findings might have particular implications for the understanding of SUD–PTSD comorbidity. PTSD has been associated with reduced basal cortisol output and supersensitive responses to cortisol that are mediated by upregulation of glucocorticoid receptors (Yehuda, 1997a, 1997b). Of interest is that a prior history of assault has been associated with reduced basal cortisol levels, whereas elevated cortisol levels are observed in newly assaulted women, particularly those who display PTSD symptoms (Resnick, Yehuda, & Acierno, 1997). In this latter study, elevated cortisol levels were particularly evident in newly assaulted women who were using alcohol and in those suffering from hyperarousal symptoms. Bremner, Licino, et al. (1997) found that combat veterans with PTSD showed higher cerebral spinal fluid corticotropin releasing factor (CRF) relative to controls. This hormone is integrally involved in the stress response (Nemeroff et al., 1984), particularly the behavioral expression of fear (including physiologic arousal). CRF and locus ceoruleus noradrenergic (LC/NE) activity are highly interrelated, and it has been suggested that they are involved in a mutually reinforcing feedback loop that responds to stressful stimuli (Southwick et al., 1999). This powerful feed-forward feature of the CRF–LC/NE system has led some researchers to suggest that this system is involved in the development of sensitized stress responding with repeated exposure to stress as well as with the pathogenesis of stress-related disorders, such as depression, panic disorder, and PTSD (Koob, 1999). The LC/NE system appears to regulate the more cognitive (e.g., attentional) aspects of alerting and fear responses in primates (Redmond, 1987), possibly through its projections from the LC to the prefrontal cortex, and is particularly susceptible to the effects of chronic and uncontrollable stress. Arnsten (1998) and Southwick et al. (1999) have argued that NE control of the prefrontal cortex modulates attentional shifting away from distracting and irrelevant sensory processing through projections to the hippocampus. This allows for focused attention and concentration on the contents of working memory (Arnsten, 1998). Such an effect appears to result in enhanced cognitive function and behavioral calming in animals (Arnsten, 1998). Drugs of abuse that have been linked with PTSD symptoms in correlational studies (i.e., alcohol, benzodiazepines, and opioids; Stewart, Conrod, et al., 1999) have been shown to interact with glucocorticoids (de Boer, Slagen, & Van der Gugten, 1992) and may produce their calming effects by interacting with this brain system.

Studies with PTSD patients have shown that auditory reminders of trauma cause an increase in NE activity and concurrent physiologic arousal, particularly heart rate reactivity (Blanchard, Kolb, Prins, Gates, & McCoy, 1991). Biologic challenge studies that involve manipulation of the NE system have suggested that PTSD patients are characterized by a hypersensitivity to

NE stimulation. For example, Southwick et al. (1993) showed that *yohimbine*, an adrenergic antagonist that results in increases in NE activity, sensitized PTSD patients to experience hyperarousal, panic, and flashbacks to their traumatic event but did not produce such symptoms in controls. Brain imaging and neuropsychological studies indicate that, like stress, yohimbine may have dose–response effects on the brain, with high doses being specifically related to decreased activation in prefrontal cortical areas that are highly innervated by NE neurons (Birnbaum, Gobeske, Auerback, Taylor, & Arnsten, 1999; Bremner, Innis, et al., 1997). For example, Bremner, Innis, et al. (1997) conducted a yohimbine-challenge study using positron emission tomography with PTSD patients and controls and showed localized dose–response effects of yohimbine on the prefrontal cortex. Although PTSD patients showed cognitive and behavioral hypersensitivity to the yohimbine challenge, they showed decreased metabolism in prefrontal cortical areas compared to controls, suggesting that their hypersensitivity to NE stimulation caused such exaggerated activation of the LC/NE system that a decrease in activation in the prefrontal cortex resulted. Southwick et al. (1999) suggested that NE sensitivity to stress and pharmacological challenge in PTSD patients results in a decrease in the normal inhibitory control that the prefrontal cortex usually exerts over responses to irrelevant and distracting information. They suggested that this may be the process by which hyperarousal and intrusion symptoms are experienced by PTSD patients; that is, that NE sensitivity to stress causes deactivation of the prefrontal cortex and subsequent release of attentional control, such that hypervigilance is provoked and traumatic memories are brought to the forefront of attention.

Although this review focuses on experimental investigations of the neuropharmacological mechanisms that might mediate PTSD symptoms and help explain SUD–PTSD comorbidity, this does not imply that such processes are necessarily the result of pharmacologically mediated pathology. For example, the pattern of responding to yohimbine challenge in PTSD patients can be explained by a cognitive sensitivity to any form of pharmacological challenge that results in sympathetic arousal, which may then serve as an interoceptive cue that triggers traumatic memories in PTSD patients. Furthermore, it is unclear whether hyperactivity of NE in PTSD patients reflects a stress-induced biological predisposition to hyperarousal or the effects of cognitive factors on the interpretation of trauma cues. In fact, research demonstrating that PTSD patients also experience panic symptoms and flashbacks to lactate infusion challenge suggests that their hypersensitivity is not exclusive to NE activation (Jensen et al., 1997). In chapter 2 of this volume we reviewed the evidence suggesting that substance abuse is most likely in PTSD patients who have catastrophic interpretations of their anxiety symptoms (anxiety sensitivity). Anxiety sensitivity is similarly associated with susceptibility to panic induction, and such susceptibility appears to be mediated by cognitive and affective factors (or at least a centrally mediated fear mechanism; e.g., Gorman et al., 2001) rather than by neuroendocrine factors or factors that occur in the periphery. Nevertheless, research on the role of NE in the pathogenesis of PTSD provides a framework for understanding how severe, uncontrollable, and chronic stress, in interaction with personality traits such as anxiety sensitivity, may produce susceptibility to hyperarousal and certain forms of psychopathology (such as PTSD, SUDs, or their combination).

With regard to the potential interaction between the NE system and substances typically abused by PTSD patients, there is some evidence that rats bred to be attracted to alcohol may have similarly downregulated, hyperactive NE systems (Hwang, Wang, Wong, Lumeng, & Li, 2000). Moreover, ethanol produces dose-dependent effects on NE in the frontal cortex in that a low dose causes higher NE output but a high dose causes reduced output (e.g., Pohorecky, 1977). The dose-dependent effects of alcohol on alertness and sedation parallel the dose-dependent effects of NE on such functions, and it has been suggested that alcohol may produce these effects by means of NE mechanisms (Pohorecky, 1977), particularly in those in the prefrontal cortex (Rossetti et al., 1992). One speculation is that alcohol, at certain doses, inhibits the facilitating effects of NE on prefrontal cortex functions, thus enhancing the sedating, calming effects of the prefrontal cortex on stress responding. The effects of alcohol and benzodiazepines on NE function may also be mediated by CRF mechanisms (Koob, 1999).

However, studies that have explored the role of NE in drinking behavior have revealed very conflicting findings. The functional effects of alcohol on NE activity are not clear and tend to depend on the type of rat strain studied, the site of NE activity observed, or the context in which alcohol is administered. For example, rats who are bred for complete deficiency in dopamine b-hydroxylase, which is required for NE synthesis, are hypersensitive to ethanol-induced sedation, but they are not prone to alcohol consumption (Weinshenker, Rust, Miller, & Palmiter, 2000). Other studies indicate that chronic alcohol intake and tolerance to the sedating effects of alcohol are associated with depletion of NE in the hippocampus and cortex (Shafik, Aiken, & McArdle, 1991), but this effect may result only from long-term chronic use (Huttunen, 1991). Further work in this area is definitely needed that might benefit SUD–PTSD patients. Specifically, this literature suggests there are implications for how stress exposure and recurrent relapse to psychopathology or substance abuse (or both) have very significant consequences for the mental health of trauma-exposed individuals. Furthermore, insight into the neuroendocrine or neuropharmacological factors involved in this CRF–LC/NE feed-forward stress–response loop (Koob, 1999; McEwen, 2000) may provide guidance on how maintenance therapies can reduce risk for relapse or future psychopathology in such individuals.

Moreover, research on the effects of acute and chronic stress on hormonal reactions has led to the recognition that stress may alter neurobiological systems (Rasmusson & Charney, 1997; McEwen, 2000). In particular, animal studies indicate that prior stress exposure alters response to subsequent experiences through the effects of glucocorticoids (possibly through glutamate and GABA-ergic mechanisms; McEwen, 2000) on hippocampal pyramidal neurons that are integrally involved in memory function (McEwen & Magarino, 1997). Deficits in hippocampal cognitive functions and reduced hippocampal size occur in humans who have been exposed to severe stress, although it is unclear whether these changes correlate with increases in HPA activity (McEwen & Magarino, 1997; Yehuda, 1997b). The hippocampus has been shown to play an inhibitory role in stress responses, particularly with respect to mediating the integration of contextual cues (relational processing) and experience (memory) on anxiety and stress reactivity (Armony & LeDoux, 1997). Deficits in such functions could have negative implications for the regulation of both tonic and phasic activation of fear, anxiety, and arousal (Davis, Walker, & Lee, 1997). Chronic alcohol exposure, especially alcohol withdrawal, stimulates corticosteroidogenesis and may have additive detrimental effects on HPA and hippocampal function (Keith, Roberts, Wiren, & Crabbe, 1995).

THE SELF-MEDICATION AND SYMPTOM MAINTENANCE MODEL: NEURAL CIRCUITS INVOLVED IN THE RELATIONSHIP BETWEEN PTSD AND SUD

Armony and LeDoux (1997) presented a model of the structures and processes involved in the brain's response to emotional and traumatic stimuli. We have adapted this model (see Figure 3.1) to provide a preliminary illustration of those neuronal circuits and processes that are implicated in the pathophysiology of PTSD and the mechanisms of action of drugs of abuse on PTSD symptoms. As illustrated in Figure 3.1, Armony and LeDoux proposed that information about the sensory features of a traumatic event are directly sent to the amygdala via the sensory thalamus or indirectly via the sensory cortex, the association cortex, or the hippocampus. The hippocampus is particularly involved in integrating memory and sensory information about the event to allow for its contextual understanding. According to a large number of studies conducted by LeDoux and his colleagues (e.g., LeDoux, 1996), the hippocampus could have inhibitory influences on stress reactivity if the event is integrated into a nonthreatening context. The hippocampus also sends information to and receives input from the prefrontal cortex, which is involved in higher order processing and abstraction. Deficits in this pathway could potentially limit the efficiency

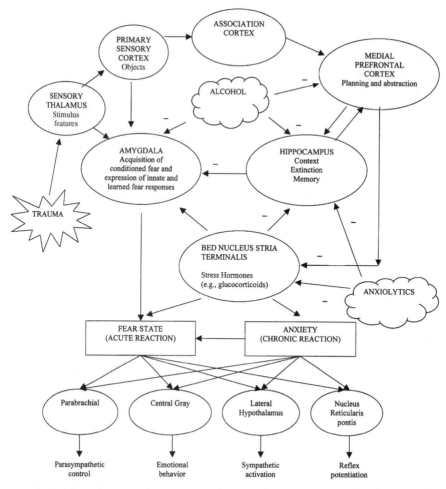

Figure 3.1. Model illustrating the neuronal circuits and processes implicated in the pathophysiology of posttraumatic stress disorder (PTSD) and the mechanisms of action of drugs of abuse on PTSD symptoms. Based on Armony and LeDoux's (1997) hypothesized neural system involved in the regulation of classic fear conditioning.

with which the hippocampus is able to apply context and past experiences to newly processed events or reprocess memories into lexical terms (Spiegel, 1997). As a consequence, such deficits are associated with less efficient inhibition of stress and fear reactions to such affectively ambiguous information (Arnsten, 1998).

The activation of the central nucleus of the amygdala and the bed nucleus stria terminalis, respectively, cause two types of responses: (a) fear and (b) anxiety (Davis et al., 1997). The fear response is more severe and more acute (because of feedback mechanisms). The anxiety response is less intense and has potential for longer term activation (Davis et al., 1997). Both structures have similar effects on hypothalamic and brain stem functions that are involved in symptoms of anxiety and fear. However, the bed of the nucleus stria terminalis is particularly susceptible to the effects of glucocorticoids and causes NE release (Koob, 1999; Lee & Davis, 1997). The neurocircuitry of this structure appears to be able to accommodate a CRF–NE feedforward loop that appears to mediate the long-term potentiation of fear and startle responses (Koob, 1999; Lee & Davis, 1997). This could explain why prior stress, psychopathology, and trauma exposure are associated with abnormalities in HPA function, stress reactivity, and PTSD susceptibility. Glucocorticoids cause dendritic atrophy in the hippocampus (McEwen, 2000), which could further interfere with information processing of future traumatic experiences based on memory of such experiences in the past. PTSD symptoms could be maintained by such deficits (whether reversible or not) in that proper integration of the trauma memory into a nonthreatening context is not achieved, thus interfering with extinction of fear responses to such memories. Alcohol, anxiolytics, and opioids are known to exert their anxiolytic effects by inhibiting activity in the bed nucleus stria terminalis and are particularly effective in reducing aspects of the startle response. Alcohol may have further inhibitory effects on startle reactivity by means of its effects on the amygdala and the prefrontal cortex (e.g., Gray, 1982; Pohorecky, 1977). It is likely that the primary reinforcing effect of such drugs of abuse is to reduce tonic levels of anxiety, which then also interfere with phasic stress and fear reactions (Davis et al., 1997). However, drugs of abuse have very short-term effects on such processes; thus, chronic use would be required to maintain anxiolytic effects. This model could also explain how PTSD symptoms could be maintained or exacerbated by chronic alcohol and anxiolytic use, as such drugs also interfere with the functioning of the hippocampus and frontal cortex (Shafik et al., 1991). As a consequence, short-term drug-induced reduction of anxiety and fear are specifically coupled with interference in functioning of brain structures that are involved in higher order processing that allows for the longer term extinction of fear. Therefore, individuals are particularly susceptible to anxiety and fear when they are not intoxicated, because they have not learned to extinguish their fear response to the stimuli that trigger trauma memories or physiologic arousal. Withdrawal from such drugs may further exacerbate sensitivity of the HPA axis, to further sensitize stress responses (Keith et al., 1995) and susceptibility to PTSD symptoms (Southwick et al., 1999).

It has also been suggested that chronic stress may further sensitize an individual to the effects of, or relapse to, drugs of abuse that possess incentive rewarding properties (e.g., alcohol and stimulants) through interactions between the CRF and dopamine-mediated psychomotor functions (e.g., Deroche, Piazza, LeMoal, & Simon, 1994). However, studies with female substance abusers suggest that PTSD is associated with a tendency to use drugs that possess anxiety-reducing properties, not stimulants (e.g., Stewart, Conrod, et al., 1999). Therefore, negative reinforcement appears to be the more dominant motivational process involved in the drug-seeking behavior of women who suffer from PTSD. Nevertheless, considering the fact that stress-induced sensitivity to the reinforcing effects of drugs of abuse (sedatives and stimulants) is mediated by neuroendocrine factors (Schulkin, Gold, & McEwen, 1998), it is highly likely that very important gender differences will be revealed with respect to how stress and trauma interact with drugs of abuse.

MEMORY NETWORK MODEL

As an alternative to these viewpoints involving physiological responses, some models of functional relations between PTSD and SUDs focus on the potentially rewarding effects of drinking and drug taking on the cognitive intrusion symptoms of PTSD (Stewart, 1996, 1997). Again, there is laboratory research relevant to this position. First, many laboratory-based studies that have used paradigms adapted from experimental cognitive psychology suggest that traumatized individuals with PTSD show content-dependent memory abnormalities in the sober state. These memory biases have been argued to underlie the intrusive cognitive symptoms of PTSD, such as traumatic memories, flashbacks, and nightmares. Specifically, PTSD patients, compared with trauma-exposed control participants with no PTSD, display memory biases favoring the recollection of trauma-relevant material (McNally, 1997). A different set of laboratory-based studies in the area of cognitive psychopharmacology has demonstrated that a variety of drugs of abuse, including benzodiazepines (e.g., Stewart, Rioux, Connolly, Dunphy, & Teehan, 1996), marijuana (e.g., Millsaps, Azrin, & Mittenberg, 1994), and alcohol (e.g., Lister, Gorenstein, Risher-Flowers, Weingartner, & Eckardt, 1991), exert significant impairments on human memory. Such memory impairments might prove rewarding for PTSD patients if they resulted in dampening of the patients' excessive memory of trauma-related material. Such a theory implicates a self-medication process, but one that is focused on the dampening of intrusive memories rather than on hyperarousal symptoms. There is in fact emerging evidence that people who report "drinking to forget" exhibit significant forgetting of emotionally charged material if memory encoding is followed by alcohol administration (Stewart, 1997). Although these laboratory studies are consistent with the notion that PTSD patients may come to abuse alcohol and certain other drugs in attempts to forget their traumatic experiences (Stewart, 1997), more direct research is required to further test this version of the self-medication model. For example, PTSD patients and controls could be tested on selective-memory tasks

(McNally, 1997) when sober and when intoxicated to test the hypothesis that alcohol and drugs of abuse selectively dampen PTSD patients' sober tendency to selectively recollect material related to their trauma.

Laboratory-based experimental cognitive research is also relevant to understanding how an SUD is maintained in an individual with PTSD. For example, memory network models propose to explain the maintenance of substance abuse (Baker, Morse, & Sherman, 1987) and may be relevant to understanding functional relations involved in SUD–PTSD comorbidity. Baker et al. (1987) suggested that urges or cravings to use alcohol and drugs are organized in a memory network that also encodes information on eliciting cues and drinking/drug-taking responses. Eliciting cues that might be encoded in such a network for a comorbid SUD–PTSD patient could be internal symptoms, such as arousal symptoms, or external cues, such as trauma reminders (see Stewart, Pihl, Conrod, & Dongier, 1998). Thus, exposure to trauma reminders, or to experience of PTSD symptoms, should serve to activate the memory network. Activation of the network in turn would lead to alcohol/drug cravings (physiological responses and subjective urges to use). Craving would presumably increase the chances that the individual will seek out the drug and engage in drinking/drug-taking behavior. Saladin et al. (2001) conducted a preliminary laboratory-based test of predictions of the memory network model as it applies to SUD–PTSD comorbidity. Specifically, they examined PTSD diagnosis and PTSD symptom severity as predictors of trauma and substance cue elicited craving among individuals with an SUD. Participants were alcohol- and cocaine-dependent crime victims, approximately half of whom were diagnosed with comorbid PTSD. Participants listened to a narrative script (their worst trauma or a neutral scene) followed by the presentation of an *in vivo* cue (their preferred drug or a neutral cue). Self-reported craving in response to both the trauma script cue and drug cue was measured. Consistent with predictions of the network model, the diagnosis of PTSD and PTSD symptom severity were significantly predictive of increased trauma cue elicited craving and drug cue elicited craving. Moreover, the findings could not be attributed to the overall greater psychological distress associated with SUD–PTSD comorbidity (Saladin et al., 2001). This model differs from the self-medication model in that, although PTSD–drug associations may be initially established through a self-medication process, at later stages of dependence substance use is maintained by an automatic activation of drug seeking without the individual having a conscious expectancy activation for symptom relief. It is known that tolerance for the subjective reinforcing properties of drugs of abuse develops with chronic use (e.g., DeWit & Griffiths, 1991). It is possible that at later stages of drug dependence SUD–PTSD patients no longer receive reinforcement from their preferred drug of abuse, but PTSD symptoms or trauma cues continue to result in activation of a memory network that automatically stimulates drug-seeking behavior. Support for the memory network model in contrast to a self-medication model would require investigating whether the enhanced alcohol cue reactivity that is observed in SUD–PTSD patients is not mediated by the effects of trauma cue exposure on arousal levels or anticipation thereof. To our knowledge, no study to date has assessed the possible mediational role of such arousal in alcohol cue reactivity in PTSD patients.

Future studies on the memory network model of SUD–PTSD comorbidity could use a variety of laboratory-based experimental paradigms to further an understanding of the processes involved in the maintenance of this form of dual disorder. For example, recent research that used priming paradigms adapted from experimental cognitive psychology has shown that exposure to negative affect primes leads to enhanced processing of alcohol cues, but only among problem drinkers with a history of drinking in response to negative affect (Zack, Toneatto, & MacLeod, 1999). This paradigm could be adapted to test memory network predictions that exposure to trauma-related primes would lead to enhanced processing of alcohol and drug cues, but only among SUD patients with a comorbid diagnosis of PTSD. Finally, future studies could directly examine alcohol/drug self-administration levels using the unobtrusive taste-rating paradigm (e.g., Conrod, Stewart, & Pihl, 1997) or drug choice paradigms (Johanson & de Wit, 1989). These behavioral paradigms could be used to test the prediction emanating from memory network theory that exposure to trauma cues or elicitation of PTSD symptoms should lead to increased drinking/drug-taking behavior among patients with comorbid SUD–PTSD.

CONCLUSION

Several recent studies that have used experimental methods to identify biological factors and brain structures that are implicated in the etiology of PTSD also shed some light on the mechanisms of action of drugs that are often abused by individuals with PTSD (i.e., alcohol, benzodiazepines, and opioids). Such studies suggest that deficits in information processing, stress reactivity, and hormonal function are associated with PTSD symptoms and vulnerability to such symptoms. Recent advancements in the understanding of the neurobiology of anxiety and fear point to the amygdala, hippocampus, and prefrontal cortex as brain structures implicated in the regulation of posttraumatic stress responses and the maintenance of PTSD symptoms. Moreover, such lines of investigation provide a context for understanding the psychobiological processes by which ingestion of alcohol, benzodiazepines, and opioids can be particularly negatively reinforcing for PTSD individuals in the short term while concurrently exacerbating or maintaining

PTSD symptoms in the longer term. The model presented in this chapter also provides a framework for understanding how the use of alcohol and prescription depressant drugs could interfere with recovery from PTSD by interfering with the integration of the traumatic event into a contextually based system of memories and beliefs. Finally, studies in the area of experimental cognitive psychology and cognitive psychopharmacology support an additional theory—namely, a memory network model—of the relationship between PTSD and SUDs. This model involves a conscious, controlled self-medication process at initial stages of development of the SUD but suggests that more automatic processes involving cue reactivity are responsible at later stages of the disorder. This alternative theory suggests that drug self-administration could be maintained as a result of trauma–drug cognitive associations without any observable self-medication processes (i.e., symptom reduction). Future research in this area should involve an integrated approach to exploring the cognitive, affective, and somatic components of the PTSD diagnosis and how drugs of abuse affect responding at all three levels of analysis. Furthermore, experimental paradigms that allow for the observation of drinking and drug use behavior in response to trauma-specific stimuli and symptoms will provide much clarification on factors that are specifically involved in the reinforcement and maintenance of drug abuse in PTSD individuals.

4

CHILDHOOD TRAUMA, POSTTRAUMATIC STRESS DISORDER, SUBSTANCE ABUSE, AND VIOLENCE

DAVID LISAK AND PAUL M. MILLER

It is the act of violence—the creation of a new victim with all the associated suffering and potential for rippling effects across time—that we seek to prevent. Thus, both conceptually and typically from a sociopolitical perspective, the perpetration of violence is viewed as the endpoint of the chain of variables that are known to be associated with it. Although the wide array of mechanisms contributing to perpetration are undoubtedly complex and intermingled, accumulation of evidence from clinical practice, forensic studies, and empirical studies of a host of populations has helped to narrow the field of factors that are most associated with the perpetration of violence. Over and over, clinicians and researchers have observed the interactive and synergistic relationships among childhood trauma, posttraumatic stress disorder (PTSD), substance abuse, and violence (see Figure 4.1).

Among the common psychological legacies of childhood trauma is PTSD, the symptoms of which often lead abuse victims to seek relief through self-medication—the consumption of mind-altering drugs and alcohol that deaden feeling, alleviate fears and anxieties, and provide temporary states of artificial euphoria. Especially when chronic, such abuse of mind-altering drugs and alcohol often contributes to a generalized deterioration in patients' lives: loss of relationships, loss of jobs. As a consequence, and possibly also as a corollary, it also often leads patients into violence—through connections with violent individuals an increasing reliance on crime to find the money to pay for the substances they are abusing, and disinhibition of violent impulses. Furthermore, some of the symptoms of PTSD itself, in particular hypervigilance and hyperreactivity to particular stimuli, may render a victim more susceptible to violent behavior, a susceptibility that may be greatly enhanced by substance abuse.

There have been some brave attempts at identifying and analyzing the enormously complex interrelationships among these variables related to violence. However, a truly comprehensive study of how these factors interrelate has not been conducted. In the absence of such a conclusive, all-encompassing study, we focus our efforts in this chapter on marshaling the evidence for the various components of the model. In doing so, we believe we provide initial empirical support for the clinical impression that the complex web of relationships among these components is indeed at work in the lives of many of our patients.

However, before cataloging this evidence, we believe a single case example of how the four components manifest themselves, both causally and interactively, in a single life, will help illuminate some of the connecting threads not yet fully documented by empirical research.

COMPOSITE CASE STUDY: THE ROAD FROM CHILDHOOD ABUSE TO DEATH ROW

Because of legal constraints, and for the preservation of confidential information, we provide a composite case study rather than a single, masked case. Although this case is a composite, the details are drawn from the actual lives of the men evaluated by David Lisak in the course of thorough forensic evaluations drawing on a wide variety of sources and resulting in detailed developmental histories of the prisoner. From Lisak's observation, the details presented in this composite transcend racial and cultural particularities and thus are meant to convey meaningful life events from across the spectrum of death row inmates with whom he has worked.

Frank was raised in an environment marked by poverty and despair, with its frequent corollaries: violence and neglect. Both of his parents abused alcohol and drugs; his mother intermittently, his father chronically and severely. Often intoxicated, or feeling the effects of intoxication, his parents

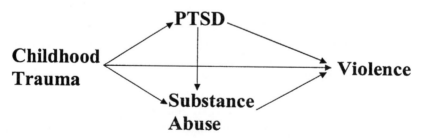

Figure 4.1. Childhood trauma, posttraumatic stress disorder (PTSD), substance abuse, and violence.

were unable to maintain steady jobs and were even less able to provide a stable environment for Frank and his siblings. Many of the most basic needs of a developing child were, in Frank, sorely neglected. He received scant attention, except when some childlike transgression provoked punishment. His diet was so erratic that a school nurse noted his bleeding gums and wondered about malnutrition.

When drunk or frustrated, either of Frank's parents could become violent, and Frank often witnessed their frequent fighting. His father's violence was particularly terrifying, and more than once Frank saw its aftermath in the form of cuts and bruises on his mother's face and body. Frank was not spared such abuse. He was routinely disciplined by "spankings" that could unpredictably escalate into beatings, with hands, fists, sticks, extension cords, and other objects at hand.

Frank's parents often threw parties, at which drugs and alcohol flowed freely, submerging the house into chaos and debauchery. By the time he was 8 years old, Frank was accustomed to seeing adults passed out from intoxication or overdoses and to seeing men and women engaged in sexual acts. It was in the chaos of one such party that Frank was sexually abused for the first time. A man took him into a room and forced Frank to orally copulate him.

By the time he was 9, Frank was himself abusing alcohol and drugs and discovering their reinforcing properties. Already scarred by neglect, physical abuse, and sexual abuse, Frank found relief and solace in marijuana and anesthetization in alcohol. There seems little doubt that his initiation into substance abuse was driven both by his need for self-medication and by virtue of his being surrounded by substance-abusing adults, most particularly his parents. Moreover, Frank often was surrounded by leftover marijuana cigarettes and unfinished drinks, so the substances themselves were easily available.

The psychological symptoms of abuse manifested themselves early in Frank's life. He was alternately depressed and withdrawn or prone to outbursts of angry defiance and disobedience. Early on he was tagged in school as a behavior problem with learning disabilities. School officials repeatedly tried to engage Frank's parents in joint efforts to help him, and repeatedly they were met with indifference. Effectively untreated, Frank's problems worsened.

No professional ever evaluated Frank for PTSD; however, an assessment of his history suggests that PTSD symptoms deriving from his abuse and neglect began emerging as Frank entered adolescence. His multiple sexual abuse experiences had left him with severe phobias surrounding sex, and so he typically avoided sexual activity. When he did counterphobically approach it, he did so in a classic state of hypervigilance and hyperreactivity. During sexual encounters he was prone to panic and almost equally prone to rage, perhaps as a secondary reaction to the panic. Frank suffered from nightmares throughout his life. At times he relived particular, terrifying scenes of his childhood. Sometimes the nightmares were disguised in content but consistent in the terror and helplessness they induced. Frank also described periods of time when he felt so hyperreactive and so full of rage that he "felt like ripping [his] skin off."

Already well versed in the mood- and mind-altering potential of drugs and alcohol, Frank became an expert in medicating his PTSD symptoms. Marijuana was his drug of choice for alleviating the chronic tension he experienced and for diverting the chronic, mounting feelings of rage with which he wrestled. Alcohol was a constant, and seemed to have a mild anesthetic effect, unless he went on a binge, in which case it disinhibited him and helped unleash his rage. To combat states of fear and to overcome his phobias, Frank would use methamphetamine. "Crank" gave him respites from fear during which he felt invulnerable and energized.

Frank was a chronic substance abuser from preadolescence; his life, and his very development, were inextricably tied to substances' psychoactive effects, the vicissitudes of their attainment, and the culture surrounding them. Drugs and alcohol were the primary coping strategies to which Frank turned when faced with life's challenges. As a consequence, he was deprived of the opportunity to develop the increasingly refined strategies needed to cope with the stresses and challenges of adult life. So imperative were drugs and alcohol that Frank devoted much of his waking life to securing their attainment. When out of work, Frank committed crimes—thefts and burglaries—to get the money he needed.

Like most people, Frank found his friends among those who shared his deepest needs and where he spent most of his time: the drug culture. He partied with other addicts, bartered with and borrowed from them, and shared his own when he was flush. During desperate times, he lived with other addicts in makeshift crash pads; in true desperation, he lived on the street. Like many addicts, Frank eventually found his way into small-time dealing, to pay off debts and to secure drugs when he was broke.

The drug scene was entirely familiar to Frank; it was an extension of his childhood environment. Its violence was also familiar. High on crank or drunk on a binge, addicts who quarreled frequently plunged into violence. Violence was the final arbiter in settling disputes, and violence was the ultimate weapon used by the dealers to control their addicted serfs. Although far from the most violent among his acquaintances, Frank was no exception to the rule of violence: He was subjected to it, and he used it. With him from earliest childhood, violence was part of his normal interpersonal landscape.

The murder that landed Frank on death row was intertwined with drugs. One night he got into a fight with an acquaintance with whom he had a long-simmering feud fed by dozens of petty grievances. Neither Frank nor his victim had the wherewithal to resolve the feud or to see through it to its meaningless source. That night, the feud erupted into violence, and Frank became a murderer. In the aftermath, Frank did what to him was obvious: He stole what valuables were to be found in the man's apartment. That act made it felony murder, and Frank was convicted and sentenced to death.

Frank's life no doubt rings familiar to many clinicians who work with substance-abusing and forensic populations. In many ways, the course of his life was dictated by the interacting phenomena addressed by this chapter: the abuse he suffered as a child, the PTSD and substance abuse that were a direct legacy of that abuse, and the violence that was laced through his life from childhood on.

The interplay among these factors has many possible permutations, but it should be noted that each factor by itself is multifactorial. Childhood trauma, for example, can only very rarely be thought of as a single variable. The most commonly studied forms of such trauma, physical abuse and sexual abuse, often if not typically involve large elements of neglect and psychological abuse. Neglect increases the risk for abuse. Most sexually abused boys, for example, are abused by someone from outside the home (in contrast to girls; Mendel, 1995). It has been widely hypothesized that neglect is often a precursor for such abuse. Psychological abuse, a negative family environment, or both, is almost always a component of other forms of abuse, and it has been noted that the commonly cited sequelae of sexual and physical abuse may in fact be attributable, to a substantial degree, to the psychological–family component (e.g., Nash, Hulsey, Sexton, Harralson, & Lambert, 1993). Finally, in the homes where such abuse and neglect are occurring, violence between the parents is not uncommon, which introduces yet another variable: the impact on the child of witnessing interspousal violence.

Neither is PTSD a factor that can be easily or simply categorized. Although it is clearly one of the potential legacies of childhood trauma, relatively little is known about what mediates the relationship: Why is PTSD sometimes expressed in overt and recognizable symptoms and at other times manifested in depression or acting-out behaviors? Similarly, the relationship between trauma and substance abuse is potentially multidetermined. Frequently, simple exposure and modeling are involved when the child is surrounded by substance-abusing adults. However, there is also strong evidence for self-medication as a motivating factor leading from trauma to the use of substances. This suggests that PTSD symptoms can function as a causal link between trauma and substance abuse. However, a synergistic relationship between the two is also plausible. Might not the abuse of such substances increase either the likelihood or the severity of PTSD symptoms?

The relationship between all of these factors and violence is clearly complex. Acts of violence can stem from relatively pure re-enactments; from unbridled rage that has its roots in experiences of victimization; and from less direct sources that still link back to trauma, such as impaired empathy and habituation to violence. PTSD symptoms—particularly hyper-vigilance and hyperarousal—create increased vulnerability to acting out violently. The well-established link between PTSD symptoms and anger is an obvious link to acts of violence. Finally, substance abuse can exacerbate all of the links noted above: through disinhibition, through altered states of consciousness, through heightened physiological arousal levels, and through chemically induced paranoia. Substance abuse also tends to create its own context of increased violence. Abusers frequently become involved in the violent drug subculture. They are likely to deteriorate in their ability to function, to hold jobs, and to sustain supportive relationships and thus are driven increasingly into criminal acts to obtain the money they need for survival and the continued use of substances.

Given the many layers of complexity just outlined, it is little wonder that researchers have not often attempted to wade into such multifactorial thickets. Nevertheless, researchers have made substantial strides, particularly during the last 10 years, in documenting and analyzing some of the links among childhood trauma, PTSD, substance abuse, and violence.

In the following sections we marshal empirical evidence to examine the component relationships among these phenomena. This review is not meant to be comprehensive; that is beyond the scope of this chapter. Rather, it is meant to combine some of the best evidence we have on the existence of the relationships among childhood abuse, PTSD, substance abuse, and violence. Although our original intent was to examine these relationships as they exist specifically among boys and men, the state of the literature does not support this intent. Characteristics of the literature that preclude such a focus are the predominance of women as subjects in the victimization literature and the predominance of men in the literatures on perpetration and on substance abuse. These imbalances, along with the relative paucity of pertinent sex difference analyses, suggest that a focus on men and boys will be a greater possibility once the imbalances in the literature have been corrected.

TRAUMA, PTSD, SUBSTANCE ABUSE, AND VIOLENCE: DIRECT EVIDENCE

Each of the factors that comprise the focus of this chapter have been linked empirically to the perpetration of violence. The respective relation-ships among childhood trauma, PTSD, substance abuse, and violence have garnered significant attention from researchers. In the following sections we summarize some of the major findings of this literature.

CHILDHOOD TRAUMA AND VIOLENCE

The relationship between childhood trauma and the later perpetration of interpersonal violence has often been termed the *cycle of violence*. As a topic of enormous social and political concern, the cycle of violence has an odd characteristic: At times, the "cycle" is described as a near inevitability; at other times it is all but denied. The topic has drawn increasing attention from the research community, in which the vacillation between inevitability and denial has had its own place, albeit in far more muted tones.

From a research perspective, there are enormous methodological difficulties in studying the cycle of violence. Perhaps the chief obstacle is the essential nature of the phenomena that comprise the cycle: acts of abuse and violence that are typically committed among intimates. Only two individuals—the victim and the perpetrator—typically witness such acts. The vast majority of these acts are never reported to authorities and never result in official records of any kind (e.g., Dodge, Bates, & Pettit, 1990; Koss, Gidycz, & Wisniewski, 1987; J. Martin, Anderson, Romans, Mullen, & O'Shea, 1993). This fact leaves researchers little alternative but to rely on the self-report of research participants. Although the accuracy of self-reports of childhood victimization has been questioned, considerable evidence indicates that retroactive self-reports are quite reliable (Brewin, Andrews, & Gotlib, 1993) and are more likely to underreport than overreport victimization (e.g., Widom & Morris, 1997; Widom & Shepard, 1996). Difficulties with the assessment of perpetration histories also pose a methodological problem. However, decades ago, researchers demonstrated that self-reports were quite reliable measures of delinquent behavior by verifying their validity through polygraph examinations and by verifying reports with already known offenses (Clark & Tifft, 1966; Gibson, Morrison, & West, 1970; Gold, 1966). In a more recent study, Maxfield, Weiler, and Widom (2000) compared official versus self-reported records of criminal behavior and concluded that studies that rely solely on official records of arrest underestimate the relationship between childhood victimization and later criminal behavior.

Despite the many complexities and pitfalls inherent in studying the cycle of violence, researchers have amassed considerable evidence indicating that individuals who suffer childhood victimization are at an increased risk for perpetrating interpersonal violence later in life. Evidence has come from the study of incarcerated criminals, sex offenders, and victimized populations.

Studies of Incarcerated Criminals

One of the most carefully crafted studies of the prevalence of childhood victimization in a sample of convicted felons was reported by Weeks and Widom (1998), who used multiple and sophisticated measures of childhood physical and sexual abuse as well as neglect. More than two thirds of the 301 male convicts they assessed reported histories of childhood victimization, with physical abuse being the most common form. Relying on institutional files for their data, Dutton and Hart (1992) reported that 41% of their sample of 604 convicted felons had experienced "serious childhood abuse." The rate of violent acts committed by abused felons was more than twice that of the nonabused felons.

Studies of Sex Offenders

Sex offenders have been a particular focus for researchers studying the cycle of violence, perhaps because popular beliefs about the link between sexual abuse and sexual perpetration have historically been very strong. Some of the earliest data in this area were published by Groth (1979), a pioneer in the study of sex offenders. On the basis of interviews and record reviews, he reported that 31% of a sample of 348 sex offenders had a history of sexual trauma. Note that neither physical abuse, the most prevalent form of victimization reported by both Dutton and Hart (1992) and Weeks and Widom (1998), nor neglect was assessed.

More recent studies of sex offenders have tended to replicate Groth's (1979) findings, as well as his exclusive focus on sexual victimization as a childhood precursor to later sexual offending. For example, Worling (1995) assessed the sexual victimization histories of 87 adolescent sex offenders, basing his assessments on months of clinical interactions with the offenders. Forty-three percent reported histories of sexual abuse, with the highest rates (71%) reported by those who had committed offenses against males. Of methodological interest, Worling noted that studies that based their assessments on pretreatment interviews reported sexual victimization rates among juvenile sex offenders in the range of 19%–25%, whereas those that based their assessments on posttreatment reviews reported rates that ranged between 47% and 55%. These findings suggest that longer term interactions reduce rates of denial among males who were sexually abused, yielding more accurate estimates of the rate of sexual victimization. Even higher rates of sexual victimization among sex offenders have been reported, from 71% (Barnard, Hankins, & Robbins, 1992) to 93% (Briggs & Hawkins, 1996).

In an exception to the exclusive focus on sexual victimization, Seghorn, Prentky, and Boucher (1987) assessed multiple forms of abuse and neglect in a sample of 151 incarcerated adult sex offenders. Based solely on record review, 58% of the offenders were victims of physical abuse, 56% were victims of neglect, and 35% were victims of sexual abuse. A study of juvenile sex offenders (Becker & Kaplan, 1991) reported somewhat lower numbers: Twenty-eight percent had been physically abused, 6.9% had been sexually abused, and 13.8% had been both physically and sexually abused (48% had suffered one or both forms of abuse).

Studies of Victimized Populations

In their review of the long-term consequences of childhood physical abuse, Malinosky-Rummell and Hansen (1993) cited an array of studies documenting a link between physical abuse and a host of violent behaviors. Rates of childhood physical abuse are significantly higher among violent juveniles, among homicidal and otherwise violent adults, among adults who abuse children, and among adolescents and adults who abuse dating partners or spouses.

In a study that relied solely on official records of abuse and later arrests, Rivera and Widom (1990) compared abused and neglected individuals to matched control participants. Childhood victimization significantly increased the risk for later violent offending as well as for an earlier onset of delinquent behavior. Similarly, a study of more than 1,500 adolescents in the Netherlands reported that sexual abuse significantly increased the risk for both aggressive and criminal behavior (Garnefski & Diekstra, 1997). Lisak, Hopper, and Song (1996) examined the relationship between childhood sexual and physical abuse and the later perpetration of various forms of interpersonal violence, from battery and rape to the abuse of children. Of the 120 men who reported some form of perpetration, 70% reported either sexual or physical abuse as children.

Studies Examining Complex Models

Although there is wide agreement that the relationship between childhood victimization and later violence is complex and mediated, empirically analyzing such a complex relationship is a daunting task. Nevertheless, some efforts have been made. For example, a longitudinal study of more than 300 juvenile detainees examined the interacting factors of (a) sexual abuse; (b) physical abuse; (c) family involvement in alcohol, drug abuse, and crime; and (d) the juveniles' own substance abuse; and delinquent behavior (Dembo, Williams, Wothke, Schmeidler, & Brown, 1992). The resulting structural equation model revealed significant relationships among the four key background variables and between each of them and delinquent behavior.

Very similar findings were reported from a very different sample: 53 adult male alcoholics in Sweden interviewed extensively on admission for inpatient treatment (Bergman & Brismar, 1994). Thirty of the men were classified as violent, having perpetrated a variety of forms of battery. These violent alcoholics differed from their nonviolent counterparts in a variety of ways: They were significantly more likely to have had a history of violence in their family of origin, they consumed significantly more alcohol, they began drinking seriously at an earlier age, and they were more likely to have attempted suicide.

The research program led by Cathy S. Widom has also attempted to identify mediating factors in the cycle of violence. Drawing from their prospective study of abused and neglected individuals who were traced and interviewed in adulthood, Weiler and Widom (1996) found that for some people psychopathy mediated the relationship between childhood victimization and adult violence. Both psychopathy scores and victimization predicted adult violence, but when psychopathy scores were introduced victimization was no longer a significant predictor of violence. In a related finding, Luntz and Widom (1994) reported that victimized individuals were significantly more likely as adults to meet diagnostic criteria for antisocial personality disorder. Kaufman and Widom (1999) examined the role of running away in mediating childhood victimization and delinquency. Although victimization increased the likelihood of running away, running away increased the risk of delinquency for both abused and nonabused individuals.

Several studies have examined the interactive effects of multiple factors associated with the perpetration of sexual violence in nonincarcerated samples of men. Lisak et al. (1996) examined the role of gender identity in a nonclinical sample of perpetrating and nonperpetrating abused men. Abused perpetrators were more rigid in their gender identities and more emotionally constricted than their abused but nonperpetrating counterparts. The findings suggest that gender-related personality variables may play a role in determining which abused men go on to perpetrate interpersonal violence. Ouimette and Riggs (1998) assessed problems in the early home environment, impulse control, hostile cognitions, and peer characteristics of sexually aggressive and nonaggressive men. Witnessing father-perpetrated domestic violence; having a poor relationship with their fathers; and having more impulse control problems, more hostile cognitions regarding women, and a larger number of antisocial peers all significantly differentiated the sexually aggressive men. These findings suggest a mediational model in which the effects of early exposure to violence are exacerbated by other familial and peer influences and by a generalized deficit in impulse control capacities.

Summary

Researchers examining the links between early trauma and later violence must grapple with enormous methodological challenges. The hidden nature of the core phenomena being studied, the often-long time lapses between the trauma and the violence, and the many intervening variables that must be accounted for all render this a complex and frustrating area of study. However, findings from a variety of population samples have been quite consistent in providing relatively strong support for the cycle-of-violence hypothesis. It is clear that future research must focus increasingly on factors that mediate and moderate the relationship between early trauma and violence. Because a very significant proportion of traumatized men and women never commit acts of violence, it is imperative that both risk and protective factors be identified that can ultimately provide the basis for intervention and prevention strategies.

PTSD AND VIOLENCE

Both the clinical literature on trauma and the emerging neurobiological literature on PTSD provide powerful bases for hypothesizing a link between PTSD symptoms and increased violence. The increased baseline arousal levels, the lowered thresholds of agitation and irritability, and the increased levels of anger that often characterize PTSD all point to an increased risk for violent behavior.

Studies of Combat Veterans

Much of the empirical data on the relationship between PTSD and violence has come from studies of Vietnam veterans. Because PTSD in Vietnam veterans is linked to combat exposure, researchers have sought to tease out the independent contribution of PTSD symptoms to violent behavior. Byrne and Riggs (1996) studied the relationship between PTSD symptoms and violence by evaluating 50 Vietnam combat veterans and their partners. On the basis of both the veterans' reports and reports of their partners, the veterans' level of violence and verbal aggression was extraordinarily high: Thirty-four percent reported at least one act of violence against their partners during the previous year, and 92% acknowledged verbal aggression. PTSD symptoms were positively related to level of violence and aggression, although the effect was mediated by relationship problems (of a nonviolent nature). Combat exposure was related both to PTSD symptoms and to violence; however, in a regression model PTSD symptoms, but not combat exposure, predicted relationship aggression.

In another approach, a large, random national sample of Vietnam-era veterans was assessed for current PTSD and a host of family and relationship problems (Jordan et al., 1992). Compared with veterans without current PTSD, those who met PTSD criteria were significantly more likely to have committed violent acts within the home during the previous year. In another study, Vietnam veterans seeking inpatient treatment for PTSD were compared with a non-PTSD inpatient control group and a group of Vietnam veterans with PTSD but who were not receiving inpatient treatment (McFall, Fontana, Raskind, & Rosenheck, 1999). The PTSD inpatients were significantly more violent than either of the comparison groups. These findings were consistent with a study comparing Vietnam combat veterans with and without PTSD, in which PTSD severity, combat exposure, and lower socioeconomic status were all related to interpersonal violence (Beckham, Feldman, Kirby, Hertzberg, & Moore, 1997).

Studies of Juvenile Offenders

Underscoring the fact that it is not simply combat-related trauma that is associated (directly or indirectly) with violent behavior are studies of male adolescent offenders that have revealed high rates of PTSD. Among 51 incarcerated juveniles who were assessed with multiple measures of PTSD, 45% rated a lifetime diagnosis of PTSD on the basis of a semistructured interview and, on the basis of a self-report checklist, 77% met the PTSD symptom threshold at least some of the time (Erwin, Newman, McMackin, Morrissey, & Kaloupek, 2000). In another study, 32% of 85 incarcerated juveniles met full criteria for current PTSD, and another 20% met partial criteria (Steiner, Garcia, & Matthews, 1997).

Summary

There is solid evidence of a link between PTSD symptoms and an increased risk for violent behavior. Like most of the relationships discussed in this chapter, establishing the precise nature of this link is made difficult by the presence of many potential confounding factors. However, there is reason for hope that advances in an understanding of the neurobiological underpinnings of PTSD may ultimately provide solid evidence of precisely how PTSD symptoms relate to violent behavior.

SUBSTANCE ABUSE AND VIOLENCE

Substances such as alcohol, cocaine, and methamphetamine have direct influences on the brain and demonstrable effects on perception and behavior. This fact lends credence to the claim for a direct relationship between the abuse of these and other substances and the perpetration of violence. There is abundant evidence that alcohol consumption is associated with violent behavior in men, women, and adolescents and that it is a factor in domestic violence. There is also experimental evidence that alcohol consumption increases violent behavior (Chermack & Giancola, 1997). Numerous studies have documented a link between alcohol and the commission of homicide; on average, more than 60% of murderers were under the influence of alcohol at the time the murder was committed (Collins & Messerschmidt, 1993). The U.S. Department of Justice reported that more than half of all individuals incarcerated in state prisons for violent crimes had consumed alcohol just prior to their offenses (Johnson & Belfer, 1995). In an integrative review and meta-analysis of research on the link between alcohol and aggression, and in particular on experimental studies, Bushman and Cooper (1990) concluded that the evidence supports a causal role for alcohol consumption in aggressive behavior. However, the evidence also clearly indicates that alcohol consumption is neither a necessary nor a sufficient explanation for violent behavior and that its influence is dependent on contextual factors such as perceived provocation, social pressure, and threat and by individual variables such as gender, aggressive disposition, psychopathology, history of victimization, and expectancies (Chermack & Giancola, 1997).

Studies of Substance Abusers and Psychiatric Patients

The complexity of the substance abuse–violence relationship was illustrated in Spunt, Goldstein, Bellucci, and Miller's (1990) ethnographic study of 185 chronic drug users in lower Manhattan. They found evidence for three dimensions of drug-related violence: (a) direct psychopharmacological effects, (b) violence in the pursuit of money to secure drugs, and (c) violence related to the sale and distribution of drugs.

Studies of psychiatric patients have sought to disentangle the relationships among psychopathology, substance abuse, and violence. Data from two of the Epidemiological Catchment Area studies indicate that both major mental disorder and substance abuse increased the probability of violent behavior (Swanson, 1993). These findings were somewhat contradicted by those of another study that compared violence committed over a 1-year period in the community by 1,136 discharged mental patients and 519 community control participants (Steadman et al., 1998). Steadman et al. (1998) found that violence commission was not related to group membership; however, they did find that for both groups substance abuse symptoms were positively related to level of violence. A study of psychiatric outpatients similarly indicated that the only significant difference between violent and nonviolent patients was substance abuse (Fulwiler, Grossman, Forbes, & Ruthazer, 1997).

Studies of Domestic Violence, Sexual Aggression, and Child Abuse

There is considerable evidence for a relationship between substance abuse and domestic violence (Hotaling & Sugarman, 1986). Kantor and Straus (1989) analyzed data from a national survey of family violence and reported that husbands' drug use and drunkenness were among a handful of variables that distinguished abusive relationships. A prospective study followed 541 couples from before the wedding to the end of the first year of marriage (Leonard & Senchak, 1996). More than a quarter of both husbands and wives reported aggression by husbands during the 1-year period, and 17% of couples reported "severe aggression." The husband's use of alcohol was one of only three variables that provided a significant longitudinal prediction of the violence.

Alcohol consumption is also a factor in sexual aggression. Studies indicate that alcohol is both a general risk factor for sexual aggression and is very often consumed at the time of perpetration by both incarcerated rapists as well as "undetected" rapists—that is, men who are never reported or prosecuted (Koss & Gaines, 1993; Ouimette, 1997; Seto & Barbaree, 1995).

Child maltreatment has also been associated with substance abuse. Drawing from a large-scale community study, parents who reported either physical abuse or neglect of their children were compared with matched control participants (Kelleher, Chaffin, Hollenberg, & Fischer, 1994). Maltreating parents were significantly more likely to report substance abuse and dependence. Famularo, Kinscherff, and Fenton (1992) reported that in 67% of 190 randomly selected cases of child maltreatment drawn from state files the parents were classified as substance abusers, a finding that is consistent with other studies (Hamilton & Browne, 1999; Kotch, Browne, Dufort, & Winsor, 1999).

Summary

The evidence of an association between substance abuse and violence is overwhelming. Furthermore, experimental evidence provides solid ground for hypothesizing a causal connection between the two, as does the known pharmacological effects of many abused substances. Beyond these direct effects, in which the neural and behavioral effects of substances cause increases in violent behavior, substance abuse also appears to act as a more indirect risk factor for violence. Substance abuse is often associated with participation in violent peer groups and with the participation in crimes in the service of securing the substances.

CONCLUSION

We began this chapter with a composite case study that depicted many of the complexities inherent in the relationships among childhood trauma, PTSD, substance abuse, and violence. Translated into research terms, the case depicted a causal link between trauma and PTSD, although one mediated by contextual factors, such as the chaos and depravity of the individual's home environment. It also depicted a causal link between trauma and substance abuse, that is, the use of substances to medicate some of the symptoms of trauma, including PTSD symptoms. Again, the case also posited a contextual link between these two variables, namely, the increased risk of traumatized children being exposed to substance-abusing family members. Finally, it depicted a complex weave of interrelationships between these phenomena and the violence that brought the person to death row. Now the question can be asked: To what extent are these depictions corroborated by the accumulated empirical research that has been reviewed?

It is our view that, although the complex and synergistic interactions suggested by the case study may, to date, remain largely beyond the scope of empirical research, the many component relationships that make up those interactions have actually received considerable evidentiary support. Traumatic experiences in childhood are linked directly to each of the outcomes in the quadratic relationship: PTSD, substance abuse, and violence. Each of the other components is, in turn, linked with all others. The evidence reviewed clearly varies in strength; in some cases it points only to an association between variables, in other cases causal inferences can be made. However, it is our view that the cumulative evidence provides a firm foundation for hypothesizing a complex, causal chain of relationships that begins with childhood trauma and ends in violence.

Much evidence remains to be gathered. In particular, it is perhaps time for researchers to test more comprehensive models than is the norm, models that integrate and test relationships among three, four, five, or all six of the relationships that we have reviewed in this chapter. It is time for researchers to more consistently control for the numerous contextual variables that may confound or explain the relationships we have observed. Moreover, now that we can be fairly confident that these relationships are not spurious or artifactual, this confidence calls for the application of longitudinal (and therefore expensive) designs for testing specific causal hypotheses. Finally, it is of vital importance to continue developing reliable and valid self-report instruments, particularly those for assessing the key input and output variables in the equation: experiences of childhood trauma and of violence perpetration. Although archival data give an assurance of validity, they do so at the expense of arbitrarily missing an enormous amount of crucial information. As researchers, we cannot escape the reality that the vast majority of childhood trauma and of violence remains invisible to our institutions and therefore missing from our archives.

II

ASSESSMENT AND TREATMENT

5

SUBSTANCE USE DISORDER–POSTTRAUMATIC STRESS DISORDER COMORBIDITY: A SURVEY OF TREATMENTS AND PROPOSED PRACTICE GUIDELINES

PAIGE OUIMETTE, RUDOLF H. MOOS, AND PAMELA J. BROWN

In this chapter we critically review empirical research on the treatment course of substance use disorder–posttraumatic stress disorder (SUD–PTSD) comorbidity. We highlight treatment implications in an attempt to profile the state of the art in treating this particular comorbidity. We hope to encourage the development of a set of evidence-based practice guidelines specific to the treatment of SUD–PTSD comorbidity.

PREVALENCE OF COMORBID SUD–PTSD

PTSD is prevalent in the general population: An estimated 9% of women and men meet criteria for lifetime PTSD (Kessler, Sonnega, Bromet, Hughes, & Nelson, 1995). Among mental health treatment-seeking samples, rates of PTSD are higher; 20%–33% of patients with SUDs meet criteria for current PTSD (Back et al., 2000; Brown, Recupero, & Stout, 1995; Najavits, Gastfriend, et al., 1998; Triffleman, Marmar, Delucchi, & Ronfeldt, 1995). PTSD is also common among veterans: In fiscal year 1998, clinician-

The Department of Veterans Affairs Mental Health Strategic Health Group and the Health Services Research and Development Service supported some of the research described in this chapter. An earlier review of the literature on the treatment of substance use disorder–posttraumatic stress disorder was published in the 1998 volume of *Addictive Behaviors*. We thank Poorni Otilingam for her help with preparing the manuscript. The views expressed in this chapter are those of the authors and do not necessarily represent the views of the Department of Veterans Affairs.

derived diagnoses indicated that about 25% of SUD patients seen in either substance abuse or psychiatric units had current PTSD (Piette, Baisden, & Moos, 1999). Given that clinical diagnoses often underestimate the actual presence of disorders, PTSD is most likely more prevalent among Veterans Affairs (VA) SUD patients than these estimates suggest.

These data are complemented by research examining rates of SUDs among Vietnam veterans. In a nationally representative community-based sample of Vietnam combat veterans, 22% of the men with current combat-related PTSD also met formal diagnostic criteria for a current SUD (Kulka et al., 1990). Among combat veterans seeking PTSD treatment, the rates of SUDs are higher: In one study sample, 84% of combat veterans with PTSD had at least one comorbid SUD (Keane & Wolfe, 1990). SUDs and PTSD thus frequently co-occur in community and clinical samples and across treatment venues.

Of significance is the negative prognostic implication of SUD–PTSD comorbidity: PTSD renders substance abuse patients more vulnerable to poorer short- and long-term treatment outcomes (P. J. Brown, Stout, & Mueller, 1996, 1999; Ouimette, Ahrens, Moos, & Finney, 1997, 1998; Ouimette, Brown, & Najavits, 1998; Ouimette, Finney, & Moos, 1999). In addition, a comorbid diagnosis of PTSD among SUD patients may have a more deleterious effect than that of other comorbid psychiatric diagnoses, encompassing substance use and psychological and psychosocial aspects of functioning (Ouimette et al., 1997, 1999; Ouimette, Ahrens, et al., 1998). Last, substance abuse is viewed as having negative implications for patients seeking PTSD treatment; patients who continue to use substances have less successful PTSD outcomes than those who abstain (Perconte & Griger, 1991).

MODELS OF SUD–PTSD COMORBIDITY
AND TREATMENT IMPLICATIONS

Self-medication theory has been proposed as an explanation for high rates of PTSD and SUD comorbidity (Khantzian, 1985, 1997). The theory proposes that, if an individual lacks the resources to cope with overwhelming and painful emotions, substances such as alcohol or drugs may be used on a regular basis to cope with these emotions. The use of these substances places the individual at risk for developing an SUD.

Applied to SUD–PTSD comorbidity, the theory suggests that an individual is exposed to trauma, develops PTSD, and then uses substances to cope with PTSD symptoms. The use of alcohol and drugs may provide temporary relief for PTSD symptoms, although with cessation of substance use PTSD symptoms re-emerge. With continual substance use, a diagnosable SUD then develops over time. In addition, intoxication may exacerbate some PTSD symptoms (e.g., cocaine use may increase hyperarousal), and withdrawal may potentiate PTSD (e.g., alcohol withdrawal can induce flashbacks). Thus, the two disorders may become intertwined in a complex fashion.

Alternatively, some patients may develop PTSD in the context of an ongoing (i.e., primary) SUD. SUDs are often associated with dangerous, risky lifestyles that expose individuals to various traumatic events. These models indicate the need to treat both PTSD and SUDs if sustained remission of both disorders is to be achieved. Our position is that the majority of patients follow a pattern in which the development of PTSD is primary (P. J. Brown et al., 1998; Bremner, Southwick, Darnell, & Charney, 1996). One implication is that, although both disorders need to be treated, change in PTSD symptoms is the more important factor in the remission of both disorders. For example, P. J. Brown (2000) reported preliminary findings that, among SUD–PTSD women, a PTSD variable (i.e., baseline number of re-experiencing symptoms) predicts substance abuse relapse and PTSD status (remitted or unremitted) at a 6-month follow-up. In contrast, no substance use variable predicts PTSD status at follow-up. Taken together, these findings suggest that PTSD cannot be considered secondary to SUDs and that treatment targeting comorbid SUD–PTSD might improve outcomes for both disorders.

However, a fundamental concern voiced by providers who treat SUD–PTSD patients is when in the treatment course to address substance use and when to address PTSD symptoms. Many providers believe that substance abuse must be treated first, and, on completion of a substantial period of abstinence, PTSD can be treated (i.e., the sequential model). The rationale for this approach is that SUD treatment will increase personal and social resources (e.g., adaptive coping skills), enabling the patient to withstand the painful emotions that may be aroused during trauma treatment. Another rationale for delaying trauma treatment is the possibility that PTSD may remit without treatment following remission of the SUD (e.g., Dansky, Brady, & Saladin, 1998). Alternatively, it has been argued that if PTSD is not addressed in treatment, the patient is at greater risk for early relapse to substance use (P. J. Brown et al., 1996; Ouimette, Moos, & Finney, in press).

Most clinical researchers recognize that SUD and PTSD symptoms are interwoven and emphasize the need for concurrent treatment of both substance use problems and PTSD symptoms (e.g., Abueg & Fairbank, 1991; Expert Consensus Guideline Series, 1999; Najavits, Weiss, & Liese, 1996; Stine & Kosten, 1995). Moreover, one recent study found that the majority of SUD–PTSD patients preferred concurrent SUD and trauma treatment

(P. J. Brown, Stout, & Gannon-Rowley, 1998). Although simultaneous treatment is advocated as the best approach, we know that, in practice, both disorders are probably treated as independent, unrelated problems.

TREATMENT OF COMORBID SUD–PTSD

Although PTSD is highly comorbid with several psychiatric disorders, including SUDs, the majority of clinical trials of PTSD treatment exclude patients with comorbidities, limiting their generalizability to patients with SUD–PTSD. Hence, this chapter focuses more on recent research on SUD–PTSD comorbidity among patients in SUD treatment, but we also include relevant work that examines substance abuse in the context of PTSD treatment settings. We concentrate specifically on empirical research relevant to the psychological treatment of SUD–PTSD comorbidity; theoretically based treatment guidelines and recommendations (e.g., Evans & Sullivan, 1995; Zweben, Clark, & Smith, 1994), as well as more conceptually focused reviews of SUD–PTSD treatment (see Kofoed, Friedman, & Peck, 1993; Najavits, Weiss, & Shaw, 1997; and Stine & Kosten, 1995), are covered elsewhere.

At present, there are no published controlled trials of concurrent SUD–PTSD treatment, but several promising research protocols are in the development and evaluation stage (e.g., Back, Dansky, Carroll, Foa, & Brady, 2001; Najavits, Weiss, Shaw, & Muenz, 1998; Triffleman, Carroll, & Kellogg, 1999). In this section we first review naturalistic studies of treatment practices that are associated with improved outcomes for SUD–PTSD patients. *Naturalistic* studies examine the effectiveness of treatments in real world settings. These studies allow natural variations in treatments and do not have stringent exclusion criteria for patients. Thus, these studies emphasize generalizability or external validity.

We also review several preliminary studies of concurrent SUD–PTSD/trauma treatment protocols. These protocols currently are being examined in randomized clinical trials, which will provide critical information on how well these treatments work under controlled conditions. It will ultimately be necessary to integrate information from research that focuses on *efficacy* (randomized clinical trials) and on *effectiveness* (real-world treatment) to identify the best treatment for SUD–PTSD patients.

Naturalistic Studies of SUD–PTSD Patients' Treatment Outcomes

One naturalistic study of veterans has investigated SUD–PTSD patients' improvement after SUD treatment, relative to improvement among SUD-only patients (Ouimette et al., 1997, 1999; Ouimette, Ahrens, et al.,

1998). SUD–PTSD patients improved on substance use outcomes following SUD treatment, albeit to a lesser degree than patients without PTSD. SUD–PTSD patients' reports of abstinence and problems from substance use were examined at 1- and 2-year follow-ups. Of the SUD–PTSD patients who were not abstinent at intake, half (49.6%) reported abstinence from alcohol and drugs at one or both follow-ups. Of SUD–PTSD patients who reported problems from substance use at intake, 38% reported no problems at either the 1- or 2-year follow-ups, or both. A study of cocaine-dependent patients entering a pharmacological trial for SUD similarly found that PTSD patients improved on substance use symptoms at a 3-month follow-up (Dansky et al., 1998). These two studies suggest that PTSD patients improve on substance use outcomes after SUD treatment, without any PTSD-specific intervention, although the amount of improvement is not as great as that for SUD patients without PTSD.

In the veteran study (Ouimette et al., 1999), although PTSD patients improved on psychological symptoms at discharge from the residential phase of treatment, they did not maintain this improvement over time; neither did they did improve on functional outcomes, such as employment status in the longer term. In the study of PTSD–cocaine-dependent patients (Dansky et al., 1998), significant improvement occurred from baseline to the 3-month follow-up on PTSD symptoms. However, at follow-up patients with PTSD had more legal problems that those without PTSD. Thus, SUD treatment by itself may not improve functional outcomes as much for SUD–PTSD patients as for SUD patients without PTSD. Psychological symptoms, including PTSD, may initially attenuate, especially following detoxification, but may worsen over time without PTSD-specific intervention.

In the veteran study (Ouimette, Ahrens, et al., 1998; Ouimette et al., 1999), specific aspects of SUD treatment and programs were examined as predictors of PTSD patients' outcomes. For SUD–PTSD patients, more outpatient substance abuse and family counseling, as well as greater participation in self-help groups during the index phase of acute treatment, were associated with better psychological functioning immediately postdischarge. Twelve-step group involvement was associated with increased use of approach coping styles (i.e., problem solving and positive reappraisal) at discharge. These associations were weaker in the SUD-only patients, suggesting that these interventions have a greater effect for SUD–PTSD patients. SUD–PTSD patients appeared to improve more on psychological symptoms in program environments that emphasized supportive and organized care than did SUD-only patients (Ouimette, Ahrens, et al., 1998).

SUD–PTSD patients' participation in outpatient treatment and course of remission from substance abuse (i.e., abstinence or nonproblematic alcohol consumption) was then examined during the 2 years following their discharge from the inpatient program (Ouimette, Moos, & Finney, 2000). SUD–PTSD patients who received more outpatient substance abuse, psychiatric, and PTSD services in the first year following treatment (and cumulatively over the 2-year follow-up) were more likely to maintain a stable course of remission from substance use. When the three types of sessions were compared, PTSD sessions in the second year and the total number of PTSD sessions over the 2 years following discharge from the index treatment episode were most strongly associated with substance use remission.

The longer the duration of PTSD care, the greater the likelihood that a patient will experience remission from substance abuse. When patients attended PTSD care consistently (two or more sessions per month) over a period of 3 months or longer, 74% experienced remission at follow-up compared with 41% of those attending inconsistently or not at all.

Last, self-help group attendance and level of participation also were examined; attendance and participation were associated with a remitted course for SUD–PTSD patients (Ouimette, Moos, & Finney, 2000; Ouimette et al., 2001). Furthermore, a specific subgroup of PTSD patients fared better with 12-step participation. Among PTSD patients who self-identified as an alcoholic or addict, participation predicted less psychological distress at both follow-ups. Conversely, among those who did not endorse an alcoholic/ addict identity, 12-step participation was associated with increased distress. Because of the emphasis on accepting a label of *alcoholic* or *addict* in 12-step groups, patients without such an identity may have found participation distressing. In addition, these patients may have been more identified with having PTSD, such as is often found with Vietnam combat veterans. Being in self-help groups that emphasize the primacy of addictions may invalidate these patients' perceptions of PTSD as their primary problem and consequently increase their distress.

Several evaluations of specialized inpatient treatment programs for PTSD have also been conducted (Fontana & Rosenheck, 1997; Johnson et al., 1996). These studies unfortunately did not include formal diagnoses of SUDs, even though a substantial proportion of the PTSD patients in these studies most likely had SUDs. However, these studies often assessed substance abuse outcomes. For example, in one study of inpatient PTSD treatment PTSD patients showed modest improvement on both PTSD and alcohol abuse outcomes (but not drug abuse) at a 4-month follow-up (Fontana & Rosenheck, 1997).

In another study of a PTSD inpatient program, neither PTSD symptoms nor substance abuse improved over an 18-month follow-up (Johnson et al., 1996). This study reported that 61% of the patients had current alcohol problems, 35% had current drug problems, and 39% had had a drug overdose in their lifetime, indicating that many of these patients had SUDs. Although it is difficult to draw conclusions without direct assessments of SUDs, it is possible that the patients' comorbid SUDs attenuated the effectiveness of the treatment programs.

Studies of Combined SUD–PTSD Treatment

Several cognitive–behavioral treatments have been shown to be efficacious in treating PTSD, including cognitive therapy, anxiety management, and real world or imaginary exposure (Meadows & Foa, 1999). In general, cognitive–behavioral techniques also are efficacious/effective in reducing substance abuse (Carroll, 1996). Accordingly, several integrated treatment protocols have been developed that adapt existing treatments for PTSD or SUD to address the other comorbidity. Some of these treatments are currently under investigation in clinical trials.

Abueg and Fairbank (1991) developed a modified relapse prevention program for combat veterans with PTSD and SUDs. Three aspects of substance abuse relapse prevention training (Marlatt & Gordon, 1985) were identified as particularly relevant for SUD–PTSD patients. First, the combined treatment protocol extended the assessment of high-risk situations for alcohol and drug use to include the assessment of emotional states (e.g., PTSD) similar to the original traumatic situations or trauma cues. Second, the protocol enhanced patients' attention to issues of self-efficacy and self-confidence in resisting alcohol or drug use, which are particularly compromised among PTSD patients. Finally, the protocol addressed the *abstinence violation effect* (i.e., the idea that a slip in perceived control of the abused substance will lead to substance abuse), which may be exaggerated among PTSD patients. Combat veterans with PTSD often overestimate the severity of mistakes because, in the context of combat, mistakes may have led to fatal consequences.

Abueg and Fairbank (1991) randomly assigned 42 alcohol-dependent veterans with PTSD to a 12-session version of the PTSD-adapted relapse prevention program as an adjunct to treatment and 42 comparable veterans to treatment as usual (PTSD inpatient treatment). At a 6-month follow-up, the SUD–PTSD patients who received the PTSD-relapse prevention treatment were more likely to be abstinent, and at a 9-month follow-up they drank less on a daily basis relative to comparison patients. However, the two groups did not differ on abstinence rates at the 9-month follow-up. Although the combined treatment enhanced substance use outcomes, this study points to the probable need for continuing care for SUD–PTSD patients to maintain treatment gains.

Najavits et al. (1996) developed a 24-session group treatment called "Seeking Safety," which combines cognitive–behavioral and interpersonal therapy techniques for patients with SUD–PTSD. Each session has an identified topic (e.g., asking for help, self-nurturing) that addresses themes relevant to both PTSD and substance abuse and that includes the development of coping skills related to the issue. In a pilot study of women with SUD–PTSD, from intake to a 3-month follow-up, significant reductions were found in substance use and trauma-related symptoms (Najavits, Weiss, Shaw, & Muenz, 1998). Patients also improved on substance use, depression, suicide risk and thoughts, dysfunctional attitudes about substance use, problem solving, and social adjustment. However, there was no improvement in PTSD symptoms, and patients reported an increase in somatic symptoms from intake to follow-up.

Patients in the Seeking Safety program rated the following treatment aspects as most helpful: the focus on abstinence and on coping skills, the therapist, and treatment overall. They gave lower helpfulness ratings to the short length of the program and to aspects of the group membership (i.e., option to call other group members outside of sessions, the assignment of a group partner, and the support of other group members). These findings suggest that integrated treatment may be effective for SUD–PTSD patients. They also indicate that patients may prefer abstinence goals, help with coping with stressors, individual treatment before group treatment, and a longer course of treatment (i.e., longer than 3 months).

Treatments That Include Exposure Techniques

Exposure treatments have been shown to be highly efficacious in the treatment of PTSD, particularly in reducing re-experiencing symptoms (Foa, 2000; Foa et al., 1999; Solomon, Gerrity, & Muff, 1992). However, these findings may not generalize to SUD–PTSD patients who typically have been excluded from the studies because of their addiction problems (Boudewyns & Hyer, 1990; Foa et al., 1999; Foa, Rothbaum, Riggs, & Murdock, 1991; Richards, Lovell, & Marks, 1994; Richards & Rose, 1991). Moreover, substance abuse was not assessed at baseline in these studies (Cooper & Clum, 1989; Keane, Fairbank, Caddell, & Zimering, 1989; Richards et al., 1994; Richards & Rose, 1991), precluding any statements about changes in alcohol and drug use over the course of treatment.

A survey of clinicians found that 27% consider a concurrent SUD to be a contraindication for exposure treatment for PTSD (Litz, Blake, Gerardi, & Keane, 1990). Clinicians' reasons for reluctance to use exposure treatment for SUD–PTSD are based on the beliefs that such patients may experience overwhelming emotions that would lead to more substance abuse or that cognitive impairment associated with the SUD could impair the patient's ability to do the necessary imagery for exposure treatment (Abueg & Fairbank, 1991). Hence, because of these clinical concerns exposure treatment has been relatively unexplored as a treatment for SUD–PTSD, although it has been seen as the treatment of choice for PTSD alone (Ballenger et al., 2000; Expert Consensus Guideline Series, 1999).

Empirical information on the effectiveness of exposure treatment for SUD–PTSD is limited to case studies and small pilot studies, the results of which generally support the effectiveness of exposure techniques (e.g., Dansky et al., 1994; Keane et al., 1989). Building on these promising pilot data, three manual-based treatments for SUD–PTSD have been developed that include exposure therapy techniques (Dansky & Brady, 1998; Donovan & Padin-Rivera, 1999; Triffleman et al., 1999). One such treatment focuses on Vietnam-era combat veterans, one focuses on PTSD in the context of cocaine dependence, and the final protocol was developed to treat SUD–PTSD in any patient population.

Donovan, Padin-Rivera, and Kowaliw (2001) developed an integrated treatment called "Transcend" for patients with combat-related SUD–PTSD comorbidity. The first phase of the program involves a 12-week partial hospitalization that focuses on decreasing PTSD symptoms and promoting an addiction-free lifestyle. The treatment approach integrates behavioral skills training; the exposure-based piece, that is, narrative trauma processing (i.e., written exercises) with an emphasis on meaning and self-acceptance/forgiveness; relapse prevention training; and peer social support. The second phase includes long-term continuing care in weekly groups for at least 6 months. These groups emphasize PTSD symptom management and relapse prevention. In a pilot evaluation of 50 male Vietnam veterans with SUD–PTSD, patients' PTSD symptoms decreased during the first phase of the program and remained stable at the 1-year follow-up.

Dansky et al. (1998; see chapter 7, this volume) developed a manual-based psychotherapy protocol for patients with PTSD and cocaine dependence that incorporates *imaginal exposure* techniques, which require patients to repeatedly recount the traumatic memory until symptoms decrease. Key features of the treatment include educating the patient about the interconnectedness of PTSD and SUD symptoms, teaching coping skills to promote abstinence, and using imaginal and in vivo exposure to try to reduce PTSD symptoms. On the basis of pilot work, Dansky et al. (1998) cautioned that individuals who have difficulty identifying an index trauma for exposure treatment, or who are unable to substantially recall their traumas, may not respond as well to the protocol.

Another protocol, "Substance Dependence PTSD Therapy," has been developed for patients with varied SUDs and traumas (Triffleman et al., 1999). This two-phase treatment has a more intensive format: twice-weekly individual sessions for 5 months. Phase I emphasizes the establishment of abstinence and education about the linkages between PTSD and SUD symptoms. Patients are taught abstinence-oriented trauma-informed coping skills (i.e., examinations of cognitions and dysphoria associated with cravings, generation of alternative cognitions, and management of emotional and physical states).

Phase II focuses on decreasing PTSD symptoms through education, stress inoculation (e.g., learning coping skills to deal with current reminders of the trauma), and in vivo exposure, with the purpose of desensitizing patients to trauma-related stimuli that they have avoided. Triffleman et al. (1999) reported that a preliminary open trial supported the efficacy of the treatment.

Implications of Treatment Studies

These findings suggest that SUD treatment for SUD–PTSD patients enhances their substance use outcomes, but not their psychosocial outcomes. For the most part, however, PTSD patients' improvement on substance use outcomes does not match the improvement of patients without PTSD. (Moreover, among the VA SUD–PTSD patients, about two thirds were not abstinent, and 75% still reported problems from substance use, at follow-up; Ouimette, 2000.)

It is clear that a comprehensive SUD–PTSD treatment plan needs to address not only substance use problems but also symptoms and quality-of-life issues (e.g., vocational problems). This recommendation is consistent with the International Society for Traumatic Stress Studies' (ISTSS) treatment guidelines for psychosocial rehabilitation treatment of PTSD, which is specifically recommended for PTSD patients who persist in substance abuse and have difficulties in several areas of functioning (ISTSS, 1997).

The findings also imply that specific types of programs and treatments may effect greater improvement in SUD–PTSD patients' outcomes. Aspects of SUD treatment that appear helpful for short-term outcomes included more intensive substance abuse counseling and involvement in family treatment. Supportive and structured treatment environments may provide a greater sense of safety that facilitates PTSD patients' short-term outcomes. Self-help participation and attendance were associated with better short- and long-term outcomes, suggesting that self-help groups provide a helpful adjunct to formal treatment for SUD–PTSD patients (Ouimette et al., 2001).

In the veterans study, PTSD-focused outpatient treatment was associated with a stable course of remission from substance abuse after the index episode of inpatient care (Ouimette, Moos, & Finney, 2000). However, only 30% of SUD–PTSD patients received PTSD outpatient care in the first year following discharge from inpatient treatment, and only 20% received PTSD outpatient care in the second year. Although PTSD care may be an essential component of treatment, only a small proportion of VA and non-VA SUD–PTSD patients receive it (see also P. J. Brown, Stout, & Mueller, 1999).

Taken together, the findings of these studies suggest that concurrent treatment is effective for patients suffering from both SUDs and PTSD. Common treatment components include education that helps patients understand SUD–PTSD and their interconnections and training in the development of adaptive coping skills. The facts that some studies found a slight deterioration after an initial improvement and that patients preferred longer term treatment highlight the need for attention to continuing care for SUD–PTSD patients.

We await the findings of ongoing controlled trials (Dansky & Brady, 1998; Najavits et al., 1996; Triffleman et al., 1999). Some limitations of the preliminary studies include lack of self-reported or structured interviews of trauma and PTSD and lack of comparison groups to evaluate whether treatments offered are more effective than simpler alternative treatments or no treatment. Future work also needs to investigate the best format in which to deliver the intervention (e.g., relapse prevention with or without imaginal, in vivo, and/or narrative exposure; individual vs. group; length of treatment).

Although pharmacological treatment of PTSD and SUD is not a focus of this chapter, there are several effective somatic treatments for PTSD (for a review, see Sutherland & Davidson, 1999). One preliminary study of SUD–PTSD patients supported the effectiveness of sertraline in decreasing both PTSD and substance use (Brady, Sonne, & Roberts, 1995). Further work is needed on the appropriate use of psychotropic medications (both alone and in conjunction with psychological interventions) for the treatment of patients with SUD–PTSD.

PROGNOSES OF COMORBID SUD–PTSD

Variables that predict SUD–PTSD patients' outcomes and explain the relationship between PTSD and poorer SUD treatment outcomes are important to identify. Prognostic characteristics could be assessed at treatment intake and used to inform treatment planning. Also, SUD–PTSD patients with the greatest "risk" could be targeted for enhanced treatment and continuing care. Hence, we next summarize empirical findings on the prognostic implications of the specific manifestation of PTSD symptoms, patients' lack of coping skills, and additional diagnostic comorbidities.

PTSD Symptom Clusters and Substance Use

Four major symptom clusters comprise the PTSD syndrome: (a) re-experiencing/intrusions (e.g., flashbacks, nightmares), (b) avoidance (e.g.,

avoiding reminders of the trauma), (c) emotional numbing, and (d) hyperarousal (e.g., hypervigilance, exaggerated startle). Avoidance and numbing
are combined into one cluster in formal diagnostic criteria but, on the
basis of empirical factor analytic studies, several authors have argued that
avoidance and numbing should be considered separate symptom clusters
(Foa, Riggs, & Gershuny, 1995; Foa, Zinbarg, & Rothbaum, 1992; Keane,
1993; Stewart, 1996; Stewart, Conrod, Pihl, & Dongier, 1999).

The literature on PTSD suggests that trauma survivors who exhibit
more dissociation are the most likely to develop chronic PTSD (Koopman,
Classen, & Spiegel, 1994) and that numbing predicts poorer treatment
response (Jaycox & Foa, 1999). However, in a study that prospectively
examined the relationship between PTSD symptom clusters and drug treatment outcome (Gil-Rivas, Fiorentine, & Anglin, 1996), neither intrusive
nor avoidance symptoms predicted relapse to drug use during the 6-month
follow-up period. More generally, the severity of these four PTSD symptom
clusters may differentially affect substance use and abuse (e.g., Schnitt &
Nocks, 1984). A better understanding of the functional relationships between PTSD symptom clusters and substance use would be helpful in predicting the course of SUD–PTSD comorbidity.

Two studies have described the concurrent relationship between PTSD
symptoms and specific substance use problems. McFall, Mackay, and Donovan (1992) compared male combat veterans with and without PTSD (as
assessed by a self-report instrument) on a measure of alcohol problems, the
Michigan Alcoholism Screening Test (Selzer, 1971), and a measure of drug
problems, the Drug Abuse Screening Test (Skinner, 1982). Patients who
had PTSD obtained higher alcohol and drug scores; patients who had more
severe intrusion symptoms also had more alcohol and drug problems. However, arousal symptoms were uniquely associated with alcohol problems,
whereas avoidance and numbing symptoms were uniquely associated with
problems related to other drugs.

In a sample of community women, the four PTSD symptom clusters
were measured by the PTSD Symptom Self-Report Scale (Foa, Riggs, Dancu,
& Rothbaum, 1993) and were examined in relation to severity of both
alcohol and prescription drug problems (Stewart, Conrod, et al., 1999).
Arousal symptoms were associated with more alcohol dependence. Numbing
and arousal symptoms were associated with more anxiolytic and analgesic
dependence, and intrusions also were associated with greater analgesic dependence. The most consistent evidence in this study was for an association
between severity of numbing and arousal symptoms and severity of substance
abuse problems.

In a study of the natural history of chronic PTSD in Vietnam veterans
(Bremner et al., 1996), patients were asked about the links between PTSD
and SUD symptoms. Patients reported that increases in their PTSD symp-

toms during and immediately after the war were associated with increased use of substances. Patients reported that heroin use relieved intrusive symptoms; in addition, alcohol reduced nightmares about the traumatic event and alleviated one specific numbing symptom: feeling cut off or detached from others. Alcohol, heroin, and benzodiazepines were reported to reduce most symptoms in the hyperarousal cluster; marijuana helped with sleep disturbances. Finally, patients reported that cocaine increased the severity of most of their hyperarousal symptoms. This naturalistic study suggested that substance use was mainly an attempt to self-medicate arousal and re-experiencing symptoms.

P. J. Brown et al. (1998) similarly found that SUD–PTSD patients reported a functional relationship between SUD and PTSD symptoms. Specifically, patients reported that an improvement in either PTSD or SUD symptoms was linked to improvement in the other set of symptoms. Deterioration in either set of symptoms resulted in worsening of the other. Patients noted that changes in PTSD symptoms were more strongly linked to changes in substance use problems than vice versa, suggesting that PTSD symptoms have a primary role in the course of SUD–PTSD comorbidity.

Coping Skills

Characteristic coping style differences may help account for PTSD patients' poorer substance use outcomes. PTSD is related to the use of more emotion-focused and fewer problem-focused coping strategies among trauma-exposed individuals (Fairbank, Hansen, & Fitterling, 1991; Nezu & Carnevale, 1987) and among substance abuse patients with and without PTSD (Ouimette et al., 1997; Ouimette, Ahrens, et al., 1998; Ouimette et al., 1999; Penk, Peck, Robinowitz, Bell, & Little, 1988). Patients with chronic PTSD may have developed a preferred or characteristic coping response to stressors. A coping style that includes ineffective strategies, such as avoidance coping, may maintain ongoing trauma-related symptoms and precipitate substance abuse. Thus, PTSD may differentially influence relapse in SUD patients through increased deficits in coping skills.

In their longitudinal evaluation of SUD–PTSD veterans, Ouimette et al. (1997) examined baseline coping styles as possible mediators of the relationship between PTSD comorbidity and poorer treatment outcomes. The association between PTSD and problems from substance use at a 1-year follow-up was partially explained by SUD–PTSD patients' greater use of emotional discharge coping (e.g., risk taking, yelling) at intake to treatment. This finding extended to patients' coping styles at treatment discharge such that PTSD patients' greater use of avoidance and emotional discharge coping at that point also partially explained their lower likelihood of remission at the 1-year follow-up.

Patients' coping at the 1-year follow-up also helped to explain the relationship between PTSD and poorer 2-year substance use outcomes (Ouimette et al., 1999). More reliance on emotional discharge and cognitive avoidance coping partially explained the association of PTSD with greater alcohol consumption and more problems from substance use. More frequent use of avoidance coping strategies and less frequent use of approach coping strategies at the 1-year follow-up partially explained the relationship between PTSD and a lower likelihood of remission at the 2-year follow-up. Coping thus should be carefully assessed at intake to treatment and be a main focus of intervention. These findings complement and support the focus on coping in several of the new interventions developed for SUD–PTSD (Dansky & Brady, 1998; Najavits et al., 1996; Triffleman et al., 1999). They also are consistent with the finding that patients report preferring help with developing adaptive coping skills (Najavits, Weiss, Shaw, & Muenz, 1998).

Additional Comorbidities

Compared with their SUD-only counterparts, SUD–PTSD patients present a more severe and complex symptom picture, including a greater likelihood of comorbid affective, anxiety, and personality disorders (Back et al., 2000; Brady, Killeen, Saladin, Dansky, & Becker, 1994; Najavits, Gastfriend, et al., 1998; Ouimette, Wolfe, & Chrestman, 1996). P. J. Brown et al. (1999) found that SUD–PTSD patients were more likely to suffer from major depressive disorder, bipolar disorder, and panic disorder than were SUD-only patients. Despite their higher rates of psychiatric comorbidity, however, SUD–PTSD patients did not use more psychiatric services (inpatient or outpatient) than SUD-only patients did in the 6 months prior to their current admission (P. J. Brown et al., 1999). Only 1 in 4 SUD–PTSD patients had received any type of psychiatric treatment; the SUD–PTSD patients averaged one outpatient psychiatric visit and two hospital overnight stays for psychiatric treatment in the prior 6 months. These findings indicate that SUD–PTSD patients may not receive adequate care for their non-PTSD psychiatric problems, which may increase their risk for poor SUD treatment outcomes.

Implications of Prognostic Indicators

These studies point to several factors that should be addressed in assessing and treating SUD–PTSD patients. The most consistent evidence is that attempts to alleviate intrusive and hyperarousal symptoms may drive the substance use of many of these patients. The findings also suggest that patients' reliance on avoidance coping may partially explain the relationship between PTSD and poorer substance use outcomes. Accordingly, treatment plans for SUD–PTSD patients should focus on how to facilitate patients' use of alternative coping strategies. Treatment of these patients' additional psychiatric comorbidities also may have a beneficial effect on coexisting SUD and PTSD symptoms.

SUD–PTSD patients with more severe intrusive and hyperarousal symptoms, poorer coping skills, and more psychiatric comorbidities may be at higher risk for relapse. Accordingly, the assessment of these three sets of factors at intake to treatment may identify SUD–PTSD patients who need more intensive treatment, referral, monitoring, and an enhanced course of continuing care. Future work on prognostic factors would be enhanced by including mixed-gender samples, assessments of *Diagnostic and Statistical Manual of Mental Disorders* (American Psychiatric Association, 1994) PTSD and SUD, multiple measures of outcomes, and prospective designs.

BARRIERS TO PTSD TREATMENT FOR SUD–PTSD PATIENTS

Practitioners need to be aware of both provider- and patient-level treatment barriers when treating individuals with SUD–PTSD. Hence, we now review recent work on access barriers to trauma and PTSD treatment for SUD–PTSD patients.

Provider-Related Barriers

Clinicians who treat patients with SUDs may not regularly diagnose PTSD or refer patients for psychological or PTSD treatment, even when PTSD is separately identified. Dansky, Roitzsch, Brady, and Saladin (1997) examined the effect of a research-based trauma/PTSD diagnostic interview on clinical practices in a substance abuse treatment unit. When research interview diagnoses were compared with discharge diagnoses in an initial sample of 95 patients, the research interview identified many more PTSD cases (40%) than did chart diagnoses (15%), indicating that clinicians had not identified PTSD in many patients. Clinical staff rarely documented PTSD despite the research interview notes, except under very specific circumstances (female patients who were victims of rape). In a second sample of 59 patients assessed after completion of the research protocol to evaluate whether the protocol had any effect on subsequent clinical practice, clinicians questioned only half of the patients about any potential victimization history. Moreover, PTSD was noted in only 5 patients at intake to treatment (all PTSD diagnoses were given by a mental health provider prior to the current hospitalization). When discharge diagnoses and plans for the 32 patients who had a history of victimization were examined, it was found that no new cases of PTSD were documented and that staff rarely, if ever, listed victimization as an issue in the treatment plan.

A survey of VA practices for PTSD found that screening for PTSD was less common in substance abuse programs than in outpatient mental health programs (Rosen et al., 2000). Although about three quarters of the clinicians in substance abuse programs regularly screened patients for depression, only half screened regularly for PTSD symptoms in patients who might have experienced a traumatic event. Thus, clinicians in VA and non-VA substance abuse treatment settings do not regularly screen for PTSD.

These data raise questions about why substance abuse clinicians do not screen for PTSD and do not refer patients for PTSD treatment. Possible reasons include lack of awareness of PTSD, discomfort in asking about trauma and PTSD, minimizing the potential effects of trauma and PTSD, lack of available PTSD or psychological counseling, and belief in the primacy of substance use problems relative to other psychiatric problems.

Patient-Related Barriers

Patients' beliefs about PTSD and trauma may affect their treatment seeking. P. J. Brown et al. (1998) asked SUD–PTSD patients about seven possible deterrents to treatment, such as difficulty in talking about their traumatic experiences with a treatment provider. The three most endorsed deterrents to PTSD treatment included emotional pain (76%), self-blame (67%), and shame (60%). Approximately 40% of the patients believed that talking about their trauma would make them worse, did not trust treatment providers, or were afraid that other people would find out about their trauma history. Only 21% of patients endorsed the belief that treatment providers were unable to deal with trauma issues. Among patients who were referred to PTSD treatment, almost 75% complied with the referral, indicating that patients' fears and concerns can be overridden by therapists' recommendations to seek PTSD treatment. When compliant and noncompliant patients were compared, noncompliant patients were more likely to indicate a lack of trust in treatment providers (P. J. Brown et al., 1998).

Implications of Barriers to Treatment

SUD–PTSD patients are not regularly screened for trauma and PTSD; neither are they regularly referred for PTSD treatment. Even when these issues are identified, they are not always addressed in treatment plans. Also, patients' specific beliefs about openly talking about trauma and PTSD may impede their seeking of appropriate treatment. Clinicians need to be aware of these provider- and patient-related tendencies and to participate in staff training in PTSD and trauma issues.

EXISTING PRACTICE GUIDELINES

Three practice guidelines have been developed for PTSD. ISTSS published the first guideline in 1997 (see also Foa, Keane, & Friedman, 2000). This guideline recommended cognitive–behavioral therapies and medication—specifically, selective serotonin reuptake inhibitors—as effective treatments for PTSD. Similarly, the Expert Consensus Guideline Series (1999) recommended exposure therapy, cognitive therapy, and anxiety management as effective psychotherapeutic techniques for PTSD, and antidepressants, particularly the selective serotonin reuptake inhibitors, as the best medication treatment for PTSD. This guideline also proposed that psychotherapy should be the first treatment choice for milder PTSD cases, with psychotherapy or adjunctive pharmacotherapy being used for more severe cases. In addition, parameters of treatment were recommended: Psychotherapy should be offered in an individual format and on a weekly basis until the patient stabilizes. The third guideline, which was designed for primary care providers (Ballenger et al., 2000), makes similar recommendations for PTSD care.

All three practice guidelines specifically developed for PTSD make treatment recommendations for comorbid addiction problems. ISTSS (1997) guidelines encourage practitioners to consult SUD treatment guidelines when SUDs are detected and to treat the SUD first. It also specifies that patients with SUD–PTSD may be more treatment resistant and engage in more high-risk behavior (e.g., suicide attempts), and may benefit more from psychosocial rehabilitation, especially if PTSD treatment is offered within that context.

The Expert Consensus Guideline Series (1999) recommend screening PTSD patients for SUDs at intake and reassessing them if there is a failure to respond to treatment. In regard to specific methods of treatment, these guidelines recommend anxiety management and encourage consideration of cognitive therapy and education techniques when addressing PTSD with comorbid SUD. Both the Expert Consensus Guideline and the Consensus Statement from the International Consensus Group on Depression and Anxiety propose that when SUD–PTSD is detected in primary care settings, providers should refer patients for specialty care (Ballenger et al., 2000; Expert Consensus Guideline Series, 1999).

Guidelines also exist for the treatment of patients with SUDs (American Psychiatric Association Practice Guidelines, 1995; American Society of Addiction Medicine, 1996; VA Clinical Practice Guideline for the Management of Persons With Substance Use Disorders, Version 1.0, Veterans Health Administration, 1999). Cognitive–behavioral, behavioral, psychodynamic–interpersonal, group–family, and self-help groups are recommended as effective treatments in these guidelines. They also note that systematic assessment and treatment of comorbid psychiatric disorders is important.

Currently, there are no practice guidelines specific to the treatment of patients with SUD–PTSD comorbidity. The documentation of SUD–PTSD patients' poorer posttreatment outcomes and increased use of costly treatment services (P. J. Brown et al., 1999) underscores the importance of developing more effective treatments and ensuring access by SUD–PTSD patients. A recent study of patients in the private health care sector estimated that SUD–PTSD patients incur approximately $3,000 more per year in addiction-related treatment costs than do patients with only SUDs (P. J. Brown et al., 1999). Thus, changes in current substance abuse treatment practices to address PTSD could result in more clinically effective and cost-effective treatments.

EMPIRICALLY BASED SUD–PTSD PRACTICE

Our findings show that comorbid PTSD is associated with poorer treatment outcomes following treatment for SUDs. On the basis of the empirical evidence reviewed in this chapter, we make the following recommendations for empirically based practice with these patients.

- *SUD patients should routinely be screened for traumatic stress experiences and PTSD.* Some studies have evaluated the use of specific instruments as screens for trauma and PTSD in SUD patients (Coffey, Dansky, Falsetti, Saladin, & Brady, 1998; Dansky, Saladin, Coffey, & Brady, 1997; Najavits, Weiss, Reif, et al., 1998). Najavits, Weiss, Reif, et al. (1998) examined the value of items from the Addiction Severity Index (ASI; McLellan et al., 1992), a commonly used assessment instrument in addiction treatment settings, as a PTSD screen. In identifying PTSD diagnoses in substance abuse patients, the lifetime ASI trauma items were highly sensitive (91% of patients with PTSD answered affirmatively to one or more of the ASI trauma items) but not very specific (only 43% of the patients who answered "yes" to a trauma item had a diagnosis of PTSD). The ASI may be cost efficient, because it is widely used in addiction treatment centers. A study of SUD patients using the PTSD Symptom Scale–Self-Report (Foa et al., 1993) as a screen found that 89% of patients were correctly classified as having PTSD when compared with a structured interview (Coffey et al., 1998). A major advantage of the PTSD Symptom Scale–Self-Report is that it requires only 10–15 minutes to complete.

Another screening instrument is the PTSD Checklist (Weathers, Litz, Herman, Huska, & Keane, 1993), which has sound psychometric properties and a brief administration time (for a more thorough review, see chapter 6, this volume).

After an initial screening is positive, a diagnosis can be confirmed using a structured clinical interview, such as the Clinician-Administered PTSD Scale (Blake et al., 1995). Providers should regularly assess and attend to PTSD symptoms, as studies of the effects of drug abstinence and withdrawal on anxiety and affective disorders suggest that some symptoms may resolve within the first 3 weeks of recovery (S. A. Brown et al., 1995; Thevos, Johnston, Latham, Randall, & Malcolm, 1991).

Another reason for screening is that individuals with trauma histories are at risk for further traumatic experiences. For example, in a pharmacologic treatment trial a higher proportion of patients with PTSD at baseline experienced a new trauma (83%) within 3 months following treatment than those without PTSD (36%; Dansky et al., 1998). Accordingly, providers should help SUD–PTSD patients understand their risk for revictimization and develop strategies to prevent such occurrences. Providers should query patients on a regular basis regarding exposure to new stressors. A measure such as the Traumatic Life Events Questionnaire (Kubany et al., 2000) may be useful in assessing exposure to potentially traumatic events (also see chapter 6, this volume). The Traumatic Life Events Questionnaire is a brief, broad-spectrum survey of traumatic life events that has yielded promising reliability and validity data (Kubany et al., 2000).

If time and resources permit, screening for additional psychopathology is recommended, along with follow-up clinical interviews to confirm diagnoses. Specifically, affective disorders and panic disorder appear to be important comorbidities to assess (P. J. Brown et al., 1999). Specific self-administered measures include the Beck Depression and Anxiety Inventories to assess depression and anxiety (Beck, Epstein, Brown, & Steer, 1988; Beck & Steer, 1987). An interview such as the Structured Clinical Interview for Diagnosis (Spitzer, Williams, Gibbon, & First, 1992) can be used to confirm the presence of comorbid affective and anxiety disorder diagnoses.

- *SUD–PTSD patients should be referred for concurrent trauma/ PTSD treatment or for psychological treatment with the recommendation that trauma/PTSD issues be addressed.* Recommended treatment methods include education, anxiety management, and cognitive–behavioral coping skills training.

- *SUD–PTSD should be referred for concurrent participation in self-help groups and, when indicated, for family treatment.* Because many addictions-focused self-help groups encourage adoption of an alcoholic or addict identity, clinicians should assess SUD–PTSD patients' identities regarding addictions and PTSD before they refer them to self-help groups. If a patient is more identified with having PTSD, exploration of whether he or she would be comfortable and still benefit from participation is important, as is monitoring the patient's distress level in regard to 12-step participation (Ouimette et al., 2001). Before making a referral for family treatment, clinicians should assess for interpersonal trauma and for the identity of the perpetrator, given that substance-dependent patients report high rates of physical assault by an intimate partner (Dansky, Byrne, & Brady, 1999).

- *Providers should offer SUD–PTSD patients continuing outpatient mental health care.* Patients who remain in outpatient care longer (i.e., regular sessions for 3 months or longer) tend to have better outcomes (Ouimette, Moos, & Finney, 2000). SUD–PTSD patients also report dissatisfaction with short-term treatments (i.e., less than 3 months; Najavits, Weiss, Shaw, & Muenz, 1998) and group formats. In line with the Expert Consensus Guideline Series (1999), we recommend individual weekly sessions for 3 months or longer, until the patient stabilizes.

Providers should also be aware of gender-related methods that may facilitate attendance at continuing care, such as providing child care, matching the gender of the therapist and the client, and keeping in mind the cultural concerns of the client (Hien & Scheier, 1996).

6

ASSESSMENT OF COMORBID SUBSTANCE USE DISORDER AND POSTTRAUMATIC STRESS DISORDER

JENNIFER P. READ, ANDREAS R. BOLLINGER, AND
ERICA SHARKANSKY

This chapter is designed to review theoretical and procedural approaches to the comprehensive assessment of comorbid substance use disorder–posttraumatic stress disorder (SUD–PTSD). We outline several widely used assessment measures as well as methods to enhance accurate assessment of PTSD and SUD symptoms, and we discuss the importance of assessing other comorbidities and present procedural and provider issues that may affect assessment.

EVALUATING TRAUMA, PTSD, AND SUD

Critical choices in the planning of an evaluation of comorbid SUD–PTSD pertain to (a) the *timing* of the assessment (i.e., when is the client most likely to provide reliable information) and (b) *measures and methods* of assessment (i.e., instruments to be used, corroborative methods).

A major concern in the assessment process is that any substance use by patients may minimize or mask PTSD symptoms. Thus, any assessment of PTSD should not occur while patients are actively drinking or drugging. PTSD assessment should ideally be conducted after the addicted individual has completed withdrawal. The withdrawal process will vary by person and by substance of abuse but will usually not exceed 1 week. Consultation with the patient's medical and psychological treatment team may help determine the patient's readiness for assessment. Diagnosing PTSD should be avoided when patients are in the acute stages of withdrawal (Hoffman & Sasaki, 1997; Saladin, Brady, Dansky, & Kilpatrick, 1995). Many withdrawal symptoms (e.g., sleep loss, nightmares, increased anxiety, and increases in intrusion of traumatic cognitions) overlap or mirror symptoms of PTSD, thereby potentially inflating estimates of PTSD or other anxiety disorders (Abueg & Fairbank, 1991). Given that memory problems are associated with withdrawal, assessment of traumatic events and associated sequelae will be more reliable after initial detoxification.

Concurrent evaluation of PTSD and SUD does not need to be time or labor intensive. A variety of measures are available that can easily be included as part of a basic assessment protocol. We provide here brief descriptions of some of the most widely used assessment tools.

Self-Report Instruments

Several self-report instruments offer a time-efficient and effective method of evaluating trauma, PTSD, and SUD. These self-report instruments can be administered in a variety of clinical and research settings and do not require specialized training of clinical personnel.

Trauma

Assessment of traumatic exposure should include attention to both parts of *Diagnostic and Statistical Manual of Mental Disorders* (4th ed.; *DSM–IV*; American Psychiatric Association, 1994) Criterion A: (a) A1, which requires experiencing or witnessing an event involving actual or threatened death or serious injury, or a threat to physical integrity, and (b) A2, which requires a response to such an event that involves intense fear, helplessness, or horror. Additional information regarding type, duration, and severity of the traumatic event may provide a better understanding of the event and its sequelae. We present self-administered instruments; interview schedules are available (e.g., the Traumatic Stress Schedule; Norris, 1990; see Norris & Riad, 1997, for more information).

The Trauma History Questionnaire (Green, 1995) is a brief self-report measure that gathers information about Criterion A and other stressful events. Information pertaining to the number of times a traumatic or stressful event occurred and the age of a patient at its occurrence is recorded. Reliability data demonstrate adequate test–retest reliability (Green, 1995, 1996).

Kubany and colleagues (2000) developed the Traumatic Life Events Questionnaire. Questionnaire items are described in behaviorally specific terms and evaluate *DSM–IV* A1 and A2 criteria and frequency of event occurrence. Emerging data on this measure suggest that it demonstrates adequate psychometric properties. Furthermore, this measure has been used successfully to assess trauma in substance-abusing populations.

PTSD

In this section we present self-report assessment instruments that offer the most promise in facilitating the detection of PTSD, particularly with respect to comorbid SUD–PTSD populations. Interested readers are referred to Norris and Riad (1997) for a more complete review.

The PTSD Symptom Scale–Self Report (PSS–SR; Foa, Riggs, Dancu, & Rothbaum, 1993) consists of 17 items designed to assess Criteria B, C, and D of the *DSM–III–R* (American Psychiatric Association, 1987) and *DSM–IV*. Falsetti, Resnick, Resick, and Kilpatrick (1993) modified the PSS–SR to measure symptom severity in addition to symptom frequency. This modified version of the PSS–SR (MPSS–SR) has demonstrated good psychometric properties in both treatment-seeking and community samples (Falsetti, Resick, Resnick, & Kilpatrick, 1992). Furthermore, this measure has been used successfully to assess PTSD symptoms in substance abuse populations and has shown strong sensitivity and specificity, as well as good reliability and validity, in these samples (Coffey, Dansky, Falsetti, Saladin, & Brady, 1998; Dansky, Saladin, Coffey, & Brady, 1997).

The PTSD Checklist (Weathers, Litz, Herman, Huska, & Keane, 1993) uses a Likert-type scale to evaluate the extent to which an individual may experience each of the 17 *DSM* cardinal symptoms. This measure is available in both *DSM–III–R* and *DSM–IV* versions and has also been revised for use with civilian populations. It has strong psychometric properties and has been used with a variety of populations (e.g., Blanchard, Jones-Alexander, Buckley, & Forneris, 1996), including people with SUDs (Najavits, Weiss, Reif, et al., 1998). However, the PTSD Checklist has not specifically been evaluated as an assessment measure to identify PTSD in SUD samples.

The Posttraumatic Stress Diagnostic Scale (PDS; Foa, 1995), which is based on the PSS–SR, consists of 49 items requiring respondents to rate symptom presence and severity on a Likert-type scale. Items are clustered around *DSM–IV* PTSD symptom clusters (re-experiencing, avoidance, and arousal). Early examination of the psychometric properties of the PDS have shown this measure to have good internal and test–retest reliability as well as strong convergent and concurrent validity. Although the PDS has been validated on a sample with diverse trauma experiences (Foa, Cashman, Jaycox, & Perry, 1997), its utility among SUD patients has not yet been established.

SUDs

Several self-report measures have been shown to be useful in screening for SUDs (see Miller, Westerberg, & Waldron, 1995). Despite the strengths of brief self-report measures, such instruments are insufficient for a formal diagnosis of SUD. Moreover, there is a paucity of empirical research examining the utility of such self-report instruments for PTSD patients.

The Alcohol Use Disorders Identification Test (Babor, de la Fuente, Saunders, & Grant, 1992; Saunders, Aasland, Babor, de la Fuente, & Grant, 1993) is a brief (10-item) measure that assesses alcohol consumption, drinking behavior, and alcohol-related problems. Its scores correlate with other self-report alcohol screening tests (J. P. Allen, Litten, Fertig, & Babor, 1997). Two other brief self-report measures with well-documented psychometric properties are the Michigan Alcoholism Screening Test (Selzer, 1971) and the Drug Abuse Screening Test (Skinner, 1982). Both measures, administered in either a paper-and-pencil or an interview format, can be used in a variety of settings with various populations.

Structured Clinical Interviews

Structured interviews in general tend to require clinical interviewers with specific training in the administration and scoring of the measures. Because of the level of detail that structured interviews cover with respect to symptomatology, they are generally viewed as confirmatory measures used to formulate a clinical diagnosis rather than as screening measures.

PTSD

Although numerous structured clinical interviews have been developed and used to assess PTSD (for reviews, see Carlson, 1997; Norris & Riad, 1997), here we highlight three of the most widely used. The Clinician-Administered PTSD Scale for *DSM–IV* (CAPS; Blake et al., 1995) assesses core and associated PTSD symptoms, both currently and over the course of the individual's lifetime (Blake et al., 1990). Presence, intensity, and frequency of each PTSD symptom in each of three symptom clusters (reexperiencing, avoidance, or hyperarousal) is assessed. The CAPS has been found to have excellent psychometric properties (Blake et al., 1995; Weathers & Litz, 1994). It has been shown to correlate significantly with other well-known measures of PTSD (Blake et al., 1995; Weathers & Litz, 1994) and has demonstrated strong diagnostic utility against the Structured Clinical Interview for the *DSM* (Weathers & Keane, 1999). Potential limitations of the CAPS include its length in administration and amount of training required for the interviewers. In addition, the intensity ratings for individual PTSD symptoms may be difficult to ascertain (Blake et al., 1995). At sites with limited clinical resources or more diverse client populations, a briefer interview, or even a self-report instrument, may be preferred.

The National Women's Study PTSD Module (Kilpatrick, Resnick, Saunders, & Best, 1989; Resnick, 1996) is a diagnostic interview that was modified from the Diagnostic Interview Schedule (DIS; Robins, Helzer, Croughan, & Ratcliff, 1981). The National Women's Study PTSD Module allows for the assessment of detailed information about a broad range of Criterion A traumatic events and B, C, and D symptoms. This measure is used for both men and women, has demonstrated good psychometric properties (Resnick, 1996; Resnick, Kilpatrick, Dansky, Saunders, & Best, 1993), and has been administered to substance abuse populations (see Coffey et al., 1998; Dansky, Saladin, et al., 1997).

The PTSD module of the Structured Clinical Interview for DSM–IV (SCID; First, Spitzer, Gibbon, & Williams, 1994) is used in the assessment of PTSD and has excellent psychometric properties (Kulka et al., 1990; McFall, Smith, Roszell, Tarver, & Malas, 1990; Schnurr, Friedman, & Rosenberg, 1993). However, the SCID requires both a substantial amount of training and a professional clinician for administration, and it primarily yields categorical or dichotomous symptom ratings (S. N. Allen, 1994; Spitzer, Williams, Gibbon, & First, 1990). Furthermore, the symptom criteria do not have behaviorally anchored rating scales, and therefore there may be undesired subjectivity in the coding of a particular response. This measure lacks the precision of a more focused interview such as the CAPS (see Weiss, 1997).

SUDs

The SCID (First et al., 1994) is among the most popular structured interviews for the assessment of SUDs. The SCID has modules for alcohol as well as other classes of drugs. This measure yields a diagnosis of substance abuse or dependence and allows for specifiers such as *mild, moderate,* or *severe,* as well as the stage of the disorder (i.e., current diagnosis, partial or full remission). The SCID has demonstrated strong psychometric properties in the assessment of SUDs (Skre, Onstad, Torgersen, & Kringlen, 1991; Williams et al., 1992); however, the SCID requires rather extensive inter-viewer training, which can be time consuming and costly.

Another DSM-based measure used for assessing SUDs is the DIS (Robins et al., 1981), which was developed originally to gather epidemiological data regarding the prevalence of SUDs (see Miller, Westerberg, & Waldron, 1995). The DIS has demonstrated good psychometric properties (Levitan, Blouin, Navarro, & Hill, 1991; Malgady, Rogler, & Tryon, 1992) and has been found to be easy to administer in the assessment of substance abuse (Fleming & Barry, 1991). Unlike the SCID, the DIS requires little clinical training and does not require clinical judgment. Furthermore, the DIS is available in both paper-and-pencil and computer-administered formats.

Two other interviewer-administered measures that are widely used as part of a comprehensive assessment for SUD are the Addiction Severity

Index (ASI; McLellan et al., 1992), and the Timeline Follow-Back (TLFB; Sobell & Sobell, 1992). It is important to note that these two measures are not diagnostic measures per se; however, they are commonly used in both clinical and research settings to gather detailed information about substance use and related consequences.

The ASI assesses the severity of SUDs based on client functioning across several unique domains (measured by independent problem scales), including alcohol, drug, medical, employment, legal, family–social, and psychiatric. The ASI also assesses for emotional, physical, or sexual abuse. The ASI has been used with several diverse client populations (Appleby, Dyson, Altman, & Luchins, 1997; Joyner, Wright, & Devine, 1996; Leonhard, Mulvey, Gastfriend, & Shwartz, 2000; Weisner, McLellan, & Hunkeler, 2000) and has demonstrated strong psychometric properties (Appleby et al., 1997; McDermott et al., 1996; McLellan et al., 1992). The ASI has traditionally been used for evaluation of substance abuse populations, yet the comprehensiveness of this measure allows for its use in screening for trauma and PTSD as well as SUD. Najavits, Weiss, Reif, et al. (1998) noted that, although the ASI is not an effective measure for diagnosing PTSD, the trauma history items on this measure could serve to alert clinicians to the possibility that a client may have comorbid PTSD–SUD.

The TLFB procedure obtains a detailed picture of alcohol and other substance use behaviors. The TLFB is structured like a calendar and broken down month by month. Using this calendar, clients are asked to identify and note memorable occasions over the past 30 days to help prompt their recall of daily alcohol and other drug use behaviors over the past month. Use of the TLFB allows for a more comprehensive understanding of a client's daily drinking and drugging patterns. For example, by calculating a client's percentage of days abstinent, and number of drinks per drinking day, the percentage of days of heavy drinking can be derived. This measure has been shown to be a valid and reliable method for assessing substance use patterns over time (Sobell & Sobell, 1995).

Corroborative Evaluation Methods: Biological

In addition to self-report and structured interview methods, several biological methods for evaluating PTSD and SUD symptoms are available.

PTSD

Psychophysiological assessment methods are promising in that they potentially offer an unbiased way of deriving information about PTSD symptoms that does not rely on self-report data or on interviewer discretion and decisions. Psychophysiological assessments have typically focused on measuring physiological responsiveness (i.e., autonomic arousal) when an individual is exposed to trauma-related stimuli (Blanchard, Kolb, Pallmeyer, & Gerardi, 1982; Blanchard, Kolb, & Prins, 1991; Everly & MacNeil-Horton, 1989; Gerardi, Blanchard, & Kolb, 1989). The assessment of autonomic arousal usually includes an electromyogram and measurements of heart rate, blood pressure, and galvanic skin response. The amount of required instrumentation and technical expertise necessary to obtain these measurements was at one time a significant practical limitation of this approach; however, advances in technology and increasing computer competence among practitioners have made psychophysiological assessment methods more viable (Orr & Kaloupek, 1997). This assessment approach may be particularly valuable in assessment contexts such as forensic or disability evaluations.

One disadvantage of psychophysiological assessment is its demonstrated poorer sensitivity than specificity, resulting in a significant number of false negatives. Thus, some relevant PTSD symptomatology may not be detected during the physiologic assessment process. Moreover, physiologic arousal is only one of several categories of posttraumatic stress symptoms; therefore, even in cases where physiologic assessment methods are implemented and used successfully to evaluate physiologic arousal in response to a stressor, not all of the PTSD criteria are being evaluated.

SUDs

Biological indicators, such as urinary or saliva analysis tests, can be used to assess use of alcohol or other drugs within approximately the past 24 hours (Bates, Brick, & White, 1993; Roffman & George, 1988; Washton, Stone, & Hendrickson, 1988). In addition, breath-analysis tests are commonly used to assess current blood alcohol concentration in patients and have been shown to provide reliable estimates (Bates et al., 1993). It is unlikely that such biological measures of recent alcohol use would flag ongoing, problematic use; however, such measures will maximize the likelihood that the person being assessed is not currently under the influence of alcohol or other substances, thus enhancing the reliability of the information derived from the assessment (e.g., Leigh & Skinner, 1988).

Elevated blood levels of gamma glutamyl transferase (GGT) and mean corpuscular volume (MCV) are among the most commonly used biological markers of problematic alcohol use (Anton, Stout, Roberts, & Allen, 1998; Leigh & Skinner, 1988). Although these markers have been linked to patterns of chronic alcohol abuse, they have not been demonstrated to reliably detect alcohol use disorders. Furthermore, they appear to add little to diagnostic accuracy beyond what would be discerned from a diagnostic interview alone (Hillman, Sykes, & McConnell, 1998). Finally, biological methods of evaluating substance abuse can be financially costly, thus making such methods impractical for most clinicians.

Corroborative Evaluation Methods: Collateral Information

More often than not, assessment of trauma history and related psychological sequelae and of substance abuse symptomatology relies on retrospective recall (see Najavits, Weiss, & Shaw, 1997). Numerous researchers have discussed the challenges that reliance on memory poses to accurate diagnostic assessment, specifically with respect to the questionable reliability of retrospective recall. Such issues become particularly salient when applied to the task of attempting to parse out the temporal relationship between trauma and substance-related symptomatology or to understanding interplay among symptoms. In addition, it has been suggested that the self-report of substance use and related symptomatology among substance abusers will be enhanced if individuals are made aware that their self-reports will be verified by other sources (see O'Farrell & Maisto, 1987). Hence, it may be useful for clinicians to broaden assessment to incorporate information from a multitude of corroborative sources, such as friends or family members or documentation from military service or medical records.

EVALUATING OTHER COMORBIDITIES

As previously noted, SUD–PTSD comorbidity has been shown to be associated with higher levels of other Axis I (e.g., depression; Bollinger, Riggs, Blake, & Ruzek, 2000; Kessler, Sonnega, Bromet, Hughes, & Nelson, 1995) and Axis II (e.g., borderline personality disorder, antisocial personality disorder; Bollinger et al., 2000; Krinsley, Young, Weathers, Brief, & Kelley, 1992; Ouimette, Wolfe, & Chrestman, 1996) disorders. Such extensive comorbidity may make it difficult to disentangle and accurately diagnose SUD and PTSD. Hence, any assessment should comprehensively evaluate the presence of other psychopathology. Several of the measures described in this chapter (e.g., SCID, DIS) can be used to evaluate other common comorbidities and symptomatology.

SPECIAL ISSUES

Attend to Nonoverlapping Symptoms

During assessment, clinicians can facilitate greater diagnostic accuracy by attending to symptom overlap and symptom differentiation. Much of the overlap between PTSD and SUD (both dependence and withdrawal) occurs among avoidance (Criterion C) and arousal (Criterion D) symptoms of PTSD, whereas re-experiencing (Criterion B) symptoms are more specific to PTSD. Saladin et al. (1995) reported that intrusive re-experiencing symptoms (e.g., unpleasant memories, nightmares, flashbacks) demonstrate minimal overlap with substance intoxication or withdrawal.

In cases where the overlap between PTSD and SUD causes difficulty in ascribing symptoms to one diagnosis or the other, it may be helpful to give particular attention to the re-experiencing of symptoms, as the presence or absence of these symptoms may help to distinguish between PTSD and SUD. In cases where hyperarousal and avoidance symptoms are heavily represented, clinicians should be aware that some variance in the experiencing of these symptoms could be due to ongoing substance abuse rather than to traumatic stress sequelae (Saladin et al., 1995).

Establish Temporal Order of Substance Use and PTSD Symptoms

In exploring relations between PTSD and SUDs, some discussion has revolved around the utility of conceptualizing one disorder or the other as *primary*, or as acting as a precipitant of the other (see Stewart et al., 1998). Some researchers have argued that SUDs often evolve in response to traumatic events, citing the preponderance of people with SUDs who previously experienced a trauma (e.g., Kilpatrick, 1990; Resnick et al., 1993; Winfield, George, Swartz, & Blazer, 1990), whereas others have suggested that substance abuse is at least as likely to be the more primary of the two disorders (e.g., Brady, Dansky, Sonne, & Saladin, 1998; Cottler, Compton, Mager, Spitznagel, & Janca, 1992). Regardless of which disorder developed first, there is evidence indicating that temporal order of symptoms may be associated with different clinical pictures (Brady et al., 1998), which suggests that the accurate identification of the primary disorder may facilitate more appropriate treatment planning.

In many cases, however, the primacy of one disorder over the other may not consistently be discernible, and some evidence points to a relationship between these two disorders that is more symbiotic than causal. Many people with SUD–PTSD have a history of early childhood trauma (Najavits et al., 1997; Ouimette et al., 1996; Triffleman, Marmar, Delucchi, & Ronfeldt, 1995). Thus, it is particularly difficult to establish symptoms in relation to a particular Criterion A event, as the event may have occurred too early for current functioning to be realistically contrasted with pretrauma functioning. Furthermore, many people with histories of trauma have experienced not one but multiple traumas (Cloitre, Tardiff, Marzuk, Leon, & Portera, 1996; Irwin, 1999), and linking posttraumatic sequelae to any single trauma is difficult, if not impossible. For example, a person who presents with apparent

SUD–PTSD symptoms may have experienced combat trauma as well as early childhood trauma. In such a situation it is difficult to ascertain which (if any) of these traumatic experiences was *the* Criterion A event. If someone was traumatized in childhood, then subsequent substance abuse symptoms might be perceived as being secondary to the trauma. Thus, the presence of multiple victimizations makes assessment of symptom onset difficult and at times arbitrary.

It is important for professionals who assess and work clinically with people with comorbid SUD–PTSD to be aware that the genesis of a disorder (i.e., which disorder came first) may not have any bearing on the current clinical picture. Thus, an understanding of the primacy of one disorder over the other may facilitate a clearer understanding of the pathology, but it should not be confused with which symptoms are at present causing the greatest amount of clinical distress or how the symptoms are currently affecting one another. Assessing not only the presence but also the severity of concurrent symptoms (Kofoed, Friedman, & Peck, 1993) will assist in the next step of treatment planning, with the most acute, severe, or debilitating symptoms being attended to first to decrease overall psychological distress and to increase level of functioning.

Explore Relations Between Trauma Symptoms and Substance Use

Research has indicated that specific substances of abuse can be linked to particular posttraumatic symptoms. For example, Bremner, Southwick, Darnell, and Charney (1996) found that patients used specific types of drugs to alleviate different types of PTSD symptoms (e.g., substances such as alcohol, heroin, and other central nervous symptom depressants were used to address hyperarousal and intrusive symptoms). Stewart, Conrod, et al. (1999) reported similar findings and noted that specific substances of abuse were differentially associated with certain constellations of PTSD symptoms. Thus, when one is assessing comorbid PTSD and SUD, particular substances of abuse may provide clues about the extent to which a particular substance may be used by the patient to alleviate specific posttraumatic symptoms. For example, a patient's frequent use of depressant drugs might alert the clinician to pay special attention during the assessment process to hyperarousal symptoms and the ways in which substances are used to medicate these symptoms.

The identification of substances that are used in response to PTSD symptomatology may also indicate the PTSD symptoms that are most problematic for the patient. Specifically, the PTSD symptoms that are most commonly linked to substance use are likely to be those that are eliciting the greatest amount of psychological distress for the patient. It is these symptoms that should be addressed first in treatment.

A client's perceptions of his or her symptoms and how these symptoms affect one another are also a valuable source of information. Simply asking patients if symptoms are related to trauma or if they may be related to substance use will help a clinician understand symptom constellations (Saladin et al., 1995). This was exemplified in a study by Brown, Stout, and Gannon-Rowley (1998), who found that patients with SUD–PTSD perceived the relationship between the two disorders to be interconnected and reported that when symptoms from one disorder either improved or became worse, symptoms from the other disorder moved in the same direction. Moreover, regardless of the accuracy of the information pertaining to the connection among symptoms, client *perceptions* about how the two disorders relate to one another is valuable clinical information and may be helpful in addressing the client's motivations for change. For example, if the client recognizes that PTSD symptoms are likely to worsen with continued substance use, then he or she may be more motivated to engage actively in treatment for substance abuse.

Be Sensitive to Stigmatization and Shame

Both victimization status (particularly sexual victimization) and substance abuse are associated with significant societal stigma (Imhof, 1996). Such a stigma can present a challenge in the process of assessing PTSD and SUDs. For example, clients who wish to avoid being labeled an alcoholic or an addict may minimize either the quantity or frequency of their drinking as well as the extent of consequences resulting from substance use (Vuchinich, Tucker, & Harllee, 1988). Concern about encountering stigma or bias may similarly influence patient reports of both trauma and substance abuse history. For example, in a study conducted by Brown et al. (1998), more than half of the patients with SUDs and PTSD indicated that shame and blame were critical deterrents to seeking psychological treatment. On a related note, more than one third of the study participants identified lack of trust in the treatment provider as another potential barrier to treatment seeking. These data underscore the importance of providing a safe and validating environment for the assessment to take place.

Attend to the Assessment Context

Shame and stigma are not the only factors that may lead to the underreporting or misrepresentation of trauma and substance abuse symptomatology. Contextual factors, such as being court-ordered to treatment, seeking disability or other financial compensation, or even cultural mores also can affect an individual's self-report of PTSD and SUD symptoms. Specifically, gender differences have been identified in symptom reporting such that women are more likely to report greater symptomatology across several areas of distress than are men (Kroenke & Spitzer, 1998; Sheridan, Mulhern, & Martin, 1999). Cultural differences regarding behaviors that are deemed acceptable or unacceptable for different genders regarding sexual behavior and substance use can also affect reporting of victimization history, trauma-associated sequelae, and substance use (Wolfe & Kimerling, 1997). For example, men may be more ready to report combat trauma than they are to report interpersonal trauma. In addition, people seeking financial compensation may be more likely to report PTSD symptoms (Frueh, Gold, & de Arellano, 1997; Frueh, Smith, & Barker, 1996). Conversely, substance abuse symptoms may be less frequently reported if patients fear that the stigma and blame associated with SUDs will negatively affect their chances for financial compensation. Clients who are seeking treatment because of pressure from employers, the criminal justice system, or family members may minimize any kinds of symptoms in the interest of presenting themselves in a more positive light. Thus, it is important for clinicians to be aware of the context or circumstances surrounding the assessment referral (Vuchinich et al., 1988).

Particularly for clinicians working with combat veterans it is important to understand specific aspects of the military culture that may contribute not only to current substance use patterns but also to the individual's attitude toward his or her substance use and resulting openness to treatment. For example, some veterans may believe that alcohol and drug use were encouraged or condoned in the military environment. Thus, it is possible that substance use may continue to be viewed as an accepted and adaptive way of coping with stressful or traumatic events. If an individual perceives his or her substance use as a normal way of coping with a traumatic event, then he or she may be likely to underestimate or minimize substance abuse symptoms or associated consequences.

Take Steps to Minimize Relapse or Worsening of Symptoms

Among SUD patients, comorbid PTSD is associated with higher rates of SUD relapse (Ouimette, Ahrens, Moos, & Finney, 1997). Although the specific mechanisms of why this comorbidity may lead to relapse are as yet unknown, it is likely that an individual's perceived inability to cope effectively with traumatic memories and trauma-related sequelae may at least partially explain this phenomenon. The process of assessment of PTSD clearly has the potential to activate traumatic memories and trauma-related symptoms and, as a result, may serve to create urges to use substances to cope with this symptomatology. Thus, clinicians need to explain to patients that they may experience an increase in symptoms as a function of the assessment and should develop contingency plans (e.g., behavioral contracts) and strategies (e.g., coping skills training; Monti, Rohsenow, Colby, & Abrams, 1995). The assessment process should include an evaluation of specific situations likely to trigger substance use, with particular attention to PTSD symptoms and the role that these serve in relation to urges to use. Conversely, it is also valuable to understand the extent to which substance use patterns are associated with PTSD symptoms, as it is possible that substance use may serve as a trigger for PTSD symptoms. Before the assessment begins, psychoeducation regarding what the assessment process entails should be offered to prepare the client for potential challenges that may arise.

PROVIDER ISSUES

In a literature review, Ouimette, Brown, and Najavits (1998) posited several reasons why clinicians may fail to sufficiently screen for and document PTSD in substance abuse treatment settings. Such reasons included underestimation of the effects of trauma and related sequelae, discomfort in discussing sensitive issues such as trauma, the belief that substance abuse symptomatology should be attended to prior to addressing other comorbid psychological issues, and insufficient knowledge or training. PTSD treatment providers may also be reluctant to inquire about substance use patterns, possibly fearing they will overwhelm clients or believing that substance use problems will automatically dissipate with PTSD treatment. Moreover, despite the prevalence of SUDs in PTSD populations (Escobar et al., 1983; Keane, Gerardi, Lyons, & Wolfe, 1988), some PTSD treatment providers may shy away from inquiring about substance abuse for fear that they lack the necessary expertise to adequately address such issues should they arise.

Providers should be aware of potential barriers to comprehensive assessment and should take steps to address these barriers in the interest of providing optimal care for clients at risk for comorbid SUD–PTSD. For example, as we have underscored in this chapter, clinicians should bear in mind the importance of concurrently evaluating SUD–PTSD instead of triaging assessment and focusing only on one disorder or the other. Furthermore, in the interest of overcoming shyness or embarrassment about potentially sensitive topics (i.e., trauma history, problematic substance use), clinicians should work with clients to establish a common language through which trauma and substance abuse experiences and symptoms may be described. This terminology should be described clearly and operationalized at the outset of the assessment process so that it is clear to both clinician and client. Terms should be behaviorally specific to maximize accuracy. The use of a specific and agreed-on common language will increase the likelihood of collecting accurate trauma and substance use data. Furthermore, such specificity will also help to normalize discussion about these topics.

ONGOING ASSESSMENT

Assessment of comorbid SUD–PTSD is not limited to the initial formulation of a diagnosis. Indeed, in addition to assessing for relevant symptoms to formulate a clinical diagnosis, clinicians should conduct an ongoing assessment to track changes in the presence and severity of symptoms. Ongoing assessment can be behavioral—measuring actual drinking behaviors or the presence of observable re-experiencing, avoidance, or arousal symptoms—or it may focus on more internal, cognitive, or emotional factors (e.g., urges to drink, difficulty concentrating, feeling as if a traumatic event is recurring). Outcome assessment should also evaluate patient progress with respect to functional impairment (i.e., the extent to which social or occupational functioning continues to be affected). Clinicians should also continuously assess relations between PTSD and SUD symptoms, with an eye toward how the amelioration or exacerbation of one set of symptoms may affect the other symptoms. One method of assessment that lends itself particularly well to developing an understanding of symptom interplay is the self-monitoring of symptoms (Shiffman, 1988). By maintaining an ongoing log of PTSD and SUD symptoms, clients and clinicians will be able to observe changes over time as well as interactions between symptom constellations.

Ongoing assessment also allows clinicians not only to evaluate client progress but also to think about this progress with respect to the diagnostic and treatment choices that were made during assessment. Specifically, through ongoing assessment, diagnostic and treatment planning decisions may be re-evaluated or tweaked in light of new developments in symptom presentation (Ruzek, Polusny, & Abueg, 1998).

SUMMARY AND CONCLUSION

Comprehensive assessment of comorbid SUD–PTSD represents the first step toward providing adequate care for people with these concomitant diagnoses. We have provided some guidelines that may enhance the accuracy of the assessment process. For example, taking such steps as assessing for PTSD and SUDs concurrently, as well as approaching the assessment process with an open mind and an awareness of other commonly comorbid diagnoses, will enhance the likelihood that important presenting symptoms are not overlooked or misdiagnosed. Screening questions for PTSD should be standard practice in all SUD treatment facilities and, conversely, PTSD treatment providers should routinely screen for SUDs among their clients. Atkinson, Henderson, Sparr, and Deale (1982) advised clinicians to make all justifiable diagnoses and to clearly associate specific symptoms with each diagnosis. Thus, clinicians should strive for accuracy over parsimony, applying multiple diagnoses if there is sufficient evidence rather than attempting to distill complex diagnostic symptom presentations into one or two simple clinical categories.

We underscore the importance of uncovering as much information as possible about the nature of and relationship among particular symptoms. To this end, strategies such as distinguishing overlapping (i.e., shared by both PTSD and SUDs) from nonoverlapping symptoms, exploring relations between trauma and substance abuse symptoms, and differentiating trauma history from PTSD are offered as a means to determine how specific symptoms may relate to a particular diagnostic category or to one another.

Understanding the context in which a client is being assessed will facilitate a clearer understanding of both the client and his or her diagnosis. Awareness of and sensitivity to contextual factors (such as the circumstances under which a patient is being evaluated, or cultural factors that may contribute to a sense of shame and stigmatization) will help minimize the possibility that such factors will bias symptom reporting. Finally, the way clinicians approach the assessment process (e.g., planning for the ways in which the assessment process may trigger worsening of symptoms or relapse, implementing ongoing assessment throughout treatment) are apt to make for a smoother evaluation and better continuity of care.

A more comprehensive approach to assessment of comorbidity can help patients begin to connect PTSD and SUD symptoms and to help them develop a model of etiology, symptomatology, and treatment. To this end, clients should receive education about both PTSD and SUD (Kofoed et al., 1993). Moreover, clinicians working with these clients should seek to validate their experiences with these two disorders and should help them understand the meaning of this comorbid diagnosis. In particular, some patients may not even be aware that it is possible to carry two diagnoses at the same time. Thus, any information that clinicians can provide to enhance the client's understanding is likely to be useful in assessment and in subsequent treatment.

The relationship between substance use and PTSD is clearly complex, which can present numerous challenges to clinicians working with at-risk clients. Furthermore, although research attempting to explore this comorbidity has increased dramatically over the last 10 years, much still remains unknown about working clinically with this population. This chapter represents an effort to present what has been established in the existing literature with respect to assessing and diagnosing comorbid SUDs and PTSD. An awareness of the commonalties and differences between these two disorders, as well as the ways in which they may affect one another, will help clinicians to provide a more comprehensive and accurate assessment for this high-risk population.

7

EXPOSURE-BASED, TRAUMA-FOCUSED THERAPY FOR COMORBID POSTTRAUMATIC STRESS DISORDER–SUBSTANCE USE DISORDER

SCOTT F. COFFEY, BONNIE S. DANSKY, AND KATHLEEN T. BRADY

There is growing evidence that the presence of posttraumatic stress disorder (PTSD) in individuals with a substance use disorder (SUD) has an adverse impact on treatment outcome (Brady, Killeen, Saladin, Dansky, & Becker, 1994; P. J. Brown, Recupero, & Stout, 1995; Brown, Stout, & Mueller, 1999; Najavits, Weiss, & Shaw, 1999; Ouimette, Brown, & Najavits, 1998). One possible explanation for this poor treatment outcome and higher addiction severity is the presence of negative emotion associated with PTSD. Significantly distressing intrusive symptoms in the form of memories, dreams, or flashbacks are one of the core diagnostic symptom clusters of PTSD according to the *Diagnostic and Statistical Manual of Mental Disorders* (*DSM–IV*; American Psychiatric Association, 1994). These intrusive symptoms give rise to negative emotional states that may adversely affect SUD–PTSD clients' substance abuse treatment by increasing drug and alcohol craving. A recent laboratory-based study provides support for this hypothesis (Coffey et al., 2002). Using relatively brief guided imagery as an analogy to trauma-related intrusive memories, investigators examined the impact of trauma-related imagery on drug craving in a sample of individuals comorbid for PTSD and either cocaine or alcohol dependence. Both cocaine- and alcohol-dependent participants reported increased craving and other drug-relevant responses following the presentation of trauma stimuli compared with neutral stimuli. The authors suggested that intrusive trauma-related memories may adversely affect SUD–PTSD comorbid individuals by increasing their level of drug craving and thus placing them at higher risk for relapse.

To address the problem of poor treatment outcome in SUD–PTSD comorbid clients, a growing number of investigators have advocated for more aggressive assessment and treatment of PTSD during substance use treatment (Coffey, Dansky, Falsetti, Saladin, & Brady, 1998; Najavits, Weiss, & Liese, 1996; Ouimette, Ahrens, et al., 1998; Sharkansky, Brief, Peirce, Meehan, & Mannix, 1999; Stewart, 1996). Many substance abuse treatment providers unfortunately focus solely on substance abuse problems and neglect assessment and treatment of trauma and PTSD (Brinson & Treanor, 1989; Hurley, 1991). For example, when Dansky, Roitzsch, Brady, and Saladin (1997) examined the prevalence of crime-related PTSD on individuals in an inpatient substance abuse treatment unit using a standardized structured interview, they found that 40% of the patients met criteria for current PTSD. The results of these research interviews were documented in the patients' medical charts, yet PTSD was mentioned in only 15% of the sample's discharge summaries. On completion of the assessment portion of the study, the charts of a new sample of patients were reviewed, and it was found that only 8% of patients had PTSD documented in their discharge summaries. This study provides strong evidence that in many substance abuse treatment programs PTSD can be underassessed and underdiagnosed and, therefore, undertreated. If PTSD is untreated in SUD samples, and PTSD symptoms increase drug craving in SUD–PTSD comorbid patients (Coffey et al., 2002), then SUD patients with undiagnosed and untreated PTSD may be at greater risk of relapse. This might help explain the poorer treatment outcome in SUD–PTSD patients that has been reported (Brady et al., 1994; Brown, Stout, & Mueller, 1999; Ouimette, Finney, & Moos, 1999).

To address the problem of untreated PTSD in SUD populations, a novel approach has been proposed by two independent research groups (Back, Dansky, Carroll, Foa, & Brady, 2001; Triffleman, Carroll, & Kellogg, 1999). The approaches use exposure-based treatment techniques for PTSD in combination with an empirically validated treatment for SUD. Clinicians treating substance-dependent clients have historically been reluctant to use exposure-based techniques for the treatment of PTSD. This reluctance may be attributed to several sources. First, some clinicians believe that SUD clients are too frail to tolerate exposure-based therapy without significantly increasing the risk of relapse (see Triffleman et al., 1999, for a discussion of this issue). Second, it has been suggested that SUD clients are too cognitively impaired to undergo some exposure-based techniques (Pitman et al., 1991). Third, some SUD clinicians report discomfort in discussing trauma issues with their clients. For some clinicians this discomfort stems from previous training that discouraged the discussion of trauma during SUD treatment, whereas for others the reluctance stems from personal discomfort in discussing trauma during therapy. We hope that this chapter will reduce some of the reluctance among clinicians to use exposure-based techniques for the treatment of PTSD when treating SUD–PTSD co-morbid clients.

Before we discuss these two approaches, we present a brief review and description of exposure-based treatments of PTSD.

EXPOSURE THERAPY FOR PTSD

Numerous therapies for PTSD have been proposed (e.g., Foa & Rothbaum, 1998; Marks, Lovell, Noshirvani, Livanou, & Thrasher, 1998; Resick & Schnicke, 1993), but exposure-based treatments have generally received the most empirical support (Foa, Rothbaum, Riggs, & Murdock, 1991; Keane, Fairbank, Caddell, & Zimering, 1989; Marks et al., 1998; Tarrier et al., 1999; Tolin & Foa, 1999). In fact, the Expert Consensus Guidelines for the treatment of PTSD recommended exposure therapy as the most rapid and effective psychotherapy for the treatment of PTSD (Foa et al., 1999). In particular, exposure therapy was recommended as a first-line treatment option when the prominent trauma symptoms were intrusive thoughts; flashbacks; or trauma-related fears, panic, and avoidance.

The objective of exposure-based treatments for PTSD is to expose a client with PTSD to trauma-related memories, objects, emotions, places, or people with the goal of reducing the emotional reactivity to these stimuli and thereby reducing PTSD symptomatology. These treatments were originally based on respondent and operant conditioning theories; specifically, Mowrer's (1960) two-factor theory was used as an early theoretical framework for exposure-based treatment of PTSD. Within this framework, fear is acquired through a classical conditioning process by which a neutral stimulus is paired with a stimulus that invokes a fear response so that the neutral stimulus elicits the fear response in the absence of the feared stimulus. Through this pairing, individuals with a fear response to places, objects, memories, or emotions undergo extinction of this response when exposed to the feared stimuli without the feared aversive consequences (cf. Kilpatrick, Veronen, & Resick, 1979).

Emotional processing theory, another prominent theory that describes the development and treatment of PTSD, has been developed by Foa and Kozak (1986, 1991). Emotional processing theory was strongly influenced by Lang's (1979) bio-informational theory of emotion and explains the reduction of fear during exposure therapy using elements of both behavioral and cognitive psychology. In brief, Foa and Kozak's model proposes that exposure is effective because the activation of fear allows for the correction of mistaken stimulus–stimulus and stimulus–response associations. Specifically, activation of the fear structure allows for the correction of mistaken beliefs about the trauma (e.g., belief that the client is responsible for his or her childhood sexual abuse, belief that all men are dangerous, etc.) and may lead to the following changed beliefs: (a) Objectively safe situations that serve as reminders of trauma are not dangerous; (b) remembering the trauma is not the same as experiencing the trauma; (c) prolonged exposure to a fear-provoking stimulus, without escape or avoidance, will lead to a reduction of fear and anxiety; (d) experiencing trauma-related symptoms does not lead to a loss of control (Foa & Rothbaum, 1998; Foa, Steketee, & Rothbaum, 1989).

Several techniques may be used to expose an individual to traumatic material. In this chapter we address two of the more common techniques: (a) exposure through imagery and (b) *in vivo* exposure.

Exposure Through Imagery

When treating trauma survivors with exposure techniques, one of the most flexible approaches is to use imagery (Cooper & Clum, 1989; Foa et al., 1991; Keane et al., 1989; Marks et al., 1998; Tarrier et al., 1999; Tolin & Foa, 1999). With this approach, the client is instructed to visualize the traumatic event in detail. The visualization can be accomplished either by the client describing the trauma aloud, the client thinking about the events of the trauma silently, or by having the therapist direct and guide the visualization process. Imagery techniques are useful because they do not rely on objects or events that may be difficult to produce or replicate. For example, it may be logistically difficult for an individual who was sexually assaulted in her childhood home and subsequently moved to another city to return to her childhood home, be exposed to relevant stimuli, and thus reduce her reactivity to the stimuli. However, by using imagery techniques the individual may bring into consciousness memories of her home and the relevant trauma-related stimuli and thereby reduce her reactivity to those memories.

A method of imaginal exposure used by Foa (Foa & Rothbaum, 1998) consists of telling the story of a trauma in detail, or "reliving" the trauma. In this method, the trauma survivor verbalizes repeatedly the details of the trauma, from the beginning of the incident to the end, over an extended period of time (e.g., 45 minutes). The memory is recounted in the first-person perspective as if the trauma were occurring at that moment. Clients are instructed to include not only the objective details of the incident (e.g., date, time, the colors of clothing worn, odors present) but also thoughts and emotions they experienced. To increase the vividness of the images, clients are encouraged to close their eyes while telling their story. Clinical experience has shown that many trauma survivors can often repeat the details of a trauma in detail without emotional reactivity; this can be especially true for those involved in the court system because of the frequency with which these individuals are required to describe their trauma. Despite the ability to describe the details of their trauma with minimal distress, many of these same trauma victims continue to suffer significant trauma-related symptomatology. Foa and Kozak (1986) theorized that trauma-related symptomatology is due to unprocessed trauma-related emotions. To reduce this residual symptomatology, a trauma survivor must not only describe the incident in detail but also emotionally process the trauma-related material. To aid the client in processing the emotional material, the therapist encourages the client to describe his or her emotions and thoughts during the reliving and to describe the event in the present tense. As the incident is recounted, the therapist asks the client to briefly rate his or her level of discomfort. A standard metric, termed *subjective units of discomfort*, is used to describe the level of distress experienced by the individual. Subjective units of discomfort ratings range from 0 to 100, with 0 representing no discomfort and 100 representing extreme discomfort. The ratings are collected at standard intervals (e.g., every 5 or 10 minutes). After an incident has been relived once, the client is instructed to repeat the description from the beginning. This process is repeated for 45–60 minutes. Therefore, if an incident requires 5 minutes to relive, the client will undergo approximately nine exposure trials during an imaginal exposure session.

As the client progresses through therapy, his or her reported distress in response to the memory of the overall event will decrease (i.e., subjective units of discomfort ratings of 15–20), although significant distress may continue to be reported in response to specific details of the trauma (e.g., "The guy takes out a big gun from his jacket and points it at me"). During later stages of therapy, when the typical subjective units of discomfort ratings are approximately 15–20, memories that elicit ratings above 20 are referred to as *hot spots*: memories that are associated with a great deal of unprocessed emotions and require a concentration of effort to process these emotions and reduce the emotional distress elicited by them. To accomplish this reduction in distress, the client is instructed to begin reliving his or her trauma as described earlier. As a hot spot is reached in the memory, the client is instructed to describe repeatedly this portion of the trauma memory. By repeating the exposure trials of this portion of the memory, the emotions are processed more rapidly, and the emotional reactivity to the memory is reduced (Foa & Rothbaum, 1998; Foa et al., 1991).

Exposure Through In Vivo Methods

Another exposure-based technique used to reduce reactivity to trauma-related material is *in vivo* exposure. Unlike imaginal exposure, in which the trauma-related stimuli are memories of the actual trauma, during *in vivo* exposure the client has prolonged contact with objects, places, or people that symbolically represent or in some other way are associated with his or her trauma. For example, stimuli used during *in vivo* exposure could include pieces of clothing worn during an assault, the site of a car accident, or staying at home alone. Stimuli that are appropriate candidates for *in vivo* exposure are those objects, places, and people that elicit distressing trauma-related memories or that are avoided because of the distressing memories or emotions that are elicited.

To select appropriate stimuli for *in vivo* exposure, the client and therapist collaborate to develop a list of stimuli that evoke trauma-related memories and responses. This list will eventually be developed into a hierarchy. Stimuli that do not evoke trauma-related responses by the fact that they are avoided should also be included on the list. In addition, cognitive and behavioral avoidance of stimuli may make it difficult for clients to remember objects that elicit trauma-related responses. For example, when creating a list, a patient may not include pieces of clothing worn during a motor vehicle accident because the garment is no longer worn, and thoughts of the garment are avoided. The patient may not even be aware of the reason that the garment is no longer worn, only that he or she has not worn it since the accident. Therefore, it is very important that the trauma, events following the trauma, and the clients' behavior following the trauma are thoroughly analyzed to reveal stimuli that may be appropriate for *in vivo* exposure.

After a list of trauma-related stimuli has been produced, each stimulus is given a subjective units of discomfort rating. The rating assigned to each stimulus on the list represents the distress experienced when the client is in contact with the stimulus or, if the stimulus is avoided, the anticipated distress associated with the stimulus. After each stimulus is rated, the list is ordered into a hierarchy from least to most distressing. It is typical for stimuli to be included in the hierarchy that may be logistically difficult to replicate. For example, the sound of a particular vehicle used during an assault may be difficult to reproduce. However, in many cases an approximation of a particular stimulus (e.g., the sound of any older vehicle in need of a new muffler) may be sufficient to elicit a trauma-related emotional response. If a stimulus cannot be approximated, or the task of doing so is unwieldy, the item should be excluded from the hierarchy, and exposure to the stimulus may be satisfied through imaginal exposure, described earlier.

An important caveat in selecting *in vivo* exposure stimuli is to be mindful of the objective safety of the stimuli. A stimulus associated with a trauma may elicit fear and avoidance in a client and may appear to be an appropriate candidate for an *in vivo* exposure trial. However, it may be discovered that exposure to that stimulus will put the client at risk for revictimization. For example, the street on which an assault occurred may evoke memories of the assault that results in a fear response and therefore is avoided. If it is revealed that the street is located in a very dangerous section of town, the client may need to be accompanied during *in vivo* exposure trials to protect his or her safety. In other cases, stimuli may need to be avoided altogether if it is believed that the stimuli may pose a risk to the physical or psychological health of the client.

To begin *in vivo* exposure, an item from the hierarchy should be selected that evokes a subjective units of discomfort rating between 40 and 60. Clients are instructed to remain in the presence of the item for 30–45 minutes or until their ratings are decreased by at least 50%. Clients record their ratings prior to exposure, and then after the exposure trial they record their highest rating during the trial and their discomfort rating at the end of the trial. They are encouraged to conduct exposure trials as often as possible and are reminded that the more exposure trials they undergo the less anxiety they will eventually experience. Clients progress to the next item on their hierarchy when the current item produces little or no discomfort (i.e., rating less than 15). For a more detailed description of exposure techniques, see Foa and Rothbaum (1998).

Client Appropriateness

Although exposure-based treatments for PTSD have a great deal of empirical support (Cooper & Clum, 1989; Foa et al., 1991; Keane et al., 1989; Marks et al., 1998; Tolin & Foa, 1999), not all clients are appropriate candidates (Coffey, 2000). Individuals with numerous traumas that occurred many years prior to treatment (e.g., severe childhood sexual abuse) are less than ideal candidates for exposure-based treatment. There are several reasons for this. First, because the client may have a large number of trauma memories, guided imagery may be an inefficient technique to reduce reactivity to the memories. Because many SUD clients have a long history of victimization, we and our colleagues have used guided imagery to treat adults with multiple traumas from childhood by creating a hierarchy of the memories. Our approach has been to address the most distressing memory first and to then progress down the hierarchy to other memories. We have found that by first treating the most disturbing memory there is a reduction in reactivity to the entire stimulus class that can be labeled *trauma memories*. This reduction in stimulus class reactivity is seen in the rapid response to treatment for the memories lower on the hierarchy. Tolin and Foa (1999) reported success using a similar approach.

A second problem that may exist when treating victims of childhood trauma is that memories of trauma can be unclear and contain only brief glimpses of trauma-related episodes (Loftus, Garry, & Feldman, 1994; Williams, 1994). Under these conditions, imaginal exposure may be of little assistance in reducing trauma-related symptomatology, and *in vivo* exposure may be a better treatment choice. However, more research is necessary to better clarify when imaginal exposure is contraindicated.

A third difficulty in treating multiple-trauma SUD clients with exposure-based treatments is that the *in vivo* hierarchy can become large and unwieldy. We and our colleagues have experimented with treating SUD–PTSD clients with large *in vivo* hierarchies and found that often many of the items belong to a stimulus class that can be presented in combination. For example, if a client suffers from PTSD related to a motor vehicle accident and reports a great deal of fear associated with objects related to the accident (e.g., accident-related clothing, vehicle involved in the accident, accident site), it may be more efficient to simultaneously expose the client to numerous stimuli (i.e., return to the accident site in the vehicle that was involved in the accident while wearing the clothes worn during the accident). Objects that are related to the medical procedures following the accident (e.g., neck brace, pictures of injuries) may form another stimulus class that can be presented in combination. By combining stimuli into classes one can reduce large hierarchies to a manageable size and make treatment more efficient.

Another issue that can be problematic for the effective treatment of PTSD is anger. Anger is very common in clients with PTSD regardless of the type of trauma that precipitated the disorder. However, extreme anger may impede PTSD treatment by blocking the emotional engagement that is necessary for the processing of trauma-related emotional distress (Foa, Riggs, Massie, & Yarczower, 1995). For many clients, intense anger is a response to current trauma-related symptomatology and, for them, as PTSD symptoms are reduced, anger is also reduced. Intense anger in PTSD treatment can be addressed in at least two ways. First, clients should be informed as to the role that anger may be playing in the maintenance of PTSD symptomatology (i.e., anger serving as an avoidance mechanism of the more distressing emotions of fear and anxiety). Clients are encouraged to postpone discussing their anger in favor of processing the trauma-related emotions of fear and anxiety. If clients are unable to postpone addressing their anger, strategies to manage anger may be used before beginning exposure treatment (Novick, 1975, 1977).

Despite the recommendations we just provided, exposure-based therapy may not be appropriate for some clients. For example, clients who suffer from severe dissociative symptoms may not benefit from or tolerate exposure-based treatments even if they have been well schooled in grounding techniques to reduce their dissociative episodes (see Najavits, 2002b). It may be helpful for a therapist to instruct a client with severe dissociative symptoms to keep his or her eyes open during imaginal exposure rather than close them. The therapist may also want to frequently remind the client that they are in the therapist's office and that the client is safe. If an initial trial of exposure therapy proves unsuccessful or intolerable, other approaches to reduce PTSD symptomatology may be initiated (e.g., Najavits, 2002b; Najavits et al., 1996; Resick & Schnicke, 1993). See the Clinical Guidelines section for recommended decision rules for deciding which SUD–PTSD clients might benefit from exposure-based therapy.

TWO EXAMPLES OF EXPOSURE-BASED TREATMENTS FOR PTSD AND SUDs

Recently, two exposure-based treatments for PTSD and substance dependence have been developed. Both projects were funded by the National Institute on Drug Abuse, each with the goal of developing a manual for the respective treatment and to test the treatments' safety and viability.

Concurrent Treatment of PTSD and Cocaine Dependence

Concurrent Treatment of PTSD and Cocaine Dependence (CTPCD) is a 16-session, twice-weekly, individual outpatient psychotherapy designed to treat individuals with comorbid PTSD and cocaine dependence (Back et al., 2001). CTPCD combines prolonged exposure (PE) for the treatment of PTSD (Foa & Rothbaum, 1998) and coping skills training (CST) for substance dependence (Carroll, 1998; Kadden et al., 1992; Monti, Abrams, Kadden, & Cooney, 1989) and is appropriate for both genders. Although CTPCD was designed to treat cocaine users, the substance use treatment component, CST, was originally intended for the treatment of alcohol dependence (Kadden et al., 1992; Monti et al., 1989). Therefore, with fairly minor modifications (e.g., substituting examples of cocaine-using situations with alcohol- or heroin-using situations), it is believed that CTPCD could serve as an appropriate treatment for individuals with PTSD and any type of drug or alcohol dependence.

CST is a cognitive–behavioral therapy initially developed by Monti et al. (1989) and later adopted as one of the three treatments in Project MATCH, the National Institute on Alcohol Abuse and Alcoholism's multi-site treatment comparison study (Kadden et al., 1992; Project MATCH Research Group, 1997). Recently, the National Institute on Drug Abuse published a modified version of CST as a treatment manual for cocaine dependence (Carroll, 1998). CST is a manual-based treatment that can be administered in a group or an individual format to either inpatients or outpatients. Each session of the treatment focuses on a specific skill important to facilitate recovery from substance dependence. The eight core sessions consist of skills thought to be the most important to successful recovery from substance dependence and are typically presented to the client first.

For example, the second session addresses an explanation of craving, craving awareness, and craving management that is based on learning theory. After the administration of the core sessions, elective sessions are presented. The four elective sessions are chosen from a menu of 14 topics through a collaborative effort between the patient and therapist. Examples of elective sessions include assertiveness training, anger management, and coping with negative moods and depression. To reinforce the skills discussed in each session, homework is assigned and is then discussed at the beginning of the next session.

The initial goal of CTPCD is to teach and establish skills necessary for sobriety. It is believed that treatment for trauma without the necessary skills needed for sobriety could increase the risk of relapse in some individuals. However, it is also believed that treatment of PTSD symptoms should be addressed as quickly as possible because of the strong relation between negative affect and craving (e.g., Cooney, Litt, Morse, Bauer, & Gaupp, 1997; Greeley, Swift, & Heather, 1992; Rubonis et al., 1994) and, more specifically, negative affect inducing trauma memories and craving (Coffey et al., 2002).

To balance the dual needs of sobriety skill building and prompt trauma treatment, the first five sessions of CTPCD focus on coping skills for cocaine dependence. The first session is a rapport-building session that introduces the concept of cocaine dependence as learned behavior and provides an overview of PE as the treatment of PTSD. PE is a structured cognitive–behavioral therapy that combines imaginal and *in vivo* exposure techniques to reduce the symptoms of PTSD (Foa & Rothbaum, 1998). The treatment was initially developed to treat victims of rape but has been adapted to treat PTSD resulting from other traumas (e.g., Tolin & Foa, 1999). In addition to exposure techniques, patients are taught breathing retraining as a method to manage symptoms of PTSD and drug dependence.

Within the next four sessions, material from CST as well as an HIV education session is presented. HIV education and prevention are presented because of the high prevalence of HIV within drug-using populations and the benefits that drug abuse treatment can have on reducing the risk of HIV exposure (Metzger, Navaline, & Woody, 2000).

Although no attempt is made to alleviate the symptoms of PTSD during the first five sessions, PTSD symptoms are used as examples when discussing triggers for substance use and potential sources of negative affect. Although there are brief discussions relating PTSD symptomatology and drug dependence throughout the first five sessions, PTSD symptomatology is not explicitly described until Session 4. This discussion is accompanied by the presentation of the Victim's Reaction Handout (VRH; National Crime Victims Research and Treatment Center, 1989). This handout describes the symptoms of PTSD and how these symptoms may develop after a trauma. It also discusses the differences between fear and anxiety and the different manifestations of fear a trauma victim may experience.

During the first half of Session 6, the purpose and theoretical underpinnings of *in vivo* exposure are presented, as are the concepts of hierarchies and of rating discomfort using subjective units of discomfort. An initial hierarchy is developed, and an appropriate stimulus from the hierarchy is selected for the *in vivo* exposure trials that will be conducted prior to the next session. The selection of appropriate stimuli for exposure is always conducted as a collaboration between the therapist and the trauma survivor. As described earlier, the selection criteria include the objective safety of the stimulus, the appropriate subjective units of discomfort level for the initial exposure trial (i.e., a rating between 40 and 60), and the replicability of the stimulus (e.g., a wooden paddle may be replicated easily, whereas an attic may be more challenging if the trauma survivor lives in an apartment complex). The number of exposure trials to be completed prior to the next session is also decided through a dialogue between the therapist and client. The client should be reminded that the decrease in trauma stimuli–related arousal is directly proportional to the number of exposure trials that are completed. The therapist should be aware of the strong avoidance reaction that some clients with PTSD may manifest and should gently encourage the client to experience as many exposure trials as are tolerable. In the last half of Session 6, previously presented coping skills for drug dependence materials are discussed. These skills are reviewed to reduce the risk of substance use relapse after the *in vivo* exposure trials.

Session 7 begins with a discussion of the trauma survivor's reaction to the *in vivo* exposures and the assignment of either the same stimulus again (if discomfort ratings have not been reduced to <15) or a different hierarchy item. Compliance and understanding of *in vivo* exposure are assessed at this time. After this discussion, a description and the rationale for imaginal exposure is presented. After the client acknowledges a clear understanding of the procedure, imaginal exposure is started. As with all of the imaginal exposure trials, the first imaginal exposure lasts approximately 45 minutes. On completion of the imaginal exposure, the client's reaction to the exercise is discussed, and coping skills for drug dependence are briefly reviewed. The client is presented with an audiotape of the imaginal exposure and is instructed to listen to the tape at least twice in the coming week and record three discomfort ratings on each occasions: (a) discomfort prior to listening to the tape, (b) highest rating during the tape, and (c) rating at the end of the tape.

Subsequent sessions follow a pattern that is designed to reduce the risk of relapse in clients. First, the *in vivo* and imaginal exposure rating sheets are discussed, as is the CST homework assignment from the previous week. Next, imaginal exposure is conducted for approximately 45 minutes.

Finally, a CST topic is presented, and homework related to that topic is assigned. The imaginal exposure intervention is presented first so that any craving that is elicited by the exposure can be addressed in the context of drug treatment. In this way, therapists are able to actively teach skills to reduce trauma-related drug craving and impulses to use addictive substances as the behavior is occurring, rather than in a retrospective fashion. Suggested session topics are presented in Table 7.1.

Substance use is monitored at each session in two ways: through (a) the completion of a Timeline Follow-Back (Sobell & Sobell, 1992), a detailed method to assess self-reported substance use during the prior week, and (b) the administration of a breath analysis and urine drug screens (UDS). Abstinence is supported through verbal reinforcement, and a functional behavioral analysis is conducted for any slips or relapses. Clients are not reprimanded for slips or relapses, and any one slip or relapse does not lead to treatment termination. Instead, slips and relapses are discussed in the context of CST (i.e., the identification of high-risk situations for substance use, identifying triggers for use, coping with cravings and thoughts about substance use, etc.). However, substance use that escalates during treatment, especially after the initiation of exposure therapy, may highlight the need for further CST. In these cases, all of the CST sessions or selected CST sessions may be presented prior to exposure therapy, depending on the skills deficits discovered during the analysis of the relapse(s). For example, if a client's relapses occur primarily in response to the experience of negative affect, the therapist may choose to administer the sessions on anger awareness, anger management, awareness of negative thinking, and management of negative thinking prior to the initiation exposure therapy. It is important to note, however, that the decision to delay exposure treatment for PTSD must be made cautiously and judiciously, because the symptoms of PTSD itself may be the primary factor contributing to the client's continued substance use, and any delay in addressing PTSD symptoms may put the client at further risk of relapse.

Preliminary data on CTPCD are promising (Brady, Dansky, Back, Foa, & Carroll, 2001), although results must be interpreted with caution, because the sample size was small ($n = 39$), the dropout rate was high (61%), and a within-subject design was used. Despite these limitations, the data suggest that CTPCD was as well tolerated as other treatments for cocaine abuse in samples of cocaine users. The treatment completion rate for CTPCD (39%), defined as receiving 10 or more of the 16 sessions, was slightly higher than that reported by the National Institute on Drug Abuse Collaborative Cocaine Treatment Study (28%; Crits-Christoph et al., 1999). CTPCD also fared well when compared with concurrent treatments for SUD–PTSD that use non-exposure-based techniques in the treatment of PTSD. For example, Najavits, Weiss, Shaw, and Muenz (1998) defined treatment com-

TABLE 7.1
Description of the 90-Minute Concurrent Treatment of Posttraumatic Stress Disorder and Cocaine Dependence Sessions Separated by Treatment Focus

Session	Treatment focus	
	Posttraumatic stress disorder	Cocaine dependence
1	Introduction and description of exposure treatment and breathing retraining	Introduction and description of Cognitive–Behavioral Coping Skills Training for substance dependence
2	Introduction and description, continued	Coping with cravings
3	Introduction and description, continued	Managing thoughts about cocaine use
4	Common reactions to victimization	Planning for emergencies
5	Common reactions to victimization	HIV education I
6	Provide rationale for *in vivo* exposure, develop hierarchy for *in vivo* exposure, assign *in vivo* exposure homework	Review of coping methods
7	Provide rationale for imaginal exposure, imaginal exposure, assign *in vivo* exposure	Review of coping methods
8	Imaginal exposure, assign *in vivo* exposure	HIV education II
9	Imaginal exposure, assign *in vivo* exposure	Anger awareness
10	Imaginal exposure, assign *in vivo* exposure	Anger management
11	Imaginal exposure, assign *in vivo* exposure	Awareness of negative thinking
12	Imaginal exposure, assign *in vivo* exposure	Managing negative thinking
13	Imaginal exposure, assign *in vivo* exposure	Review of coping
14	Imaginal exposure, assign *in vivo* exposure	Assertiveness
15	Imaginal exposure, assign *in vivo* exposure	HIV review
16	Review and termination	Review and termination

pleters as those who attended at least 25% of the therapy sessions. Using their criteria, Najavits, Weiss, Shaw, and Muenz (1998) reported a 63% completion rate, whereas 69% of the participants in CTPCD attended at least 25% of the sessions.

In addition to being well tolerated, CTPCD appears to be effective in reducing substance use and PTSD symptomatology. The use of any illicit drug, as measured by UDS, was low throughout the 16-week treatment trial, and there appeared to be a slight reduction in substance use over the course of the treatment. For example, during the first half of treatment 88% of the UDS were drug free, whereas 90% of the UDS were drug free during the second half of treatment. It is important to note that drug use did not escalate during the second half of treatment, when the majority of the exposure sessions occurred. PTSD symptoms, as measured by the Clinician Administered PTSD Scale (Blake et al., 1995) dropped significantly over the course of treatment, as did self-reported depressive symptoms.

Historically, a concern regarding the use of exposure-based techniques in the treatment of comorbid SUD–PTSD has been the fear of exposure-related relapse (Pitman et al., 1991). The average number of sessions attended by CTPCD treatment completers was approximately 15, whereas treatment noncompleters attended approximately 4 sessions. Of the participants who did not complete at least 10 of 16 therapy sessions, 75% of them dropped out before the first exposure session, suggesting that their decision to terminate treatment was not a direct result of the exposure therapy. Thus, preliminary data suggest that CTPCD is well tolerated, may prove to be an effective treatment for co-occurring PTSD and cocaine dependence, and that exposure-based PTSD treatment does not appear to increase the risk of substance use relapse in this comorbid population.

Substance Dependence PTSD Therapy

A second exposure-based treatment for PTSD and substance dependence was proposed by Triffleman et al. (1999). Substance Dependence PTSD Therapy (SDPT) is an integration of three empirically validated treatment approaches for substance dependence (i.e., CST), trauma (i.e., Stress Inoculation Training [SIT]; Meichenbaum & Deffenbacher, 1988; Meichenbaum & Novaco, 1985), and *in vivo* exposure. Like CTPCD, SDPT is appropriate for both genders and for patients with diverse trauma histories. However, Triffleman et al. (1999) cautioned that individuals with prolonged childhood sexual or physical abuse histories may require continued therapy at the conclusion of SDPT. This caution is also relevant for CTPCD.

SDPT is a highly structured 5-month, twice-weekly treatment with two phases. Phase I, which lasts 12 weeks, is referred to as *trauma-informed, addictions-focused treatment* and consists of five treatment modules taken largely from CST, described earlier. Modules may involve one to four sessions, depending on the treatment needs of the particular patient. The module topics are (a) introduction to SDPT, (b) coping with craving and drug use triggers, (c) relaxation training, (d) HIV risk behaviors, and (e) anger awareness and management. As the title suggests, the focus of Phase

I is twofold: (a) the establishment of sobriety and (b) education about PTSD and the relation between PTSD and substance use.

Patients with a significant period of abstinence from substance use should also be administered Phase I. Triffleman et al. (1999) made this recommendation for three reasons. First, Phase I topics overlap with issues that many trauma victims have, such as anger awareness and anger management. Second, Phase I serves as a review of coping skills that are helpful for continued abstinence, and it serves as a vehicle to anticipate problem areas. Third, the module topics may provide an opportunity to discuss previously unexplored problem areas in the patient's life (Triffleman et al., 1999).

The decision to transition from Phase I to Phase II is based on clinical judgment. Substance use during Phase I is a critical piece of information when making this decision; however, it is not the only information that is used. If at the end of Phase I substantial progress toward sobriety has been made, even though total abstinence has not been reached, and it appears that the client has the necessary skills to tolerate the increased negative affect associated with trauma-focused treatment, then the client is transitioned to Phase II. If the client does not possess the substance use coping skills needed to tolerate trauma-focused therapy without relapsing to substance use, then Phase I should be continued until those skills are acquired. Evidence that clients have the necessary skills needed to progress to Phase II might include the ability to cope with stressful life situations (e.g., argument with spouse, denial of public assistance) without using substances or the increased ability to modulate one's affect in a healthy manner (e.g., take a walk when angry at his or her child rather than yell at the child).

Phase II is described as *trauma-focused, addictions-informed* therapy and is an 8-week program aimed at reducing PTSD symptomatology in the addicted client. The PTSD treatment takes two forms. The first portion of Phase II is referred to as *Anti-Avoidance I* and consists of the presentation of a modified version of SIT. In SIT, coping skills and cognitive restructuring strategies are taught to the client to assist him or her in reinterpreting both cognitive distortions about the trauma and the symbolic meaning associated with trauma-related stimuli (Foa et al., 1991; Meichenbaum & Cameron, 1983). In preparation of the *in vivo* exposure, clients are taught strategies to address avoided situations. Clients are taught how to approach an avoided situation, how to confront the situation, skills to use if overwhelmed by an avoided situation, and how to deal with the aftermath that may follow. Anti-Avoidance I usually lasts 2 to 4 sessions.

During *Anti-Avoidance II*, which usually lasts 6 to 12 sessions, SIT is combined with *in vivo* exposure to reduce cognitive, emotional, and physiological reactivity to trauma-related stimuli. Whereas both *in vivo* and imaginal exposure techniques are used in CTPCD, only *in vivo* exposure is used in SDPT. Another difference between SDPT and CTPCD is the duration of the *in vivo* exposure trials: CTPCD recommends more traditional exposure durations (i.e., durations recommended for nonaddicted trauma populations), whereas SDPT recommends that clients "remain in the situation only as long as they can tolerate the arousal," which may be as little as 30 seconds (Triffleman et al., 1999, p. 11). Throughout Phase II, substance use should be monitored by UDS at least once per week, preferably twice a week because of the short half-life of cocaine.

An open trial of SDPT is currently under way. Preliminary data suggest that SDPT is effective at reducing PTSD severity and that the treatment appears to be well tolerated.

CASE EXAMPLE OF EXPOSURE-BASED TREATMENT FOR COMORBID SUD–PTSD

C.W., a 38-year-old man seeking treatment for his cocaine use, presented with current PTSD and cocaine dependence. His cocaine use consisted primarily of crack cocaine use that began following the murder of his niece approximately 2½ years prior to treatment. His niece was shot by strangers and died in his arms. Following a brief diagnostic screen by clinical staff, C.W. was referred to the CTPCD research staff for a full evaluation. The research protocol was explained to C.W., and he consented to enter the psychotherapy trial. Although C.W. reported occasional recreational use of powder cocaine (i.e., three or four times per year), and met criteria for past alcohol abuse, he did not meet criteria for any substance abuse disorder at the time of his trauma. Moreover, at the time of the trauma he was gainfully employed but was unemployed on treatment entry. In addition to meeting diagnostic criteria for PTSD and cocaine dependence, C.W. met criteria for panic disorder without agoraphobia and for major depression. In addition to the structured interviews that were administered, various self-report measures were administered to measure changes in symptom reporting across time. At baseline, distress produced by trauma symptoms, as measured by the Impact of Event Scale (Horowitz, Wilner, & Alvarez, 1979), was 55, and depressive symptoms, as measured by the Beck Depression Inventory (Beck, Ward, Mendelson, Mock, & Erbaugh, 1961), were 13 (indicating mild depression). Over the course of treatment, no cocaine use was detected through weekly UDS or by self-reported use.

Treatment consisted of 14 sessions, although treatment likely would have been terminated sooner in a clinical treatment setting. Additional sessions were required to adequately adhere to the research protocol. As per the protocol, *in vivo* exposure began at Session 6, and imaginal exposure began at Session 7. Of the 14 sessions, 6 involved imaginal exposure. The final 2 sessions did not involve imaginal or *in vivo* exposure and focused on coping skills for substance users, because C.W. did not report any significant trauma symptoms. Imaginal exposure consisted of C.W. repeatedly "reliving" the murder. At each session, an audiotape was made of the imaginal exposure and given to C.W. so that the he could listen to it between sessions. *In vivo* exposure items included looking at pictures of his niece, looking at drawings she had made for C.W., visiting the child's gravesite, and returning to the scene of the murder. During the first 3 imaginal exposure sessions C.W. became quite tearful but was encouraged to continue imaging the scene and to experience the emotions elicited by the memory. By Sessions 5 and 6 C.W. was reporting low subjective units of distress ratings during the imaginal exposure and could revisit the scene of the murder, his most distressing hierarchy item, with minimal discomfort (distress ratings ≤10). At treatment termination, C.W. reported minimal PTSD symptoms (Impact of Event Scale score = 9) and no depressive symptoms (Beck Depression Inventory score = 0) and reported a desire to begin work again.

CLINICAL GUIDELINES

Although exposure-based therapies for PTSD show promise in the treatment of SUD–PTSD clients, the use of these techniques in this population requires a clinician to have experience in at least three areas: (a) experience treating PTSD with exposure techniques, (b) experience treating SUD clients with CST, and (c) a working knowledge of current learning theories on which exposure and CST are based. In the absence of direct experience in these areas, clinicians should seek peer supervision when treating this challenging population.

As stated previously, not all trauma survivors are best treated with exposure-based techniques. During the development of the CTPCD manual, our research group found that individuals with extremely poor memories of their trauma (beyond typical memory gaps that are often present), individuals who experienced marked dissociation during exposure and were unable to use techniques to ground them in reality (see Najavits, 2002b), individuals with a poor ability to develop vivid images of any kind, and individuals with an inability to tolerate or modulate distress caused by exposure were poor candidates for exposure-based techniques. Although individuals with these characteristics made up the minority of patients treated during the study, a set of decision rules was developed to assist us in screening out the few patients who were poorly suited for exposure therapy. We developed the decision rules using three sources of information: (a) clinical experience of the project investigators and therapists, (b) feedback from patients treated in the project, and (c) the Expert Consensus Guidelines on the Treatment of PTSD (Foa et al., 1999). On the basis of these sources of information, the following guidelines were developed to select those SUD–PTSD patients best suited for treatment by exposure-based techniques (Coffey, 2000):

- history of a single trauma or multiple discrete traumas;
- relatively clear memories of the trauma(s);
- if multiple traumas occurred, the traumas did not occur before the age of 15;
- relatively minor dissociation during exposure therapy techniques;
- ability to develop vivid images;
- intrusive memories, flashbacks, fear–avoidance, or hyperarousal being the most prominent trauma symptoms.

Clinicians should be mindful, however, that these guidelines have not been empirically validated and should serve only as general recommendations.

As when treating trauma victims with any therapeutic approach, clinicians should warn clients, prior to the onset of exposure, that their PTSD symptoms will likely escalate during the initial phase of treatment (i.e., the first month or so). Clients should be informed that, although very uncomfortable, this escalation of symptoms is a normal process of treatment that is attributed to their exposure to trauma-related memories and stimuli. Clients should be further informed that their symptoms will decrease soon if they continue the exposures. During this initial phase of exposure therapy it is important to review coping skills necessary to maintain sobriety.

Finally, some trauma victims with an SUD may not recognize the need for concurrent treatment for their two disorders. SUD–PTSD individuals may seek treatment for what they consider their primary disorder and may minimize the need to treat their "secondary" disorder. Avoidance and minimization are prominent symptoms in both SUDs and PTSD and should be addressed by conducting a functional behavioral analysis of the client's substance use and trauma histories. The goal of the functional behavioral analysis is to present the relation between the client's substance use and trauma so that he or she can make an informed treatment decision. Areas to investigate may include (a) when the escalation in their substance use occurred in relation to their trauma, (b) whether their substance use puts them at risk for further victimization, (c) their craving response to trauma memories, and (d) their use of substances as a mechanism to cope with trauma symptoms. For more information regarding this motivational approach for the treatment of substance dependence, see Miller and Rollnick (1992).

FUTURE DIRECTIONS

Both of the treatments described in this chapter are in the initial stages of treatment development. Specifically, the authors of the two treatments have recently completed their therapy manuals and have tested the viability of the treatments in an open-label fashion. During this initial phase there were no comparison or control groups; therefore, the analyses were strictly within subject. Outcome measures collected throughout the treatment process suggest the treatments are efficacious, but without appropriate control groups any conclusions must remain tentative.

Therefore, an obvious next step in the therapy development process is to test the efficacy of the treatments in between-subjects designs with random assignment. A no-treatment control group (i.e., for which a "treatment" would consist of the outcome measures and attention from a research assistant) would help clarify whether the treatments contained active agents or whether a nonspecific treatment factor was responsible for any observed change. Nonspecific factors could include social contact in a supportive environment, completing assessments about substance use and trauma symptomatology, or simply the act of coming to treatment. Because of clinical considerations, a more feasible approach would involve a *dismantling* study, in which a three-group study within an SUD–PTSD comorbid sample, comparing CTPCD against PE alone and CST alone, would address whether combined PTSD and SUD treatment improves treatment outcome (defined by both a reduction in substance use and a reduction in PTSD severity) over the two treatments separately. This design would also address the impact that PTSD treatment alone may have on subsequent substance use and the impact that SUD treatment alone may have on PTSD symptoms.

In time, exposure-based treatments for comorbid SUD–PTSD should be compared with other non-exposure-based treatments (e.g., Evans & Sullivan, 1995; Najavits et al., 1996). For example, Najavits, Weiss, Shaw, and Muenz (1998) recently developed a cognitive–behavioral concurrent treatment for comorbid SUD–PTSD that shows promise and appears to be well tolerated (see Najavits, 2002b). How exposure-based approaches for the treatment of comorbid SUD–PTSD compare to these non-exposure-based treatments should be tested in the future.

The timing of trauma-focused treatment in concurrent SUD–PTSD therapy is also an important consideration. Although some individuals advocate for SUD treatment prior to trauma-focused interventions, and some advocate for trauma-focused interventions prior to SUD treatment (Brinson & Treanor, 1989; Hurley, 1991; Stewart, 1996), the question remains an empirical one at this time. Both of the treatment approaches described in this chapter take a middle-of-the-road approach, providing a foundation of substance abuse treatment first but treating PTSD symptoms early in the therapeutic process. However, CTPCD, compared with SDPT, appears to take a slightly more aggressive approach when treating PTSD in that it uses both imaginal and *in vivo* exposure and addresses PTSD symptoms earlier in the treatment. How quickly PTSD symptoms should be addressed remains an important question.

Several other issues need to be addressed, including whether exposure-based treatment for comorbid SUD–PTSD is better suited for men or for women, is better suited for certain types of trauma or substances, or is better suited in certain treatment settings. However, despite the questions that remain, exposure-based approaches show great promise for the treatment of comorbid SUD–PTSD.

8

SEEKING SAFETY: A NEW PSYCHOTHERAPY FOR POSTTRAUMATIC STRESS DISORDER AND SUBSTANCE USE DISORDER

LISA M. NAJAVITS

In 1993 I began developing a cognitive–behavioral therapy (CBT) for the dual diagnosis of posttraumatic stress disorder (PTSD) and substance use disorder (SUD), under a grant from the Behavioral Therapies Development Program of the National Institute on Drug Abuse. At that point, there were no published treatment outcome studies nor any empirically studied psychosocial treatments for this population. Through trial and error, the Seeking Safety treatment manual (Najavits, 2002b) was developed while simultaneously tested on patients in a variety of settings. Seeking Safety is the first treatment for PTSD and substance abuse with published outcome results (Najavits, Weiss, Shaw, & Muenz, 1998). The goal was to mold a therapy—by listening to patients very closely in the context of treating them, reading available literature, and conducting empirical research on the treatment—that would best fit their needs.

Seeking Safety has shown positive outcomes in four studies thus far that tap a range of subpopulations with this dual diagnosis: women in prison, inner-city women, adult outpatient women, and adult outpatient men. Other studies are currently underway.

This chapter provides (a) a description of Seeking Safety and how it was developed, (b) a comparison with existing treatments, (c) a review of outcome research on it, and (d) ideas for future directions. An earlier article describing the treatment (Najavits, Weiss, & Liese, 1996) is now outdated, as the treatment has evolved considerably with empirical testing and implementation in various populations. For example, Seeking Safety was originally designed for women but has since been expanded to men. Although it was originally designed as a group treatment, it has been adapted for individual therapy as well. Treatment topics, format, and training have also changed over time.

The term *substance abuse* is used throughout this chapter, as it is commonly used in clinical settings. However, Seeking Safety was designed to address both substance *abuse* (the less severe version of the disorder) and substance *dependence* (the most severe version), both of which are subsumed within the term *substance use disorder* in the fourth edition of the *Diagnostic and Statistical Manual of Mental Disorders* (American Psychiatric Association, 1994). Note that *substance dependence* is used for any studies that specifically target that syndrome.

DESCRIPTION OF THE TREATMENT

The Seeking Safety treatment comprises 25 topics that are approximately evenly divided among cognitive, behavioral, and interpersonal domains (see Exhibit 8.1 for a brief description of all topics). Each addresses a "safe coping skill" designed to help the patient attain safety from both PTSD and substance abuse. The topics are designed to be written in simple language; to be as emotionally compelling as possible; to provide a respectful tone that honors patients' courage in fighting the disorders; and to teach new ways of coping that convey the idea that, no matter what happens, they can learn to cope in safe ways—without substances and other destructive behavior.

Key Principles

Seeking Safety is based on five principles.

1. Safety as the Priority of This First-Stage Treatment

The title of the treatment—"Seeking Safety"—expresses its central idea: When a person has both active substance abuse and PTSD, the most urgent clinical need is to establish safety. *Safety* is an umbrella term that signifies various elements: safety from substances; safety from dangerous relationships (including domestic violence and drug-using friends); and safety from extreme symptoms, such as dissociation and self-harm. Many of these self-destructive behaviors re-enact trauma—having been harmed through trauma, patients are now harming themselves. *Seeking safety* refers to helping patients free themselves from such negative behaviors and, in so doing, to move toward freeing themselves from trauma at a deep emotional level.

The treatment fits what has been described as *first-stage therapy* for each of the disorders. Experts within the PTSD and substance abuse fields

EXHIBIT 8.1
The 25 Seeking Safety Treatment Topics (and Domains)

1. **Introduction to Treatment/Case Management**
   Covers (a) introduction to the treatment, (b) getting to know the patient, and (c) assessment of case management needs.

2. **Safety (combination)**
   Safety is described as the first stage of healing from both PTSD and substance abuse and is the key focus of the treatment. A list of more than 80 safe coping skills is provided, and patients explore what safety means to them.

3. **PTSD: Taking Back Your Power (cognitive)**
   Four handouts are offered: (a) "What is PTSD?" (b) "The Link Between PTSD and Substance Abuse," (c) "Using Compassion to Take Back Your Power," and (d) "Long-Term PTSD Problems." The goal is to provide information as well as a compassionate understanding of the disorder.

4. **Detaching From Emotional Pain: Grounding (behavioral)**
   A powerful strategy, *grounding*, is offered to help patients detach from emotional pain. Three types of grounding are presented (mental, physical, and soothing), with an experiential exercise to demonstrate the techniques. The goal is to shift attention toward the external world, away from negative feelings.

5. **When Substances Control You (cognitive)**
   Eight handouts are provided, which can be combined or used separately: (a) "Do You Have a Substance Abuse Problem?"; (b) "How Substance Abuse Prevents Healing From PTSD"; (c) "Choose a Way to Give Up Substances"; (d) "Climbing Mount Recovery," an imaginative exercise to prepare for giving up substances; (e) "Mixed Feelings"; (f) "Self-Understanding of Substance Use"; (g) "Self-Help Groups"; and (h) "Substance Abuse and PTSD: Common Questions."

6. **Asking for Help (interpersonal)**
   Both PTSD and substance abuse lead to problems in asking for help. This topic encourages patients to become aware of their need for help and provides guidance on how to obtain it.

7. **Taking Good Care of Yourself (behavioral)**
   Patients explore how well they take care of themselves using a questionnaire listing specific behaviors (e.g., "Do you get regular medical check-ups?"). They are asked to take immediate action to improve at least one self-care problem.

8. **Compassion (cognitive)**
   This topic encourages the use of compassion when trying to overcome problems. Compassion is the opposite of "beating oneself up," a common tendency for people with PTSD and substance abuse. Patients are taught that only a loving stance toward the self produces lasting change.

9. **Red and Green Flags (behavioral)**
   Patients explore the up-and-down nature of recovery in both PTSD and substance abuse through discussion of "red and green flags" (signs of danger and safety). A Safety Plan is developed to identify what to do in situations of mild, moderate, and severe relapse danger.

10. **Honesty (interpersonal)**
    Patients discuss the role of honesty in recovery and role-play specific situations. They are asked to explore the cost of dishonesty, when it's safe to be honest, and how to handle it if the other person can't accept honesty.

(continued)

EXHIBIT 8.1 (Continued)

11. **Recovery Thinking (cognitive)**
Thoughts associated with PTSD and substance abuse are contrasted with healthier "recovery thinking." Patients are guided to change their thinking using rethinking tools such as *List Your Options*, *Create a New Story*, *Make a Decision*, and *Imagine*. The power of rethinking is demonstrated through think-aloud exercises.

12. **Integrating the Split Self (cognitive)**
Splitting is identified as a major psychic defense in both PTSD and substance abuse. Patients are guided to notice splits (e.g., different sides of the self, ambivalence, denial) and to strive for integration as a means to overcome these.

13. **Commitment (behavioral)**
The concept of keeping promises, both to self and others, is explored. Patients are offered creative strategies for keeping commitments, as well as the opportunity to identify feelings that can get in the way.

14. **Creating Meaning (cognitive)**
Meaning systems are discussed with a focus on assumptions specific to PTSD and substance abuse, such as Deprivation Reasoning, Actions Speak Louder Than Words, and Time Warp. Meanings that are harmful versus healing in recovery are contrasted.

15. **Community Resources (interpersonal)**
A lengthy list of national nonprofit resources is offered to aid patients' recovery (including advocacy organizations, self-help, and newsletters). Also, guidelines are offered to help patients take a consumer approach in evaluating treatments.

16. **Setting Boundaries in Relationships (interpersonal)**
Boundary problems are described as either too much closeness (difficulty saying "no" in relationships) or too much distance (difficulty saying "yes" in relationships). Ways to set healthy boundaries are explored, and domestic violence information is provided.

17. **Discovery (cognitive)**
Discovery is offered as a tool to reduce the cognitive rigidity common to PTSD and substance abuse (called "staying stuck"). Discovery is a way to stay open to experience and new knowledge, using strategies such as Ask Others, Try It and See, Predict, and Act "As If". Suggestions for coping with negative feedback are provided.

18. **Getting Others to Support Your Recovery (interpersonal)**
Patients are encouraged to identify which people in their lives are supportive, neutral, or destructive toward their recovery. Suggestions for eliciting support are provided, as well as a letter that they can give to others to promote understanding of PTSD and substance abuse. A safe family member or friend can be invited to attend the session.

19. **Coping With Triggers (behavioral)**
Patients are encouraged to actively fight triggers of PTSD and substance abuse. A simple three-step model is offered: change who you are with, what you are doing, and where you are (similar to "change people, places, and things" in Alcoholics Anonymous).

20. **Respecting Your Time (behavioral)**
Time is explored as a major resource in recovery. Patients may have lost years to their disorders, but they can still make the future better than the past. They are asked to fill in schedule blanks to explore whether they use their time well and whether recovery is their highest priority. Balancing structure versus spontaneity; work versus play; and time alone versus in relationships are also addressed.

(continued)

EXHIBIT 8.1 (Continued)

21. **Healthy Relationships (interpersonal)**
    Healthy and unhealthy relationship beliefs are contrasted. For example, the unhealthy belief "Bad relationships are all I can get" is contrasted with the healthy belief "Creating good relationships is a skill to learn." Patients are guided to notice how PTSD and substance abuse can lead to unhealthy relationships.
22. **Self-Nurturing (behavioral)**
    Safe self-nurturing is distinguished from unsafe self-nurturing (e.g., substances and other "cheap thrills"). Patients are asked to create a gift to the self by increasing safe self-nurturing and decreasing unsafe self-nurturing. Pleasure is explored as a complex issue in PTSD/substance abuse.
23. **Healing From Anger (interpersonal)**
    Anger is explored as a valid feeling that is inevitable in recovery from PTSD and substance abuse. Anger can be used constructively (as a source of knowledge and healing) or destructively (a danger when acted out against self or others). Guidelines for working with both types of anger are offered.
24. **The Life Choices Game (combination)**
    As part of termination, patients are invited to play a game as a way to review the material covered in the treatment. Patients pull from a box slips of paper that list challenging life events (e.g., "You find out your partner is having an affair"). They respond with how they would cope, using game rules that focus on constructive coping.
25. **Termination**
    Patients express their feelings about the ending of treatment, discuss what they liked and disliked about it, and finalize aftercare plans. An optional Termination Letter can be read aloud to patients to validate the work they have done.

Note. Each topic represents a safe coping skill relevant to both PTSD and substance abuse. Domains (cognitive, behavioral, interpersonal, or a combination) are listed in parentheses.

(e.g., Herman, 1992; E. Kaufman & Reoux, 1988) have independently described an extremely similar first stage of treatment that prioritizes stabilizing the patient, teaching coping skills, and reducing the most destructive symptoms (Najavits, 2002b). Later stages, again quite similar for the two disorders, are *mourning* (facing one's past by exploring the impact of trauma and substance abuse) and *reconnection* (attaining a healthy engagement with the world through work and relationships), to use the language of Herman (1992). The first stage, safety, is an enormous therapeutic task for some patients, and thus the Seeking Safety treatment addresses only that stage. Throughout the treatment, safety is addressed over and over, including, the topic "Safety," a list of safe coping skills, a Safe Coping Sheet to explore recent unsafe incidents, a Safety Plan to identify stages of danger and how to address them, a Safety Contract, and a report of unsafe behaviors at each session's check-in. The concepts of safety and first-stage treatment are designed to protect the therapist as well as the patient. By helping patients move toward safety, therapists are protecting themselves from the sequelae of treatment that could move too fast without a solid foundation: vicarious traumatization, medico–legal liability, and dangerous transference dilemmas (Chu, 1988; Pearlman & Saakvitne, 1995). In particular, eliciting trauma memories too early in treatment when safety has not been established may have harmful consequences (Chu, 1988; Ruzek, Polusny, & Abueg, 1998). Increased substance use and suicidality are of particular concern in this vulnerable dual-diagnosis population (Chu, 1988). Thus, seeking safety is, hopefully, both the patient's and the therapist's goal.

2. Integrated Treatment of PTSD and Substance Abuse

The treatment is designed to continually integrate attention to both disorders; that is, both are treated at the same time by the same clinician. This *integrated* model contrasts with a *sequential* model, in which the patient is treated for one disorder, then the other; a *parallel* model, in which the patient receives treatment for both disorders, but by different treaters; or a *single* model, in which the patient receives only one type of treatment (Weiss & Najavits, 1997). An integrated model is consistently recommended as the treatment of choice for this dual diagnosis (Abueg & Fairbank, 1991; Brady, Killeen, Saladin, Dansky, & Becker, 1994; Brown, Recupero, & Stout, 1995; Evans & Sullivan, 1995; Kofoed, Friedman, & Peck, 1993; Najavits et al., 1996; Ruzek et al., 1998). Indeed, a survey of patients with this dual diagnosis found that they also prefer simultaneous treatment of both disorders (Brown, Stout, & Gannon-Rowley, 1998). In practice, how-ever, the two disorders are not usually treated simultaneously. Indeed, it is still the norm for patients to be told that they need to become abstinent from substances before working on PTSD, which does not work for many patients. In many settings clinical staff are reluctant to even assess for the other disorder; and patients' own shame and secrecy about trauma and substance abuse can further reinforce treatment splits (Brown, Recupero, & Stout, 1995). Integration is thus, ultimately, an intrapsychic goal for patients as well as a systems goal: to "own" both disorders, to recognize their interrelationship, and to fall prey less often to the vulnerability of each disorder triggering the other. Thus, the treatment provides opportunities for patients to discover connections between the two disorders in their lives: in what order they arose and why, how each affects healing from the other, and their origins in other life problems (e.g., poverty). The therapist, too, is guided to use each disorder as leverage to help patients overcome the other disorder, as patients often have initially stronger motivation to work on one rather than the other. Finally, integration also occurs at the intervention level. Each safe coping skill in the treatment can be applied to both PTSD and substance abuse. For example, setting boundaries in relationships can apply to PTSD (e.g., leaving an abusive relationship) and to substance abuse (e.g., asking a friend to stop offering drugs).

3. A Focus on Ideals

It is difficult to imagine two mental disorders that each individually, and especially in combination, lead to such demoralization and loss of ideals. In PTSD this loss of ideals has been written about, for example, in work on "shattered assumptions" (Janoff-Bulman, 1992) and the "search for meaning" (Frankl, 1963). Some research has found that trauma survivors who are able to create positive meanings from their suffering fare better than those who do not (Janoff-Bulman, 1997). With substance abuse there is also a loss of ideals—life narrows in focus and, in its severe form, the person "hits bottom." It is notable that the primary treatment for substance abuse for most of this century, Alcoholics Anonymous (AA), is the only treatment for a mental disorder with a heavily spiritual component. The AA goal of living a life of moral integrity is an antidote to the deterioration of ideals inherent in substance abuse.

Thus, Seeking Safety explicitly seeks to restore ideals that have been lost. The title of each topic is framed as a positive ideal, one that is the opposite of some pathological characteristic of PTSD and substance abuse. For example, the topic "Honesty" combats denial, lying, and the false self. "Commitment" is the opposite of irresponsibility and impulsivity. "Taking Good Care of Yourself" is a solution for bodily self-neglect. Throughout, the language of the treatment emphasizes values such as respect, care, integration, protection, and healing. By aiming for what can be, the hope is that patients can summon the motivation for the incredibly hard work of recovery from two difficult disorders.

4. Four Content Areas: Cognitive, Behavioral, Interpersonal, and Case Management

CBT is the basis for this treatment, because it so directly meets the needs of first-stage treatment through its high degree of structure, focus on problem solving in the present, educational emphasis, and time-limited framework. Moreover, in outcome studies CBT has been found to be one of the most promising approaches for the treatment of each of the disorders (PTSD and substance abuse) when treated separately (Najavits et al., 1996). Whereas originally the treatment was solely cognitive and behavioral, interpersonal and case management domains were added when the need for them became apparent in working with patients. Interpersonal topics now comprise one third of the topics, and case management is begun in the first session and addressed at every session throughout the treatment. The interpersonal domain is an area of special need, because most PTSD arises from trauma inflicted by others (e.g., in contrast to natural disasters or accidents; Kessler, Sonnega, Bromet, Hughes, & Nelson, 1995). Whether the trauma involved childhood physical or sexual abuse, combat, or crime victimization, all have an interpersonal valence that may evoke distrust of others, confusion over what can be expected in relationships, and concern over re-enactments of abusive power (Herman, 1992). Substance abuse similarly is often associated with relationships. It is typically initiated in interaction with others and is frequently used to cope with interpersonal conflicts and anxiety in social situations (e.g., Marlatt & Gordon, 1985). The case management component arose because data in the first Seeking Safety pilot study showed that many patients were engaged in few treatment services (Najavits, Dierberger, & Weiss, 1999). Most participants required significant assistance getting the care they needed, such as psychopharmacology, job counseling, and housing. Thus, case management (termed *community resources*) is heavily emphasized, with the idea that psychological interventions can work only if patients have an adequate treatment base.

5. Attention to Therapist Processes

Research shows that for substance abuse patients in particular (and psychotherapy in general), the effectiveness of treatment is determined as much or more by the therapist as by any particular theoretical orientation or patient characteristics (Najavits, Crits-Christoph, & Dierberger, 2000; Najavits & Weiss, 1994). With dual-diagnosis patients, who are often considered "difficult," "severe," or "extreme" (Kofoed et al., 1993), providing effective therapy is a major challenge. Moreover, in conducting workshops for clinicians and listening to hundreds of therapy tapes using the model, it has become clear that some of the most frequent dilemmas are about process: for example, how to calm agitated patients and how to confront a patient who has lied about substance abuse. Therapist processes emphasized in Seeking Safety include compassion for patients' experience, using the treatment's coping skills in one's own life (not asking the patient to do things that one cannot do oneself), giving patients control whenever possible (as loss of control is inherent in trauma and substance abuse), modeling what it means to try hard by meeting the patient more than halfway (e.g., heroically doing anything possible within professional bounds to help the patient get better), listening to patients' behavior more than their words, learning to give both positive and negative feedback, and obtaining feedback from patients about their reactions to the treatment. The flip side of such positive therapist processes is negative countertransference, including harsh confrontation; sadism; inability to hold patients accountable because of misguided sympathy; becoming victim to patients' abusiveness; power struggles; and, in group treatment, allowing a patient to be scapegoated. As Herman (1992) suggested, therapists may unwittingly repeat the trauma roles of victim, perpetrator, or bystander. Attention is also directed to what I call the *paradox of countertransference* in PTSD and substance abuse; that is, each disorder appears to evoke opposite counter-transference reactions that are difficult for therapists to balance. PTSD tends to evoke identification with patients' vulnerability, which, if taken too far, may lead to excessive support at the expense of growth. Substance abuse tends to evoke anxiety about the patient's substance use, which, if extreme, can become harsh judgment and control (e.g., "I won't treat you if you keep using"). The goal is thus for the therapist to integrate support and accountability, which are viewed as the two central processes in the treatment.

Training methods for the treatment (Najavits, 2000) emphasize these various process issues as well as observation of the therapist in action (e.g., taped sessions) and intensive training experiences (e.g., watching videotapes of good vs. poor sessions, rehearsal of "tough-case" scenarios, peer supervision, role plays, knowledge tests, identifying key themes, and think-aloud modeling).

What Is Not Part of the Treatment

There are two main areas that this treatment explicitly omits, particularly when it is offered in group format: (a) exploration of past trauma and (b) interpretive psychodynamic work.

Exploration of past trauma is, in and of itself, a major treatment intervention for PTSD. As noted above, it is conceptualized as the second stage of treatment, after the patient has attained a foundation of safety (Herman, 1992; E. Kaufman & Reoux, 1988). A variety of PTSD treatment methods have as their central goal the evocation of traumatic memories as a means to process them. These include mourning (Herman, 1992), exposure therapy (e.g., Foa & Rothbaum, 1998), eye movement desensitization reprocessing (Shapiro, 1995), the counting method (Ochberg, 1996), the rewind method (Muss, 1991), and thought field therapy (Figley, Bride, & Mazza, 1997). When trauma memories are directly processed, they no longer hold such emotional power over the patient.

Despite the known importance of such treatments for PTSD (e.g., Marks, Lovell, Noshirvani, Livanou, & Thrasher, 1998), numerous experts have recommended that such work not begin for substance abusers until they have achieved a period of stable abstinence and functionality (Chu, 1988; Keane, 1995; Ruzek et al., 1998; Solomon, Gerrity, & Muff, 1992). The concern is that if patients are overwhelmed by painful memories from the past, their substance use could worsen in a misguided attempt to cope. Thus far, only two studies of patients with PTSD and substance abuse have used exploration of past trauma as a key intervention: a study by Brady and colleagues (Brady, Dansky, Back, Foa, & Carroll, 2001; see also chapter 7, this volume) and a study by Najavits and colleagues that combined Seeking Safety plus exposure therapy–revised (Najavits, Schmitz, Gotthardt, & Weiss, 2002; see also the section entitled Research on Seeking Safety). In the study by Brady and colleagues, results indicated that the 39% of their sample who were able to complete at least 10 of the 16 sessions showed positive outcomes in PTSD and cocaine use (as well as other symptoms), which were maintained at 6-month follow-up. However, most patients were noncompleters, and they excluded patients with suicidal ideation, and thus likely selected a less impaired sample. In the study by Najavits and colleagues, positive outcomes were found in various domains, including psychiatric and substance abuse symptoms. However, a large number of modifications to standard exposure therapy were created, the treatment was conducted individually, and various "safety parameters" were put in place to maximize patients' ability to safely tolerate the work.

Thus, until further research explores the use of exposure techniques with this dual-diagnosis population, it is not included as part of Seeking Safety. Also, Seeking Safety was initially tested in a time-limited group format, which did not appear to be an appropriate context in which to conduct exposure methods for victims of repeated early trauma, who represent a large number of patients with this dual diagnosis (Najavits, Weiss, & Shaw, 1997). Even small mention of trauma experiences has been found to trigger other patients, and in a short-term group treatment there may be insufficient ability to fully process the material.

Interpretive psychodynamic work is also specifically avoided in Seeking Safety. There is little, if any, exploration of the patient's relationship with the therapist or, in group treatment, of members' relationships with each other. There is also no interpretation of intrapsychic motives or dynamic insights. Although these powerful interventions can be helpful in later stages of treatment, they are believed too potentially upsetting for patients at this stage.

Treatment Format

For each of the 25 treatment topics, the following are provided in the Seeking Safety manual (Najavits, 2002b):

1. A brief *Summary*.
2. A *Therapist Orientation* that provides background about the topic, clinical strategies for conducting the session, and discussion of countertransference issues.
3. A *Quotation* that is read aloud at the start of each session to emotionally engage patients. For example, the quotation for the topic "PTSD: Taking Back Your Power" is from the politi-

cal leader Jesse Jackson: "You are not responsible for being down, but you are responsible for getting up" (p. 11, Marlatt & Gordon, 1985).

4. A *Patient Handout* that summarizes the main points in the session and offers ideas for "commitments" (i.e., homework patients can do between sessions; see Exhibit 8.2 for an example of a patient handout).

5. A segment on *Tough Cases* of treatment challenges that the therapist can rehearse.

Additional materials include a background chapter on PTSD and substance abuse and an in-depth chapter on how to conduct the treatment (including emergency situations).

Topics can be conducted in any order, with the order selected by patients, therapists, or both. Many topics include a variety of handouts, from which patients and therapists can select those that are most relevant to cover. Moreover, each topic can be conducted as a single session or over multiple sessions, depending on the patient's length of stay. The treatment is thus both highly structured yet also extremely flexible—characteristics that may be particularly important when working with severe populations. The multiple needs, impulsivity, and intense affect of such a population can lead to derailed sessions if the therapist does not impose clear structure. Yet the treatment is also highly flexible, which allows patients' most important concerns to be kept primary, to allow adaptation to a variety of settings, to respect therapists' clinical judgment, and to encourage therapists to remain inspired and interested in the work. These concerns are believed paramount for a population such as this, where the risks of patient dropout and therapist burnout are high (Najavits, 2001). Moreover, they were designed to adapt to the managed care era, in which many patients will have limited access to treatment. Thus, the treatment can be used for just one or a few sessions, or can be extended to long-term treatment. The therapy is also designed to be integrated with other treatments. Although it can be conducted as a stand-alone intervention, the severity of patients' needs usually suggests that they be in several treatments at the same time (e.g., 12-step groups, pharmacotherapy, individual therapy, group therapy). Thus, not only was the treatment designed to be used in conjunction with other treatments, but it also includes an intensive case management component to help engage patients in them.

The treatment has been conducted in a variety of formats thus far, including group and individual; open and closed groups; 50- and 90-minute sessions; singly and co-led sessions; weekly and twice weekly; outpatient, inpatient, and residential; integrated with other treatments or as a stand-alone therapy; and single-gender or mixed-gender. The four empirical studies

EXHIBIT 8.2
Excerpt From a Patient Handout

Taking Good Care of Yourself

DO YOU. . .

- ♥ Associate only with safe people who do not abuse or hurt you? YES ___ NO ___
- ♥ Eat a healthful diet? (healthful foods and not under- or overeating)
  YES ___ NO ___
- ♥ Have safe sex? YES ___ NO ___
- ♥ Travel in safe areas (e.g., avoid being alone in deserted places)?
  YES ___ NO ___
- ♥ Get enough sleep? YES ___ NO ___
- ♥ Keep up with daily hygiene (e.g., clean clothes, showers, brushing teeth)?
  YES ___ NO ___
- ♥ Get adequate exercise (not too much nor too little)? YES ___ NO ___
- ♥ Take all medications as prescribed? YES ___ NO ___
- ♥ Maintain your car so it is not in danger of breaking down? YES ___ NO ___
- ♥ Avoid walking or jogging alone at night? YES ___ NO ___
- ♥ Spend within your financial means? YES ___ NO ___
- ♥ Have annual medical check-ups with each of the following: Doctor? Dentist?
  Eye doctor? Gynecologist (women only)? YES ___ NO ___
- ♥ Know who to call if you are facing domestic violence? YES ___ NO ___
- ♥ Have safe housing? YES ___ NO ___
- ♥ Always drive substance-free? YES ___ NO ___
- ♥ Refrain from bringing strangers home to your place? YES ___ NO ___
- ♥ Carry cash, ID, and a health insurance card in case of danger? YES ___ NO ___
- ♥ Currently have at least two drug-free friendships? YES ___ NO ___
- ♥ Not smoke cigarettes? YES ___ NO ___
- ♥ Have at least one hour of free time to yourself per day? YES ___ NO ___
- ♥ Do something pleasurable every day (e.g., go for a walk)? YES ___ NO ___
- ♥ Take vitamins daily? YES ___ NO ___
- ♥ Have at least one person that you can truly talk to (therapist, friend, sponsor,
  spouse)? YES ___ NO ___
- ♥ Use contraceptives as needed? YES ___ NO ___
- ♥ Have at least one social contact every week? YES ___ NO ___
- ♥ Attend treatment regularly (e.g., therapy, group, self-help groups)?
  YES ___ NO ___
- ♥ Have at least 10 hours per week of structured time? YES ___ NO ___
- ♥ Have a daily schedule and "to-do" list to help you stay organized? YES ___
  NO ___
- ♥ Attend religious services (if you like them)? YES ___ NO ___ N/A ___

YOUR SCORE: (total # of "no"s) ___

Notes on self-care:

Self-Care and PTSD. People with PTSD often need to learn to take good care of
themselves. For example, if you were abused as a child you got the message
that your needs were not important. You may think, "If no one else cares about
me, why should I?" Now is the time to start treating yourself with respect and
dignity.

(continued)

EXHIBIT 8.2 (Continued)

Self-Care and Substance Abuse. Substance abuse is one of the most extreme forms of self-neglect because it directly harms your body. And, the more you abuse substances the more you are likely to neglect yourself in other ways too (e.g., poor diet, lack of sleep).

Note. From *Seeking Safety: A Treatment Manual for PTSD and Substance Abuse* (p. 179) by L. M. Najavits, 2002b, New York: Guilford Press. Copyright 2002 by Guilford Press. Reprinted with permission.

of the treatment conducted thus far, however, were conducted under constrained conditions to evaluate gains within the typical limits of managed care treatment. The treatments were time-limited (typically twice per week for three months), with one session per topic, and two of the studies used a group modality.

Patient Selection

Although the treatment was formally tested on patients who met current diagnostic criteria for both PTSD and substance dependence, it has also been used clinically on patients who did not fully meet these criteria. This includes, for example, a patient struggling with PTSD who has a prior substance abuse history but no current use or, conversely, a patient who abuses substances and has a trauma history but not PTSD. Indeed, it appears helpful to guide patients to apply the treatment's coping skills to whatever problems are most important to them right now. The substance abuse material may be especially relevant for other impulse-control disorders such as binge eating, gambling, workaholism, and sex addiction.

Also notable is the wide range of clinicians who have used the treatment, including those with diverse specialties (addiction counseling, psychology, social work), primary foci (mental health, substance abuse), and orientations (psychodynamic, 12-step, cognitive–behavioral). It appears that far more important than any such characteristics are a high degree of empathy, a willingness to cross-train (i.e., for mental health clinicians to learn about substance abuse and vice versa), positive attitudes toward this patient population, and a strong ability to hold patients accountable and work with aggression (Najavits, 2000). Future research is needed to evaluate the benefit of the treatment based on particular patient and clinician characteristics.

Conducting the Session

Exhibit 8.3 summarizes the format of the session, which comprises four parts: (a) check-in, (b) quotation, (c) relate the topic to patients' lives, and (d) check-out. Optional additional elements are urinalysis testing (con-

EXHIBIT 8.3
Session Format

1. CHECK-IN
The goal of the check-in is to find out how patients are doing (up to 5 minutes per patient). Patients report on five questions: "Since the last session (a) How are you feeling? (b) What good coping have you done? (c) Describe your substance use and any other unsafe behavior; (d) Did you complete your Commitment?" and (e) Community Resource update.

2. QUOTATION
The quotation is a brief device to help emotionally engage patients in the session (up to 2 minutes). A patient reads the quotation out loud. The therapist asks "What is the main idea in the quotation?" and links it to the topic of the session.

3. RELATE THE TOPIC TO PATIENTS' LIVES
The therapist and/or patient select any of the 25 treatment topics (listed in Exhibit 8.1) that feels most relevant. This is the heart of the session, with the goal of meaningfully connecting the topic to patients' experience (30–40 minutes). Patients look through the handout for a few minutes, which may be accompanied by the therapist summarizing key points (especially for patients who are cognitively impaired). Patients are asked what they most relate to in the material, and the rest of the time is devoted to addressing the topic in relation to specific and current examples from patients' lives. As each topic represents a safe coping skill, intensive rehearsal of the skill is strongly emphasized.

4. CHECK-OUT
The goal is to reinforce patients' progress and give the therapist feedback (a few minutes per patient). Patients answer two questions: (a) "Name one thing you got out of today's session (and any problems with it)" and (b) "What is your new commitment?"

Note. From *Seeking Safety: A Treatment Manual for PTSD and Substance Abuse* (p. 54) by L. M. Najavits, 2002b, New York: Guilford Press. Copyright 2002 by Guilford Press. Reprinted with permission.

ducted prior to the session to assess recent drug use) and a feedback questionnaire for patients to rate the helpfulness of the session. The structure is designed to model how to make good use of time, how to "contain" appropriately, and how to set goals and stick to them. For patients with PTSD and substance abuse, who are often impulsive and overwhelmed, the predictable structure of the session helps them know what to expect. It offers, moreover, in its process, a mirror of the careful planning and focus that are needed for recovery from the disorders.

Most of the session is devoted to any 1 of the 25 topics described in Exhibit 8.1, with emphasis on relating it to current and specific problems in patients' lives. Priority is placed on attending to any unsafe behavior the patient reported during the check-in. Thus, the tone of the treatment, when conducted well, feels like deep therapy rather than simply psychoeducation or "school." Each topic represents a safe coping skill, and strong emphasis is placed on having patients try out the skill during the session, using any method the therapist prefers:

- *Do a "walk-through."* Ask patients to identify a situation in which the safe coping skill might help, then describe how they would use it. For example, in the topic "Asking for Help": "If you feel like cutting your arm, whom could you call? What would you say?"
- *In-session experiential exercise.* Some topics lend themselves to guiding patients through an experience rather than just talking about it. For example, the skill of grounding is demonstrated in a 10-minute exercise during the session.
- *Role play.* This is one of the most popular methods, particularly for interpersonal topics.
- *Identify role models.* Ask patients to try to think of someone who already knows the skill and explore what that person does. For the topic "Commitment," one can ask the patient "Do you know anyone who follows through on promises?"
- *Think aloud.* This is particularly useful for the cognitive sessions. Patients practice out loud a new way of talking to themselves. For example, on the topic "Compassion," one can ask "When you were fired from your job this week, how could you have talked to yourself compassionately?"
- *Process obstacles.* Ask patients to anticipate what might happen if they try to implement the skill. For example, in "Setting Boundaries in Relationships," one can ask the patient "What might your partner say if you requested safe sex?"
- *Involve safe family and friends.* Some topics encourage the patient to obtain help from safe people, such as "Getting Others to Support Your Recovery."
- *Replay the scene.* Ask patients to identify something that went wrong and then go through it again as if they could relive it ("What would you do differently this time?"). A Safe Coping Sheet was designed for this process, or it can be done more informally.
- *Discussion questions.* For each topic, ideas to generate discussion are offered.
- *Make a tape.* Create an audiotape for patients to use outside of sessions as a way to literally "change old tapes." In the topic "Compassion," for example, kind, encouraging statements can be recorded.
- *Review key points.* Ask patients to summarize the main points of the handout that are meaningful to them.
- *Question and answer.* Ask patients questions to see what they do and do not know about the topic; for example, "Does anyone know what the letters 'PTSD' stand for?"

Throughout, patients are encouraged to identify ways that they can cope safely with any life situations that arise. They can draw from the list of more than 80 safe coping skills (which is posted on the wall and provided as a handout in the topic "Safety"), and are encouraged to discover which ones work for them. They can also fill out the Safe Coping Sheet, which guides them to contrast their old way of coping with a new way that is safe. This sheet was derived from forms used in CBT (e.g., Beck's [1979] dysfunctional thought record) but is modified to be simpler and to have patients rate the safety of their old and new ways of coping. Patients are encouraged to seek explanations, but not excuses, for their unsafe behavior. The goal is to understand why they might be coping in poor ways (e.g., through substance use or self-harm) but to learn that no matter what happens in life, there is always a way to cope constructively rather than destructively.

At the end of each session patients are asked to select a commitment to try before the next session. Commitments are very much like CBT homework, but the language is changed to emphasize that patients are making a promise—to themselves, to the therapist, and, in group treatment, to the group—to promote their recovery by taking at least one action step forward. Also, commitments do not have to be written, as clinical experience with this population indicates that some patients do not like written assignments. Examples of commitments include "Ask your partner not to offer you any more cocaine," "Read a book on parenting," "Try calling a hotline," and "Write a supportive letter to the young side of you that feels scared." Ideas for commitments are offered at the end of each patient handout, but therapists are encouraged to customize them to best fit each patient. Therapists are also offered strategies for working with patients who repeatedly do not complete their commitments.

How the Treatment Was Developed

When beginning Seeking Safety in 1993, I selected a sample of women, given the high prevalence of this dual diagnosis in female substance abusers, and chose a format of time-limited group therapy for cost effectiveness. In addition to reading literature on PTSD and substance abuse, I drew from the traditions of several clinical areas: substance abuse treatment (Beck, Wright, Newman, & Liese, 1993; Carroll, Rounsaville, & Keller, 1991; Marlatt & Gordon, 1985; Miller, Zweben, DiClemente, & Rychtarik, 1995), PTSD treatment (Chu, 1988; Davis & Bass, 1988; Herman, 1992; Van der Kolk, 1987), CBT (Beck, 1979), women's treatment (Jordan, Stiver, & Surrey, 1991; Lerner, 1988), and the field of education (Najavits & Garber, 1989).

The process of developing the therapy involved a large amount of trial and error over several studies (see the section Research on Seeking Safety) and a variety of clinical settings. On these projects, I conducted some of the treatment directly, supervised other therapists in conducting it, listened to tapes of many sessions, and worked closely with therapists to identify what did and did not work. The manual was also reviewed by several experts in the field, and patients' response to various aspects of the treatment and their suggestions provided important feedback. Several related studies provided additional input, including a literature review on women with PTSD and substance abuse (Najavits et al., 1997), a descriptive study of women with PTSD and substance abuse (Najavits, Weiss, & Shaw, 1999), a study of cocaine-dependent patients with and without PTSD (Najavits, Gastfriend, et al., 1998), an assessment study (Najavits, Weiss, Reif, et al., 1998), a survey of therapists on their views of treatment manuals (Najavits, Weiss, Shaw, & Dierberger, 2000), and a survey of clinicians on their difficulties and gratifications in treating patients with this dual diagnosis (Najavits, 2002a).

HOW IS SEEKING SAFETY DIFFERENT FROM EXISTING TREATMENTS?

Broadly speaking, Seeking Safety differs from existing treatments in its theory (i.e., safety as the target goal), its emphasis on humanistic themes (e.g., compassion, honesty, commitment), its attempt to make CBT accessible and interesting to patients who may be difficult to reach, its strong focus on case management, its format (e.g., the use of quotations), its detailed therapist and patient materials for each topic, and its attention to process issues. Several manual-based and empirically studied treatments that would appear to be most closely related are contrasted with Seeking Safety here.

CBT

CBT is one of the most widely used treatments. It has been adapted in recent years for PTSD (Ruzek et al., 1998) and for substance abuse (Beck et al., 1993; Carroll et al., 1991); however, none of these adaptations were designed for the combination of PTSD and substance abuse. In addition, the characteristics of Seeking Safety described above are not typically part of CBT. The same applies to two close cousins of CBT: relapse prevention (an offshoot of CBT developed for substance abuse) and coping skills training (e.g., Monti, Abrams, Kadden, & Cooney, 1989).

Dialectical Behavior Therapy

Dialectical behavior therapy (DBT) uses a coping skills approach and has recently been adapted for substance abuse (Linehan et al., 1999); however, it was designed for patients with borderline personality disorder and does not attempt to diagnose, describe, or treat PTSD. Although some patients have both borderline personality disorder and PTSD, they are separate disorders, with only a minority of patients having both (Herman, 1992; Linehan et al., 1999; Najavits, Weiss, Shaw, & Muenz, 1998). DBT is also a much longer, more intensive treatment with a full year of treatment in both group and individual concurrent therapies totaling over 3 hours per week plus as-needed phone coaching (Linehan et al., 1999). Seeking Safety was designed as a lower cost treatment (e.g., originally tested as a short-term group treatment with one leader) with expansion to more intensive and lengthy formats if patients have access to more care. The format of DBT, many of the skills it teaches, and its language and level of abstraction are also different.

Motivational Enhancement Therapy

Motivational enhancement therapy for substance abuse (Miller & Rollnick, 1992) seeks to engage and retain patients in treatment by focusing on positive interpersonal therapy processes (e.g., "roll with resistance," "express empathy," "avoid argumentation"). However, it does not include rehearsal of coping skills, does not address dual diagnosis or PTSD in particular, and is not cognitive–behavioral.

Twelve-Step Treatment

Although 12-step treatments such as AA are highly compatible with Seeking Safety and many other psychotherapy treatments, they focus on substance abuse only (not PTSD), advocate an abstinence model only (i.e., they reject a harm-reduction approach), are not designed to be led by professional treaters, and do not provide explicit rehearsal of coping skills. Some psychotherapy adaptations of 12-step models (Mercer, Carpenter, Daley, Patterson, & Volpicelli, 1994) provide the last two characteristics, however.

Specific Treatments for PTSD

A variety of treatments have been designed specifically for PTSD (for a description, see Schiraldi, 2000). However, none of these have been designed for or evaluated in this dual-diagnosis population, except for exposure therapy, which is discussed in the next two sections.

Treatments for PTSD and Substance Abuse

Several treatments have been developed for patients with a dual diagnosis of PTSD and substance abuse. In addition to Seeking Safety, three others have undergone pilot empirical testing: (a) Concurrent Treatment of PTSD and Cocaine Dependence (Back, Dansky, Carroll, Foa, & Brady, 2001); Substance Dependence Posttraumatic Stress Disorder Therapy (Triffleman, Carroll, & Kellogg, 1999); and Transcend (Donovan, Padin-Rivera, & Kowaliw, 2001).

Back et al.'s (2001) treatment is a 16-session model that adapts a combination of Foa's exposure therapy for PTSD (Foa & Rothbaum, 1998), relapse prevention (Carroll, 1998), and psychoeducation about PTSD and cocaine dependence. It differs from Seeking Safety in its inclusion of exposure techniques, shorter length, limited range of substances being addressed (i.e., cocaine only), format, and particular skills. Triffleman et al.'s (1999) treatment differs from Seeking Safety in its inclusion of in vivo exposure techniques for PTSD, format, and particular skills. Donovan et al.'s (2001) treatment is a 12-week program developed for veterans that comprises 10 hr/week of group treatment, mandatory attendance in a substance abuse rehabilitation program, and supplementary activities (e.g., volunteer community service). Six weeks focus on skills development, and 6 weeks on trauma processing, based on a combination of concepts derived from constructivist, existential, dynamic, cognitive–behavioral, and 12-step theories. It differs from Seeking Safety in its design as an intensive partial-hospital program, its skills, its target population (veterans), and its focus on trauma processing. Finally, five other models have been described but have not yet been empirically tested: books by Trotter (1992) and by Evans and Sullivan (1995), both in the 12-step tradition; a book by Miller and Guidry (2001); a chapter by Abueg and Fairbank (1991) that describes a behavioral model developed in a Veterans Administration setting; an article by Bollerud (1990) on an eclectic model for inpatient care; and a chapter by Meisler (1999) on group treatment for PTSD and alcohol abuse.

RESEARCH ON SEEKING SAFETY

Four outcome studies on Seeking Safety have been completed. Each is briefly described here.

Women Outpatients

In this study (Najavits, Weiss, Shaw, & Muenz, 1998), outcome results were reported for 17 female outpatients who completed group modality Seeking Safety treatment, with 25 sessions over 3 months. Completion of the treatment was defined as six or more sessions (met by 63% of the 27 who enrolled). All the women met criteria for current substance dependence and PTSD. All had experienced five or more lifetime traumas, with an average age of 7 at the time of the first trauma. Sixty-five percent of the sample had one or more co-occurring personality disorders. Forty-one percent had drug dependence, 41% had alcohol dependence, and 18% had both. Assessments were conducted at pretreatment, posttreatment, and 3-month follow-up.

Results showed significant improvements in substance use (both alcohol and drug), trauma-related symptoms, suicide risk, suicidal thoughts, social adjustment, family functioning, problem solving, depression, cognitions about substance use, and didactic knowledge related to the treatment. The only negative finding was a worsening of somatic symptoms (which may have been a function of substance withdrawal). Patients' treatment attendance (67% of available sessions), alliance, and satisfaction were also very strong. Treatment completers were more impaired than dropouts yet more engaged in the treatment. Overall, the data suggest that women with PTSD and substance abuse can be helped when provided with a treatment adapted to them. All results are clearly tentative, however, because of the lack of a control group, external treatments the patients may have engaged in, multiple comparisons, and the lack of assessment on dropouts.

Women in Prison

This was a study of 17 women in a minimum-security correctional setting using group modality Seeking Safety treatment, with 25 sessions over 3 months (Zlotnick, Najavits, & Rohsenow, 2002). All participants met criteria for current PTSD and substance dependence, and all had histories of repeated physical abuse, sexual abuse, or both (with an average age of 8 at the first trauma). The most common drug of choice was cocaine. All of the women who were offered treatment began treatment.

The attendance rate was 83% of sessions, and measures of client satisfaction and alliance were high. Results showed that, of the 17 women, 9 (53%) no longer met criteria for PTSD at the end of the 3-month treatment; at a follow-up 3 months later, 46% still no longer met criteria for PTSD. PTSD symptoms decreased significantly from pretreatment to posttreatment, and this was maintained at the 3-month follow-up. During incarceration, random urinalysis showed that none of the women were using a substance.

A follow-up 6 weeks after release from prison indicated that 29% were using an illegal substance, and at 3 months after release the rate was 35%. A significant decrease in drug and alcohol use and legal problems was found from pretreatment to both 6 weeks after release and 3 months after release. Recidivism rate (return to prison) was 33% at 3-month follow-up, a rate typical of this population. The participants rated the treatment as equally helpful for both PTSD and substance abuse.

Low-Income Urban Women

This study of 100 outpatient low-income urban women compared Seeking Safety in individual format to relapse prevention treatment (RPT) in a randomized controlled trial, with a "treatment-as-usual" nonrandomized control condition (Hien, Cohen, Litt, Miele, & Capstick, 2002). Twenty-five sessions were conducted over a 3-month period, and all participants met current criteria for PTSD and SUD. At the end of treatment, patients in both Seeking Safety and RPT had significant reductions in substance use frequency and intensity, PTSD symptoms, and psychiatric symptom severity, whereas participants in the treatment-as-usual comparison group did not show any significant changes. Improvements in PTSD severity were sustained at the 6-month follow-up point but not at 9 months for patients in both treatment groups. Although statistically significant improvements in substance use and psychiatric severity were not maintained for either of the treatments at the 6-month follow-up, trends in the direction of lower substance use and psychiatric severity were found. Results of the study were interpreted to suggest that carefully conducted cognitive–behavioral interventions can substantially decrease current symptoms of both PTSD and SUD in a relatively brief period with an exceedingly hard-to-reach population.

Outpatient Men

This study of 5 outpatient men evaluated a combination of Seeking Safety plus Exposure Therapy–Revised, using individual treatment (Najavits, Schmitz, et al., 2002). They were offered 30 sessions over 5 months, with the option to select how much of each type of treatment they preferred on a session-by-session basis. All patients met criteria for current PTSD and substance dependence, with childhood trauma the basis of the PTSD. They had an average of 9.6 different types of trauma (all noncombat), with an average first trauma at 8 years of age. They reported an average of 22 days of drug problems in the prior month and 6 days of alcohol problems. The Exposure Therapy–Revised component was an adaptation of Foa and Rothbaum's (1998) exposure therapy, modified for PTSD and SUD. The modifications were designed to increase the acceptability and safety of exposure therapy in substance abuse patients by using a variety of "safety parameters."

Outcome results showed significant improvements in drug use, family and social functioning, trauma symptoms, anxiety, dissociation, sexuality, hostility, overall functioning, meaningfulness, and feelings and thoughts related to safety. All 5 patients attended all 30 sessions, and they chose an average of 21 Seeking Safety sessions and 9 Exposure Therapy–Revised sessions. Treatment satisfaction and alliance were very high. The need for further evaluation using more rigorous methodology is discussed.

Current Studies

Other studies are currently underway, including a study of homeless female veterans at 10 Veterans Administration sites, a study of women in substance abuse treatment at four sites, a brief version of the treatment (12 sessions) in the Clinical Trials Network of the National Institute on Drug Abuse, a randomized controlled trial of women in prison, and a study of women in residential treatment.

FUTURE WORK

Several issues may be particularly interesting to address in future research:

- *How long should the Seeking Safety treatment be?* In research, patients' main critique of the treatment has been that it is too short. Therapists, too, have conveyed that they would prefer a longer treatment, with the possibility of conducting each topic over several sessions. Conversely, in many clinical settings, therapists report that they have far fewer than 25 sessions available per patient. Study designs could address this issue by offering different numbers of sessions and then evaluating the degree to which they impact outcomes.
- *What adjunctive treatments are most helpful in combination with Seeking Safety?* Exposure treatment has successfully been combined with Seeking Safety (Najavits et al., 2002b). Also, data are currently being analyzed on the amount of 12-step self-help group participation by patients in the treatment. These and other future projects may help elucidate optimal combinations of treatments.
- *Does Seeking Safety provide differential benefit for particular types of symptoms?* Although the four studies thus far have shown a

positive impact on various symptoms, it will be important over time to determine whether the treatment differentially affects PTSD symptoms, substance abuse symptoms, and other key areas.

- *What are the treatment's active mechanisms?* For example, some topics may be much more helpful than others; or some domains (cognitive, behavioral, interpersonal, case management) may have different degrees of impact.

- *How can training boost the power of the treatment?* Training clinicians has proved to be an area ripe with questions (Najavits, 2000). How can training be more effective and more transportable to a variety of settings (especially when the weekly hour-long supervision typical of research studies is not available)? How can therapists be identified who are likely to be most effective with this population? What methods of training are most helpful?

- *What degree of benefit can be expected?* One of patients' most common questions is "Will I really get better?" Answering this in relation to Seeking Safety (or any other treatment) will require empirical data to determine how much and what types of improvement can be expected, over what timeframe, and under what conditions. The notion of what *recovery* means for either PTSD or substance abuse is complex, with some people believing full recovery is possible and others believing that adaptation to lifelong disorders is more realistic.

In short, a great deal is unknown at this point. Learning from a variety of patients, clinicians, settings, and studies will be an evolving process. In closing, a paraphrase of a quotation by Jacob (1997), from the topic "Discovery," is apt:

> Progress . . . begins with the invention of a possible world . . . which is then compared by experimentation with the real world. And it is this constant dialogue between imagination and experiment that allows . . . an increasingly fine-grained conception of what is called reality.

9

COMORBID POSTTRAUMATIC STRESS DISORDER AND SUBSTANCE USE DISORDERS: TREATMENT OUTCOMES AND THE ROLE OF COPING

PAMELA J. BROWN, JENNIFER P. READ, AND
CHRISTOPHER W. KAHLER

In this chapter we describe a study that examines the prospective relationship between posttraumatic stress disorder (PTSD) and substance use disorders (SUDs) among patients recently treated for substance abuse or dependence. To provide a context for this study, we survey the relevant prospective literature on SUD–PTSD comorbidity and review factors suggested by this literature to affect symptom presentation, treatment, and remission of these two disorders. Specifically, we discuss the role of gender and coping skills in the relationship between SUDs and PTSD.

STUDIES ASSESSING THE EFFECT OF COMORBID PTSD ON SUD OUTCOME

Emerging research has identified comorbid PTSD as a poor prognostic factor for SUD patients. Two published studies have used prospective designs and repeated assessments with structured interviews to examine substance use outcomes in patients with PTSD versus patients without PTSD. Brown, Stout, and Mueller (1996) compared substance-dependent women with and without a comorbid diagnosis of PTSD on their alcohol and drug use 3 months after completing inpatient substance abuse treatment. Although rates of relapse did not significantly differ by PTSD status, proportional hazards regression analyses revealed that women with PTSD relapsed more quickly (mean number of days = 26.48) than did women without PTSD (mean number of days = 54.53). Study results also indicated that women with PTSD reported greater general psychiatric distress than women without PTSD, perhaps reflecting the additive effects of their two disorders. However, in contrast to current PTSD status, psychiatric distress was not found to be a significant predictor of relapse. Study limitations include solely measuring substance use outcome dichotomously (relapse vs. no relapse) rather than continuously (e.g., percentage days of abstinence) and the restriction of study participants to women only.

Ouimette et al. (1997) compared patients with both substance abuse and PTSD (SUD–PTSD) to patients with substance abuse and another non-PTSD Axis I psychiatric diagnosis (SUD–PSY) and those with only substance use diagnoses (SUD-only) on substance use and psychosocial outcomes 1 year after substance abuse treatment. Although the three groups did not differ on symptoms of alcohol dependence or average daily alcohol consumption at follow-up, SUD–PTSD patients reported more substance-related problems as well as greater psychological distress and less support from friends than both SUD–PSY and SUD-only patients. Compared with SUD-only patients, SUD–PTSD patients were more likely to be readmitted for inpatient/residential treatment and less likely to be employed during follow-up. At a 2-year follow-up (Ouimette, Finney, & Moos, 1999), the differences among these three groups on substance use and psychological and psychosocial functioning became more pronounced. Considered collectively, these findings suggest that poorer outcomes may be specific to PTSD rather than to psychiatric comorbidity in general and that the scope of poorer treatment outcomes extends to psychosocial functioning. Ouimette et al. (1997) noted that the generalizability of the study's findings is limited to male substance abuse patients in Veterans Affairs treatment centers. Another major study limitation is that PTSD status was determined by chart diagnoses and not by structured clinical interview.

Despite different methodologies and different sampling procedures, these research findings indicate that comorbid PTSD may render SUD patients more vulnerable to poor outcomes. However, both studies treated PTSD status as a static variable and did not investigate how changes in PTSD over the course of follow-up (e.g., possible remission) affect alcohol and drug use outcomes. Moreover, both studies were limited to single-sex samples, preventing any examination of possible gender differences.

STUDIES ASSESSING THE EFFECT OF COMORBID SUDs ON PTSD OUTCOME

A few published studies have examined the impact of comorbid SUDs on PTSD outcome. Zlotnick et al. (1999) examined the course of PTSD in patients with another comorbid anxiety disorder and found that a history of alcohol abuse or dependence was predictive of increased time to remission from PTSD (remission was defined as 8 consecutive weeks of no or minimal symptoms). No patient with a history of alcohol abuse or dependence (n = 20) experienced a remission during the 5-year follow-up period. This study suffered from several limitations, including the small sample size and the fact that PTSD patients were recruited into the study for an anxiety disorder other than PTSD and thus may not be representative of PTSD patients without other anxiety disorders. Another methodological problem is the use of lifetime (not current) alcohol diagnoses.

In another study on PTSD outcome, Bremner, Southwick, Darnell, and Charney (1996) recruited a sample of Vietnam combat veterans with chronic PTSD and examined retrospectively the longitudinal course of PTSD symptoms and alcohol and drug abuse. The results showed that increases in substance abuse mirrored increases in PTSD symptoms in the period during and immediately after the war. Several design limitations, including retrospective reports for the past 20 years and long-interval symptom assessments (every 2 years), raise concerns about reliability. Moreover, the findings may not be generalizable to individuals with PTSD related to noncombat stressors (e.g., sexual assault), which may have a different symptom course.

GENDER AND SUD–PTSD COMORBIDITY

Although early SUD–PTSD comorbidity research focused primarily on male combat veterans, research on women with these concomitant diagnoses has expanded in the past few years (see review by Najavits, Weiss, & Shaw, 1999). Studies that have examined comorbidity rates in clinical samples and in the general population indicate that comorbid SUD–PTSD is a significant problem for both men and women (e.g., see reviews by Keane & Kaloupek, 1997; Stewart, Pihl, Conrod, & Dongier, 1998); however, examinations of gender-specific risk rates for one disorder in the presence of the other (i.e., SUD in the presence or absence of PTSD, and vice versa) suggest that women may be more vulnerable than their male counterparts to SUD–PTSD comorbidity (see review by Stewart, Ouimette, & Brown, in press). Gender also may influence the way that SUDs and PTSD are interrelated. For example, women may be at higher risk than men to the form of comorbidity in which the PTSD develops first (e.g., Kessler, Sonnega, Bromet, Hughes, & Nelson, 1995). SUD–PTSD women also may be less likely to drink or use drugs in "positive" situations, such as pleasant times with others (e.g., Sharkansky, Brief, Peirce, Meehan, & Mannix, 1999), and they may make excessive use of medical services (see review by Stewart et al., in press). Evidence of such gender differences raises concerns about the possible role of gender in SUD–PTSD treatment outcome and whether gender-specific treatments are needed. Although extant research suggests that SUD–PTSD patients have relatively poorer outcomes compared with patients with either of these disorders alone (e.g., Brown et al., 1996, Ouimette et al., 1997), to date no single study has examined whether such outcomes vary by patient gender.

COPING AS A POTENTIAL MEDIATOR
OF TREATMENT OUTCOME

Although still little is known about factors that potentially mediate the relationship between PTSD and substance use, theoretically guided studies of substance abusers consistently show that coping skills play an important role in the relapse–recovery process (see Marlatt, 1996; Monti, Rohsenow, Colby, & Abrams, 1995). For example, studies show that the more frequent use of cognitive coping predicts abstinence at 6 months posttreatment (Ito & Donovan, 1990) and that the use of coping strategies is significantly associated with the prevention of relapse (Wells et al., 1989). Other investigations have similarly shown that increased drinking after substance abuse treatment is associated with both skills deficits (Marlatt & Gordon, 1985) and the failure to use alternative coping responses (Cronkite & Moos, 1980).

Coping deficits also have been associated with a diagnosis of PTSD. For example, several studies show that PTSD patients have more avoidant coping styles than their non-PTSD counterparts (e.g., Fairbank, Hansen, & Fitterling, 1991; Foa, Steketee, & Rothbaum, 1989). Fairbank et al. (1991) speculated that PTSD patients with a long history of coping with their trauma symptomatology may have developed a preferred or characteristic coping response to stressors. Thus, PTSD may differentially influence substance abuse relapse through deficits in coping skills.

In a longitudinal study of veterans seeking substance abuse treatment, Ouimette et al. (1997) examined coping and cognitive styles as possible mediators of the relationship between PTSD and poorer substance use outcomes. The association between PTSD and problems from substance use at a 1-year follow-up was partially explained by SUD–PTSD patients' greater use of emotional discharge coping (e.g., risk taking, yelling), decreased expectations of benefits from quitting drinking/drugging, and greater substance use reinforcement expectancies. In a subsequent article, Ouimette et al. (1999) examined SUD–PTSD veterans' coping at the 1-year follow-up as an explanatory variable of the relationship found between PTSD and poorer 2-year substance use outcomes. As the researchers predicted, emotional discharge and cognitive avoidance coping both partially explained the impact of PTSD on greater alcohol use, more substance use–related problems, and lower probability of SUD remission.

THE PRESENT STUDY

The present study builds on previous research and examines the relationship between PTSD and SUD outcomes as well as the relationship between alcohol and drug use and PTSD outcomes. We also explored how adaptive and maladaptive coping influence the SUD–PTSD relationship. Because our study sample consists of both male and female patients, we also analyzed data for possible gender differences and assessed the impact of gender on both SUD and PTSD outcomes.

Participants and Procedure

Participants were individuals receiving inpatient substance abuse treatment at a free-standing, private, university-affiliated hospital. Recruitment was nonrandom; we attempted to oversample women and minorities. To be eligible for the study, patients had to be literate, between the ages of 18 and 55, and able to provide the name and address of one collateral who could serve as a corroborative source. Exclusionary criteria included significant organic impairment, psychosis, and homelessness.

Three patients who agreed to participate left the inpatient unit against medical advice and did not complete the intake assessment. Medical records indicated that one of these patients carried a diagnosis of PTSD. Baseline data were analyzed on the remaining 133 participants.

The sample was roughly evenly divided by gender (68 women and 65 men). The average age of participants was 37 years ($SD = 9.07$), and ages ranged from 18 to 55 years. The sample was predominantly Caucasian (90%, $n = 120$). The modal personal income was in the $0–$9,999 range. More detailed demographic descriptions are provided in Table 9.1.

Approximately 71% of participants carried an additional Axis I diagnosis other than PTSD or substance abuse or dependence. Sixty-one percent ($n = 81$) of participants met criteria for a current affective disorder, and approximately 47% ($n = 62$) met criteria for a current (non-PTSD) anxiety disorder.

A total of 120 patients completed a follow-up assessment 6 months after their hospital discharge, resulting in a follow-up rate of 90%. Of the 13 who did not complete the follow-up assessment, 1 was too ill to complete the assessment, 1 refused to complete the assessment, and the remainder could not be located or contacted. Follow-up rates did not differ by gender or PTSD status.

TABLE 9.1
Sample Demographic Characteristics at Baseline

Demographic variables	%	n
Employment status		
Unemployed/disabled	46	54
Employed full time	47	63
Employed part time	12	16
Marital status		
Single/never been married	24	32
Married/committed relationship	39	52
Separated/divorced	37	49
Education		
Less than high school education	14	18
Completed high school	38	50
At least some college	49	65

Measures

A battery of interviewer-administered and paper-and-pencil measures pertaining to traumatic exposure, PTSD status, substance use, psychiatric distress, and coping was administered at baseline and again at 6 months postdischarge.

Traumatic Exposure

The Life Stressor Checklist–Revised (Wolfe & Kimerling, 1997) was used to assess traumatic exposure. This 30-item screening measure queries about a broad range of stressful events, such as natural disasters, physical or sexual assault, life-threatening illness, accident or injury, and catastrophic death of a loved one. Age at the time of the trauma is recorded, allowing for a distinction between childhood and adulthood trauma. An event was defined as traumatic if it involved actual or threatened serious injury or death to the participant or another person, and if the participant's reaction to this event involved intense fear, helplessness, or horror (Criterion A of the PTSD diagnosis; *Diagnostic and Statistical Manual of Mental Disorders* [4th ed.; *DSM–IV*], American Psychiatric Association, 1994).

PTSD

Patients who reported experiencing a traumatic event were interviewed using the Clinician Administered PTSD Scale (CAPS; Blake et al., 1995). This structured interview assesses the frequency and severity of the 17 symptoms of PTSD as defined by *DSM–IV* (American Psychiatric Association, 1994). The CAPS has been shown to possess sound psychometric properties and excellent diagnostic utility against the Structured Clinical Interview for *DSM–IV* PTSD module (Blake et al., 1995). For the purposes of the present study, we used the number of PTSD criteria met as a general indicator of PTSD severity.

Substance Use

To establish substance use history, all participants were administered the SUD modules of the Structured Clinical Interview for *DSM–IV* (First, Spitzer, Gibbon, & Williams, 1994). At both baseline and follow-up, the Timeline Follow-Back method (Sobell & Sobell, 1995) was used to determine percentage days abstinent during the previous 6 months.[1] At intake, all patients were asked to indicate the age at which they began using substances problematically and the number of years their substance use had been problematic.

General Psychiatric Distress

General psychiatric distress was assessed with the Symptom Checklist–90–Revised (Derogatis, 1977). This 90-item, Likert-type self-report measure is widely used and yields a single overall score of psychiatric distress, with higher numbers indicating greater levels of distress.

Coping

Coping style was evaluated with the 71-item COPE (Carver, Scheier, & Weintraub, 1989), which assesses different ways in which individuals respond to stressful or traumatic events. The measure asks participants to rate on a scale that ranges from 1 (*not at all*) to 4 (*a lot*) the extent to which they use various strategies to cope with stress. The COPE has been shown to assess as many as 14 different dimensions of coping. In this study, principal-components analyses indicated strong support for a two-factor solution. These factors were interpreted as (a) Positive/Adaptive Coping (acceptance, active coping, suppression of competing activities, planning, positive reinterpretation and growth, religion, restraint, seeking of emotional support, and seeking of instrumental support) and (b) Negative/Maladaptive Coping (alcohol and other drug use, behavioral disengagement, mental disengagement, denial).

---

[1]Collaterals were interviewed near the time of patients' baseline and follow-up assessments and provided data on their respective patients' percentage days abstinent during the previous 180 days. Agreement regarding both baseline and follow-up was good (intraclass coefficients of .50 and .43, respectively).

Rates of Traumatic Exposure and Comorbid PTSD

Traumatic Exposure

An overwhelming majority (94.7%, *n* =126) of this sample reported having experienced intense trauma (i.e., catastrophic death of a loved one, physical abuse, sexual violence). Participants also reported past exposure to a broad range of other types of traumatic or stressful events (see Table 9.2). The high rates of trauma exposure reported in the sample are consistent with other studies of people with SUDs (e.g., Najavits, Weiss, & Shaw, 1999) and suggest that traumatic histories are the norm rather than the exception in this type of population. Gender differences were noted with respect to trauma exposure rates, with women more likely to experience both childhood and adulthood physical abuse. Women also were significantly more likely to experience forced sexual touching and forced sex in adulthood than were men in this sample. These gender differences are disturbing, as interpersonal violence and sexual victimization in particular have been linked to a greater risk for the development of PTSD than other types of trauma (Kendall-Tackett, Williams, & Finkelhor, 1993; Norris, 1992). Thus, these data suggest that women may be at greater risk for exposure to events that are more likely to lead to posttraumatic stress symptoms than are men.

PTSD

We found high rates of PTSD in our sample: Forty-one percent (*n* = 55) met diagnostic criteria for current PTSD at baseline, as measured by the CAPS (Blake et al., 1995). At follow-up, 38 patients diagnosed with PTSD at baseline still suffered from PTSD, and 14 patients' PTSD had

TABLE 9.2
Rates of Exposure to Traumatic Events

Traumatic event	%	*n*
Catastrophic loss of a loved one	67	89
Victim of robbery, mugging	43	57
Serious accident	49	65
Serious physical or mental illness	50	67
Physical abuse		
Childhood	39	52
Adulthood	34	45
Forced sexual touching		
Childhood	43	57
Adulthood	14	18
Forced sex		
Childhood	23	31
Adulthood	17	23

remitted (i.e., they no longer met full criteria for a PTSD diagnosis). Of the 68 patients who did not have PTSD at baseline assessment, 6 patients had a PTSD diagnosis at the end of the follow-up, whereas the other 62 remained without a PTSD diagnosis.

We compared patients with and without PTSD at baseline on several baseline variables to characterize similarities and differences between these two groups (see Table 9.3). PTSD patients reported significantly greater levels of general psychiatric distress and higher levels of negative and maladaptive coping at baseline than their non-PTSD counterparts. In addition, PTSD patients reported an earlier age of onset of problematic substance use compared to non-PTSD patients. Accordingly, PTSD patients had more years of problematic substance use. No differences were found between PTSD and non-PTSD patients on age, percentage days abstinent, or positive and adaptive coping strategies.

In keeping with the increased levels of interpersonal violence and sexual victimization among women in our sample (Kendall-Tackett et al., 1993; Norris, 1992), chi-square analyses revealed that women in the present study had higher rates of PTSD at baseline (50%) than men (32%). No other gender differences on baseline measures were found.

Impact of PTSD on Substance Use Outcomes

Research has indicated that comorbid SUD–PTSD is associated with greater involvement with alcohol and other drugs than SUD alone (Brady, Killeen, Saladin, Dansky, & Becker, 1994; Najavits, Weiss, & Shaw, 1999).

TABLE 9.3
Baseline Differences Between Posttraumatic Stress Disorder (PTSD)
and Non-PTSD Patients

	PTSD		No PTSD	
Measure	M	SD	M	SD
Substance use				
Percentage days abstinent	46.5	37.0	41.4	35.5
Age of problematic use onset***	19.6	8.0	26.5	10.8
Years of problematic use***	17.0	10.5	11.2	10.0
General psychiatric distress[a],***	169.9	65.5	112.2	64.2
Coping[b]				
Positive/Adaptive	83.2	18.6	84.4	17.3
Negative/Maladaptive**	42.0	7.2	38.5	7.8

Note. [a]General psychiatric distress was assessed with the Symptom Checklist–90–Revised (Derogatis, 1977). [b]Possible scores on the Positive/Adaptive coping subscale range from 36 to 144; possible scores on the Negative/Maladaptive coping subscale range from 13 to 52. Higher scores indicate greater use of that particular coping type.
**$p < .01$. ***$p < .001$.

To determine the prospective influence of a PTSD diagnosis at baseline on substance use outcomes, we examined differences between patients diagnosed with PTSD and those without a PTSD diagnosis at baseline assessment on percentage days of substance use at 6-month follow-up. No significant between-group differences were found.

PTSD Status From Baseline to Follow-up

Because baseline PTSD status did not predict SUD outcome, we next examined whether changes, or lack thereof, in PTSD status between baseline and follow-up assessments were associated with substance use outcomes. On the basis of the CAPS baseline and follow-up results, we classified patients into three groups: (a) PTSD unremitted (i.e., they had PTSD at baseline and still met diagnostic criteria for PTSD at follow-up; $n = 38$), (b) PTSD remitted (i.e., they had PTSD at baseline but no longer met PTSD diagnostic criteria at follow-up; $n = 14$), and (c) no PTSD at baseline and follow-up ($n = 62$).[2]

To test the effects of PTSD changes on substance use outcome, we conducted a multiple regression analysis with follow-up percentage days abstinent as the dependent variable (see Table 9.4). We dummy coded the PTSD group using the non-PTSD group as the reference group. The results of these analyses revealed that, after controlling for baseline psychiatric distress and baseline percentage days abstinent, patients with continued PTSD had poorer substance use outcomes (i.e., fewer percentage days abstinent) than did those who had never carried a PTSD diagnosis. No significant

TABLE 9.4
Prediction of Follow-Up Percentage Days Abstinent

Predictor	B	SE B	Beta	t
Baseline % days abstinent	0.00	.00	.18	1.89
Sex	−0.02	.09	−.02	−0.17
Baseline PTSD severity	−0.00	.01	−.07	−0.75
Baseline SCL−90−R	−0.00	.00	.14	1.36
Comparison of no PTSD and unremitted PTSD	−0.22	.11	−.22	−2.04*
Comparison of no PTSD and remitted PTSD	0.07	.14	.05	0.51

Note. $R^2 = .08$. SCL−90−R = Symptom Checklist−90−R.
*$p < .05$.

---

[2]Six patients did not meet criteria for PTSD at baseline but did so at the end of follow-up. Although this group of patients whose PTSD developed over the course of follow-up are of clinical interest, given the small sample size we did not include this group in subsequent data analyses.

differences were found between individuals with remitted PTSD and individuals who had never carried a PTSD diagnosis.

On the basis of the findings presented here, it is possible that continued PTSD symptoms represent an impediment to abstinence from alcohol and drugs. Alternatively, as examined below, it is possible that abstinence or reduction in substance use is associated with improvements in PTSD symptoms.

Factors Associated With PTSD Remission

To examine potential predictors of remission from PTSD, we conducted a series of *t* tests to compare participants who had remitted from PTSD and those who had not remitted on several baseline and follow-up variables.

Baseline

First, we tested differences between the remitted and unremitted PTSD groups on baseline variables, including gender, general psychiatric distress, PTSD severity, and positive and negative coping. As shown in Table 9.5, the remitted PTSD group had less severe PTSD and general psychiatric distress at baseline than did the unremitted PTSD group.

Second, we examined differences between the two groups of interest on substance use variables at baseline. The results of these analyses revealed

TABLE 9.5
Baseline Comparisons of Posttraumatic Stress Disorder (PTSD)
Remitted and Unremitted Patients

	PTSD status at follow-up							
	Remitted				Unremitted			
Measure	n	%	M	SD	n	%	M	SD
Gender								
Male	6	30.0			14	70.0		
Female	8	25.0			24	75.0		
Substance use								
% Days abstinent			41.0	38.4			48.2	37.4
Years of problematic use			18.9	11.5			17.0	10.5
PTSD severity[a]			10.2	2.2			11.5	1.6
General psychiatric distress[b,*]			134.4	50.7			181.6	68.2
Coping								
Positive/Adaptive			86.9	20.7			83.0	18.1
Negative/Maladaptive			42.8	7.1			41.4	7.3

Note. [a]PTSD severity is based on the number of PTSD symptoms. [b]General psychiatric distress was assessed with the Symptom Checklist–90–Revised (Derogatis, 1977).
$*p < .05$.

no statistically significant differences between individuals in the remitted and unremitted PTSD groups on baseline percentage days abstinent from alcohol/drugs or years of problematic substance use. Thus, substance involvement at baseline does not appear to be associated with remission from PTSD at follow-up.

Follow-up

With a second set of *t* tests we examined differences between participants with remitted and unremitted PTSD on follow-up psychosocial and substance use variables (see Table 9.6). These variables included general psychiatric distress, positive and negative coping, and percentage days abstinent. Remitted and unremitted groups differed significantly on general psychiatric distress, both positive and negative coping, and percentage days abstinent. Compared with the unremitted PTSD group, patients in the remitted group reported lower levels of overall psychiatric distress, higher levels of positive coping, lower levels of negative coping, and a higher number of percentage days abstinent at follow-up.

To examine the unique contributions of relevant psychosocial and substance use variables, we used logistic regression to examine predictors of PTSD outcomes (remitted vs. unremitted), controlling for variables that were demonstrated in group difference analyses (see preceding paragraphs) to be associated with PTSD remission, as well as continued substance use at follow-up (percentage days abstinent). Thus, this logistic regression model included baseline PTSD symptom severity, baseline and follow-up psychiatric distress, positive and negative coping at follow-up, and percentage days abstinent at follow-up (see Table 9.7). Results of these analyses revealed no significant effect of percentage days abstinent on PTSD remission status.

TABLE 9.6
Follow-Up Comparisons of Posttraumatic Stress Disorder (PTSD)
Remitted and Unremitted Patients

| | PTSD status at follow-up | | | |
| | Remitted | | Unremitted | |
Measure	M	SD	M	SD
Substance use[a],*	90.0	14.7	76.0	31.1
General psychiatric distress[b],***	58.3	47.6	153.2	77.6
Coping				
Positive/Adaptive**	101.1	16.8	83.2	19.4
Negative/Maladaptive***	27.0	8.4	38.4	8.4

Note. [a]Substance use is based on the percentage of days abstinent. [b]General psychiatric distress was assessed with the Symptom Checklist–90–Revised (Derogatis, 1977).
*$p < .05$. **$p < .01$. ***$p < .001$.

TABLE 9.7
Predictors of Posttraumatic Stress Disorder Outcomes

Predictor	Beta	SE	Odds ratio
Baseline PTSD severity	−0.31	0.27	0.74
SCL–90–R		0.01	0.99
Baseline	−0.01		
Follow-up	−0.01	0.01	0.99
Follow-up % days abstinent	−0.73	1.15	0.48
Follow-up positive coping	0.04	0.04	1.04
Follow-up negative coping*	−0.27	0.12	0.76

Note. SCL–90–R = Symptom Checklist–90–R.
*$p < .05$.

In fact, the only significant predictor of PTSD remission in this logistic regression model was negative coping at follow-up. Controlling for the other variables, higher levels of negative coping were associated with reduced odds of PTSD remission.

The logistic regression model suggests that the relationship between substance use outcomes and PTSD status may be influenced by other variables. Specifically, after controlling for psychiatric distress and including follow-up coping in the model, the relationship between percentage days abstinent and PTSD remission was no longer significant. These findings underscore the complex, dynamic relationship between SUD–PTSD comorbidity and suggest that the relationship is affected by a third variable: coping.

PTSD and Substance Use Outcomes: The Role of Coping

To examine relations between coping and substance use outcome in our sample of men and women, we compared PTSD and non-PTSD participants' scores on positive/adaptive and negative/maladaptive dimensions of coping at follow-up. Results of analyses of variance were consistent with earlier comparisons of remitted versus unremitted PTSD patients with respect to coping and indicated that participants who had remitted from PTSD at follow-up reported significantly greater levels of positive coping and lower levels of negative coping than those in the unremitted group. Furthermore, individuals who never had PTSD reported significantly lower levels of negative coping at follow-up than those with unremitted PTSD.

We then examined whether changes in coping occurred over time as a function of PTSD status. Using multiple regression analyses, and controlling for respective baseline coping variables, we found that non-PTSD patients and remitted patients engaged in greater positive coping at follow-up compared to unremitted patients (see Table 9.8). In addition, participants who never carried a PTSD diagnosis reported significantly less negative

TABLE 9.8
Prediction of Follow-Up Coping

Predictor	B	SE B	Beta	t
Positive coping				
Baseline positive coping***	0.33	0.89	.32	3.74***
Comparison of no PTSD and unremitted PTSD*	−7.29	3.45	−.19	−2.11*
Comparison of no PTSD and remitted PTSD*	9.67	4.91	.18	1.97*
Negative coping				
Baseline negative coping**	0.27	0.10	.22	2.73**
Comparison of no PTSD and unremitted PTSD***	8.57	1.65	.44	5.19***
Comparison of no PTSD and remitted PTSD	−3.14	2.35	−.11	−1.33

Note. R^2 for positive coping = .20, R^2 for negative coping = .30. PTSD = posttraumatic stress disorder.
*$p < .05$. **$p < .01$. ***$p < .001$.

coping than those whose PTSD symptoms were unremitted. No differences in negative coping were found between the no-PTSD and remitted PTSD groups.

In light of our findings regarding the effect of follow-up PTSD status on coping, we sought to ascertain whether these variables were associated with substance use outcome (see Table 9.9). Accordingly, we added positive and negative coping at follow-up to our regression equation examining the relationship between PTSD status at follow-up and substance use outcomes. Both positive and negative coping were found to contribute significantly to percentage days abstinent from substances. Furthermore, when these two domains of coping were included in the regression model, differences between substance use outcomes for PTSD and no-PTSD groups were no longer significant. Follow-up analyses covarying for baseline coping did not affect these results.

TABLE 9.9
Prediction of Follow-Up Coping

Predictor	B	SE B	Beta	t
Baseline % days abstinent	0.00	.00	0.16	1.85
Baseline positive coping	−0.00	.00	−0.10	−1.06
Baseline negative coping	0.01	.01	0.12	1.37
Follow-up positive coping	0.01	.00	0.26	2.78**
Follow-up negative coping	−0.02	.01	−0.43	−4.24***
Comparison of no PTSD to unremitted PTSD	0.08	.10	0.08	0.77
Comparison of no PTSD to remitted PTSD	−0.04	.13	−0.03	−0.32

Note. R^2 = .26. PTSD = posttraumatic stress disorder.
**$p < .01$. ***$p < .001$.

Summary of Findings and Implications for Treatment

Almost all the patients in our study reported experiencing a traumatic event in their lifetime. Consistent with the literature on PTSD rates among substance abusers in treatment (e.g., Brady et al., 1994; P. J. Brown et al., 1995; Fullilove et al., 1993; Sharkansky et al., 1999), a sizable percentage of our sample (over 40%) met diagnostic criteria for PTSD at the baseline assessment. It is clear that clinicians need to be alert to the high rates of trauma and concomitant PTSD among patients seeking substance abuse treatment. At the very least, addiction treatment intake procedures should include a PTSD screening measure to help identify individuals with possible comorbid PTSD (see chap. 6, this volume, for a review of PTSD measures). It is unfortunate that, in practice, many treatment providers focus exclusively on alcohol and drug problems and neglect the assessment and treatment of PTSD (e.g., Brinson & Treanor, 1989; Dansky, Roitzsch, Brady, & Saladin, 1997). A recent study by Dansky, Roitzsch, et al. (1997) showed that PTSD evaluations conducted as part of a research protocol on an inpatient SUD unit had little impact on diagnostic procedures subsequently practiced by clinical staff. Although staff appeared to recognize the importance of screening for sexual and physical abuse histories, they tended to overlook the evaluation of PTSD. In light of the high rates of co-occurrence of these two disorders in this sample, careful assessment of PTSD as part of addiction treatment evaluation procedures appears warranted.

In our study, female gender was associated with an increased risk of exposure to childhood and adulthood physical abuse as well as adulthood forced sexual touching. The disproportionate occurrence of these particular traumas in women relative to men may explain the higher rate of PTSD among women in our sample. Alternatively, there may be a gender-related vulnerability to PTSD, independent of the type of traumatic event(s) experienced. This vulnerability may be due to a host of factors, such as number of previous traumas, trauma severity, and social support at the time of the trauma and following the trauma (e.g., Yehuda & McFarlane, 1995).

Given the high rates of traumatic exposure and PTSD among women in our sample, we recommend that treatment providers screen for PTSD in all women presenting for substance abuse treatment. Other red flags for possible PTSD include SUD patients who present with high levels of general psychiatric distress, those who report an early age of onset of problematic alcohol/drug use, and those with many years of problematic use.

In contrast to previous research (e.g., Brown et al., 1996; Ouimette et al., 1997, 1999), our findings indicate that baseline PTSD status alone does not predict substance use outcome; rather, it is *no change* in PTSD status over the course of follow-up (i.e., unremitted PTSD) that is related to poorer substance use outcomes. This finding leads us to speculate that an intervention that improves PTSD symptoms may have a similar impact on substance use outcomes. The absence of significant differences in substance use outcomes between the remitted PTSD group and the non-PTSD group suggests that there is no residual deleterious effect of PTSD symptoms on substance use if these symptoms lessen. Therefore, it is *continued* PTSD that appears to be a critical factor in the relationship between PTSD and substance abuse outcomes. Even in the absence of definitive data on the mechanisms by which continued PTSD affects substance use outcomes, the value of educating both treatment providers and patients about the interplay between these two disorders seems clear.

One possible explanation for differing study findings regarding the predictive value of a baseline diagnosis of PTSD may relate to chronicity. It may not be PTSD per se but rather PTSD chronicity that predicts poor substance use outcomes. Community-based studies suggest that approximately half of the individuals with PTSD are in episode for more than 1 year (Breslau & Davis, 1992; Kessler et al., 1997). In a clinical study of 54 patients with PTSD and another comorbid anxiety disorder, Zlotnick et al. (1999) found that the average length of index episode of PTSD for patients was 19 years. In their sample, the likelihood of full remission from PTSD during a 5-year follow-up was only .18. In contrast, other studies have reported that nearly 50% or more of patients with PTSD recovered from this disorder within 1 year (Rothbaum & Foa, 1993; Rothbaum, Foa, Riggs, Murdock, & Walsh, 1992). As Zlotnick et al. noted, these other studies assessed the course of PTSD in patients who had suffered a more recent traumatic event. Hence, differences in remission rates across studies may be related to the time elapsed since the traumatic event. In our study, we unfortunately did not assess the length of time patients had suffered from PTSD and could not control for this variable in analyses and determine how it affects the course of comorbid SUDs. Hence, PTSD chronicity is an important variable that should be assessed and controlled for in future SUD–PTSD studies.

In the present study, unremitted PTSD was associated with poorer substance use outcomes. In contrast, neither baseline nor follow-up substance use was associated with PTSD outcomes. Taken together, these findings suggest that comorbid SUDs and PTSD cannot be treated as independent, unrelated problems. Although most clinical researchers advocate the need for simultaneous treatment for patients suffering from comorbid SUDs and PTSD (e.g., Ouimette, Brown, & Najavits, 1998), we know that in practice this is the exception rather than the norm. Treatment providers should be warned against viewing PTSD as secondary to SUDs and assuming that successfully treating the alcohol/drug problem alone will somehow result in improved PTSD symptoms. However, the most effective focus and timing of such trauma/PTSD treatment remains to be determined.

The data presented here regarding coping suggest that persons with a PTSD diagnosis may present to treatment with poorer coping skills. Furthermore, 6 months after inpatient substance abuse treatment, participants who still meet criteria for PTSD demonstrate poorer coping than those whose PTSD symptoms have remitted or those who never had PTSD. Although the temporal order of relations among variables cannot be determined, the present data do suggest that patients in substance abuse treatment experienced changes in coping from baseline to follow-up assessment. Furthermore, it appears that these changes are associated with better substance use outcomes. A focus on coping approaches may facilitate enhanced outcomes for both substance abuse and PTSD.

Our study provides support for the critical role of coping in the relationship between PTSD and SUD. Although PTSD and substance use consistently demonstrated associations with one another, regression models that included coping styles negated the relationship between these two variables. In view of the demonstrated relationship that coping has shown with both PTSD and SUD outcomes, clinicians may wish to focus on helping their SUD–PTSD patients decrease their maladaptive coping approaches and learn or master more adaptive coping strategies as part of a comprehensive approach to treatment of these comorbid disorders.

Several skills-training interventions have been developed and implemented with substance abusers (Kadden et al., 1992; Monti, Abrams, Kadden, & Cooney, 1989) and with PTSD patients (Echeburua, de-Corral, Sarasua, & Zubizarreta, 1996; Frueh, Turner, Beidel, Mirabella, & Jones, 1996). Indeed, preliminary findings from SUD–PTSD treatment studies that have a strong coping-skills emphasis appear very promising (see chap. 8, this volume, as well as an unpublished study by Donovan, Padin-Rivera, & Kowaliw cited in Donovan & Padin-Rivera, 1999). For example, Donovan et al. (unpublished, cited in Donovan & Padin-Rivera, 1999) evaluated a 12-week partial-hospitalization group treatment for male veterans with comorbid SUD–PTSD that included problem solving as a program element. Significant reductions in PTSD symptoms and substance use were achieved during treatment and maintained at follow-up. However, because the intervention included numerous components other than coping and problem-solving, no definitive conclusion about the unique effects of coping skills training can be made.

A major goal of this chapter was to assess the impact of gender on the course of PTSD and alcohol and drug use. Although women were more likely to experience certain traumatic events and had higher rates of PTSD (see previous discussion), we did not find gender to be related to either PTSD or SUD outcomes. Moreover, no gender differences were found for either baseline or follow-up coping. Thus, it appears that although women are at increased risk for exposure to trauma and to subsequent development of PTSD, female gender is not necessarily a risk factor for poorer long-term PTSD outcomes. Our conclusions are similar for SUD outcomes. Although some researchers and clinicians have called for gender-specific treatment for substance abuse (e.g., Nelson-Zlupko, Dore, Kauffman, & Kaltenbach, 1996), the data suggesting the necessity of such specialized treatment approaches have been inconclusive (e.g., Alterman, Randall, & McLellan, 2000; Rice, Longabaugh, Beattie, & Noel, 1993). The findings here suggest that men and women demonstrate similar substance use outcomes following treatment and therefore do not suggest the need for a more gender-specialized approach. Furthermore, the absence of gender-based differences in coping also suggests that women are not at greater risk for maladaptive coping approaches that may interfere with recovery from PTSD or substance abuse.

In interpreting our results it is important to note several limitations in our study. First, our follow-up assessment occurred only 6 months after hospital discharge. Research has suggested that the trajectory of substance abuse patterns may vary over time (e.g., Longabaugh, Wirtz, Zweben, & Stout, 1998; Project MATCH Research Group, 1997). In light of this, many treatment outcome studies monitor patients over the course of 1 year or more after treatment to evaluate longer term outcome (e.g., Humphreys, Moos, & Finney, 1995; Longabaugh et al., 1998; Ouimette et al., 1999). It is possible that our relatively short (6-month) follow-up period may have minimized outcome differences for PTSD versus non-PTSD patients. Second, as noted above, we did not assess certain variables—specifically, PTSD chronicity—that may be significant predictors of both PTSD and SUD outcome. Third, we do not know how treatment experiences during the follow-up period may have affected study results. Hence, treatment for SUDs or PTSD, or both, subsequent to hospital discharge may be a confounding variable. Fourth, our study focused exclusively on PTSD diagnoses and did not examine the unique impact of each of the three PTSD symptom constellations (re-experiencing, avoidance–numbing, hyperarousal) on SUD outcome. Specific PTSD symptoms, rather than a PTSD diagnosis per se, may ultimately be more helpful in understanding the course of SUD–PTSD comorbidity and pinpointing particularly effective areas of intervention.

III

SPECIFIC POPULATIONS

10

CONCURRENT POSTTRAUMATIC STRESS DISORDER AND SUBSTANCE USE DISORDER AMONG VETERANS: EVIDENCE AND TREATMENT ISSUES

JOSEF I. RUZEK

In recent years, clinicians and researchers have become more aware of the relationships among exposure to traumatic events, posttraumatic stress disorder (PTSD), and substance abuse problems (e.g., Ruzek, Polusny, & Abueg, 1998; Stewart, 1996). These connections have been especially clear to individuals who work with combat veterans. In a large epidemiological study of Vietnam veterans (National Vietnam Veterans Readjustment Study; Kulka et al., 1990), 73% of male Vietnam veterans who met diagnostic criteria for PTSD also qualified for a lifetime diagnosis of alcohol abuse or dependence. This strong association between the two sets of problems presents real challenges to clinicians. Perhaps because the PTSD afflicting most of these veterans and their families has been of extremely long duration (around 30 years in the Vietnam veterans who comprise the largest group of such patients), it is extremely treatment resistant. Patients present with problems that are not easily addressed and that may limit veterans' ability to benefit from substance use disorder (SUD) programs. The levels of emotional distress and practical problems in living experienced by veterans with both sets of problems exceed those whose SUD is uncomplicated by PTSD, and their home environments provide little scaffolding for continued sobriety; most are unemployed, financially challenged, lacking in routine family contact, relatively socially isolated, and devoid of daily purposeful activity. Because substantial numbers of veteran patients experience difficulties related to PTSD and SUD in combination, and because they are difficult to treat, increasing consideration is being given to the potential benefits of addressing the two problems in a more integrated fashion. In this chapter I describe the literature related to this dual diagnosis in specific groups of veterans, identify clinical practices helpful in working with these veterans, and explore key challenges to the better integration of PTSD and SUD treatment.

PTSD, TRAUMA EXPOSURE, AND SUBSTANCE ABUSE IN VETERANS

Vietnam Veterans

Most of the empirical research examining the relationships among PTSD, trauma exposure during military service, and SUD problems in veterans has been conducted with veterans of the Vietnam war. This research has focused on general community samples as well as two major groups of help seekers: (a) individuals seeking treatment for PTSD and (b) those being treated for alcohol or drug problems. Among male veterans seeking treatment for combat-related PTSD, high rates of lifetime alcohol disorders (ranging from around 40% to 85%) and lifetime drug abuse and dependence (range: 25%–56%) have been consistently documented (e.g., Roszell, McFall, & Malas, 1991; Sierles, Chen, McFarland, & Taylor, 1983). Evidence also shows that PTSD is commonly found in Vietnam veterans seeking help for SUD problems (e.g., Hyer, Leach, Boudewyns, & Davis, 1991; McFall, Mackay, & Donovan, 1992; Triffleman, Marmar, Delucchi, & Ronfeldt, 1995). For example, Triffleman et al. (1995) administered the Structured Clinical Interview for DSM–III–R (Spitzer, Williams, & Gibbon, 1987) PTSD module to 40 veteran SUD inpatients and found that 40% had a lifetime history of combat-related PTSD, 58% had a lifetime history of PTSD due to combat or other traumatic exposure, and 38% had current PTSD. Research on national samples of Vietnam veterans supports these clinical studies in indicating high rates of SUD–PTSD comorbidity (e.g., Centers for Disease Control and Prevention, 1988; Kulka et al., 1990).

Relative to other veteran groups, several themes are perhaps more often encountered by clinicians who work with Vietnam veterans. Some have to do with the fact that public support for the Vietnam war was so mixed. More so than in other wars and conditions of deployment, there was widespread opposition to the war among the general population. Far from having their sacrifices be acknowledged and being received as heroes, veterans routinely describe bad homecoming experiences (indifference, insults, and ridicule from civilians, e.g., being spit on or called "baby killers"). Since that time they have come to expect negative attitudes from civilians and have felt alienated from the American public. For many, these expectations have remained relatively unchanged across the years, in part because they have had little interpersonal contact with others. It is also true that many veterans themselves experienced the war as senseless and lacked a clear conviction of its moral correctness. Many perceive their government as having lied to them and their military leaders as having mismanaged the conduct of, and therefore lost, the war. Mistrust of authority (including treatment providers) and hostility toward the government are common. These feelings were not helped by their early experiences with Veterans Affairs (VA) health care services, when the psychological impact of the war was not recognized and their right to compensation for psychological problems was questioned; indeed, many veterans remain reluctant to use available services. When compared with older veterans of World War II and Korea, Vietnam veterans more frequently describe as traumatic their experience of being exposed to brutality, mutilated bodies, the death of children, and the loss of friends (Davidson, Kudler, Saunders, & Smith, 1990). It is likely that these factors have set the scene for Vietnam veterans to experience greater personal guilt related to specific acts during the war for which they feel responsible. They have also meant that these veterans, unlike those who served in many other conflicts, sometimes cannot take refuge in a range of positive beliefs that may help to buffer their distress (e.g., "I served my country honorably"; "I'm proud of what I accomplished"; "Others appreciate my sacrifice"; "We won the war"; "It was terrible, but it was the right thing to do"). It is also apparent that the occupational lives of Vietnam veterans, perhaps more than those of veterans of World War II or Korea, have been characterized by an inability to maintain employment because of anger and anxiety, the holding of many short-term jobs, a general sense of failure, and a current decision not to seek future employment. Greater levels of alienation from civilian society, trauma-related guilt, and problems in maintaining employment have all contributed to the relatively greater social isolation seen in veterans of Vietnam.

Veterans of World War II and Korea

World War II and Korean conflict veterans are less likely than those who served in Vietnam to have sought help for PTSD in the years following their military service. Often, these older veterans appear to have indeed suffered with chronic PTSD for many years before seeking help, but they coped by working long hours (workaholism), drinking, or both. Lower past rates of help seeking may be due to factors such as less availability of mental health services, less awareness (both by veterans and health care professionals) of the chronicity of emotional problems associated with combat, a skepticism about the concept of PTSD among some older veterans, a greater perceived stigma associated with seeking help for mental illness, and a stronger generational emphasis on the minimization and nondisclosure of distressing emotions. This reticence to retell the trauma story and acknowledge problems means that PTSD may be easily missed by health care professionals (Druley & Pashko, 1988; Macleod, 1994); possible problems with recognition of these problems are also compounded by the finding that, in elderly combat veterans, PTSD self-report scale cutoff scores that are lower than those applicable to other age groups discriminate among respondents with and without PTSD (Summers, Hyer, Boyd, & Boudewyns, 1996).

Experience with these older veterans suggests that as they age they increasingly face a number of stressors—health problems, bereavement, and retirement—that are often associated with an activation or worsening of PTSD symptoms (Macleod, 1994). This is, of course, not surprising, given that illness and the temporal proximity of death are reminders of previous war-related experiences with personal death threat and that exposure to the death of significant others is a direct reminder of war zone grief. These problems bring up feelings of vulnerability, loss of control, dependency on others, and helplessness, which are important themes for individuals struggling with PTSD. Also, when veterans retire, they lose an important avoidance strategy that may have reduced the frequency or intensity of PTSD symptoms.

The military and postmilitary experiences of veterans of the Korean conflict are in some ways similar to those experienced by Vietnam veterans and dissimilar to those of World War II veterans. The Korean conflict involved heavy casualties, territorial stalemate, and an end with no clear victor. Returning veterans received little or no public recognition, and there was some public condemnation of them for supposed poor combat performance. As a group, they were ignored and "forgotten." Fontana and Rosenheck (1994) and McCranie and Hyer (2000) have suggested that these differences in military outcome and homecoming experience may in part account for a higher severity of PTSD symptoms and more severe psychosocial adjustment problems observed in treatment-seeking Korean versus World War II veterans.

Although clinical experience indicates that alcohol problems and PTSD often co-occur in older veterans, little research has addressed this issue. Some limited evidence suggests that Korean veterans may demonstrate alcohol problems at rates similar to Vietnam veterans and that excessive alcohol use is correlated with combat exposure (e.g., Branchey, Davis, & Lieber, 1984); Korean conflict prisoners of war also show a high (20%) prevalence of alcohol abuse (Sutker, Winstead, Galina, & Allain, 1990). Although World War II veterans in general may consume alcohol at levels lower than Vietnam veterans, high rates of alcohol consumption have been reported among American World War II prisoners of war (e.g., Engdahl, Speed, Eberly, & Schwartz, 1991; Sutker, Allain, & Winstead, 1993). Herrmann and Eryavec (1996) found a high level of lifetime alcohol abuse

(53%, and 8% had a current diagnosis of alcohol abuse) and a positive correlation between combat exposure and alcohol abuse in a sample of elderly Canadian World War II veterans residing in a veterans' long-term care facility (in whom lifetime prevalence of PTSD was 23%; Herrmann & Eryavec, 1994). Davidson et al. (1990) compared rates of alcohol problems in World War II and Vietnam veterans with PTSD and reported that 47% of the World War II patients received a lifetime diagnosis of alcoholism, compared with 68% of the Vietnam group, a nonsignificant difference. Engdahl, Dikel, Eberly, and Blank (1998) studied former prisoners of war (including both World War II and Korea veterans) and found that current PTSD was associated with significantly increased risk of lifetime (but not current) alcohol abuse and dependence. By contrast, some studies have indicated that PTSD does not predict alcohol abuse (e.g., Herrmann & Eryavec, 1996). In Herrmann and Eryavec's (1996) study, however, 64% of the veterans with PTSD also met criteria for alcohol problems.

Studies of older veterans also suggest that PTSD is generally the primary diagnosis with respect to alcohol abuse and dependence (e.g., Engdahl et al., 1998). Davidson et al. (1990) found that in their subsample of World War II veterans the onset of alcoholism followed the onset of PTSD, at a mean of 6.9 years later; and only five cases of alcohol abuse/dependence were reported by Engdahl et al. (1998) to have preceded combat exposure and the onset of PTSD. These findings suggest that veterans turned to alcohol to self-medicate their symptoms.

Veterans of More Recent Deployments

In recent years, there have been many military deployments encompassing war (e.g., Operation Desert Storm), peacekeeping (e.g., Haiti, Bosnia, Kosovo), and peace enforcement (e.g., Somalia). In general, the younger veterans affected by traumatic experiences connected with their military service have appeared somewhat reluctant to join extant treatment services dominated by older Vietnam veterans, and their rates of utilization of PTSD and SUD services in the VA are relatively low. That they are of a different generation is sometimes a perceived barrier to help seeking, and veterans of recent conflicts (e.g., the Gulf War) and peacekeeping efforts often express the view that their service was less traumatic than Vietnam, World War II, or Korea. In fact, these younger veterans almost always receive a strong welcome from their older comrades. Also, most treatment programs strongly emphasize that it is inappropriate to compare one's trauma to that of others.

Among Gulf War veterans seeking health-related care the most commonly diagnosed medical conditions include PTSD, alcohol abuse and dependence, and medically unexplained physical symptom syndromes (Engel et al., 1999). Compared with military personnel not deployed to the Persian

Gulf, those who participated in the war show higher rates of PTSD and SUD, although absolute levels of PTSD appear lower than in previous wars (Iowa Persian Gulf Study Group, 1997). Two years after the war, Wolfe, Erickson, Sharkansky, King, and King (1999) found a rate of PTSD of 8%. Despite limited American casualties, the conflict did include "pockets of trauma" in which such events as intense combat and death by friendly fire occurred. Some veterans found themselves exposed to high levels of trauma by nature of their job assignments. Sutker, Uddo, Brailey, Vasterling, and Errera (1994), for example, found high rates of PTSD (48% current, 65% lifetime) in non-help-seeking Desert Storm troops assigned grave-registration duties. In this sample, PTSD diagnoses were frequently documented in association with alcohol use disorders. Sutker, Uddo, Brailey, Allain, and Errera (1994) found a significant positive correlation between combat exposure and alcohol problems in African American troops who performed these same duties. Studies of Gulf War veterans suggest that clinicians need to attend to many of the same issues so prominent in Vietnam veterans with PTSD, including the prevention of occupational performance problems (Engel et al., 1999), the management of anniversary reactions (Morgan, Hill, Fox, Kingham, & Southwick, 1999), and the reduction of psychological stress associated with exposure to environmental toxins. They should remember, however, that increased health symptom reporting is unlikely to be exclusively psychogenic in origin; it is associated with exposure to environmental pesticides, debris from Scud missiles, chemical and biological warfare agents, and smoke from tent heaters, after controlling for war zone exposure and PTSD (Proctor et al., 1998).

Although the stresses encountered on peacekeeping missions may differ somewhat from combat stressors, studies of veterans serving in these nontraditional military roles indicate that experiences associated with peacemaking or peacekeeping can also cause PTSD, high levels of general psychological distress, or both (e.g., Fontana, Litz, & Rosenheck, 2000; Litz, Orsillo, Friedman, Ehlich, & Batres, 1997; Stuart & Halverson, 1997). For example, 8% of Somalia peacekeepers met criteria for PTSD 5 months after their return to the United States (Litz et al., 1997), and more than one third of participants met criteria for general "psychiatric caseness" (Orsillo, Roemer, Litz, Ehlich, & Friedman, 1998). This is perhaps not surprising, given that such humanitarian missions can involve, in addition to conventional military dangers, exposure to extreme climates; mass suffering and death; body handling; violent confrontations with locals; and an inability to prevent harm to starving, impoverished noncombatants. In these last few situations, personnel may be required to witness violence without being able to intervene. In a study of Somali peacekeepers, Fontana et al. (2000) found that severity of PTSD in both men and women was related not only to exposure to combat but also to exposure to the dying of the Somali people and to sexual harassment from military personnel. Clinicians should take note of this last finding and assess previous experiences with sexual harassment in their male, as well as female, patients.

FEMALE VETERANS

Only a few studies of the relationships among trauma, PTSD, and SUD in female veterans have been performed to date. In the National Vietnam Veterans Readjustment Study (Kulka et al., 1990), female Vietnam veterans with PTSD showed a lifetime rate of 29% for alcohol disorders, higher than those without PTSD; 10% of female veterans with current PTSD had a current alcohol use disorder, compared with less than 2% of women without PTSD. Lifetime rates of alcohol abuse or dependence among Vietnam theatre veterans were greater than those observed in era veterans or civilians. In a national study of the health status of female veterans seeking ambulatory care, Hankin, Spiro, Miller, and Kazis (1999) found that those who reported being sexually assaulted while in the military were twice as likely to screen positive for symptoms of current alcohol abuse than those who did not.

Ouimette, Wolfe, and Chrestman (1996) examined the characteristics of PTSD–alcohol abuse comorbidity in a group of 52 non-help-seeking female veterans. Their sample included 12 women diagnosed with PTSD and alcohol abuse/dependence, 13 women with PTSD only, and 22 control participants with neither diagnosis; all had served during the Vietnam era. A useful aspect of the study was the separation of gender-based stressors (e.g., sexual harassment) from "traditional" military stressors. Results indicated that women diagnosed with PTSD and alcohol abuse/dependence were more likely to report a history of childhood sexual abuse, and they reported a greater number of childhood traumas, more sexual assaults as adults, and more gender-based wartime stress than both comparison groups. They did not differ in terms of other trauma variables, including exposure to traditional war zone stressors. In relation to symptoms, dual-diagnosis women reported more PTSD, dissociation, and borderline personality disorder symptoms than the comparison groups.

Taken together, these findings are similar to those obtained with male veterans, in that trauma exposure and PTSD are both associated with alcohol abuse/dependence (see also Davis & Wood, 1999) and survivors with both PTSD and alcohol problems experience more symptoms than those with PTSD only. However, childhood sexual abuse, sexual assault, and gender-based stressors, rather than levels of exposure to traditional war stressors, appear most related to concurrent PTSD and alcohol problems. Clinically speaking, this means that treatment is often focused on their experience of sexual assault rather than combat trauma. The presence of men can often act as a powerful trauma reminder, which means that if male helping professionals are part of the treatment team, they must be well trained and sensitive to the experience of sexual assault survivors.

ASSESSMENT AND INTERVENTION

Treatment Outcome Research

It is possible that SUD–PTSD veterans will have worse outcomes following treatment than those with either disorder alone. Ouimette and her colleagues (Ouimette, Ahrens, Moos, & Finney, 1997, 1998; Ouimette, Moos, & Finney, 2000) have published a series of reports following the course of treatment for male veterans being seen in VA SUD programs. Their work suggests that patients with concurrent PTSD and SUD appear to benefit less from treatment than both those with SUD only and those with comorbid Axis I disorders. Ouimette, Ahrens, et al. (1998) compared male veterans with concurrent SUD and PTSD (SUD–PTSD), those with SUD problems only (SUD), and substance-abusing patients with another (non-PTSD) Axis I disorder (SUD–PSY) in terms of changes during treatment. Compared with SUD patients, those with concurrent PTSD improved less during treatment in several domains of change: psychological distress, coping skills, and adaptive cognitions. Relative to the SUD–PSY group, SUD–PTSD patients reported more distress and expected fewer benefits from stopping substance use. One year after termination of treatment, SUD–PTSD patients were significantly worse than both comparison groups on measures of problems due to substance use, psychological distress, and support from friends (Ouimette et al., 1997). Compared with SUD patients, they were less likely to be employed and had higher rates of readmission for SUD or psychiatric treatment. Overall, these findings suggest that a diagnosis of PTSD limits the effectiveness of conventional SUD treatment. However, PTSD status in these studies was established by chart diagnoses, the reliability and validity of which are unknown and probably resulted in an underestimation of rates of PTSD. It is possible that patients in these studies who were diagnosed with PTSD presented with more severe symptoms or otherwise differed from patients whose PTSD went unrecognized. Research using standardized diagnostic interviews is required before these findings can be extended to include the general population of veterans with chronic PTSD who are seen in SUD treatment settings.

Many researchers and clinicians have argued that treatment for veterans who suffer with both PTSD and SUD problems, like their civilian counterparts, will be more effective if both sets of problems are addressed explicitly in treatment. However, there is little empirical evidence to support such arguments at present. Some unpublished studies do suggest that integrated SUD–PTSD treatment may be effective (e.g., Abueg, Fairbank, Penk, & Gusman, 1995; Donovan, Padin-Rivera, & Kowaliw, 2001). For example, Donovan et al. (2001; Donovan & Padin-Rivera, 1999) evaluated a comprehensive 12-week partial hospitalization treatment for 46 veterans with PTSD and polysubstance (70%) or alcohol dependence (30%) diagnoses. Their comprehensive approach involves 10 hours of group therapy per week and includes a wide range of program elements. It emphasizes peer support, includes attention to both childhood and war zone issues, and incorporates a variety of therapeutic methods (e.g., sand tray exercises, skills training, behavioral homework, drug-free housing). Veterans were treated in cohorts of up to 8 clients and were assessed at pre- and posttreatment and at 6- and 12-month follow-ups. The researchers reported significant reductions in Clinician-Administered PTSD Scale scores (Blake et al., 1990) from pre- to posttreatment, and most gains in PTSD symptoms were maintained at both follow-up periods. Significant reductions in substance use (days of alcohol use, alcohol use to intoxication, and polysubstance use) were achieved during treatment and maintained at follow-ups. Although the study's strengths include use of a manual-based protocol, assessment by an independent evaluator, and a 12-month follow-up period, in the absence of a control group the observed gains cannot be attributed to the treatment. Also, veterans included in the study were required to have participated in conventional SUD treatment before entering the dual-diagnosis program, and posttreatment substance use variables were compared with substance use before completion of the traditional program, so any improvements cannot be attributed to the latter program. Overall, the study suggests that PTSD and SUD problems can be significantly improved by treatment, but the study design limits any strong conclusions as to the actual benefits of an *integrated* SUD–PTSD treatment.

Other research has suggested that treatment for PTSD can enhance SUD treatment outcomes. Ouimette, Moos, and Finney (2000) found that amount of outpatient PTSD service use after completion of inpatient SUD treatment was a major predictor of SUD outcomes. Relative to other types of visits (psychiatric, SUD), number of PTSD visits in the second year and total number of PTSD visits over the 2 years after hospitalization had the largest effects on remission from SUDs. Consistency of PTSD care (two or more sessions per month for varying lengths of time) also predicted remission: A significantly higher proportion of SUD–PTSD patients who received consistent care for 3 months or longer were in remission from SUD and substance dependence. However, as the authors acknowledged, one cannot conclude from this study that PTSD treatment causes increased rates of remission from SUD. Patients may have self-selected into participation in

PTSD outpatient care on the basis of various other characteristics that may have affected outcome. Nonetheless, the findings cited here provide some suggestive preliminary evidence that addressing traumatic stress and PTSD in SUD treatment will improve outcomes for veterans. Further development of approaches that integrate treatment of the two disorders is needed, and randomized controlled trials are necessary to demonstrate that such treatments improve on conventional services.

Clinical Care

As indicated above, the treatment of veterans with PTSD and SUD is more art than science; practice guidelines based on empirical studies are not yet available. Nonetheless, it is possible to outline some practical implications of existing research and note potentially important treatment considerations.

First, clinicians who work with veterans should routinely assess substance use patterns and routinely screen for trauma exposure and PTSD. This may be especially important in work with female veterans. Grossman, Willer, Stovall, Maxwell, and Nelson (1997) examined discharge diagnoses of male and female veterans hospitalized at an urban VA medical center and found evidence of the underdiagnosis of both PTSD and SUDs in their sample of women. With regard to screening for trauma history, it is important to recognize that screening should extend to all types of trauma. Exposure to non-combat-related trauma is common among veterans (Hankin et al., 1999). Investigations of male substance-abusing veterans particularly indicate high rates of childhood physical and sexual abuse (e.g., Krinsley, Brief, Weathers, & Steinberg, 1994; Schaefer, Sobieraj, & Hollyfield, 1988; Triffleman et al., 1995). Triffleman et al. (1995) administered the Trauma Antecedents Questionnaire (Herman, Perry, & Van der Kolk, 1989) to 44 veteran SUD inpatients and found that 77% reported being exposed to at least one type of severe childhood trauma, and 48% had experienced two or more childhood traumas. These rates of exposure mean that veterans seeking SUD treatment often have PTSD as a result of traumatic experiences, especially childhood trauma, that are not related to combat. In fact, Triffleman et al. (1995) found that of veterans receiving inpatient SUD treatment and diagnosed with lifetime PTSD, 28% were cases of non-combat-related PTSD. A variety of instruments have been developed to systematically assess past history of exposure to both military (Keane, Newman, & Orsillo, 1997) and civilian (Norris & Riad, 1997) traumatic events, and PTSD screening tools have been developed for use in medical settings (e.g., Andrykowski, Cordova, Studts, & Miller, 1998) and epidemiological research (e.g., Breslau, Peterson, Kessler, & Schultz, 1999).

If a veteran is being treated for PTSD and an SUD problem is detected, it is very possible that motivation to change alcohol or drug use will be low. The patient may see his or her SUD problem as less important than PTSD, or alcohol and drugs may be perceived as a helpful ways of coping with trauma-related distress. Clinicians should therefore assess patients' motivation to abstain and set specific treatment goals with regard to all substances; often veterans may see the need to change their use of one substance but plan on continuing use of another. Attention to motivation may be especially important during the initial period of abstinence, when substance-abusing patients with comorbid PTSD will require strong support. There is significant overlap between symptoms of PTSD and opiate withdrawal (Salloway, Southwick, & Sadowsky, 1990), which may in part explain why anecdotal reports indicate that withdrawal symptoms may be associated with an increase in traumatic memories; exacerbation of PTSD symptoms; and, possibly, increased suicide risk (e.g., Daniels & Scurfield, 1992; Kosten & Krystal, 1988). Clinicians should prepare their patients for possible short-term worsening of PTSD symptoms and teach them strategies for managing symptoms and urges to drink or use other drugs. In general, clinicians should be alert to risk of dropout from care. Boudewyns, Woods, Hyer, and Albrecht (1991) reported that violation of a treatment policy prohibiting substance use was the primary reason among veterans with combat-related PTSD for not completing inpatient PTSD treatment.

If PTSD is identified in a veteran who is being treated for SUD, a number of considerations are in order. Research suggests that male substance-abusing veterans with PTSD (e.g., Hyer et al., 1991; Schaefer et al., 1988; Sharkansky, Brief, Peirce, Meehan, & Mannix, 1999) or with histories of childhood trauma (e.g., Krinsley et al., 1994) experience higher levels of subjective distress and other problems than SUD patients without PTSD or childhood trauma. Such problems may include more years of substance use, more symptoms of substance dependence, and more treatment episodes. They may also include a greater number of problems in living, including legal problems, social conflicts, violent behavior, assault charges, and suicide attempts. Female substance-abusing veterans with PTSD have been found to report more severe PTSD symptoms than women with PTSD only (Ouimette et al., 1996). These increased rates of problems mean that these veterans will often require more frequent practitioner contact and longer treatment.

Much of the treatment of SUD, of course, involves training in skills for managing problem situations without drinking or using other drugs. With SUD–PTSD veterans it is important to supplement general relapse prevention methods with attention to potential trauma-related relapse situations (Abueg & Fairbank, 1991). A key role of the clinician is to help the patient identify individual high-risk situations and prepare him or her to cope with them. Part of the task is to motivate the veteran to change. A general commitment to PTSD or alcohol treatment may not extend to a similar desire to reduce violence, confront avoided situations, develop more intimacy with others, or reduce hypervigilance behaviors. The nonconfrontational motivation-building approaches developed by Miller and Rollnick (1992) may be especially helpful in this regard. Murphy, Cameron, Sharp, and Ramirez (1999) recently described a manual-based group intervention that applies these approaches to veterans with PTSD to encourage them to contemplate and commit to changing a range of trauma-related problems.

Although all veterans will need to cope with many, many situations that provoke PTSD symptoms, or urges to use substances, or both, and there is great variation in the individual profile of such situations, especially important for many will be skills for coping with commonly occurring (but difficult to manage) relapse triggers: PTSD symptoms themselves, interpersonal anger and conflict, trauma-related guilt, and social isolation.

Veterans report frequent use of alcohol and drugs in response to PTSD symptoms and lack confidence in their ability to manage symptoms without resorting to substance use. The literature specifically suggests that veterans with PTSD may use alcohol to reduce symptoms of arousal. In addition to anxiety management skills (i.e., muscular or imaginal relaxation, breathing retraining, self-talk), tools for staying "grounded" and avoiding being overwhelmed by emotion are important. The Seeking Safety treatment protocol developed by Najavits (Najavits, Weiss, Shaw, & Muenz, 1998; see also chapter 8, this volume) includes a variety of useful grounding tactics, including repeating "safety statements" (e.g., "My name is _____ and I am safe right now," "I am in the present, not the past"), touching objects in the immediate environment and noticing how they feel, and looking at the photographs of loved ones.

Research has documented significant anger control problems (e.g., Chemtob, Hamada, Roitblat, & Muraoka, 1994) and violence (McFall, Fontana, Raskind, & Rosenheck, 1999) in veterans with PTSD. Aggression and hostility in substance-abusing veterans are associated with use of more negative coping strategies (escape–avoidance, distancing, and confrontational coping) and less confidence in personal ability to resist substances when confronted with high-risk situations, especially unpleasant internal states, rejection, and conflict with family and friends (McCormick & Smith, 1995). PTSD-related anger is usually experienced by the veteran as rapid in onset (all or nothing), intense, and difficult to control. Anger treatments designed specifically for veterans with PTSD have been described (Novaco & Chemtob, 1998; Reilly, Clark, Shopshire, Lewis, & Sorensen, 1994), and preliminary evidence supports their utility (Chemtob, Novaco, Hamada, & Gross, 1997).

Some of the distress associated with war-related memories is generated by feelings of guilt. In fact, nearly two thirds of Vietnam veterans may experience moderate or greater guilt related to war experiences (Kubany et al., 1996). Veterans often experience these guilt feelings as relatively intractable, grounded in fact rather than being a product of interpretation or judgment. Simple discussion usually fails to modify these beliefs, and clinicians, like patients, can feel unsure of how to address them. Kubany's (1998) systematic cognitive therapy approach provides people who work with veterans with a helpful analysis of the nature of thinking errors and faulty conclusions that drive trauma-related guilt, procedures for guilt assessment, and practical advice for restructuring guilt cognitions.

Skills for escaping social isolation are also important in recovery. Many veterans with chronic PTSD and SUD problems have only occasional and brief contacts with others. Social isolation contributes to loneliness and a sense of purposelessness in their lives, and it creates a fertile ground for negative thinking. Isolated veterans lack companionship, friendship, emotional intimacy, and emotional and practical support for sobriety, factors that could in principle aid in their recovery. Probably the major factor motivating veterans to endure the stresses of psychological treatment is a desire to improve their relationships with partners and family members. Also, when veterans enter residential PTSD or SUD treatment settings, they usually greatly value the connection with other veterans; it often appears that the mutual support, understanding, and friendship evident among the patients deserves much credit for whatever therapeutic improvement is observed. For these reasons, it is crucial that counselors work with veterans to reduce social anxiety, improve communication and friendship skills, and increase participation in social activities. For this to happen, however, it is not enough to simply offer brief training in generic communication skills. Rather, social connection should be made a specific and sustained target of treatment, accompanied by regular therapeutic assignments to participate in family activities, join in social contact with other veterans, participate in appropriate volunteer and veterans' organizations, or some combination of these. As veterans experiment with these situations they will need ongoing support, help in solving problems, and instruction in managing conflicts.

In part because many veterans with SUD–PTSD are socially isolated and lack a social group that will support their abstinence, 12-step programs can play a potentially very important role in their recovery. In this context, attendance at Alcoholics Anonymous or Narcotics Anonymous meetings provides an opportunity to make a positive change in the social environment of veterans. Moreover, it provides a "laboratory" in which to address many of their interpersonal problems: social anxiety, social skills deficits, difficulties with intimacy and trust, feeling unsafe in groups of people, and so on.

Although it has often been assumed that veterans with PTSD will have special difficulties in affiliating with the groups (Satel, Becker, & Dan, 1993), some recent research suggests that they have similar rates of posttreatment participation as veterans with substance abuse problems only (Ouimette et al., 2001). However, rates of participation are modest for both groups, and clinicians should, when appropriate, target affiliation as a treatment goal. It is important to assess for and, where necessary, address, negative attitudes toward participation in support groups as well as significant levels of social anxiety and deficits in social skills that may interfere with participation. With regard to women, consideration should be given to the fact that exposure to 12-step groups composed largely of men may present a real problem for those with a history of male-perpetrated sexual assault; use of women's meetings may be preferable, especially early in recovery. Consistent with clinical experience suggesting the utility of self-help group participation, Ouimette, Ahrens, et al. (1998) found that greater 12-step involvement was associated with a number of positive changes during treatment for participants with both PTSD and SUD: greater use of positive appraisal and problem-solving coping, less use of emotional discharge coping, and fewer psychological symptoms at discharge. Greater posthospital 12-step group participation has also been found to be associated with remission from SUDs over a 2-year period following inpatient hospitalization for SUD (Ouimette, Moos, & Finney, 2000).

Summary

Data that indicate whether addressing traumatic stress and PTSD in the context of SUD treatment will improve outcomes for veterans are extremely limited at present. It is clear that veterans with an SUD–PTSD dual diagnosis experience higher levels of distress and more problems in living than veterans with SUD only, and there is some suggestion that substance-abusing veterans with concurrent PTSD will have worse outcomes after treatment. Clinicians should routinely screen for SUD, trauma history, and PTSD in their veteran patients; set specific treatment goals for all substances; provide strong support during the initial period of abstinence; provide training in management of PTSD symptoms, interpersonal anger and conflict, trauma-related guilt, and social isolation; and take concrete steps to increase affiliation and engagement with self-help support groups.

CHALLENGES IN SERVICE DEVELOPMENT

An extensive network of treatment services is available for veterans experiencing PTSD, SUD, or both within the national Veterans Health

Administration, the VA's health care system. At the current time, 173 medical centers are supplemented by more than 391 outpatient, community, and outreach clinics, including the VA's 205 Readjustment Counseling Service Vietnam Veteran Outreach Centers ("Vet Centers"). These helping services address PTSD and SUD by means of general mental health counseling; specialist SUD detoxification, residential, and outpatient services; specialist PTSD residential and outpatient services; and a smaller number of dual-disorder SUD–PTSD services that attempt to integrate treatment for the disorders. Veterans commonly receive help for their problems in sequential fashion, first participating in SUD treatment and then being referred for treatment focusing on PTSD. PTSD services routinely address SUD recovery as part of their care.

In the past, the VA has not provided an environment that is sensitive to the needs of female veterans with dual PTSD and SUD. Women have sometimes been treated in inpatient units surrounded by male patients, which is a major problem given that sexual assault is so commonly part of their history. To receive help, women have had to enter a hospital environment peopled largely by men, to see primarily male treatment providers. With the development around the country of a number of women's outpatient trauma treatment services, the establishment of women's residential programs specializing in treatment of PTSD, and the designation of women's coordinators at all VA medical facilities, this situation is changing for the better. At the current time, the VA treatment system is a rich resource for veterans with PTSD and SUD, providing easy and widespread access to services targeting both disorders. Clinicians treating veterans in non-VA treatment settings are therefore in a position to supplement their care with referrals to relatively intensive specialized services to address the needs of their patients with PTSD, SUD, or both.

Although the VA has been a leader in explorations of integration of PTSD and SUD treatment (e.g., with the establishment of dual-diagnosis substance use and PTSD treatment programs), it is interesting to note that awareness of the link between the two disorders has failed to effectively penetrate traditional SUD treatment services in the VA. Ouimette, Ahrens, et al. (1998), in their study of outcomes for SUD–PTSD patients in VA inpatient SUD programs, noted that none of the 15 programs studied included PTSD-focused treatment components. If a better integration of treatment for these disorders is to be achieved, it will be necessary to identify and explore ways of challenging the barriers to such integration.

A first barrier is the need to persuade individuals in decision-making positions that an integrated approach to treatment will help veterans. A proximal step in accomplishing such persuasion will be the implementation of improved PTSD and trauma screening by SUD treatment staff. Systematic screening will increase rates of identification of veterans with trauma histories and PTSD and increase awareness on the part of clinicians and administrators. Better dissemination of the kind of information presented in this chapter will be helpful in the persuasion effort, but it is incumbent on the individuals advocating change to empirically demonstrate improved outcomes for veterans when trauma and PTSD are addressed during SUD treatment. Particularly useful will be comparisons of sequential versus integrated treatment of the two disorders.

Barriers also exist at the level of the individual provider. The vast majority of those who provide traditional SUD counseling services to veterans have received little education or training about trauma and PTSD. Most believe that substance use problems should be the central focus of their attention and that other issues (e.g., trauma history) are better tackled at a later time. It is likely that some staff will not see it as part of their role to address PTSD, and some staff (and patients) will be generally fearful of discussing traumatic experiences. Some specialized SUD–PTSD interventions (e.g., therapeutic exposure) are likely to be difficult to implement in the absence of experienced trauma therapists and therefore unlikely to be delivered widely. Training will be required if SUD programs are to increase rates of assessment of PTSD and delivery of PTSD-informed treatment. At the present time, materials to assist providers in bringing trauma-related issues into SUD treatment for veterans are not widely available.

At the organizational level, the separation of SUD and PTSD treatment services means that providers treating the two disorders may be physically separated and limited in their knowledge of each other's relevant expertise and services. Moreover, the reality of separate services sometimes sets up turf battles in which different programs compete for access to patients. Perhaps the greatest barrier is simply the fact that existing programs have their own traditional way of doing things. It is important, therefore, that those interested in bringing PTSD issues into SUD treatment be sensitive to the traditions and strengths of that treatment and design their approaches in ways that are compatible with existing substance care and that attempt to complement rather than supplant that care.

As a final comment on service development, it is important to note that awareness of the SUD–PTSD relationship should reach beyond specialized mental health and SUD treatment services into other settings where these patients may present themselves. In particular, primary care physicians and nurses should be trained to better identify and respond to the needs of SUD–PTSD patients. Davis and Wood (1999) suggested that female veterans with SUD and sexual trauma histories show physical health problems and are likely to seek help in primary care clinics. Hankin et al. (1999) studied a representative sample of 2,160 male veterans being seen in Boston ambulatory care facilities and reported that patients who experienced a traumatic event in the past year or during their lifetime were twice as likely to meet criteria for an alcohol-related disorder as those with no such experience. Of patients who screened positive for PTSD, 24% also screened positive for an alcohol-related disorder. Of those who met screening criteria for alcohol problems, 39% screened positive for PTSD.

Although many clinicians and researchers have spoken to the need to better integrate treatment for the two sets of problems, practical models of such integration require further systematic development. The ability to design more effective treatments for veterans will depend on better understanding of the impact of alcohol and other drugs on PTSD symptoms and of the effects of PTSD on SUD recovery. That treatment informed by this understanding will achieve greater reductions in PTSD symptoms, other trauma-related problems, and use of substances remains to be demonstrated through careful evaluative research.

11

POSTTRAUMATIC STRESS DISORDER AND SUBSTANCE USE DISORDER AMONG INCARCERATED WOMEN

CYNTHIA L. BATTLE, CARON ZLOTNICK, LISA M. NAJAVITS, MARYSOL GUTIERREZ, AND CELIA WINSOR

Over the past 20 years, there has been a dramatic increase in the number of women housed in U.S. jails and prisons. According to a report from the Bureau of Justice Statistics (U.S. Department of Justice, 1999b), approximately 3.2 million women were arrested in 1998, representing 22% of all arrests made that year. These arrests resulted in more than 950,000 women incarcerated or placed on probation by the U.S. correctional system, with roughly 85,000 confined to state or federal prisons. These numbers reflect a substantial increase over arrest and incarceration rates of women 10 and 20 years ago, with a significantly larger proportion of adult women having some involvement with the corrections system. Between 1985 and 1998, the rate of women confined to state or federal prisons increased by 238%, from 1 woman in 4,167 imprisoned in 1985 to 1 woman in 1,230 imprisoned in 1998; during that same 13-year period, the per capita rate of women in jails also nearly doubled (U.S. Department of Justice, Bureau of Justice Statistics, 1999b). Furthermore, the incarceration rate for women is growing at a considerably faster pace than that of men. For example, between 1990 and 1996, felony convictions among women in the state court system increased by 44%, a growth rate 2.5 times greater than that of male defendants (U.S. Department of Justice, Bureau of Justice Statistics, 1999b).

In the following sections we review empirical findings regarding the two most prevalent psychiatric disorders found among this growing population of incarcerated women: substance use disorder (SUD) and posttraumatic stress disorder (PTSD), as well as existing and developing treatments designed to address these complex interconnected problems. We also review the most common offenses leading to women's incarceration, sociodemographic characteristics of this population, and the connections among women's victimization, substance use, and criminality. Our discussion of "incarcerated women" includes women detained in county jails (typically awaiting trial or convicted of misdemeanor offenses), women confined in state and federal prisons (typically serving longer sentences for felony convictions) and, when data are available, adolescent female offenders serving time in juvenile detention centers or training schools. Although the focus of this chapter is on incarcerated women with PTSD and SUD, these problems are clearly salient for men as well. For more information on the prevalence of PTSD, SUD, and other disorders among male inmates, readers may refer to Gibson et al. (1999); Powell, Holt, and Fondacaro (1997); and Teplin (1994). Treatment outcome data on substance abuse programs for male offenders have recently been presented by Hiller, Knight, and Simpson (1999); Martin, Butzin, and Inciardi (1995); and Wexler, De Leon, Thomas, Kressel, and Peters (1999).

OFFENSES LEADING TO WOMEN'S INCARCERATION

The crimes that most typically result in women's incarceration are nonviolent and substance-related. Drug offenses are currently the single most common type of criminal behavior resulting in women's incarceration. The Bureau of Justice Statistics reported that nearly three quarters of women in federal prisons in 1998 were incarcerated for drug offenses and that these types of convictions have increased sharply in recent decades (U.S. Department of Justice, 1999b). In 1986, 1 out of every 8 female inmates in the state prison system was serving time for a drug offense; by 1991, 1 in 3 female inmates was serving time for this type of offense (U.S. Department of Justice, Bureau of Justice Statistics, 1994). Between 1990 and 1996, the rate of women's drug possession convictions increased by 41%, and drug trafficking convictions rose by 34% (U.S. Department of Justice, Bureau of Justice Statistics, 1999b).

Even when drug possession and trafficking do not constitute the primary reason for the arrest, evidence suggests that women's criminal behavior is frequently drug related. A 1997 survey of state prisoners documented that over 40% of female inmates were under the influence of drugs at the time of their offense, compared with 32% of male inmates (U.S. Department of Justice, Bureau of Justice Statistics, 1999a). Furthermore, 62% of female inmates surveyed in 1997 reported drug use in the month prior to their offense, a rate that is significantly higher than the 56% of men who reported such use. With regard to male and female detainees in U.S. jails, the Bureau of Justice Statistics reported that 70% were either regular drug users or had committed a drug offense and that 16% of all offenses had been committed to obtain money for drugs (U.S. Department of Justice, 2000b).

Although media reports have suggested that women are perpetrating violent offenses at an increasing rate, crime statistics have shown that women are responsible for only a small percentage of such offenses, and this number is on the decline. On the basis of a survey of victims of violent crimes between 1993 and 1997, the vast majority of violent offenders (86%) were men (U.S. Department of Justice, Bureau of Justice Statistics, 1999b). A recent epidemiologic study of 805 female prisoners reported that only 11% had been incarcerated for violent crimes (Jordan, Schlenger, Fairbank, & Caddell, 1996). Moreover, the Bureau of Justice Statistics reported that the number of violent crimes committed by women in 1997 had decreased 25% compared with that reported in 1994, just 3 years earlier (U.S. Department of Justice, 1999b).

CHARACTERISTICS OF FEMALE PRISONERS

Although women of every age, race, and socioeconomic group are incarcerated in U.S. jails and prisons, certain groups are clearly overrepresented. What qualities characterize the "typical" incarcerated woman? In Table 11.1 some key sociodemographic characteristics of female prisoners are presented. A nationwide survey of state prison inmates (U.S. Department of Justice, Bureau of Justice Statistics, 1994) indicates that the majority of female prisoners are unmarried women of color between the ages of 25 and 34. Black, non-Hispanic women comprise the single, largest racial group. Most incarcerated women have a high school diploma or a general equivalency diploma but have not obtained higher education beyond that degree. Just over half of the incarcerated women surveyed (53%) were unemployed at the time of their arrest. The majority come from economically impoverished circumstances: Thirty-seven percent of women surveyed in 1997 reported an income of under $600 per month prior to their arrest, and 30% were receiving welfare assistance.

Most women in U.S. jails and prisons are mothers. Roughly 7 out of 10 women involved in the correctional system have children under the age of 18, including 65% of women serving sentences in state prisons and 59% of women confined in federal prisons. In addition, between 5% and 6% of women are pregnant at the time of their admission to state prisons and county jails (U.S. Department of Justice, Bureau of Justice Statistics, 1999b), and one study documented that 25% were either currently pregnant or recently postpartum (Leukefeld, 1995, cited by Veysey, 1998). Incarcerated women are likely to be the parent with primary custodial responsibility prior

TABLE 11.1
Sociodemographic Characteristics of Female Prisoners

Characteristic	Percentage of female inmates
Race/ethnicity[a]	
White, non-Hispanic	36.2
Black, non-Hispanic	46.0
Hispanic	14.2
Other	3.6
Age (years)[a]	
17 or younger	0.1
18–24	16.3
25–34	50.4
35–44	25.5
45–54	6.1
55 or older	1.7
Education[a]	
8th grade or less	16.0
Some high school	45.8
High school graduate	22.7
Some college or more	15.5
Marital status[a]	
Married	17.3
Widowed	5.9
Divorced	19.1
Separated	12.5
Never married	45.1
Family characteristics	
Women with children under age 18[b]	65.0
Employment[a]	
Employed	46.7
Unemployed	53.3

[a]Based on data from the Bureau of Justice Statistics (U.S. Department of Justice, 1994).
[b]Based on data from the Bureau of Justice Statistics (U.S. Department of Justice, 1999b).

to their admission to prison. Whereas 90% of male prisoners with minor children reported that another parent had custody of their children, only 25% of female inmates reported that they did not have primary custody (U.S. Department of Justice, Bureau of Justice Statistics, 1994). Most incarcerated mothers have two or more children, and the Bureau of Justice Statistics has estimated that there are over 1.3 million American children with mothers under some form of correctional sanction (U.S. Department of Justice, Bureau of Justice Statistics, 1999b).

In terms of family background, the majority of women in prison (58%) grew up in a household without both parents present. Many female inmates reported that at least one family member had been previously incarcerated (46%), and one third reported a parental history of drug or alcohol abuse (U.S. Department of Justice, Bureau of Justice Statistics, 1994).

Prevalence of Psychiatric Disorders Among Incarcerated Women

Recent research has revealed that a strikingly high percentage of incarcerated women and adolescent female offenders suffer from psychiatric disorders. Prevalence rates for many of these disorders are elevated not only in comparison to the general female population but also when compared with incarcerated males (Cauffman, Feldman, Waterman, & Steiner, 1998; Jordan et al., 1996; Teplin, Abram, & McClelland, 1996; Veysey, 1998). Table 11.2 displays findings from two recent epidemiologic studies demonstrating prevalence rates of PTSD, SUD, and traumatic exposure in this population: Teplin et al.'s (1996) investigation of psychiatric disorders among 1,272 female pretrial jail detainees in Chicago and Jordan et al.'s (1996) study of 805 women admitted to the North Carolina prison system.

SUD is by far the most prevalent disorder among incarcerated women. Seventy percent of all female jail detainees had either a drug or alcohol use disorder (32.3% met criteria for alcohol abuse or dependence, and 63.6% met criteria for drug abuse or dependence). In the prison population, the rate of SUDs was also high, with 38.6% of female prisoners meeting criteria for alcohol use or dependence and 44.2% diagnosed with drug abuse or dependence (Jordan et al., 1996). PTSD was the next most prevalent psychiatric disorder, affecting 33.5% of women surveyed (Teplin et al., 1996). Although the exact prevalence of PTSD was not obtained in the prison study, Jordan et al. (1996) reported that 30% of their sample had experienced a serious traumatic event and also suffered from six or more PTSD symptoms

TABLE 11.2
Lifetime Prevalence Rates of Psychiatric Disorders and Exposure to Traumatic Events Among Incarcerated Women

Diagnosis	Pretrail jail detainees[a]	Prisoners[b]
Alcohol use/dependence	32.3	38.6
Drug use/dependence	63.6	44.2
Posttraumatic stress disorder	33.5	30.0[c]
Exposure to traumatic events	—	78.0
Any of the disorders assessed	80.6	64.0

Note. All table values are percentages. Dash indicates data were not reported.
[a]*N* = 1,272. The data in column 1 are from "Prevalence of Psychiatric Disorders Among Incarcerated Women: 1. Pretrial Jail Detainees," by L. A. Teplin, K. M. Abram, and G. M. McClelland, 1996, *Archives of General Psychiatry, 53*, p. 507. Copyright 1996 by the American Medical Association. Reprinted with permission.
[b]*N* = 805. The data in column 2 are from "Prevalence of Psychiatric Disorders Among Incarcerated Women: 2. Convicted Felons Entering Prison," by B. K. Jordan, W. E. Schlenger, J. A. Fairbank, and J. M. Caddell, *Archives of General Psychiatry, 53*, pp. 515–517. Copyright 1996 by the American Medical Association. Reprinted with permission.
[c]Reflects percentage of women who reported both exposure to a traumatic event as well as six or more symptoms of posttraumatic stress disorder.

during the 6 months prior to the interview. Following SUD and PTSD, the next most common psychiatric disorders were major depressive episode (16.9% among jail detainees, 13% among prisoners), antisocial personality disorder (13.8% among jail detainees, 11.9% among prisoners), and dysthymia (9.6% among jail detainees, 7.1% among prisoners). Altogether, over 80% of the women in the jail sample and 64% of women in the prison sample met criteria for at least one psychiatric disorder at some point in their lifetime.

Results from independent quantitative and qualitative studies of incarcerated populations have supported the finding that SUDs and PTSD are two of the most prevalent mental health problems among incarcerated women in the United States (Cauffman et al., 1998; Fogel & Belyea, 1999; Greene, Haney & Hurtado, 2000; McClellan, Farabee, & Crouch, 1997; Owen & Bloom, 1995; Peters, Strozier, Murrin, & Kearns, 1997; Richie & Johnson, 1996; Sanders, McNeill, Rienzi, & DeLouth, 1997; Welle, Falkin, & Jainchill, 1998; Zlotnick, 1997), and the high rate of these disorders is frequently hypothesized to be a significant contributor to criminal recidivism in this population. Using structured diagnostic interviews to assess for PTSD and a range of psychiatric disorders among a randomly selected sample of 85 incarcerated women, Zlotnick (1997) found that 68% of these women met criteria for current or lifetime PTSD. In the first study of PTSD among incarcerated female delinquents, Cauffman et al. (1998) conducted structured diagnostic interviews with 96 incarcerated female adolescents aged 13–22 and determined that over 65% of respondents had experienced PTSD at some point in their lives, and an additional 9.5% met partial diagnostic criteria for lifetime PTSD.

Compared with the general population of women in the United States, incarcerated women are substantially more likely to have SUD or PTSD. Based on the findings of Teplin et al. (1996) reported above, rates of PTSD among incarcerated women (33.5%) are three times higher than rates of PTSD reported in a sample of community women (10.4%; Kessler, Sonnega, Bromet, Hughes, & Nelson, 1995). Prevalence rates of SUDs are even more discrepant when compared with the general population. Jordan et al. (1996) and Teplin et al. (1996) contrasted their findings with data from the Epidemiologic Catchment Area Study (Robins & Regier, 1991) and found that incarcerated women were at least six times more likely to have an alcohol use disorder, and at least seven times more likely to have a drug use disorder, depending on age and ethnicity. For example, 41.7% of White female jail detainees between the ages of 18 and 25 were diagnosed with alcohol use or dependence, whereas 6.7% of White women in the community met criteria for this diagnosis.

It is interesting that the difference in prevalence rates between incarcerated and nonincarcerated women varied by racial group. Among both jail detainees and state prisoners, rates of most psychiatric disorders were considerably higher among non-Hispanic White women than among African American and Hispanic women. For example, of the seven disorders assessed in Jordan et al.'s (1996) prison study, the lifetime prevalence rate was significantly higher among White women for five of the disorders (major depressive episode, dysthymia, panic disorder, alcohol use or dependence, and drug use or dependence). Jordan et al. interpreted this to indicate that "among white women, only the most deviant or disturbed are likely to be incarcerated, whereas African American women may be incarcerated for less serious or frequent offenses" (p. 518). Teplin et al. (1996) also suggested that the higher rates of disorder among White people may reflect biases against racial minority groups and the poor. They noted that racial minority arrestees are often poorer than their White counterparts and may therefore be unable to afford bail or the legal representation necessary to facilitate an immediate release.

In sum, psychiatric morbidity is very common among incarcerated women, with 64%–80% of this population meeting criteria for a psychiatric disorder at some point in their lifetime. SUD is the most prevalent disorder in both jail and prison populations, followed by PTSD. Rates of both SUD and PTSD are markedly elevated among incarcerated women compared with community populations. In the following sections we review research findings regarding patterns of drug and alcohol use and the types of traumatic events experienced by female offenders prior to their incarceration.

Patterns of Substance Abuse Among Incarcerated Women

What substance abuse patterns are characteristic of incarcerated women? Among female state prison inmates, the most commonly used drug 1 month prior to the offense was cocaine/crack (36.5%; U.S. Department of Justice, 1994). Marijuana was the second most common drug (20.5%), followed by heroin/opiates (15.9%), stimulants (7.6%), depressants (5.0%), and hallucinogens (2.2%). The high prevalence of crack and cocaine use by female offenders represents a shift in drug use patterns. According to the Bureau of Justice Statistics (U.S. Department of Justice, 1994), in the mid-1980s marijuana was a more frequently used drug among female prisoners than crack/cocaine. By 1991, however, prevalence rates of marijuana use had declined from 30.5% to 20.5%, and rates of crack/cocaine use had become more popular, increasing from 23.3% to 36.5% in this population.

Research indicates that patterns of alcohol and drug use between male and female inmates differ in important ways. Compared with their male counterparts, women in prison generally report heavier and more frequent drug use, including greater use in the month before their offense (U.S. Department of Justice, Bureau of Justice Statistics, 1999b), and greater likelihood of using drugs at the time of their offense (Peters et al., 1997; U.S. Department of Justice, Bureau of Justice Statistics, 1994). Moreover, 1 out of every 4 female prisoners stated that they had committed their crime to pay for drugs, compared with 1 out of every 6 male prisoners (U.S. Department of Justice, Bureau of Justice Statistics, 1994). Female prisoners are also more likely than male prisoners to report a history of intravenous drug use and a history of sharing needles for the injection of illicit drugs. Henderson (1998) reviewed empirical research on female offenders' substance abuse patterns and noted that women's initiation into drug use often stems from opposite-sex relationships, a route of entry into the drug culture less frequently reported by men. Although female inmates report a higher prevalence of drug use than their male counterparts, men report significantly higher levels of alcohol use and dependence (U.S. Department of Justice, Bureau of Justice Statistics, 1994). Among state prison inmates, 72.8% of men reported that they had used alcohol sometime during the year prior to their offense, compared with 57.7% of women. Furthermore, about one third of male inmates indicated that they used alcohol on a daily basis, compared with 19% of female inmates (U.S. Department of Justice, Bureau of Justice Statistics, 1994).

Types of Traumatic Exposure Among Incarcerated Women

It is possible that the most universal experience among incarcerated women is a history of exposure to traumatic events. Research on female prison and jail inmates have found that an exceedingly high percentage of this population—between 77% and 90%—has a history of some type of traumatic exposure (Browne, Miller, & Maguin, 1999; Cauffman et al., 1998; Fogel & Belyea, 1999; Greene et al., 2000; Jordan et al., 1996; Lake, 1993; Owen & Bloom, 1995; Richie & Johnson, 1996; Zlotnick, 1997). Investigators have used several different methods to assess the types of antecedent traumas experienced by incarcerated women, some with questions exclusively about childhood events (e.g., physical or sexual abuse by a caretaker) and others that assess adult experiences as well (e.g., rape, domestic assault, physical assault by a stranger). Between 29% and 70% of women in these studies reported a history of childhood physical abuse; sexual abuse ranged from 18% to 59%. Greene et al. (2000) reported that 60% of their sample had witnessed domestic assault as a child. Owen and Bloom (1995) found that 40% recalled experiencing childhood emotional abuse. In terms of traumatic events during adulthood, domestic violence was the most frequently reported experience, affecting between 59% and 90% of incarcerated women (Browne et al., 1999; Fogel & Belyea, 1999; Lake, 1993; Owen & Bloom, 1995). Other common victimization experiences in adulthood included rape (30% in Lake's sample; 32% in Owen & Bloom's sample), robbery (41%; Lake, 1993), and physical assault by a stranger (37%; Lake, 1993).[1]

Exposure to traumatic events is considerably lower in nonincarcerated populations. On the basis of data from the National Comorbidity Survey, Kessler et al. (1995) found that 51.2% of the survey's 5,877 female respondents reported exposure to at least one traumatic event, compared with 77%–90% in samples of incarcerated women.

In sum, the vast majority of women in jails and prisons report exposure to traumatic events, with childhood abuse and domestic assault most commonly reported. Even when compared with the high base rate of traumatic exposure among community women, traumatic exposure among incarcerated women is markedly elevated.

Comorbidity of PTSD and SUD Among Incarcerated Women

Although SUDs and PTSD are the most prevalent clinical disorders among incarcerated women and perhaps the most critical, intertwined causes of recidivism, very little data have been published regarding the prevalence of SUD–PTSD comorbidity within this population. In a study of 85 randomly selected women prisoners, Zlotnick (1997) found that 58 participants (68% of the sample) met criteria for current or lifetime PTSD; these inmates were significantly more likely to have a concurrent SUD compared with those without PTSD (91.4% of women with PTSD reported a history of SUD, in contrast to 66.7% of women without PTSD). The co-occurrence of PTSD and SUD is well documented in the general community. For example, Kessler et al. (1995) reported that when participants in the National Comorbidity Survey had a PTSD diagnosis there was a 2.5-fold increase in the risk for alcohol abuse or dependence and a 4.5-fold increase in the risk for drug abuse or dependence. On the basis of these high rates of comorbidity of PTSD and SUD in the general community, and the fact that incarcerated women report high rates of both SUD alone and PTSD alone, the dual diagnoses of SUD and PTSD is a likely phenomenon among women prisoners, albeit an understudied one.

CONNECTIONS AMONG WOMEN'S VICTIMIZATION, SUBSTANCE USE, AND CRIMINALITY

The steady influx of women into U.S. jails and prisons, coupled with the predominance of substance abuse and traumatic histories in this

---

[1] All of the above findings were subject to some degree of self-report bias: either underreporting (e.g., lack of disclosure due to shame regarding the victimization experience or anxiety related to self-disclosure) or overreporting (e.g., embellishing or fabricating events to "justify" one's involvement in

population, has spurred a growing literature examining the complex and interconnected relationships among women's victimization experiences, substance use, and criminal behavior. Informed by psychological, sociological, medical, legal, and criminal justice perspectives, theories have pointed to family histories of violence and substance abuse as critical factors that increase a young woman's risk for future problems such as running away from home, becoming involved in violent adult relationships, abusing drugs and alcohol, and ultimately engaging in criminal behavior (Browne et al., 1999; Chesney-Lind, 1997; Covington, 1999; Gilfus, 1992; Peugh & Belenko, 1999; Sable, Fieberg, Martin, & Kupper, 1999; Veysey, 1998). The impact of socioeconomic factors such as racism and poverty on the lives of these women has also been emphasized. For example, racial biases may directly or indirectly influence arrest and sentencing decisions; a poor woman's lack of financial resources may limit access to adequate legal representation.

Prospective longitudinal studies that can help clarify the temporal and causal relationships between these problems are rare. However, some empirical research has shown a correlational link between exposure to traumatic experiences—such as childhood abuse, adult rape, or domestic violence—and future criminal acts. Using cross-sectional data, Lake (1993) found that women who had been victims of domestic violence had significantly more arrests for criminal behavior than women who had not experienced domestic assault. Owen and Bloom (1995) summarized findings from several studies suggesting that women who are convicted of murder were likely to target their violence toward men who had previously abused them. Perhaps most convincing in establishing an association between childhood victimization and criminality is Widom's (1989) prospective, longitudinal study of abused and nonabused girls. Widom found that the study's matched cohort of abused girls were significantly more likely to engage in future adult criminal activity (15.9%) than girls who were not abused (9.0%).

Two general hypotheses explain the association between exposure to trauma and criminality. First, as Widom's (1989) study suggests, early victimization may be a precursor to criminal behavior, either directly or mediated by substance abuse-related crimes. The association between traumatic exposure and substance abuse is frequently explained with the *self-medication hypothesis* (cf. Khantzian, 1985), which posits that an overwhelming traumatic experience (such as childhood abuse) occurs, and the survivor turns to drugs or alcohol to treat distressing symptoms of PTSD, such as the re-experiencing of traumatic memories and persistent increased arousal. A woman's comorbid substance dependence can, in turn, then lead to

---

crime). Although the authors of these studies generally suspected that underreporting is much more of an issue in distorting results, the extent or exact nature of the bias is unknown.

criminal involvement, by means of drug possession or trafficking charges or other crimes committed to obtain drugs or drug money. Excessive anger and risk-taking behavior stemming from past victimization may also increase a woman's risk for arrest.

Second, the link between criminal behavior and exposure to trauma may be explained by the increased vulnerability to traumatic events (such as physical assault or rape, or both) or involvement in high-risk criminal behavior such as prostitution and illegal drug use. On the basis of the results from their study of 150 female inmates in New York, Browne et al. (1999) highlighted the early timing of victimization experiences reported by these women and asserted that it is "unlikely that victimization precipitated simply by drug use or criminal activity increased the cumulative lifetime prevalence figure significantly" (p. 317). Because the studies just discussed were all based on correlational data, a causal link between past trauma and criminal behavior cannot be assumed, because other, nonidentified intervening factors, such as the relational quality of the family of origin and socioeconomic factors, may account for the relationship between interpersonal violence and criminality.

Another factor in understanding the rise in women's incarceration rates in the past 20 years are changes in the drug use patterns in recent decades, particularly the increase in cocaine and crack addiction among women in the 1980s and 1990s and the use of prostitution and other criminal behavior to maintain access to these drugs (Chesney-Lind, 1997; Henderson, 1998; Peugh & Belenko, 1999). These changes in patterns of drug use, combined with a nationwide trend toward harsher sentences for drug-related crimes (e.g., mandatory minimum sentencing requirements such as "three-strikes" laws), have resulted in more women serving sentences for crimes that in previous years would not have led to incarceration. The nationwide movement to "get tough on crime" was welcomed by many Americans as a way to address the public's growing fear of crime; however, this legislative movement and the resultant influx of criminals into the country's jails and prisons has also been criticized as expensive and only minimally effective, or ineffective, in reducing crime rates (see Glaser, 1997). Owen and Bloom (1995) asserted that "the criminality of women has not increased; instead, the legal response to drug-related behavior has become increasingly punitive, resulting in a flood of less serious offenders in the State and Federal prison systems" (p. 175).

Finally, in a unique study of both incarcerated women and their children, Greene et al. (2000) emphasized the cyclical and intergenerational quality of the problems associated with women's incarceration. On the basis of interviews with 102 incarcerated mothers in three correctional institutions in California, they found that the majority of children of incarcerated women had experienced the same kind of criminologic influences (witnessing violence, experiencing physical or sexual abuse) that the mothers had experienced. The authors reported that the "parallels in their traumatic social histories were dramatic and disturbing . . . 83% of the [incarcerated] mothers' children had either been sexually or physically abused, or had witnessed violence in the home, almost identical to the frequency among the mothers themselves" (p. 11).

TREATMENT FOR INCARCERATED WOMEN WITH PTSD AND SUD

In spite of the growing demand for services to address the needs of incarcerated women, particularly those with PTSD, SUD, or both, resources for treatment remain sparse. As of yet there are no empirically validated treatments to address comorbid SUD and PTSD in this population. Most jail- and prison-based programs that do exist are designed for male inmates with substance abuse problems and do not systematically address victimization issues or the specific needs of women (Henderson, 1998; Peters et al., 1997; Peugh & Belenko, 1999; Prendergast, Wellisch, & Falkin, 1995). Browne et al. (1999) argued that targeted interventions to address posttraumatic symptomatology within the prison or jail setting will improve women's psychological and behavioral adjustment both prior to and following their release into the community. Peugh and Belenko (1999) also stressed the importance of recognizing incarcerated women's histories of victimization and designing appropriate interventions to address their problems. In a comprehensive review of the needs and rights of female jail detainees with mental disorders, Veysey (1998) similarly urged for more comprehensive PTSD assessment and treatment for incarcerated women. Some evidence suggests that attention to women's victimization histories during their incarceration may help lower recidivism rates. Canestrini (1994, cited by Browne et al., 1999) followed 220 women who participated in 6–12 months of treatment in a program for survivors of family violence and found that these women were half as likely to be convicted of a subsequent crime compared with those who did not participate in the treatment program. Incarcerated women themselves appear motivated to receive services for both substance abuse and interpersonal violence. In a recent survey designed to assess the needs of incarcerated women, the service most frequently rated as very important was a service related to childhood physical and sexual abuse, and over 80% of the women rated drug dependency/addiction-related services as very important (Sanders et al., 1997).

Project WORTH (Women's Options for Recovery, Treatment and Health) researchers Welle et al. (1998) conducted an in-depth ethnographic study to examine treatment approaches used within eight prison and community-based programs serving substance-abusing female offenders in

New York and Oregon. Although the programs they studied were primarily designed to treat substance abuse, the authors noted that these programs have increasingly made efforts to address women's extensive victimization histories. Such efforts included establishing safe, therapeutic environments that use therapeutic sanctions rather than punitive sanctions; decreasing or eliminating use of confrontational techniques commonly used in this type of treatment; and continuing support services after release to assist women who relapse. Emphasizing the high percentage of incarcerated women with traumatic histories, they argued that "in drug treatment for women offenders, it is no longer adequate to address women's criminal activity without also addressing women's experiences as crime victims" (p. 160).

In designing and implementing appropriate treatments for female inmates with PTSD and SUD, the individual needs of incarcerated women and how these needs are influenced by their larger context (i.e., the prison setting and their community) need to be considered. Several issues on both the individual level and the system level must be taken into account.

The Needs of the Incarcerated Woman

Female offenders typically enter jail or prison with multiple interpersonal and socioeconomic stressors. As noted earlier, most incarcerated women are economically impoverished, unemployed, and have limited education. Many are unmarried mothers of young children. The majority has experienced traumatic events, frequently childhood abuse, domestic assault, or both. In developing programs for incarcerated women, researchers have stressed the need for services that address women's victimization experiences and substance abuse problems, as well as their physical health needs (e.g., treatment and risk reduction of HIV and sexually transmitted diseases) and their roles as custodial parents (e.g., promoting reunification after release and providing parenting classes; Chesney-Lind, 1997; Covington, 1999; Fogel & Belyea, 1999; Greene et al., 2000; Peters et al., 1997; Peugh & Belenko, 1999; Pollack, 1998; Sanders et al., 1997; Veysey, 1998). Furthermore, researchers have recommended a more integrated continuum of care for female substance abusers in the criminal justice system. Compared with nonincarcerated substance abusing clients, these women often face a wider range of problems, such as the perceived stigma of a criminal record and dual challenges of recovery and re-entry into society (Barthwell et al., 1995; Hiller et al., 1999; Peters et al., 1997). Also, treatment interventions need to help female substance abusers released from prison face the many challenges that may place them at risk for returning to substance use. After release some women will return to high-risk drug neighborhoods and families that provide little support for continuation of treatment (Peters et al., 1997), and some women will return to partners who physically and emotionally assault them (Richie, 2000).

Treatment Within a Jail or Prison System

Systemic issues have significant impact on the delivery and effectiveness of treatment within a jail or prison environment. As noted earlier, treatments targeting inmates' PTSD symptomatology are considerably less common than those addressing substance abuse. This relative inattention to offenders' traumatic histories could be due to lack of specialized mental health training for counselors serving this population and to lack of readily available and empirically valid treatments to address PTSD and SUD, as well as to a general concern among corrections staff regarding "opening up" trauma-related issues in this population.

The prison setting also poses challenges for incarcerated women in that inmates are typically afforded very little privacy and control while incarcerated. For women who have been victimized, particularly those suffering from PTSD, the coercive nature and lack of control inherent in the confinement setting may be particularly threatening (e.g., pat downs, strip searches, inmate counts in the middle of the night) and may make it difficult to reduce PTSD symptoms even when treatment is available. Some researchers have suggested that aspects of jail and prison environments can inadvertently retraumatize women with PTSD, ultimately exacerbating symptoms and increasing behavioral problems (Covington, 1999; Heney & Kristiansen, 1997; Maeve, 2000; Veysey, 1998).

Prendergast et al. (1995) conducted a survey of 234 prison, jail, and community-based programs serving offenders with substance abuse problems across the United States, with the aim of assessing the availability and appropriateness of services for women. Although these researchers acknowledged the increase in gender-specific services for incarcerated women, they also identified several obstacles that limit female offenders' access to effective treatment, including a general lack of programming, poor assessment of women's mental health needs (beyond substance abuse issues), and poor linkages with follow-up and transitional programs. Prendergast et al. concluded that "the availability of treatment for women offenders falls far short of what is needed, and the treatment that is available does not necessarily offer the types of services that women need" (p. 246).

FUTURE TREATMENTS FOR FEMALE OFFENDERS WITH COMORBID SUD–PTSD

Although there currently are no empirically validated treatments for incarcerated women with a dual diagnosis of PTSD and SUD, some emerging treatments may be relevant to this population. One such program is Najavits and colleagues' Seeking Safety treatment, a 24-session cognitive–behavioral group program designed specifically for women with both PTSD and SUD (Najavits, Weiss, & Liese, 1996; Najavits, Weiss, Shaw, & Muenz, 1998; chapter 8, this volume). In contrast to treatments designed for men with combat-related PTSD, this treatment emphasizes issues that have increased relevance for women, such as the tendency to engage in self-blame and experience revictimization (Najavits et al., 1996). The primary goals of the treatment are (a) to achieve abstinence from substances and (b) personal safety. Strong emphasis is also placed on the development of self-care skills and avoiding relationship patterns that re-evoke past abusive relationships. In focusing on personal safety, self-care, and abstinence—rather than the exploration of traumatic events—this treatment is consistent with first-stage or early treatment recommendations for both PTSD and SUD (Najavits et al., 1996).

Several aspects of the Seeking Safety treatment may make it particularly useful in treating comorbid PTSD and SUD. First, the treatment uses cognitive–behavioral self-control strategies such as impulse control methods, cognitive restructuring, and anger management and cue exposure, techniques that have been successfully used in the past to treat both disorders. Second, the treatment teaches participants how to successfully manage negative affect; this skill is important to individuals with PTSD and SUD, who may experience anger, episodic depression, anxiety, and irritability, all of which can interfere with daily functioning as well as the therapeutic process. Third, the treatment teaches functional behaviors that may have never been learned or may have deteriorated because of substance use or the sequelae of trauma (e.g., relationship skills, self-nurturing, problem solving, adaptive lifestyle skills). Fourth, the treatment offers explicit training in relapse prevention, another critical skill area for this population. Findings from a preliminary outcome study of the Seeking Safety treatment on a small sample of dually diagnosed nonincarcerated women indicate that this treatment may be effective in increasing abstinence, decreasing substance use, reducing subtle PTSD symptoms, and improving participants' interpersonal problems (Najavits, Weiss, Shaw, & Muenz, 1998).

With regard to serving the specific needs of incarcerated women, one helpful aspect of the Seeking Safety treatment is that it uses various strategies to make the material engaging and accessible for women in early recovery who may suffer from poor concentration and impulse control problems. The strategies used (e.g., visual aids, role preparation, memory enhancement techniques) may prove particularly helpful for incarcerated women with PTSD and SUD, who typically present with concentration difficulties, poor impulse control, dissociative symptoms, and anger management problems (Zlotnick, 1999). The Seeking Safety treatment also targets many of the deficits found in the population of incarcerated women that may interfere with their recovery and place them at higher risk for reoffending—in particular impulsiveness, anger dyscontrol, and maladaptive lifestyle activities. Zlotnick and her colleagues Lisa Najavits and Damaris Rohsenow are currently conducting a pilot study to examine the feasibility, acceptability, and initial efficacy of the Seeking Safety program in treating incarcerated women with both PTSD and SUD.

ALTERNATIVES TO INCARCERATION

In light of the increasingly high cost of incarceration and the low threat to society that most female offenders pose, several researchers have advocated community-based alternatives to incarceration. These proposed programs emphasize maintaining relationships with children; achieving family stability; changing "negative lifestyles"; and focusing on women's strengths, development, and empowerment (Browne et al., 1999; Buccio-Notaro, Molla, & Stevenson, 1996; Covington, 1999; Owen & Bloom, 1995). Advocates of this approach suggest that treatment efforts are more likely to be successful when implemented outside of a confinement setting and that community-based programs will have a more positive impact not only on the women themselves but also on their children and families.

California's Options for Recovery (OFR) is an example of an innovative community-based pilot program for female offenders. OFR was designed for pregnant and parenting female offenders with SUDs; instead of incarceration, this program allowed women to live in the community and maintain closer connections to their children, while receiving intensive substance abuse treatment and case management services. Berkowitz, Brindis, Clayson, and Peterson (1996) conducted a multimethod evaluation of the OFR program. Outcome data regarding reductions in drug use and criminal activity were not reported; however, qualitative findings from interview and survey data indicated that the program had a positive impact on interagency relationships, increased public and judicial awareness regarding the complex issues associated with substance-abusing female offenders, and prompted significant expansion in the continuum of services available to women. Of interest is that although the services provided to participants and their children were quite extensive, OFR's approach to treatment was found to have significantly lower costs than those associated with traditional incarceration with a substance abuse treatment component. From a therapeutic standpoint, the risk of the traditional prison setting exacerbating symptoms of women with PTSD and SUD is an additional reason to explore alternatives to incarceration for this population. With regard to the complex array of problems in the lives of female offenders, Berkowitz et al. argued:

> Unlike prisons, community-based programs are better equipped to address the multiple needs of female offenders, including drug addiction,

physical and sexual abuse, unemployment, and family relationships. Without these treatment components, the web of poverty, addiction, and social dysfunction that afflicts the lives of many chemically dependent women is likely to remain unbroken. (p. 32)

CONCLUSION

Women comprise a rapidly growing proportion of inmates in U.S. prisons and jails, and research has indicated that these women are primarily convicted of nonviolent, drug-related crimes. An expanding body of literature has examined the characteristics and needs of this population and has revealed that a remarkably high percentage of incarcerated women have experienced victimization as children and adults and often enter prison with existing SUDs. Recent epidemiologic findings suggest that prevalence rates of both PTSD and SUD among female inmates are significantly elevated— more than twice as high as rates of these disorders among women in the general community. In spite of the increased need for services for female prisoners with PTSD and SUD, treatment options remain limited, and the interconnected problems of PTSD and substance dependence are hypothesized to be major causes of recidivism in this population. To address these issues, researchers have advocated for the development and implementation of more appropriate gender-specific treatments for incarcerated women, including greater emphasis on the long-term impact of childhood victimization and increased use of community-based alternatives to incarceration. Although there are currently no empirically validated treatments to treat incarcerated women with SUD–PTSD, some emerging treatments may be relevant in meeting the needs of this population. Mental health professionals have a key role in providing comprehensive assessment and treatment for incarcerated women with these disorders.

12

COMORBIDITY OF SUBSTANCE USE DISORDERS AND POSTTRAUMATIC STRESS DISORDER IN ADOLESCENTS

ROSE M. GIACONIA, HELEN Z. REINHERZ, ANGELA D. PARADIS, AND CECILIA K. STASHWICK

Few studies have investigated the comorbidity of substance use disorders (SUDs) and posttraumatic stress disorder (PTSD) among adolescents, despite overwhelming evidence that contemporary adolescents are at substantial risk for developing SUD (Johnston, O'Malley, & Bachman, 2000; Kessler et al., 1994; Reinherz, Giaconia, Lefkowitz, Pakiz, & Frost, 1993; Warner, Kessler, Hughes, Anthony, & Nelson, 1995) and experiencing serious traumas and PTSD (Deykin, 1999; Giaconia et al., 1995; March & Amaya-Jackson, 1993; Pfefferbaum, 1997; Saigh, Green, & Korol, 1996). There is a growing body of research with adult populations concerning the prevalence, onset, course, sequelae, and treatment of SUD–PTSD comorbidity (Breslau et al., 1998; Brown & Wolfe, 1994; Kessler et al., 1997; Najavits, Weiss, & Shaw, 1997; Ouimette, Brown, & Najavits, 1998), but there is little corresponding research about SUD–PTSD comorbidity among adolescent populations. Studies of adults can provide clues about the link between adolescent SUD and traumas/PTSD, but they may not accurately reflect the increased levels of risk for SUD and PTSD faced by more recent generations of adolescents (Cottler, Compton, Mager, Spitznagel, & Janca, 1992; Johnson & Gerstein, 1998; Norris, 1992). Neither can these adult studies adequately appraise the impact of SUD–PTSD comorbidity on psychosocial functioning during adolescence, a distinct and critical developmental period when youth are still acquiring the social, educational, and occupational skills they will need throughout adulthood (Arnett, 2000; Newcomb & Bentler, 1988; Parrish, 1994).

This chapter focuses on SUD–PTSD comorbidity research studies conducted with clinical and community samples of adolescents. The goals of this review are to: (a) evaluate the prevalence, patterns of onset, and impact of SUD–PTSD comorbidity on psychosocial functioning; (b) assess whether research with adolescents supports current explanations for the link between SUD and PTSD; (c) identify key areas in which additional research is needed; and (d) provide implications for the identification, assessment, and treatment of comorbid SUD–PTSD.

RISKS FOR SUD AND PTSD AMONG ADOLESCENTS

Two complementary lines of research strongly demonstrate that all of the requisite elements for SUD–PTSD comorbidity—substance use, SUD, traumas, and PTSD—are not only prevalent among adolescents in the general population, but may be increasing. Considered collectively, these studies emphasize the potential for extensive SUD–PTSD comorbidity among adolescents and underscore the importance of examining the prevalence and onset of this comorbidity during adolescence, when it is likely to first emerge.

Rates of SUD in Adolescents

The first line of research on SUD highlights that adolescent alcohol and drug use disorders are widespread and emerging at increasingly earlier ages. Cross-generational epidemiological studies of SUD have uniformly identified middle to late adolescence as a peak risk period for first onset of serious alcohol and drug abuse or dependence and have documented a marked increase in lifetime rates in recent generations (Burke, Burke, Rae, & Regier, 1991; Kessler et al., 1994; Warner et al., 1995). In addition, recent community studies of adolescents have established that lifetime rates of SUD are substantial (10%–32%). Lewinsohn, Hops, Roberts, Seeley, and Andrews (1993) reported that 10.8% of their community sample of youth in Grades 9–12 met diagnostic criteria for alcohol or drug abuse or dependence as defined by the *Diagnostic and Statistical Manual of Mental Disorders* (3rd edition, revised [DSM–III–R]; American Psychiatric Association, 1987). Reinherz et al. (1993) found even higher lifetime rates in a predominately White, working-class community of 18-year-olds; 32.4% met *DSM–III–R* criteria for alcohol abuse or dependence, and 9.8% had a lifetime diagnosis of drug abuse or dependence. In a subsequent report examining the ages of onset of these disorders, Giaconia et al. (1994) found that approximately one third of adolescents with lifetime alcohol (32.2%) or drug (36.8%) disorders experienced the onset of these disorders by as early as age 14. Furthermore, ongoing national research initiatives targeting school-age youth continue to chronicle alarming rates of the alcohol and drug use that are precursors of later SUD in adolescents, as well as increasingly earlier ages of initiation into substance use (Centers for Disease Control and Prevention [CDC], 2000; Segal & Stewart, 1996; Weinberg, Rahdert, Colliver, & Glantz, 1998). For example, before age 13, nearly one third (32.2%) of youth nationwide have consumed alcohol, and 11.3% have used marijuana (CDC, 2000).

Rates of Traumas and PTSD in Adolescents

A second, parallel line of research on traumas and PTSD has firmly established the vulnerability of children and adolescents for experiencing a wide range of serious traumatic events and subsequently developing PTSD (Cuffe et al., 1998; Deykin, 1999; Giaconia et al., 1995; March & Amaya-Jackson, 1993; Pfefferbaum, 1997; Saigh et al., 1996). Although most studies of PTSD in adolescents have focused on youth exposed to specific traumas such as natural disasters, crime, and war (Saigh, Yasik, Sack, & Koplewicz, 1999), a small number of community studies have investigated the prevalence of a full range of traumas and PTSD among children and adolescents (Deykin, 1999). These community studies have demonstrated that, with the obvious exception of combat, adolescents are at risk for all types of "qualifying" traumas required for a diagnosis of PTSD (*DSM–III–R* and *DSM–IV*; American Psychiatric Association, 1987, 1994), including rape, physical assault, seeing someone hurt or killed, natural disasters, threat of injury or harm, narrow escape, sudden injury or accident, receiving news about the sudden death or injury of someone close, and learning that any of these events happened to a close friend or relative. Giaconia et al. (1995) reported that 43% of their sample had experienced at least one *DSM–III–R* trauma, and 6.3% overall (or 14.5% of those exposed to traumas) subsequently developed PTSD. Cuffe et al. (1998) determined that 16% of their sample of adolescents and young adults aged 16–22 years experienced a lifetime *DSM–IV* trauma, and 12.4% of those exposed to traumas met criteria for a current (past-year) diagnosis of PTSD. Perkonigg, Kessler, Storz, and Wittchen (2000), whose sample included German adolescents and young adults aged 14–24 years, found that 21.4% reported any *DSM–IV* trauma, and 7.8% of those with lifetime traumas subsequently developed PTSD. Similarly, among the youngest group (aged 15–24 years) included in the U.S. National Comorbidity Survey, 8% met lifetime *DSM–III–R* criteria for PTSD (Kessler, Sonnega, Bromet, Hughes, & Nelson, 1995).

Adolescents are especially vulnerable for experiencing traumas involving interpersonal violence, such as assault, rape, and robbery (CDC, 2000; U.S. Department of Justice, Bureau of Justice Statistics, 2000a), types of traumas that are most frequently linked to PTSD in both adolescents and adults (Cuffe et al., 1998; Deykin & Buka, 1997; Giaconia et al., 1995;

Kessler et al., 1995). Boney-McCoy and Finkelhor (1995) found that 41% of a U.S. nationwide sample of youth aged 10–16 years had experienced some type of violent victimization such as physical or sexual assault. Similarly, in a more recent survey of a nationally representative sample of U.S. youth aged 12–17 years, Kilpatrick et al. (2000) determined that 47% had either experienced lifetime victimization or had witnessed violence; 5% of youth in the sample met *DSM–IV* criteria for a current (past-year) diagnosis of PTSD. Mazza and Reynolds (1999) reported substantially higher rates among young adolescents in an inner-city neighborhood; 93% had been exposed to at least one violent event in the past year, and 6.4% manifested clinically significant levels of PTSD symptoms.

PREVALENCE OF COMORBID SUD–PTSD

The preceding findings on the prevalence of substance use, SUD, traumas, and PTSD among adolescents illustrate the potential magnitude of SUD–PTSD comorbidity among youth. Three additional types of information may be more directly valuable in understanding the actual scope of SUD–PTSD comorbidity among adolescents: (a) estimates of the overall prevalence of SUD–trauma and SUD–PTSD in community groups; (b) rates of traumas and PTSD among adolescents with SUD (or, conversely, rates of SUD among youth exposed to traumas or with PTSD); and (c) indexes summarizing the extent to which SUD, traumas, and PTSD are associated (e.g., chi-square tests of independence and odds ratios indicating degree to which youth with SUD are at greater risk for traumas/PTSD than their peers without SUD).

Overall Rates of SUD–Traumas and SUD–PTSD

Estimates of the overall prevalence of SUD–PTSD comorbidity among adolescents in the general population serve several purposes. First, this basic information can alert clinicians, teachers, and others who work with adolescents about the level of risk for SUD–PTSD comorbidity faced by youth in community settings. Second, these prevalence estimates can be used by policymakers in formulating decisions about the allocation of resources for prevention and treatment efforts (Saigh et al., 1996).

The scant research on overall rates of SUD–PTSD comorbidity among adolescents in community settings suggests that these disorders frequently co-occur and may pose a serious threat to the mental health of contemporary youth. In a study of 18-year-olds in a predominately White, working-class community, Giaconia et al. (2000) determined that 18.5% of these adolescents met *DSM–III–R* criteria for a lifetime SUD (alcohol or drug abuse or dependence) and had experienced at least one qualifying trauma; 3.6% of the total sample (or 8.5% of those exposed to traumas) met all DSM–III–R lifetime criteria for both SUD and PTSD. There were no significant gender differences in lifetime rates of SUD–PTSD comorbidity, although females were at somewhat greater risk for SUD–PTSD than their male counterparts (5.2% of females vs. 2.1% of males). These findings are consistent with community studies of adults that have documented substantial comorbidity of SUD and PTSD in the general population (Breslau, Davis, Andreski, & Peterson, 1991; Breslau et al., 1998; Kessler et al., 1995).

Rates of Traumas and PTSD in Adolescents With SUD

Documenting the prevalence of traumas and PTSD in adolescents with SUD can play a crucial role in informing those who work with this client group about the likelihood that these adolescents will currently have or subsequently experience these additional difficulties. Descriptive findings from clinical and community studies consistently demonstrate that substantial proportions of adolescents with SUD have also experienced serious traumas (50%–75%), developed PTSD (11%–47%), or both. In a study of adolescents with alcohol dependence, Clark, Lesnick, and Hegedus (1997) reported that 59% of these adolescents (aged 14–18 years) experienced one or more DSM–III–R trauma, and 13% met DSM–III–R lifetime criteria for PTSD. Deykin and Buka (1997) determined that three quarters (74.7%) of the chemically dependent adolescent inpatients in their study had been exposed to DSM–III–R traumas, and 30% had a lifetime diagnosis of PTSD. In another study of inpatient adolescents aged 13–19, Koltek, Wilkes, and Atkinson (1998) found that 47% of the adolescents with SUD also experienced PTSD.

Community studies have found similarly high rates of trauma and PTSD among adolescents with SUD. Giaconia et al. (2000) established that 55.5% of 18-year-olds with SUD reported at least one lifetime trauma, and 10.9% met DSM–III–R lifetime criteria for PTSD. Similarly, in a nationwide sample of adolescents, Kilpatrick et al. (2000) determined that 51.9% of adolescents with current (past-year) alcohol abuse or dependence had been physically assaulted, 75% had witnessed violence, and 16% met criteria for current PTSD. Among adolescents with a current marijuana disorder, 46.4% had been physically assaulted, 84% had witnessed violence, and 22% had current PTSD.

Rates of SUD in Adolescents With Traumas and PTSD

Although less frequently reported than rates of PTSD among youth with SUD, rates of SUD among adolescents who have experienced traumas and PTSD are also substantial. Data from a community study of 14- to 24-year-olds (Perkonigg et al., 2000) indicate that 34.7% of participants who had experienced *DSM–IV* traumas also had a lifetime *DSM–IV* SUD. Among those with a diagnosis of PTSD, 5.3% had a comorbid SUD. Furthermore, Lipschitz, Winegar, Hartnick, Foote, and Southwick (1999) reported that, among inpatient adolescents aged 11–18 years, 25% with PTSD also had a current diagnosis of alcohol abuse.

Relationship Between SUD and Traumas/PTSD

Complementing descriptive findings about rates of traumas and PTSD among adolescents with SUD are correlational findings characterizing the extent to which youth with SUD are at increased risk for traumas and PTSD, as compared with their peers without SUD. Studies that included a community comparison group uniformly demonstrate that adolescents with SUD are at a significantly elevated risk for experiencing any lifetime trauma (two- to fivefold) and for developing PTSD (four- to ninefold; Clark et al., 1997; Giaconia et al., 2000; Kilpatrick et al., 2000). Adolescents with SUD are especially at a heightened risk (two- to fivefold) for experiencing the types of traumas most likely to result in PTSD, including violent victimization, such as physical and sexual assault, and witnessing violence or harm to others (Clark et al., 1997; Giaconia et al., 2000; Kilpatrick et al., 2000). Kilpatrick et al. (2000) further demonstrated that risk for PTSD varied by type of SUD. Compared with their non-SUD peers, adolescents with alcohol abuse or dependence were at a fourfold risk for PTSD, whereas those with marijuana abuse or dependence were at a sixfold risk, and adolescents with hard drug abuse or dependence were at the greatest risk for subsequently developing PTSD (ninefold risk).

PATTERNS OF ONSET OF SUD–PTSD COMORBIDITY

As with the treatment of adults, identifying the temporal patterns of onset of SUD–PTSD comorbidity in adolescents can facilitate an understanding of the etiology of this pair of disorders and can aid in planning treatment interventions. Research findings about sequencing of onset typically are based on cross-sectional data that compare self-reported respective ages of onset of SUD and trauma/PTSD and classify *onset* as: (a) SUD precedes trauma/PTSD, (b) SUD and trauma/PTSD occur at the same age, or (c) SUD follows the onset of trauma/PTSD. Recent studies, both within and across clinical and community studies of adolescents, have found no overall sequencing of onset that definitively characterizes this comorbidity;

rather, results indicate that there are diverse and multiple pathways leading to the comorbidity of SUD and trauma/PTSD during adolescence and suggest that patterns of onset may differ depending on type of SUD, type of trauma, and gender.

Onset of SUD and Traumas

Results from Giaconia et al.'s (2000) study reflect the finding that no overall pattern of sequencing of onset has been reported for SUD and traumas; for about half (56.3%) of the adolescents in the sample the onset of SUD preceded that of the earliest trauma, for 18.3% both occurred during the same year, and for 25.4% the SUD emerged later than the trauma. Yet results from Perkonigg et al.'s (2000) study illustrate that the onset of disorder may be influenced by type of SUD. In their study, alcohol disorders were almost equally likely to precede (45.0%) and to follow (39.7%) trauma, with a smaller portion of SUD and traumas emerging in the same year (15.3%). For drug disorders, however, SUD preceded trauma for 65.9%, followed trauma for 31.8%, and occurred in the same year for only 2.3%. Clark et al. (1997) determined that although traumas preceded SUD in 76% of their inpatient adolescents, the sequencing of onset varied substantially by type of trauma: Traumas preceded SUD for 40% of adolescents who had witnessed violence and only 23% of those who had experienced violent victimization. Considered collectively, these results indicate that the development of SUD–trauma is a complex process that may be influenced by both the type of SUD and the type of trauma.

Onset of SUD and PTSD

Studies determining the patterns of onset for comorbid SUD–PTSD also suggest that there are multiple patterns of onset, and a few have highlighted possible factors, such as gender and type of SUD, that may be associated with particular pathways to this comorbidity in adolescence. Giaconia et al. (2000) established that for 50% of adolescents with comorbid SUD–PTSD, the onset of SUD preceded that of PTSD; for 35.7% SUD and PTSD developed during the same year; and for 14.3% the SUD developed more than 1 year later than the PTSD. Perkonigg et al. (2000) determined that patterns of onset varied somewhat by type of SUD. For drug disorders, the SUD preceded PTSD in 75% of the comorbid participants, whereas for alcohol disorders the SUD preceded PTSD for 55.5% of the participants. Deykin and Buka (1997) found that although there was no clear pattern of sequencing among chemically dependent inpatient adolescents overall, there were significant gender differences in onset patterns. For males with SUD–PTSD, SUD followed the onset of PTSD for only 27.8%. In contrast, for females SUD followed onset of PTSD for 58.8%. Similarly, Brady, Dansky, Sonne, and Saladin (1998) found that females were more likely than males to have a primary onset of PTSD before developing cocaine dependence.

One limitation of the findings about patterns of onset from cross-sectional studies is that they are based on retrospective reports of ages of onset and may be subject to errors in recall (Cottler et al., 1992; Stewart, 1996). However, this may be less problematic for adolescent respondents than for adult participants in prior community studies, because these events (trauma, PTSD, and SUD) are more recent for these youth (Giaconia et al., 2000; Stewart, 1996).

IMPACT OF COMORBID SUD–PTSD ON PSYCHOSOCIAL FUNCTIONING

The impact of comorbid SUD–PTSD on adolescent psychosocial functioning, like other aspects of this comorbidity, has not been widely researched. Two key issues are (a) determining whether this comorbidity is associated with greater impairments than either disorder alone and (b) identifying the specific types of psychosocial impairments associated with this comorbidity. Although some indication of social or occupational impairment is one criterion required for a *DSM–III–R* or *DSM–IV* diagnosis of SUD or PTSD (American Psychiatric Association, 1987, 1994), few studies of adolescents have delineated specific types of psychosocial deficits associated with SUD–PTSD comorbidity. There is some evidence that patterns of impairment for adolescents with SUD differ from those of adolescents with PTSD, raising the possibility that youth with comorbid SUD–PTSD may experience a wider range of difficulties than youth with either disorder alone. For example, in a primarily clinical sample, Clark and Kirisci (1996) established that adolescents with PTSD exhibited adverse effects in several areas of psychological, physical, and social functioning, including less life satisfaction, greater anxiety, more health complaints, and less social competence. In contrast, adolescents with SUD showed deficits in role functioning, reflecting poorer academic achievement and more school adjustment difficulties. Similarly, in a community study of adolescents, Reinherz et al. (1993) found that whereas PTSD was associated with poorer self-esteem, more interpersonal problems, and lower grades, SUDs were associated only with poorer school performance and course failure.

Determining the relationship between SUD–PTSD comorbidity and age-appropriate functioning during adolescence is particularly crucial, because many of the social, educational, and behavioral difficulties that emerge in adolescence may have long-term consequences for subsequent functioning in adulthood (Giaconia et al., 2000; Kandel, Davies, Karus, & Yamaguchi, 1986; Newcomb & Bentler, 1988). Moreover, identifying specific patterns of impairment associated with SUD–PTSD comorbidity can aid in designing treatments that address both the comorbidity and its concomitant impairments.

In one of the only published studies that evaluated a broad range of psychosocial difficulties linked to SUD–PTSD in adolescents, Giaconia et al. (2000) compared the psychosocial functioning of three groups of 18-year-olds: (a) those with SUD only, (b) those with comorbid SUD–PTSD, and (c) those with no SUD or PTSD. A fourth group with only PTSD was excluded because of the small number of criterion-meeting participants. The results demonstrated that comorbid SUD–PTSD was generally associated with a wider range of impairments than SUD alone and that the types of impairments found for the SUD–PTSD group reflected a combination of deficits: those typically associated with SUD as well as those often linked to PTSD.

Compared with their peers with neither disorder, youth with SUD–PTSD comorbidity and those with only SUD both demonstrated significantly greater externalizing behavior problems, including delinquent and aggressive behavior; poorer school performance, including more course failures, expulsions, suspensions, and absences; an increased likelihood of criminal arrests in the past year; and serious suicidal behavior (Giaconia et al., 2000). These are areas of impairment typically associated with SUD (Kandel & Davies, 1996; Parrish, 1994; Reinherz et al., 1993; Segal & Stewart, 1996). However, there were additional impairments unique to the youth with comorbid SUD–PTSD that were not experienced by youth with SUD only. Comorbid youth manifested marked internalizing behavior problems, such as anxiety and withdrawn behavior; expressed greater problems in communicating with others; viewed their health as poorer; and were more likely to identify somatic complaints, such as headaches. These are areas of impairment often linked to PTSD in both adolescents (Giaconia et al., 1995; Reinherz et al., 1993) and adults (Amaya-Jackson et al., 1999; Friedman & Schnurr, 1995; Solomon & Davidson, 1997; Warshaw et al., 1993).

These cross-sectional findings cannot be interpreted as indicating that SUD–PTSD comorbidity caused these deficits; other pre-existing factors may have caused both comorbidity and poor outcomes in late adolescence. However, they do strongly illustrate that SUD–PTSD comorbidity in adolescence is an identifier of youth who are functioning poorly in almost every age-appropriate area and whose subsequent psychosocial functioning might be seriously compromised if these difficulties are left untreated.

EXPLANATIONS FOR THE LINK BETWEEN SUD AND PTSD AMONG ADOLESCENTS

Researchers and clinicians who work with adult populations have proposed several explanations for the link between SUD and PTSD. Research findings from the studies of adolescents we review in this chapter suggest that no single explanation best fits the data. Instead, the evidence suggests that there are diverse and multiple pathways leading to this comorbidity for adolescents.

One proposed explanation for the SUD–PTSD association is that substance use and SUD increase risk for exposure to traumas because substance users may engage in risky behaviors that enhance the likelihood of experiencing traumas (Brown & Wolfe, 1994; Deykin & Buka, 1997; Saladin, Brady, Dansky, & Kilpatrick, 1995). Two types of evidence from studies of adolescents partially support this view. First, findings about patterns of onset illustrate that, for at least some adolescents with SUD–trauma (45%–66%), SUD preceded the onset of these traumas (Clark et al., 1997; Giaconia et al., 2000; Perkonigg et al., 2000). Second, studies have demonstrated that adolescents with SUD are significantly more likely than non-SUD youth to have experienced traumas involving harm to themselves (two- to fivefold) and traumas that entail witnessing harm to others (three- to fivefold; Clark et al., 1997; Giaconia et al., 2000; Perkonigg et al., 2000), that is, traumas that might plausibly result from engaging in risky behavior.

Giaconia et al. (2000) found more direct evidence of this proposed link between substance use/SUD and risky behavior; nearly three quarters (74%) of adolescents with lifetime SUD acknowledged that they had been under the influence of alcohol or drugs in situations where it increased their chances of getting hurt. Recent studies of substance use in community samples of adolescents confirm the association between substance use and behaviors that may increase the likelihood of experiencing harm or injury, including risk-taking behavior such as hitchhiking, walking in unsafe neighborhoods, and driving after using alcohol or drugs (CDC, 2000; Windle, 1994). For example, nearly one third (31.2%) of male students in Grade 12 nationwide acknowledged driving after drinking alcohol at least once in the past 30 days (CDC, 2000).

A second explanation for the relationship between SUD and PTSD is that substance use increases the likelihood of developing PTSD following trauma because it interferes with an individual's ability to cope effectively with the trauma (Brown & Wolfe, 1994; Meisler, 1996; Saladin et al., 1995). As indirect evidence for this explanation, one community study reported that even after controlling for exposure to trauma, adolescents with SUD continued to be at greater risk (twofold) for developing PTSD following trauma than their peers without SUD (Giaconia et al., 2000). Although there was no direct evidence documenting how SUD interfered with the adolescents' ability to manage trauma, these researchers suggested that extensive psychosocial impairments found for adolescents with SUD in their study and others (Kandel & Davies, 1996) support the view that youth with SUD may lack the skills needed to cope with trauma and its aftermath.

A third explanation for SUD–PTSD comorbidity, the *self-medication hypothesis*, suggests that substance use begins after the onset of traumas or PTSD in an attempt to manage the distressing symptoms associated with traumas or PTSD (Brown & Wolfe, 1994; Saladin et al., 1995). Findings from both clinical and community studies of adolescents about the sequencing of onset of SUD–traumas and SUD–PTSD provide partial support for this proposition. For at least some adolescents, the onset of SUD followed the onset of trauma (25%–76%) and occurred after the onset of PTSD (14%–59%; Clark et al., 1997; Deykin & Buka, 1997; Giaconia et al., 2000; Perkonigg et al., 2000). However, there was no direct evidence that this temporal pattern reflected the adolescents' attempts to self-medicate.

AREAS FOR ADDITIONAL RESEARCH

Research investigating the comorbidity of SUD and PTSD among adolescents has lagged far behind research conducted with adults. Nonetheless, the limited research on adolescents provides an emerging picture of SUD–PTSD comorbidity as prevalent, with multiple patterns of onset, and associated with substantial and wide-ranging impairments that may compromise subsequent functioning in adulthood. These findings, viewed in light of the more extensive body of research on adults, point to several areas that warrant further investigation in adolescent populations.

First, more community-based studies targeting adolescents of both genders and from a variety of ethnic and socioeconomic status (SES) groups are needed to provide basic information about the scope and key correlates of SUD–PTSD comorbidity among youth in the general population. There is some limited evidence from the clinical studies reviewed that female adolescents are at greater risk for SUD–PTSD comorbidity than their male counterparts (Clark et al., 1995; Deykin & Buka, 1997), a finding more consistently found in studies of adults (Najavits et al., 1997). Future research should assess whether this gender difference holds true with more diverse community groups of adolescents. Similarly, are there differences in the prevalence of SUD–PTSD comorbidity among different ethnic and SES groups? Equally important, are there any interactions among gender, SES, and ethnicity indicating that one particular subgroup of youth is most at risk for SUD–PTSD?

There is little available research on the role of gender, SES, and ethnicity in SUD–PTSD comorbidity among adolescents, but these relationships are likely to be complex, because no single group is at greater risk for all of the requisite elements for this comorbidity. For example, adolescent males are more likely to use alcohol and drugs and develop SUD than are adolescent females (CDC, 2000; Reinherz et al., 1993). In contrast, adolescent females are substantially more likely to develop PTSD than their male counterparts (Cuffe et al., 1998; Deykin & Buka, 1997; Giaconia et al., 1995). Similarly, whereas most types of substance use/SUD are more prevalent among Whites and Hispanics than among African American adolescents (CDC, 2000; Johnston et al., 2000; Kilpatrick et al., 2000), African American adolescents are at an increased risk for experiencing traumas leading to PTSD (Bell & Jenkins, 1991; Cuffe et al., 1998; Fitzpatrick & Boldizar, 1993; McGruder-Johnson, Davidson, Gleaves, Stock, & Finch, 2000; Schwab-Stone et al., 1995). The associations of SES with SUD and PTSD are even less definitive. There is conflicting evidence about whether lower SES is associated with greater risk for substance use/ SUD (Johnston et al., 2000; Kessler et al., 1994) as well as mixed findings about the relationship between SES and exposure to traumas and PTSD (Foy & Goguen, 1998; Giaconia et al., 1995; U.S. Department of Justice, Bureau of Justice Statistics, 2000a). Community-based studies of adolescents that include representative samples of males and females, all ethnic groups, and youth from all SES groups are essential in order to establish the differential roles played by gender, ethnicity, and SES in SUD–PTSD comorbidity.

The studies we have reviewed also point to differences in rates of SUD–PTSD comorbidity that vary by type of SUD (Kilpatrick et al., 2000). This type of research must be extended to develop a fuller picture of the interplay of SUD and trauma in SUD–PTSD comorbidity and to aid in the identification of youth most at risk. For example, are adolescents with drug abuse or dependence at greater risk for SUD–PTSD comorbidity than those with alcohol abuse or dependence? Are traumas involving directly experienced physical violence more likely to lead to SUD–PTSD comorbidity than traumas involving witnessed violence? Are different types of SUD associated with exposure to different types of traumas?

Second, the patterns of onset of SUD–PTSD among adolescents warrant further research. Cross-sectional studies of onset patterns should be supplemented with prospective longitudinal studies that trace the development of SUD–PTSD comorbidity among participants known to be disorder free at an initial or baseline assessment, a method that was used in two recent studies of adults (Chilcoat & Breslau, 1998a; Kilpatrick, Acierno, Resnick, Saunders, & Best, 1997). Another promising approach is to directly assess the subjective perceptions of individuals with comorbid SUD–PTSD about how the two disorders are related (Brown, Stout, & Gannon-Rowley, 1998; Stewart, 1996).

In addition, research studies that identify the correlates, course, and consequences of different patterns of onset hold promise for increasing the understanding of this comorbidity. The significant gender differences in SUD–PTSD onset patterns among adolescent inpatients reported by Deykin and Buka (1997), who found that PTSD was more likely to precede SUD in female adolescents and develop subsequent to the onset of SUD in males, highlight the importance of evaluating gender and other sociodemographic correlates. Specifically, do the pathways leading to SUD–PTSD differ by gender, SES, and ethnicity? Clinical studies of adolescents similarly suggest that sequencing of onset varies by type of trauma (Clark et al., 1997) and by type of SUD (Perkonigg et al., 2000). Moreover, research with adults suggests that the pattern of SUD–PTSD onset is significantly associated with the subsequent degree of impairment (Brady et al., 1998). These findings offer a starting point for further research about the origins and consequences of different onset patterns.

Third, longitudinal studies that trace the natural course and long-term sequelae of SUD–PTSD comorbidity are essential to understanding the likely duration and developmental consequences of this comorbidity. The widespread impairments identified for adolescents with SUD–PTSD comorbidity in one analysis (Giaconia et al., 2000) underscore the need to determine whether these current impairments in adolescence foreshadow subsequent difficulties in later adulthood. Three lines of research suggest that continued impairments for youth with SUD–PTSD comorbidity are likely. First, longitudinal studies of substance use and SUD in adolescence provide compelling evidence that psychosocial impairments associated with substance abuse extend well beyond adolescence and into adulthood (Kandel et al., 1986; Newcomb & Bentler, 1988). Second, studies of PTSD in children and adolescents illustrate that this disorder may have a chronic, long course (American Academy of Child and Adolescent Psychiatry [AACAP], 1998) and is associated with significant social, interpersonal, and academic deficits (Giaconia et al., 1995; Reinherz et al., 1993). Third, studies of adults have demonstrated that SUD–PTSD comorbidity is linked to a more prolonged course and poorer psychosocial functioning than either disorder alone (Najavits, Gastfriend, et al., 1998; Najavits et al., 1997; Ouimette, Brown, & Najavits, 1998; Ouimette, Finney, & Moos, 1999; Warshaw et al., 1993). In addition to prospective studies that document the course and sequelae of SUD–PTSD among adolescents, studies that identify factors that alter the trajectory of this pair of disorders would be useful in developing interventions that promote recovery.

Fourth, studies that identify risk and protective factors for SUD–PTSD comorbidity can play an important role in developing strategies designed to limit the onset and scope of this comorbidity. Specifically, what psychosocial factors predict which youth who have either SUD or PTSD will subsequently develop the other disorder? Do these risks include the common antecedents hypothesized by some researchers, such as early conduct problems, antisocial behavior, anxiety, or other pre-existing disorders (Brown & Wolfe, 1994; Deykin & Buka, 1997; Stewart, 1996)? As is true of types of impairment, are these risks likely to reflect a wider range of psychosocial variables than those typically associated with SUD alone and with PTSD alone? Alternatively, what psychosocial factors, such as social support and a stable childhood home environment (Najavits, Weiss, & Shaw, 1999; Stewart, 1996), promote resistance to developing this comorbidity in at-risk adolescents?

Fifth, although there is expanding research on the efficacy of treatment programs for SUD–PTSD in adults (Najavits, Weiss, & Liese, 1996; Ouimette, Moos, & Finney, 2000; Triffleman, Carroll, & Kellogg, 1999), there are no studies about treatments for SUD–PTSD comorbidity in adolescents. Treatment studies specifically targeting adolescents are vital, because these treatments should differ somewhat from those designed for adults, by recognizing the specific developmental needs of adolescents (AACAP, 1997). However, one of the key findings from studies of adults that should be evaluated with adolescents is the importance of treatments that address both SUD and PTSD (Ouimette, Brown, & Najavits, 1998; Ouimette, Moos, & Finney, 2000).

IMPLICATIONS FOR IDENTIFICATION, ASSESSMENT, AND TREATMENT OF SUD–PTSD COMORBIDITY

Despite the lack of research on the treatment of SUD–PTSD comorbidity in adolescents, the studies we review in this chapter provide several implications for the identification, assessment, and follow-up of adolescents at risk for, or who have already developed, comorbid SUD–PTSD. First, because so little has been written about SUD–PTSD comorbidity in adolescents, it is essential that research findings about the scope of this comorbidity be broadly disseminated to clinicians who may be presented with this client group. Current treatment guidelines for PTSD (AACAP, 1998), as well as those for SUD (AACAP, 1997) note the general importance of assessing for other comorbid disorders. Specific information highlighting the magnitude of SUD–PTSD comorbidity can inform assessment and treatment decisions by increasing clinicians' awareness that SUD and traumas/PTSD will frequently co-occur.

Second, there is also a need to increase awareness about SUD–PTSD comorbidity among non-mental health clinicians who work with adolescents, such as school personnel and health care providers. Because adolescents are at an age when self-referral for treatment is unlikely to occur, the responsibility for identifying and referring youth at risk for, or with, SUD–PTSD rests with parents, teachers, and health care providers. The types of impairments associated with SUD–PTSD comorbidity suggest alternative avenues for the identification and treatment of this comorbidity. For example, the failing grades and frequent absences that characterize youth with SUD–PTSD comorbidity indicate that the school setting may serve as one source for targeting these youth (Giaconia et al., 2000; Pfefferbaum, 1997). For some youth, school-based services may also provide a more developmentally appropriate environment than other treatment settings (AACAP, 1997; Foy & Goguen, 1998; Pfefferbaum, 1997). Similarly, the somatic complaints, poor perceived health, and large number of sick days reported by youth with comorbid SUD–PTSD suggest that the primary health care setting may provide an opportunity to identify youth at risk for, or with, this comorbidity (Friedman & Schnurr, 1995; Giaconia et al., 2000; Solomon & Davidson, 1997).

Third, as emphasized in recent studies of adolescents in inpatient substance treatment programs (Clark et al., 1997; Deykin & Buka, 1997), youth presenting with SUD, like their adult counterparts, should routinely be screened for traumas and PTSD. Conversely, adolescents presenting with traumas or PTSD should be assessed for SUD.

Fourth, the consistent finding that only a subset of youth with SUD–PTSD comorbidity developed both disorders in the same year (Giaconia et al., 2000; Perkonigg et al., 2000) indicates the need for continued monitoring and follow-up of youth with SUD because they remain at risk for subsequently experiencing traumas and developing PTSD. Likewise, youth with PTSD are at continued risk for SUD even more than 1 year following the onset of PTSD.

Fifth, for youth presenting with comorbid SUD–PTSD, the sequencing of onset for this pair of disorders should be evaluated. An individualized clinical evaluation prior to treatment should consider factors that have been associated with particular pathways leading to comorbid SUD–PTSD, such as gender and type of trauma experienced, as well as subjective perceptions about how the two disorders are related (Brown et al., 1998; Stewart, 1996). The temporal relationship between SUD and PTSD is important to ascertain for each patient, because it may influence the design of treatment programs (Deykin & Buka, 1997). For example, successful treatment efforts for individuals with primary PTSD, who may have developed substance problems in an effort to alleviate PTSD symptoms through self-medication, would differ from efforts used with primary-SUD patients, whose SUD developed prior to the onset of PTSD (Brown & Wolfe, 1994; Saladin et al., 1995). The initial goal of treatment for primary-PTSD patients would be to address the trauma in therapy and to find more effective methods of coping with PTSD symptoms. In contrast, efforts should be made to stop the substance abuse and lower the risk-taking behaviors in primary-SUD patients before moving on to therapy aimed at reducing PTSD symptoms (Brady et al., 1998; Deykin & Buka, 1997).

Finally, findings about the extensive social, educational, health, and psychological impairments, including suicidal behaviors in adolescence, that are associated with comorbid SUD–PTSD underscore the need for early intervention to limit the sequelae of these disorders in later adulthood. Furthermore, the specific types of impairments associated with SUD–PTSD comorbidity for adolescents might serve as additional foci for continuing treatment and follow-up efforts.

EPILOGUE: FUTURE DIRECTIONS

PAIGE OUIMETTE AND PAMELA J. BROWN

In this book, we provide the latest findings with regard to the etiology, assessment, and treatment of co-occurring posttraumatic stress disorder (PTSD) and substance use disorder (SUD). Special attention was paid to specific populations for which this dual diagnosis provides a particular challenge. In this summary we suggest practical implications for clinicians and future directions for researchers.

What is known about etiology? Converging evidence supports self-medication theory as important in the initial development of SUD–PTSD (chapter 1), with more complex functional relations in regard to the maintenance of the disorders (chapters 2 and 3). As noted in Part I, alternative pathways to the development of SUD–PTSD (i.e., etiological subgroups) may exist with important prognostic and treatment implications.

For clinical necessity, treatments often develop prior to or in tandem with research on etiology and theory development as with SUD–PTSD treatments. We hope that as more knowledge is gained about theoretically important variables, treatments can be better tailored to both the general population and subgroups of individuals (Part IV) who experience SUD–PTSD.

In regard to treatment of SUD–PTSD, there is a clear consensus among researchers that both disorders need to be addressed in treatment. That patients prefer concurrent treatment bolsters this view (Brown et al., 1998). On the basis of the findings presented in this volume, we make the following general suggestions for clinicians.

1. SUD and PTSD assessment should be a routine part of screening at SUD- and PTSD-specific treatment facilities (chapter 6).
2. During initial assessments it is important to pay attention to process and inform patients about the link between the two

disorders (e.g., that trauma assessment may exacerbate urges to use substances; chapter 6).

3. SUD–PTSD patients should receive treatment that addresses both conditions. Recommended treatment methods include education, anxiety management, and cognitive–behavioral coping skills training (chapter 5). As reviewed in chapter 8, Seeking Safety is one potential manual-based treatment, which is backed up by data suggesting effectiveness, for the first stage of SUD–PTSD intervention.

4. Exposure treatment should be considered under the guidelines outlined in chapter 7, possibly as a second-stage intervention.

5. Adjunctive treatments, such as self-help, should be considered when appropriate (chapter 5).

6. Providers should be aware of the need for continuing ongoing mental health care for these individuals (chapter 5).

7. Given the link between gender and type of trauma, the patient's gender should be considered. If treatments are conducted using group formats, single-gender groups are recommended.

To further inform theory, treatment, and practice guidelines for the treatment of SUD–PTSD comorbidity, we recommend the following avenue of research.

1. Experimental research on functional relations as recommended in chapter 3. Studies could focus on cognitive factors, P300 deficits, psychophysiology (e.g., startle), neuroendocrine indices, neuropsychology, and neuroimaging. Important to this research would be an integrated approach that examines responding at multiple levels of analysis (e.g., cognitive, affective, somatic).

2. Longitudinal studies of adolescents that can examine potential causal pathways among traumatic exposure, PTSD, and stages of substance use and abuse (see chapters 1 and 12).

3. Controlled trials comparing new treatments for SUD–PTSD (chapters 7 and 8) as well as examination of patient–treatment matching variables. Patients who leave treatment should be evaluated for reasons for dropout.

4. Survey development and administration to assess current mental health provider/program practices for patients with SUD–PTSD (for an example, see Rosen et al., 2000).

5. Development and administration of complementary patient and provider surveys to assess perceived barriers to obtaining and delivering empirically supported best care.

6. Implementation of a naturalistic longitudinal study of SUD–PTSD patients that assesses PTSD, SUD, prognostic factors, service utilization, and outcomes.
7. Research on the etiology and treatment of SUD–PTSD among specific subpopulations.

Understanding the etiology of SUD–PTSD comorbidity and treating individuals who have this dual diagnosis are relatively new endeavors for clinician–scientists. We hope that this book stimulates new and creative research ideas among former, current, and future clinician–researchers in the field of SUD–PTSD comorbidity. Moreover, we hope that it raises awareness about the unique clinical issues associated with SUD–PTSD comorbidity and inspires clinicians providing the front-line services to learn about and integrate empirically based practices into their treatments.

REFERENCES

Abueg, F. R., & Fairbank, J. A. (1991). Behavioral treatment of the PTSD–substance abuser: A multidimensional stage model. In P. Saigh (Ed.), *Posttraumatic stress disorder: A behavioral approach to assessment and treatment* (pp. 111–146). New York: Pergamon Press.

Abueg, F. R., Fairbank, J. A., Penk, W., & Gusman, F. D. (1995). *Interim findings from a randomized controlled trial of trauma relevant relapse prevention training (TRRPT) in PTSD and alcoholism.* Paper presented at the annual meeting of the International Society of Traumatic Stress Studies, Chicago, Illinois.

Acierno, R., Resnick, H., Kilpatrick, D. G., Saunders, B., & Best, C. L. (2000). Risk factors for rape, physical assault, and posttraumatic stress disorder in women: Examination of differential multivariate relationships. *Journal of Anxiety Disorders, 13,* 541–563.

Allen, J. P., Litten, R. Z., Fertig, J. B., & Babor, T. (1997). A review of research on the Alcohol Use Disorders Identification Test (AUDIT). *Alcoholism: Clinical and Experimental Research, 21,* 613–619.

Allen, S. N. (1994). Psychological assessment of post-traumatic stress disorder: Psychometrics, current trends, and future directions. *Psychiatric Clinics of North America, 17,* 327–349.

Alterman, A. I., Randall, M., & McLellan, A. T. (2000). Comparison of outcomes by gender and for fee-for-service versus managed care: A study of nine community programs. *Journal of Substance Abuse Treatment, 19,* 127–134.

Amaya-Jackson, L., Davidson, J. R., Hughes, D. C., Swartz, M., Reynolds, V., George, L. K., & Blazer, D. G. (1999). Functional impairment and utilization of services associated with posttraumatic stress in the community. *Journal of Traumatic Stress, 12,* 709–724.

American Academy of Child and Adolescent Psychiatry. (1997). Practice parameters for the assessment and treatment of children and adolescents with substance use disorders. *Journal of the American Academy of Child and Adolescent Psychiatry,* 36(Suppl. 10), 140S–156S.

American Academy of Child and Adolescent Psychiatry. (1998). Practice parameters for the assessment and treatment of children and adolescents with posttraumatic stress disorder. *Journal of the American Academy of Child and Adolescent Psychiatry, 37*(Suppl. 10), 4S–26S.

American Psychiatric Association. (1980). *Diagnostic and statistical manual of mental disorders* (3rd ed.). Washington, DC: Author.

American Psychiatric Association. (1987). *Diagnostic and statistical manual of mental disorders* (3rd ed., rev.). Washington, DC: Author.

American Psychiatric Association. (1994). *Diagnostic and statistical manual of mental disorders* (4th ed.). Washington, DC: Author.

American Psychiatric Association. (1995). *Practice guidelines for treatment of patients with substance use disorders: Alcohol, cocaine, opioids.* Washington, DC: Author.

American Society of Addiction Medicine. (1996). *Patient placement criteria for the treatment of substance-related disorders* (2nd ed.). Chevy Chase, MD: Author.

Andrykowski, M. A., Cordova, M. J., Studts, J. L., & Miller, T. W. (1998). Posttraumatic stress disorder after treatment for breast cancer: Prevalence of diagnosis and use of the PTSD Checklist—Civilian Version (PCL–C) as a screening instrument. *Journal of Consulting and Clinical Psychology, 66,* 586–590.

Annis, H. M., Graham, J. M., & Davis, C. S. (1987). Inventory of Drinking Situations (IDS) user's guide. Toronto, Ontario, Canada: Addiction Research Foundation.

Annis, H. M., Turner, N. E., & Sklar, S. M. (1996). Inventory of Drug-Taking Situations (IDTS) user's guide. Toronto, Ontario, Canada: Addiction Research Foundation.

Anton, R. F., Stout, R. L., Roberts, J. S., & Allen, J. R. (1998). The effect of drinking intensity and frequency on serum carbohydrate-deficient transferrin and gamma-glutamyl transferase levels in outpatient alcoholics. *Alcoholism: Clinical and Experimental Research, 22,* 1456–1462.

Appleby, L., Dyson, V., Altman, E., & Luchins, D. J. (1997). Assessing substance use in multiproblem patients: Reliability and validity of the Addiction Severity Index in a mental hospital population. *Journal of Nervous and Mental Disease, 185,* 159–165.

Armony, J. L., & LeDoux, J. E. (1997). How the brain processes emotional information. In R. Yehuda & A. C. McFarlane (Eds.), *Psychobiology of posttraumatic stress disorder* (Vol. 821, pp. 259–270). New York: New York Academy of Sciences.

Arnett, J. J. (2000). Emerging adulthood: A theory of development from the late teens through the twenties. *American Psychologist, 55,* 469–480.

Arnsten, A. F. T. (1998, June 12). The biology of being frazzled. *Science, 280,* 1711–1712.

Atkinson, J. H., Slater, M. A., Patterson, T. L., Grant, I., & Garfin, X. (1991). Prevalence, onset, and risk of psychiatric disorders in men with chronic low back pain: A controlled study. *Pain, 45*, 111–121.

Atkinson, R. M., Henderson, R. G., Sparr, L. F., & Deale, S. (1982). Assessment of Vietnam veterans for posttraumatic stress disorder in Veterans Administration disability claims. *American Journal of Psychiatry, 139*, 1118–1121.

Babor, T. F., de la Fuente, J. R., Saunders, J., & Grant, M. (1992). *The Alcohol Use Disorders Identification Test: Guidelines for use in primary health care*. Geneva, Switzerland: World Health Organization.

Back, S., Dansky, B. S., Carroll, K., Foa, E. B., & Brady, K. T. (2001). Exposure therapy in the treatment of PTSD among cocaine dependence dependent individuals: Description of procedures. *Journal of Substance Abuse Treatment, 21*, 35–45.

Back, S., Dansky, B. S., Coffey, S. F., Saladin, M. E., Sonne, S., & Brady, K. T. (2000). Cocaine dependence with and without posttraumatic stress disorder: A comparison of substance use, trauma history, and psychiatric comorbidity. *American Journal on Addictions, 9*, 51–62.

Baker, T. B., Morse, E., & Sherman, J. E. (1987). The motivation to use drugs: A psychobiological analysis of urges. In P. C. Rivers (Ed.), *Nebraska Symposium on Motivation: Alcohol use and abuse* (pp. 257–323). Lincoln: University of Nebraska Press.

Ballenger, J. C., Davidson, J. R., Lecrubier, Y., Nutt, D. J., Foa, E. B., Kessler, R. C., et al. (2000). Consensus statement on posttraumatic stress disorder from the International Consensus Group on Depression and Anxiety. *Journal of Clinical Psychiatry, 61*(Suppl.), 60–66.

Barnard, G. W., Hankins, G. C., & Robbins, L. (1992). Prior life trauma, post-traumatic stress symptoms, sexual disorders, and character traits in sex offenders: An exploratory study. *Journal of Traumatic Stress, 5*, 393–420.

Barthwell, A. G., Bokos, P., Bailey, J., Nisenbaum, M., Deverux, J., & Senay, E. C. (1995). Interventions/Wilmer: A continuum of care for substance abusers in the criminal justice system. *Journal of Psychoactive Drugs, 27*, 39–47.

Bates, M. E., Brick, J., & White, H. R. (1993). The correspondence between saliva and breath estimates of blood alcohol concentration: Advantages and limitations of the saliva method. *Journal of Studies on Alcohol, 54*, 17–22.

Beck, A. T. (1979). *Cognitive therapy of depression*. New York: Guilford Press.

Beck, A. T., Epstein, N., Brown, G., & Steer, R. A. (1988). An inventory for measuring clinical anxiety: Psychometric properties. *Journal of Counseling and Clinical Psychology, 56*, 893–897.

Beck, A. T., & Steer, R. A. (1987). *The Beck Depression Inventory manual*. Toronto, Ontario, Canada: Psychological Corporation.

Beck, A. T., Ward, C. H., Mendelson, M., Mock, J., & Erbaugh, J. (1961). An inventory for measuring depression. *Archives of General Psychiatry, 4*, 561–571.

Beck, A. T., Wright, F. D., Newman, C. F., & Liese, B. S. (1993). *Cognitive therapy of substance abuse*. New York: Guilford Press.

Becker, J. V., & Kaplan, M. S. (1991). The incidence of depressive symptomatology in juvenile sex offenders with a history of abuse. *Child Abuse & Neglect, 15*, 531–536.

Beckham, J. C., Feldman, M. E., Kirby, A. C., Hertzberg, M. A., & Moore, S. D. (1997). Vietnam veterans with chronic posttraumatic stress disorder. *Journal of Clinical Psychology, 53*, 859–869.

Begleiter, H., Porjesz, B., Bihari, B., & Kissin, B. (1984, September 28). Event-related brain potentials in boys at risk for alcoholism. *Science, 225*, 1493–1495.

Bell, C. C., & Jenkins, E. J. (1991). Traumatic stress and children. *Journal of Health Care for the Poor and Underserved, 2*, 175–185.

Bergman, B., & Brismar, B. (1994). Characteristics of violent alcoholics. *Alcohol & Alcoholism, 29*, 451–457.

Berkowitz, G., Brindis, C., Clayson, Z., & Peterson, S. (1996). Options for recovery: Promoting success among women mandated to treatment. *Journal of Psychoactive Drugs, 28*, 31–38.

Berkson, J. (1946). Limitations of the application of fourfold table analysis to hospital data. *Biometrics, 2*, 47–53.

Birnbaum, S., Gobeske, K. T., Auerbach, J., Taylor, J. R., & Arnsten, A. F. T. (1999). A role for norepinephrine in stress-induced cognitive deficits: Alpha-1-adrenoceptor mediation in the prefrontal cortex. *Biological Psychiatry, 46*, 1266–1274.

Blake, D. D., Weathers, F. W., Nagy, L. M., Kaloupek, D. G., Gusman, F. D., Charney, D. S., & Keane, T. M. (1995). The development of a clinician-administered PTSD scale. *Journal of Traumatic Stress, 8*, 75–90.

Blake, D. D., Weathers, F. W., Nagy, L. M., Kaloupek, D. G., Klauminizer, G., Charney, D. S., & Keane, T. M. (1990). A clinician rating scale for assessing current and lifetime PTSD: The CAPS–1. *Behavior Therapy, 13*, 187–188.

Blanchard, E. B., Hickling, E. J., Barton, K. A., Taylor, A. E., Loos, W. R., & Jones-Alexander, J. (1996). One-year prospective follow-up of motor vehicle accident victims. *Behaviour Research and Therapy, 34*, 775–786.

Blanchard, E. B., Jones-Alexander, J., Buckley, T. C., & Forneris, C. A. (1996). Psychometric properties of the PTSD Checklist (PCL). *Behaviour Research and Therapy, 34*, 669–673.

Blanchard, E. B., Kolb, L. C., Pallmeyer, T. P., & Gerardi, R. J. (1982). A psychophysiological study of post-traumatic stress disorder in Vietnam veterans. *Psychiatric Quarterly, 54*, 220–229.

Blanchard, E. B., Kolb, L. C., & Prins, A. (1991). Psychophysiological responses in the diagnosis of posttraumatic stress disorder in Vietnam veterans. *Journal of Nervous and Mental Disease, 179*, 97–101.

Blanchard, E. B., Kolb, L. C., Prins, A., Gates, S., & McCoy, G. C. (1991). Changes in plasma norepinephrine to combat-related stimuli among Vietnam veterans with post traumatic stress disorder. *Journal of Nervous and Mental Disease, 179,* 371–373.

Bollerud, K. (1990). A model for the treatment of trauma-related syndromes among chemically dependent inpatient women. *Journal of Substance Abuse Treatment, 7,* 83–87.

Bollinger, A. R., Riggs, D. S., Blake, D. D., & Ruzek, J. I. (2000). Prevalence of personality disorders among combat veterans diagnosed with posttraumatic stress disorder. *Journal of Traumatic Stress, 13,* 255–270.

Boney-McCoy, S., & Finkelhor, D. (1995). Psychosocial sequelae of violent victimization in a national youth sample. *Journal of Consulting and Clinical Psychology, 63,* 726–736.

Boscarino, J. A. (1995). Post-traumatic stress and associated disorder among Vietnam veterans: The significance of combat exposure and social support. *Journal of Traumatic Stress, 8,* 317–336.

Boudewyns, P. A., & Hyer, L. (1990). Physiological response to combat memories and preliminary treatment outcome in Vietnam veteran PTSD patients treated with direct therapeutic exposure. *Behavior Therapy, 21,* 63–87.

Boudewyns, P. A., Woods, M. G., Hyer, L., & Albrecht, J. W. (1991). Chronic combat-related PTSD and concurrent substance abuse: Implications for treatment of this frequent "dual diagnosis." *Journal of Traumatic Stress, 4,* 549–560.

Brady, K. T., Dansky, B. S., Back, S. E., Foa, E. B., & Carroll, K. M. (2001). Exposure therapy in the treatment of PTSD among cocaine-dependent individuals: Preliminary findings. *Journal of Substance Abuse Treatment, 21,* 47–54.

Brady, K. T., Dansky, B. S., Sonne, S. C., & Saladin, M. E. (1998). Posttraumatic stress disorder and cocaine dependence: Order of onset. *American Journal on Addictions, 7,* 128–135.

Brady, K. T., Killeen, T., Saladin, M., Dansky, B. S., & Becker, S. (1994). Comorbid substance abuse and PTSD: Characteristics of women in treatment. *American Journal on Addictions, 3,* 160–164.

Brady, K. T., Sonne, S. C., & Roberts, J. M. (1995). Sertraline treatment of comorbid posttraumatic stress disorder and alcohol dependence. *Journal of Clinical Psychiatry, 56,* 502–505.

Branchey, L., Davis, W., & Lieber, C. S. (1984). Alcoholism in Vietnam and Korea veterans: A long term follow-up. *Alcoholism: Clinical and Experimental Research, 8,* 572–575.

Bremner, J. D., Innis, R. B., Ng, C. K., Staib, L., Salomon, R., Bronen, R. A., et al. (1997). Positron emission tomography measurement of cerebral metabolic correlates of yohimbine administration in combat-related posttraumatic stress disorder. *Archives of General Psychiatry, 54,* 246–256.

Bremner, J. D., Licino, J., Darnel, A., Krystal, J. H., Owens, M. J., & Southwick, S. M. (1997). Elevated CSF corticotropin-releasing factor concentrations in posttraumatic stress disorder. *American Journal of Psychiatry, 154,* 624–629.

Bremner, J. D., Southwick, S. M., Darnell, A., & Charney, D. S. (1996). Chronic PTSD in Vietnam combat veterans: Course of illness and substance abuse. *American Journal of Psychiatry, 153*, 369–375.

Breslau, N., & Davis, G. C. (1992). Posttraumatic stress disorder in an urban population of young adults: Risk factors for chronicity. *American Journal of Psychiatry, 149*, 671–675.

Breslau, N., Davis, G. C., & Andreski, P. (1995). Risk factors for PTSD-related traumatic events: A prospective analysis. *American Journal of Psychiatry, 152*, 529–535.

Breslau, N., Davis, G. C., Andreski, P., & Peterson, E. (1991). Traumatic events and posttraumatic stress disorder in an urban population of young adults. *Archives of General Psychiatry, 48*, 216–222.

Breslau, N., Kessler, R. C., Chilcoat, H. D., Schultz, L. R., Davis, G. C., & Andreski, P. (1998). Trauma and posttraumatic stress disorder in the community: The 1996 Detroit Area Survey of Trauma. *Archives of General Psychiatry, 55*, 626–632.

Breslau, N., Peterson, E. L., Kessler, R. C., & Schultz, L. R. (1999). Short screening scale for *DSM–IV* posttraumatic stress disorder. *American Journal of Psychiatry, 156*, 908–911.

Brewin, C. R., Andrews, B., & Gotlib, I. H. (1993). Psychopathology and early experience: A reappraisal of retrospective reports. *Psychological Bulletin, 113*, 82–98.

Briggs, F., & Hawkins, R. M. F. (1996). A comparison of the childhood experiences of convicted male child molesters and men who were sexually abused in childhood and claimed to be nonoffenders. *Child Abuse & Neglect, 20*, 221–233.

Brinson, T., & Treanor, V. (1989). Alcoholism and posttraumatic stress disorder among combat Vietnam veterans. *Alcoholism Treatment Quarterly, 5*, 65–82.

Brown, P. J. (2000). Outcome in female patients with both substance use and posttraumatic stress disorders. *Alcoholism Treatment Quarterly, 18*, 127–135.

Brown, P. J., Recupero, P. R., & Stout, R. L. (1995). PTSD substance abuse comorbidity and treatment utilization. *Addictive Behaviors, 20*, 251–254.

Brown, P. J., Stout, R. L., & Gannon-Rowley, J. (1998). Substance use disorder— PTSD comorbidity: Patients' perceptions of symptom interplay and treatment issues. *Journal of Substance Abuse Treatment, 15*, 445–448.

Brown, P. J., Stout, R. L., & Mueller, T. (1996). Posttraumatic stress disorder and substance abuse relapse among women: A pilot study. *Psychology of Addictive Behaviors, 10*, 124–128.

Brown, P. J., Stout, R. L., & Mueller, T. (1999). Substance use disorder and posttraumatic stress disorder comorbidity: Addiction and psychiatric treatment rates. *Psychology of Addictive Behaviors, 13*, 115–122.

Brown, P. J., & Wolfe, J. (1994). Substance abuse and post-traumatic stress disorder comorbidity. *Drug and Alcohol Dependence, 35*, 51–59.

Brown, S. A., Inaba, R. K., Gillin, J. C., Schuckit, M. A., Stewart, M. A., & Irwin, M. R. (1995). Alcoholism and affective disorder: Clinical course of depressive symptoms. *American Journal of Psychiatry, 152,* 45–52.

Browne, A., Miller, B., & Maguin, E. (1999). Prevalence and severity of lifetime physical and sexual victimization among incarcerated women. *International Journal of Law and Psychiatry, 22,* 301–322.

Buccio-Notaro, P., Molla, B., & Stevenson, C. (1996, November). *Social Justice for Women creates alternative sentencing services and alternative sites for women involved in the criminal justice system.* Paper presented to the American Society of Criminology, Chicago.

Burke, K. C., Burke, J. D., Rae, D. S., & Regier, D. A. (1991). Comparing age at onset of major depression and other psychiatric disorders by birth cohorts in five US community populations. *Archives of General Psychiatry, 48,* 789–795.

Bushman, B. J., & Cooper, H. M. (1990). Effects of alcohol on human aggression: An integrative research review. *Psychological Bulletin, 107,* 341–354.

Butler, R. W., Braff, D. L., Rausch, J., Jenskins, M. A., Sproch, J., & Geyer, M. A. (1990). Physiological evidence of exaggerated startle response in a subgroup of Vietnam veterans with combat-related posttraumatic stress disorder. *American Journal of Psychiatry, 147,* 1308–1312.

Byrne, C. A., & Riggs, D. S. (1996). The cycle of trauma: Relationship aggression in male Vietnam veterans with symptoms of posttraumatic stress disorder. *Violence and Victims, 11,* 213–225.

Carlson, E. B. (1997). *Trauma assessments.* New York: Guilford Press.

Carroll, K. M. (1996). Relapse prevention as a psychosocial treatment: A review of controlled clinical trials. In A. G. Marlatt & G. R. VandenBos (Eds.), *Addictive behaviors: Readings on etiology, prevention, and treatment* (pp. 697–717). Washington, DC: American Psychological Association.

Carroll, K. M. (1998). A cognitive–behavioral approach: Treating cocaine addiction. In Alan I. Leshner (Ed.), *NIDA Therapy Manual for Drug Addiction* (Manual 1, DHHS Publication No. 98-4308). Washington, DC: U.S. Government Printing Office.

Carroll, K., Rounsaville, B., & Keller, D. (1991). Relapse prevention strategies for the treatment of cocaine abuse. *American Journal of Drug and Alcohol Abuse, 17,* 249–265.

Carver, C. S., Scheier, M. F., & Weintraub, J. K. (1989). Assessing coping strategies: A theoretically based approach. *Journal of Personality and Social Psychology, 56,* 267–283.

Cauffman, E., Feldman, S. S., Waterman, J., & Steiner, H. (1998). Posttraumatic stress disorder among female juvenile offenders. *Journal of the American Academy of Child and Adolescent Psychiatry, 37,* 1209–1216.

Centers for Disease Control and Prevention. (1988). Vietnam Experience Study: Health status of Vietnam veterans. I: Psychosocial characteristics. *Journal of the American Medical Association, 259,* 2701–2707.

Centers for Disease Control and Prevention. (2000, June 9). CDC surveillance summaries. *Morbidity and Mortality Weekly Report 2000, 49*(No. SS-5).

Chemtob, C. M., Hamada, R. S., Roitblat, H. L., & Muraoka, M. Y. (1994). Anger, impulsivity, and anger control in combat-related posttraumatic stress disorder. *Journal of Consulting and Clinical Psychology, 62,* 827–832.

Chemtob, C. M., Novaco, R. W., Hamada, R. S., & Gross, D. M. (1997). Cognitive–behavioral treatment for severe anger in post-traumatic-stress disorder. *Journal of Consulting and Clinical Psychology, 65,* 184–189.

Chermack, S. T., & Giancola, P. R. (1997). The relation between alcohol and aggression: An integrated biopsychosocial conceptualization. *Clinical Psychology Review, 17,* 621–649.

Chesney-Lind, M. (1997). *The female offender: Girls, women and crime.* Thousand Oaks, CA: Sage.

Chilcoat, H. D., & Breslau, N. (1998a). Investigations of causal pathways between PTSD and drug use disorders. *Addictive Behaviors, 23,* 827–840.

Chilcoat, H. D., & Breslau, N. (1998b). Posttraumatic stress disorder and drug disorders: Testing causal pathways. *Archives of General Psychiatry, 55,* 913–917.

Chilcoat, H. D., & Breslau, N. (1999). Pathways from ADHD to early drug use. *Journal of the American Academy of Child & Adolescent Psychiatry, 38,* 1347–1354.

Chu, J. A. (1988). Ten traps for therapists in the treatment of trauma survivors. *Dissociation: Progress in the Dissociative Disorders, 1,* 24–32.

Clark, D. B., Bukstein, O. G., Smith, M. G., Kaczynski, N. A., Mezzich, A. C., & Donovan, J. E. (1995). Identifying anxiety disorders in adolescents hospitalized for alcohol abuse or dependence. *Psychiatric Services, 46,* 618–620.

Clark, D. B., & Kirisci, L. (1996). Posttraumatic stress disorder, depression, alcohol use disorders, and quality of life in adolescents. *Anxiety, 2,* 226–233.

Clark, D. B., Lesnick, L., & Hegedus, A. M. (1997). Traumas and other adverse life events in adolescents with alcohol abuse and dependence. *Journal of the American Academy of Child and Adolescent Psychiatry, 36,* 1744–1751.

Clark, J. P., & Tifft, L. L. (1966). Polygraph and interview validation of self-reported deviant behavior. *American Sociological Review, 31,* 516–523.

Cloitre, M., Tardiff, K., Marzuk, P. M., Leon, A. C., & Portera, L. (1996). Childhood abuse and subsequent sexual assault among female inpatients. *Journal of Traumatic Stress, 9,* 473–482.

Coffey, S. F. (2000, November). Prolonged exposure versus Seeking Safety: Lessons from a project examining the concurrent treatment of cocaine dependence and PTSD. In B. Wolfsdorf (Chair), *Treatment of substance abuse and posttraumatic stress disorder: Applications of the Seeking Safety model.* Clinical roundtable presented at the 34th annual convention of the Association for Advancement of Behavior Therapy, New Orleans, LA.

Coffey, S. F., Dansky, B. S., Falsetti, S. A., Saladin, M. E., & Brady, K. T. (1998). Screening for PTSD in a substance abuse sample: Psychometric properties of a modified version of the PTSD Symptom Scale Self-Report. *Journal of Traumatic Stress, 11,* 393–399.

Coffey, S. F., Saladin, M. E., Drobes, D. J., Brady, K. T., Dansky, B. S., & Kilpatrick, D. G. (2002). Trauma and substance cue reactivity in individuals with comorbid posttraumatic stress disorder and cocaine or alcohol dependence. *Drug and Alcohol Dependence, 65,* 115–127.

Collins, J. J., & Messerschmidt, P. M. (1993). Epidemiology of alcohol-related violence. *Alcohol Health & Research World, 17,* 93–100.

Connor, K. M., & Davidson, J. R. T. (1997). Familial risk factors in posttraumatic stress disorder. In R. Yehuda & A. C. McFarlane (Eds.), *Psychobiology of posttraumatic stress disorder* (Vol. 821, pp. 35–51). New York: New York Academy of Sciences.

Conrod, P. J., Pihl, R. O., Stewart, S. H., & Dongier, M. (2000). Validation of a system of classifying female substance abusers on the basis of personality and motivational risk factors for substance abuse. *Psychology of Addictive Behaviors, 14,* 243–256.

Conrod, P. J., Pihl, R. O., & Vassileva, J. (1998). Differential sensitivity to alcohol reinforcement in groups of men at risk for distinct alcoholism subtypes. *Alcoholism: Clinical and Experimental Research, 22,* 585–597.

Conrod, P. J., Stewart, S. H., & Pihl, R. O. (1997). Validation of a measure of excessive drinking: Frequency per year that BAL exceeds 0.08%. *Substance Use and Misuse, 32,* 587–607.

Conrod, P. J., Stewart, S. H., Pihl, R. O., Côté, S., Fontaine, V., & Dongier, M. (2000). Efficacy of brief coping skills interventions that match different personality profiles of female substance abusers. *Psychology of Addictive Behaviors, 14,* 243–256.

Cooney, N. L., Litt, M. D., Morse, P. A., Bauer, L. O., & Gaupp, L. (1997). Alcohol cue reactivity, negative-mood reactivity, and relapse in treated alcoholic men. *Journal of Abnormal Psychology, 106,* 243–250.

Cooper, N. A., & Clum, G. A. (1989). Imaginal flooding as a supplementary treatment for PTSD in combat veterans: A controlled study. *Behavior Therapy, 20,* 381–391.

Cottler, L. B., Compton, W. M., Mager, D., Spitznagel, E. L., & Janca, A. (1992). Posttraumatic stress disorder among substance users from the general population. *American Journal of Psychiatry, 149,* 664–670.

Covington, S. (1999). *Helping women recover: A program for treating substance abuse: A facilitator's guide.* San Francisco: Jossey-Bass.

Crits-Christoph, P., Siqueland, L., Blaine, J., Frank, A., Luborsky, L., Onken, L. S., et al. (1999). Psychosocial treatments for cocaine dependence: National Institute on Drug Abuse Collaborative Cocaine Treatment Study. *Archives of General Psychiatry, 57,* 493–502.

Cronkite, R. C., & Moos, R. H. (1980). Determinants of the posttreatment functioning of alcoholic patients: A conceptual framework. *Journal of Consulting and Clinical Psychology, 48,* 305–316.

Cuffe, S. P., Addy, C. L., Garrison, C. Z., Waller, J. L., Jackson, K. L., McKeown, R. E., & Chilappagari, S. (1998). Prevalence of PTSD in a community sample of older adolescents. *Journal of the American Academy of Child and Adolescent Psychiatry, 37,* 147–154.

Daniels, L. R., & Scurfield, R. M. (1992). War-related post-traumatic stress disorder, chemical addictions and non-chemical habituating behaviors. In M. B. Williams & J. F. Sommer (Eds.), *Handbook of post-traumatic therapy* (pp. 205–218). Westport, CT: Greenwood Press.

Danksy, B. S., & Brady, K. T. (1998). *Exposure therapy for posttraumatic stress disorder and substance abuse.* Unpublished manuscript, Medical University of South Carolina.

Dansky, B. S., Brady, K. T., & Saladin, M. E. (1998). Untreated symptoms of PTSD among cocaine-dependent individuals: Changes over time. *Journal of Substance Abuse Treatment, 15,* 499–504.

Dansky, B. S., Byrne, C. A., & Brady, K. T. (1999). Intimate violence and post-traumatic stress disorder among individuals with cocaine dependence. *American Journal of Drug and Alcohol Abuse, 25,* 257–268.

Dansky, B. S., Roitzsch, J. C., Brady, K. T., & Saladin, M. E. (1997). Posttraumatic stress disorder and substance abuse: Use of research in a clinical setting. *Journal of Traumatic Stress, 10,* 141–148.

Dansky, B. S., Saladin, M., Brady, K. T., Killeen, T., Becker, S., & Roitzsch, J. C. (1994, November). *Concurrent treatment of PTSD and substance abuse in women.* Presentation conducted at the annual meeting of the International Society of Traumatic Stress Studies, Chicago.

Dansky, B. S., Saladin, M. E., Coffey, S. F., & Brady, K. T. (1997). Use of self-report measures of crime-related posttraumatic stress disorder with substance use disordered patients. *Journal of Substance Abuse Treatment, 14,* 431–437.

Davidson, J. R. T., Kudler, H. S., Saunders, W. B., & Smith, R. D. (1990). Symptom and comorbidity patterns in World War II and Vietnam veterans with posttraumatic stress disorder. *Comprehensive Psychiatry, 31,* 162–170.

Davidson, J. R. T., Smith, R. D., & Kudler, H. S. (1989). Familial psychiatric illness in chronic posttraumatic stress disorder. *Comprehensive Psychiatry, 30,* 339–345.

Davidson, J. R. T., Tupler, L. A., Wilson, W. H., & Connor, K. M. (1998). A family study of chronic post-traumatic stress disorder following rape trauma. *Journal of Psychiatric Research, 32,* 301–309.

Davis, E., & Bass, L. (1988). *The courage to heal: A guide for women survivors of child sexual abuse.* New York: Harper & Row.

Davis, M. (1984). The mammalian startle response. In R. E. Eaton (Ed.), *Neural mechanisms of startle behavior* (pp. 287–342). New York: Plenum.

Davis, M. (1986). Pharmacological and anatomical analysis of fear-conditioning using the fear-potentiated startle paradigm. *Behavioral Neuroscience, 100,* 814–824.

Davis, M., Falls, W. A., Campeau, S., & Munsoo, K. (1993). Fear-potentiated startle: A neural and pharmacological analysis. *Behavioral Brain Research, 58*, 175–198.

Davis, M., Walker, D. L., & Lee, Y. (1997). Roles of the amygdala and bed nucleus of the stria terminalis in fear and anxiety measured with the acoustic startle reflex: Possible relevance to PTSD. In R. Yehuda & A. C. McFarlane (Eds.), *Psychobiology of posttraumatic stress disorder* (Vol. 821, pp. 305–331). New York: New York Academy of Sciences.

Davis, T. M., & Wood, P. S. (1999). Substance abuse and sexual trauma in a female veteran population. *Journal of Substance Abuse Treatment, 16*, 123–127.

Deahl, M., Srinivasan, M., Jones, N., Thomas, J., Neblett, C., & Jolly, A. (2000). Preventing psychological trauma in soldiers: The role of operational stress training and psychological debriefing. *British Journal of Medical Psychology, 73*, 77–85.

De Boer, S. F., Slagen, J. L., & Van der Gugten, J. (1992). Brain benzodiazepine receptor control of stress hormones. In R. Kvetnansky (Ed.), *Stress: Neuroendocrine and molecular approaches* (vols. 1–2, pp. 719–734). Philadelphia: Gordon and Breach Science Publishers.

Dembo, R., Williams, L., Wothke, W., Schmeidler, J., & Brown, C. H. (1992). The role of family factors, physical abuse, and sexual victimization experiences in high-risk youths' alcohol and other drug use and delinquency: A longitudinal model. *Violence and Victims, 7*, 245–266.

Deroche, V., Piazza, P. V., LeMoal, M., & Simon, H. (1994). Social isolation-induced enhancement of the psychomotor effects of morphine depends on corticosterone secretion. *Brain Research, 640*, 136–139.

Derogatis, L. R. (1977). *SCL–90: Administration, scoring, and procedures manual: I. For the revised version.* Baltimore: Johns Hopkins University, Clinical Psychometrics Research Unit.

DeWit, H., & Griffiths, R. R. (1991). Abuse liability of anxiolytic and hypnotic drugs. *Drug and Alcohol Dependence, 28*, 83–11.

Deykin, E. Y. (1999). Posttraumatic stress disorder in childhood and adolescence: A review. *Medscape Mental Health, 4*, 1–11. Retrieved February 25, 2000, from http://www.medscape.com/Medscape/psychiatry/journal/1999/v04.n04/mh3048.deyk/mh3048.deyk-01.html

Deykin, E. Y., & Buka, S. L. (1997). Prevalence and risk factors for posttraumatic stress disorder among chemically dependent adolescents. *American Journal of Psychiatry, 154*, 752–757.

Dodge, K. A., Bates, J. E., & Pettit, G. S. (1990, December 21). Mechanisms in the cycle of violence. *Science, 250*, 1678–1683.

Donovan, B. S., & Padin-Rivera, E. (1999). Transcend: A program for treating PTSD and substance abuse in Vietnam combat veterans. *National Center for PTSD Clinical Quarterly, 8*, 51–53.

Donovan, B., Padin-Rivera, E., & Kowaliw, S. (2001). Transcend: Initial outcomes from a posttraumatic stress disorder/substance abuse treatment program. *Journal of Traumatic Stress, 14*, 757–772.

Druley, K. A., & Pashko, S. (1988). Posttraumatic stress disorder in World War II and Korean combat veterans with alcohol dependency. In M. Galanter (Ed.), *Recent developments in alcoholism* (Vol. 6, pp. 89–101). New York: Plenum.

Dutton, D. G., & Hart, S. D. (1992). Evidence for long-term specific effects of childhood abuse and neglect on criminal behavior in men. *International Journal of Offender Therapy and Comparative Criminology, 36,* 129–137.

Echeburua, E., de-Corral, P., Sarasua, B., & Zubizarreta, I. (1996). Treatment of acute posttraumatic stress disorder in rape victims: An experimental study. *Journal of Anxiety Disorders, 10,* 185–199.

Engdahl, B. E., Dikel, T. N., Eberly, R. E., & Blank, A. S. (1998). Comorbidity and course of psychiatric disorders in a community sample of former prisoners of war. *American Journal of Psychiatry, 155,* 1740–1745.

Engdahl, B. E., Speed, N., Eberly, R. E., & Schwartz, J. (1991). Comorbidity of psychiatric disorders and personality profiles of American World War II prisoners of war. *Journal of Nervous and Mental Disease, 179,* 181–187.

Engel, C. C., Ursano, R. J., Magruder, C., Tartaglione, R., Jing, Z., Labbate, L. A., & Debakey, S. (1999). Psychological conditions diagnosed among veterans seeking Department of Defense care for Gulf War-related health concerns. *Journal of Occupational and Environmental Medicine, 41,* 384–392.

Epstein, J. N., Saunders, B. E., Kilpatrick, D. G., & Resnick, H. S. (1998). PTSD as a mediator between childhood rape and alcohol use in adult women. *Child Abuse & Neglect, 22,* 223–234.

Erwin, B. A., Newman, E., McMackin, R. A., Morrissey, C., & Kaloupek, D. G. (2000). PTSD, malevolent environment, and criminality among criminally involved male adolescents. *Criminal Justice and Behavior, 27,* 196–215.

Escobar, J. I., Randolph, E. T., Puente, G., Spiwak, F., Asamen, J. K., Hill, M., & Hough, R. L. (1983). Posttraumatic stress disorder in Hispanic Vietnam veterans: Clinical phenomenology and sociocultural characteristics. *Journal of Nervous and Mental Disease, 171,* 585–596.

Evans, K., & Sullivan, J. M. (1995). *Treating addicted survivors of trauma.* New York: Guilford Press.

Everly, G. S., & MacNeil-Horton, A. (1989). Neuropsychology of posttraumatic stress disorder: A pilot study. *Perceptual & Motor Skills, 68,* 807–810.

Expert Consensus Guideline Series. (1999). Treatment of posttraumatic stress disorder: The Expert Consensus Panels for PTSD. *Journal of Clinical Psychiatry, 60*(Suppl. 16), 3–76.

Fairbank, J. A., Hansen, D. J., & Fitterling, J. M. (1991). Patterns of appraisal and coping across different stressor conditions among former prisoners of war with and without posttraumatic stress disorder. *Journal of Consulting and Clinical Psychology, 59,* 274–281.

Falsetti, S. A., Resick, P. A., Resnick, H. S., & Kilpatrick, D. (1992, November). *Posttraumatic stress disorder: The assessment of frequency and severity of symptoms in clinical and non-clinical samples.* Paper presented at the annual convention for the Association for Advancement of Behavior Therapy, Boston.

Falsetti, S. A., Resnick, H. S., Resick, P. A., & Kilpatrick, D. (1993). The Modified PTSD Symptom Scale: A brief self-report measure of posttraumatic stress disorder. *Behavior Therapist, 16,* 161–162.

Famularo, R., Kinscherff, R., & Fenton, T. (1992). Parental substance abuse and the nature of child maltreatment. *Child Abuse & Neglect, 16,* 475–483.

Figley, C. R., Bride, B. E., & Mazza, N. (Eds.). (1997). *Death and trauma: The traumatology of grieving.* Washington, DC: Taylor & Francis.

First, M. B., Spitzer, R. L., Gibbon, M., & Williams, J. B. W. (1994). *Structured Clinical Interview For Axis I DSM–IV Disorders—Patient Edition (SCID–I/P, Version 2.0).* New York: Biometrics Research Department, New York State Psychiatric Institute.

Fitzpatrick, K. M., & Boldizar, J. P. (1993). The prevalence and consequences of exposure to violence among African-American youth. *Journal of the American Academy of Child and Adolescent Psychiatry, 32,* 424–430.

Fleiss, J. L. (1981). *Statistical methods for rates and proportions* (2nd ed.). New York: Wiley.

Fleming, M. F., & Barry, K. L. (1991). The effectiveness of alcoholism screening in an ambulatory care setting. *Journal of Studies on Alcohol, 52,* 33–36.

Foa, E. B. (1995). *Posttraumatic Stress Diagnostic Scale.* Minneapolis, MN: National Computer Systems.

Foa, E. B. (2000). Psychosocial treatment of posttraumatic stress disorder. *Journal of Clinical Psychiatry, 61*(Suppl.), 43–48.

Foa, E. B., Cashman, L., Jaycox, L., & Perry, K. (1997). The validation of a self-report measure of posttraumatic stress disorder: The Posttraumatic Diagnostic Scale. *Psychological Assessment, 9,* 445–451.

Foa, E. B., Davidson, J. R. T., Frances, A., Culpepper, L., Ross, R., & Ross, D. (1999). The Expert Consensus Guideline Series: Treatment of posttraumatic stress disorder. *Journal of Clinical Psychiatry, 60*(Suppl. 16).

Foa, E. B., Keane, T. M., & Friedman, M. J. (2000). *Effective treatments for PTSD: Practice guidelines from the International Society for Traumatic Stress Studies.* New York: Guilford Press.

Foa, E. B., & Kozak, M. J. (1986). Emotional processing of fear: Exposure to corrective information. *Psychological Bulletin, 99,* 20–35.

Foa, E. B., & Kozak, M. J. (1991). Emotional processing: Theory, research, and clinical implications for anxiety disorders. In J. D. Safran & L. S. Greenberg (Eds.), *Emotion, psychotherapy, and change* (pp. 21–49). New York: Guilford Press.

Foa, E. B., Riggs, D. S., Dancu, C. B., & Rothbaum, B. O. (1993). Reliability and validity of a brief instrument for assessing post-traumatic stress disorder. *Journal of Traumatic Stress, 6,* 459–473.

Foa, E. B., Riggs, D. S., & Gershuny, B. S. (1995). Arousal, numbing and intrusion: Symptom structure of PTSD following assault. *American Journal of Psychiatry, 152,* 116–120.

Foa, E. B., Riggs, D. S., Massie, E. D., & Yarczower, M. (1995). The impact of fear activation and anger on efficacy of exposure treatment for PTSD. *Behavior Therapy*, 26, 487–499.

Foa, E. B., & Rothbaum, B. O. (1998). *Treating the trauma of rape: Cognitive–behavioral therapy for PTSD*. New York: Guilford Press.

Foa, E. B., Rothbaum, B. O., Riggs, D., & Murdock, T. B. (1991). Treatment of posttraumatic stress disorder in rape victims: A comparison between cognitive–behavioral procedures and counseling. *Journal of Consulting and Clinical Psychology*, 59, 715–723.

Foa, E. B., Steketee, G., & Rothbaum, B. O. (1989). Behavioral/cognitive conceptualization of posttraumatic stress disorder. *Behavior Therapy*, 20, 155–176.

Foa, E. B., Zinbarg, R., & Rothbaum, B. O. (1992). Uncontrollability and unpredictability in post-traumatic stress disorder: An animal model. *Psychological Bulletin*, 112, 218–238.

Fogel, C. I., & Belyea, M. (1999). The lives of incarcerated women: Violence, substance abuse, and at risk for HIV. *Journal of the Association of Nurses in AIDS Care*, 10, 66–74.

Fontana, A., Litz, B. T., & Rosenheck, R. A. (2000). Impact of combat and sexual harassment on the severity of posttraumatic stress disorder among men and women peacekeepers in Somalia. *Journal of Nervous and Mental Disease*, 188, 163–169.

Fontana, A., & Rosenheck, R. (1994). Traumatic war stressors and psychiatric symptoms among World War II, Korean, and Vietnam War veterans. *Psychology and Aging*, 9, 27–33.

Fontana, A., & Rosenheck, R. (1997). Effectiveness and cost of the inpatient treatment of posttraumatic stress disorder: Comparison of three models of treatment. *American Journal of Psychiatry*, 154, 758–765.

Foy, D. W., & Goguen, C. A. (1998). Community violence-related PTSD in children and adolescents. *PTSD Research Quarterly*, 9, 1–6.

Frankl, V. E. (1963). *Man's search for meaning*. New York: Pocket Books.

Friedman, M. J., & Schnurr, P. P. (1995). The relationship between trauma, posttraumatic stress disorder, and physical health. In M. J. Friedman, D. S. Charney, & A. Y. Deutch (Eds.), *Neurobiological and clinical consequences of stress: From normal adaptation to PTSD* (pp. 507–524). Philadelphia: Lippincott-Raven.

Frueh, B. C., Gold, P. B., & de Arellano, M. A. (1997). Symptoms overreporting in combat veterans evaluated for PTSD: Differentiation on the basis of compensation seeking status. *Journal of Personality Assessment*, 68, 369–384.

Frueh, B. C., Smith, D. W., & Barker, S. E. (1996). Compensation seeking status and psychometric assessment of combat veterans seeking treatment for PTSD. *Journal of Traumatic Stress*, 9, 427–439.

Frueh, B. C., Turner, S. M., Beidel, D. C., Mirabella, R. F., & Jones, W. J. (1996). Trauma Management Therapy: A preliminary evaluation of a multicomponent behavioral treatment for chronic combat-related PTSD. *Behaviour Research and Therapy, 34,* 533–543.

Fullilove, M. T., Fullilove, R. E., Smith, M., Winkler, K., Michael, C., Panzer, P. G., & Wallace, R. (1993). Violence, trauma, and posttraumatic stress disorder among women drug users. *Journal of Traumatic Stress, 6,* 533–543.

Fulwiler, C., Grossman, H., Forbes, C., & Ruthazer, R. (1997). Early-onset substance abuse and community violence by outpatients with chronic mental illness. *Psychiatric Services, 48,* 1181–1185.

Garnefski, N., & Diekstra, R. F. W. (1997). Child sexual abuse and emotional and behavioral problems in adolescence: Gender differences. *Journal of the American Academy of Child and Adolescent Psychiatry, 36,* 323–329.

Gerardi, R. J., Blanchard, E. B., & Kolb, L. C. (1989). Ability of Vietnam veterans to dissimulate a psychophysiological assessment for post-traumatic stress disorder. *Behavior Therapy, 20,* 229–243.

Giaconia, R. M., Reinherz, H. Z., Hauf, A. C., Paradis, A. D., Wasserman, M. S., & Langhammer, D. M. (2000). Comorbidity of substance use and post-traumatic stress disorders in a community sample of adolescents. *American Journal of Orthopsychiatry, 70,* 253–262.

Giaconia, R. M., Reinherz, H. Z., Silverman, A. B., Pakiz, B., Frost, A. K., & Cohen, E. (1994). Ages of onset of psychiatric disorders in a community population of older adolescents. *Journal of the American Academy of Child and Adolescent Psychiatry, 33,* 706–717.

Giaconia, R. M., Reinherz, H. Z., Silverman, A. B., Pakiz, B., Frost, A. K., & Cohen, E. (1995). Traumas and posttraumatic stress disorder in a community population of older adolescents. *Journal of the American Academy of Child and Adolescent Psychiatry, 34,* 1369–1380.

Gibson, H. B., Morrison, S., & West, D. J. (1970). The confession of known offenses in response to a self-reported delinquency schedule. *British Journal of Criminology, 10,* 277–280.

Gibson, L. E., Holt, J. C., Fondacaro, K. M., Tang, T. S., Powell, T. A., & Turbitt, E. L. (1999). An examination of antecedent traumas and psychiatric comorbidity among male inmates with PTSD. *Journal of Traumatic Stress, 12,* 473–484.

Gilfus, M. E. (1992). From victims to survivors to offenders: Women's routes of entry and immersion into street crime. *Women and Criminal Justice, 4,* 63–89.

Gil-Rivas, V., Fiorentine, R., & Anglin, M. D. (1996). Sexual abuse, physical abuse, and posttraumatic stress disorder among women participating in outpatient drug abuse treatment. *Journal of Psychoactive Drugs, 28,* 95–102.

Glaser, D. (1997). *Profitable penalties: How to cut both crime rates and costs.* Thousand Oaks, CA: Pine Forge.

Gold, M. (1966). Undetected delinquent behavior. *Journal of Research in Crime and Delinquency, 3,* 27–46.

Gorman, J. M., Kent, J., Martinez, J., Browne, S., Coplan, J., & Papp, L. A. (2001). Physiological changes during carbon dioxide inhalation in patients with panic disorder, major depression, and premenstrual dysphoric disorder: Evidence for a central fear mechanism. *Archives of General Psychiatry, 58,* 125–131.

Gray, J. A. (1982). *The neuropsychology of anxiety: An inquiry into the functions of the septo-hippocampal system.* Oxford, England: Oxford University Press.

Greeley, J., Swift, W., & Heather, N. (1992). Depressed affect as a predictor of increased desire for alcohol in current drinkers of alcohol. *British Journal of Addiction, 87,* 1005–1012.

Green, B. L. (1995). *Trauma History Questionnaire.* Unpublished instrument and data (Available from Bonnie L. Green, Department of Psychiatry, Georgetown University School of Medicine, 37th and O Street, NW, Washington, DC 20057).

Green, B. L. (1996). Trauma History Questionnaire. In B. H. Stamm (Ed.), *Measurement of stress, trauma, and adaptation* (pp. 366–369). Lutherville, MD: Sidran Press.

Greene, S., Haney, C., & Hurtado, A. (2000). Cycles of pain: Risk factors in the lives of incarcerated mothers and their children. *Prison Journal, 80,* 3–24.

Grillon, C., Sinha, R., & O'Malley, S. S. (1994). Effects of ethanol on the acoustic startle reflex in humans. *Psychopharmacology, 114,* 167–171.

Grossman, L. S., Willer, J. K., Stovall, S. G., Maxwell, S., & Nelson, R. (1997). Underdiagnosis of PTSD and substance use disorders in hospitalized female veterans. *Psychiatric Services, 48,* 393–395.

Groth, A. N. (1979). Sexual trauma in the life histories of rapists and child molesters. *Victimology: An International Journal, 4,* 10–16.

Gurvits, T. V., Gilbertson, M. W., Lasko, N. B., Tarhan, A. S., Simeon, D., Macklin, M. L., et al. (2000). Neurologic soft signs in chronic posttraumatic stress disorder. *Archives of General Psychiatry, 57,* 181–186.

Gurvits, T. V., Shenton, M. R., Hokama, H., Ohta, H., Lasko, N. B., Gilbertson, M. W., et al. (1996). Magnetic resonance imagining study of hippocampal volume in chronic, combat-related posttraumatic stress disorder. *Biological Psychiatry, 40,* 1091–1099.

Hamilton, C. E., & Browne, K. D. (1999). Recurrent maltreatment during childhood: A survey of referrals to police child protection units in England. *Child Maltreatment: Journal of the American Professional Society on the Abuse of Children, 4,* 275–286.

Hankin, C. S., Spiro, A., Miller, D. R., & Kazis, L. (1999). Mental disorders and mental health treatment among U.S. Department of Veterans Affairs outpatients: The Veterans Health Study. *American Journal of Psychiatry, 156,* 1924–1930.

Harvey, E. M., Rawson, R. A., & Obert, J. L. (1994). History of sexual assault and the treatment of substance abuse disorders. *Journal of Psychoactive Drugs, 26,* 361–367.

Helzer, J. E., Robins, L. N., & McEvoy, L. (1987). Post-traumatic stress disorder in the general population. *New England Journal of Medicine, 317,* 1630–1634.

Henderson, D. J. (1998). Drug abuse and incarcerated women: A research review. *Journal of Substance Abuse Treatment, 15,* 579–587.

Heney, J., & Kristiansen, C. M. (1997). An analysis of the impact of prison on women survivors of childhood sexual abuse. *Women and Therapy, 20,* 29–44.

Herman, J. L. (1992). *Trauma and recovery.* New York: Basic Books.

Herman, J. L., Perry, J. C., & Van der Kolk, B. A. (1989). Childhood trauma in borderline personality disorder. *American Journal of Psychiatry, 146,* 490–495.

Herrmann, N., & Eryavec, G. (1994). Posttraumatic stress disorder in institutionalized World War II veterans. *American Journal of Geriatric Psychiatry, 2,* 324–331.

Herrmann, N., & Eryavec, G. (1996). Lifetime alcohol abuse in institutionalized World War II veterans. *American Journal of Geriatric Psychiatry, 4,* 339–345.

Hien, D. A., Cohen, L. R., Litt, L. C., Miele, G. M., & Capstick, C. (2002). *Promising empirically supported treatments for women with comorbid PTSD and substance use disorders.* Manuscript submitted for publication.

Hien, D., & Scheier, J. (1996). Trauma and short-term outcome for women in detoxification. *Journal of Substance Abuse Treatment, 13,* 227–231.

Hijzen, T. H., Houtzager, S. W., Joordens, R. J., Oliver, B., & Slangen, J. L. (1995). Predictive validity of the potentiated startle response as a behavioral model for anxiolytic drugs. *Psychopharmacology, 118,* 150–154.

Hiller, M. L., Knight, K., & Simpson, D. D. (1999). Prison-based substance abuse treatment, residential aftercare and recidivism. *Addiction, 94,* 833–842.

Hillman, A., Sykes, R. A., & McConnell, A. A. (1998). Limitations in the use of gamma-glutamyl transferase estimations in alcohol-dependent subjects. *Alcohol and Alcoholism, 33,* 626–630.

Hoffman, K., & Sasaki, J. (1997). Comorbidity of substance abuse and PTSD. In C. Fullerton & R. Ursano (Eds.), *Posttraumatic stress disorder: Acute and long-term responses to trauma and disaster. Progress in Psychiatry Series* (No. 51, pp. 159–174). Washington, DC: American Psychiatric Press.

Horowitz, M. J., Wilner, N., & Alvarez, W. (1979). Impact of Event Scale: A measure of subjective stress. *Psychosomatic Medicine, 41,* 209–218.

Hotaling, G. T., & Sugarman, D. B. (1986). An analysis of risk markers in husband to wife violence: The current state of knowledge. *Violence and Victims, 1,* 101–124.

Humphreys, K., Moos, R. H., & Finney, J. W. (1995). Two pathways out of drinking problems without professional treatment. *Addictive Behaviors, 20,* 427–441.

Hurley, D. L. (1991). Women, alcohol and incest: An analytic review. *Journal of Studies on Alcohol, 52,* 253–268.

Huttunen, P. (1991). Microdialysis of extracellular noradrenaline in the hippocampus of the rat after long-term alcohol intake. *Brain Research, 560,* 225–228.

Hwang, B. H., Wang, G. M., Wong, D. T., Lumeng, L., & Li, T. K. (2000). Norepinephrine uptake sites in the locus coeruleus of rat lines selectively bred for high and low alcohol preference: A quantitative autoradiographic binding study using [–sup-3H]-Tomoxeting. *Alcoholism: Clinical and Experimental Research, 24,* 588–594.

Hyer, L., Leach, P., Boudewyns, P. A., & Davis, H. (1991). Hidden PTSD in substance abuse inpatients among Vietnam veterans. *Journal of Substance Abuse Treatment, 8,* 213–219.

Imhof, J. E. (1996). Overcoming countertransference and other attitudinal barriers in the treatment of substance abuse. In A. M. Washington (Ed.), *Psychotherapy and substance abuse: A practitioner's handbook* (pp. 3–22). New York: Guilford Press.

International Society for Traumatic Stress Studies. (1997). *PTSD Treatment Guidelines Task Force: Draft practice guidelines for the treatment of posttraumatic stress disorder.* Northbrook, IL: Author.

Iowa Persian Gulf Study Group. (1997). Self-reported illness and health status among Gulf War veterans: A population-based study. *Journal of the American Medical Association, 277,* 238–245.

Irwin, H. J. (1999). Violent and nonviolent revictimization of women abused in childhood. *Journal of Interpersonal Violence, 14,* 1095–1110.

Ito, J. R., & Donovan, D. M. (1990). Predicting drinking outcome: Demography, chronicity, coping, and aftercare. *Addictive Behaviors, 15,* 553–559.

Jacob, F. (1997). *The statue within: An autobiography.* New York: Basic Books.

Janoff-Bulman, R. (1992). *Shattered assumptions: Towards a new psychology of trauma.* New York: Free Press.

Janoff-Bulman, R. (1997). The impact of trauma on meaning: From meaningless world to meaningful life. In M. J. Power & C. R. Brewin (Eds.), *The transformation of meaning in psychological therapies: Integrating theory and practice* (pp. 91–106). Chichester, England: Wiley.

Jaycox, L., & Foa, E. B. (1999). Cognitive–behavioral theory and treatment of posttraumatic stress disorder. In D. Spiegel (Ed.), *Efficacy and cost-effectiveness of psychotherapy* (pp. 23–61). Washington, DC: American Psychiatric Association.

Jensen C. F., Keller T. W., Peskind, E. R., McFall, M. E., Veith, R. C., Martin, D. et al. (1997). Behavioral and neuroendocrine responses to sodium lactate infusion in subjects with posttraumatic stress disorder. *American Journal of Psychiatry, 154,* 266–268.

Johanson, C. E., & de Wit, H. (1989). The use of choice procedures for assessing the reinforcing properties of drugs in humans. Testing for abuse liability of drugs in humans. In M. W. Fischman & N. K. Mello (Eds.), *Testing for abuse liability of drugs in humans* (NIDA Research Monograph No. 92, pp. 123–146). Washington, DC: U.S. Government Printing Office.

Johnson, D. R., Rosenheck, R., Fontana, A., Lubin, H., Charney, D., & Southwick, S. (1996). Outcome of intensive inpatient treatment for combat-related posttraumatic stress disorder. *American Journal of Psychiatry, 153,* 771–777.

Johnson, E. M., & Belfer, M. L. (1995). Substance abuse and violence: Cause and consequence. *Journal of Health Care for the Poor and Underserved, 6,* 113–123.

Johnson, R. A., & Gerstein, D. R. (1998). Initiation of use of alcohol, cigarettes, marijuana, cocaine, and other substances in US birth cohorts since 1919. *American Journal of Public Health, 88,* 27–33.

Johnston, L. D., O'Malley, P. M., & Bachman, J. G. (2000). *The Monitoring the Future national results on adolescent drug use: Overview of key findings, 1999* (NIH Publication No. 00-4690). Washington, DC: U.S. Government Printing Office.

Jordan, B. K., Schlenger, W. E., Fairbank, J. A., & Caddell, J. M. (1996). Prevalence of psychiatric disorders among incarcerated women: II. Convicted felons entering prison. *Archives of General Psychiatry, 53,* 513–519.

Jordan, J. V., Stiver, I. P., & Surrey, J. L. (1991). *Women's growth in connection: Writings from the Stone Center.* New York: Guilford Press.

Jordan, K. B., Marmar, C. R., Fairbank, J. A., Schlenger, W. E., Kulka, R. A., Hough, R. L., & Weiss, D. S. (1992). Problems in families of male Vietnam veterans with posttraumatic stress disorder. *Journal of Consulting and Clinical Psychology, 60,* 916–926.

Joyner, L. M., Wright, J. D., & Devine, J. A. (1996). Reliability and validity of the Addiction Severity Index among homeless substance misusers. *Substance Use and Misuse, 31,* 729–751.

Kadden, R., Carroll, K. M., Donovan, D., Cooney, N., Monti, P., Abram, D., et al. (1992). *Cognitive–behavioral coping skills therapy manual: A clinical research guide for therapists treating individuals with alcohol abuse and dependence* (NIAAA Project MATCH Monograph Series, Vol. 3, DHHS Publication No. AOM 92-1895). Washington, DC: Government Printing Office.

Kandel, D. B., & Davies, M. (1996). High school students who use crack and other drugs. *Archives of General Psychiatry, 53,* 71–80.

Kandel, D. B., Davies, M., Karus, D., & Yamaguchi, K. (1986). The consequences in young adulthood of adolescent drug involvement: An overview. *Archives of General Psychiatry, 43,* 746–754.

Kantor, G. K., & Straus, M. A. (1989). Substance abuse as a precipitant of wife abuse victimizations. *American Journal of Drug and Alcohol Abuse, 15,* 173–189.

Kaufman, E., & Reoux, J. (1988). Guidelines for the successful psychotherapy of substance abusers. *American Journal of Drug and Alcohol Abuse, 14,* 199–209.

Kaufman, J. G., & Widom, C. S. (1999). Childhood victimization, running away, and delinquency. *Journal of Research in Crime & Delinquency, 36,* 347–370.

Keane, T. M. (1993). Symptomatology of Vietnam veterans with posttraumatic stress disorder. In J. R. T. Davidson & E. B. Foa (Eds.), *Posttraumatic stress disorder: DSM–IV and beyond* (pp. 99–111). Washington, DC: American Psychiatric Press.

Keane, T. M. (1995). The role of exposure therapy in the psychological treatment of PTSD. *National Center for Posttraumatic Stress Disorder Clinical Quarterly, 5,* 1, 3–6.

Keane, T. M., Fairbank, J. A., Caddell, J. M., & Zimering, R. T. (1989). Implosive (flooding) therapy reduces symptoms of PTSD in Vietnam combat veterans. *Behavior Therapy, 20,* 245–260.

Keane, T. M., Gerardi, R. J., Lyons, J. A., & Wolfe, J. (1988). The interrelationship of substance abuse and posttraumatic stress disorder. In M. Galanter (Ed.), *Recent developments in alcoholism* (Vol. 6, pp. 27–48). New York: Plenum.

Keane, T. M., & Kaloupek, D. G. (1997). Comorbid psychiatric disorders in PTSD: Implications for research. *Annals of the New York Academy of Sciences, 821,* 24–34.

Keane, T. M., Newman, E., & Orsillo, S. M. (1997). Assessment of military-related posttraumatic stress disorder. In J. P. Wilson & T. M. Keane (Eds.), *Assessing psychological trauma and PTSD* (pp. 267–290). New York: Guilford Press.

Keane, T. M., & Wolfe, J. (1990). Comorbidity in post-traumatic stress disorder: An analysis of community and clinical studies. *Journal of Applied Social Psychology, 20,* 1776–1788.

Keith, L. D., Roberts, A., Wiren, K. M., & Crabbe, J. C. (1995). Corticosteroid–alcohol interactions. In W. A. Hunt & S. Zakhari (Eds.), *Stress, gender, and alcohol-seeking behavior* (NIDA Research Monograph No. 29, pp. 181–196). Bethesda, MD: National Institutes of Health.

Kelleher, K., Chaffin, M., Hollenberg, J., & Fischer, E. (1994). Alcohol and drug disorders among physically abusive and neglectful parents in a community-based sample. *American Journal of Public Health, 84,* 1586–1590.

Kendall-Tackett, K. A., Williams, L. M., & Finkelhor, D. (1993). Impact of sexual abuse on children: A review and synthesis of recent empirical literature. *Psychological Bulletin, 113,* 164–180.

Kessler, R. C. (2000). Posttraumatic stress disorder: The burden to the individual and to society. *Journal of Clinical Psychiatry, 61,* 4–12.

Kessler, R. C., Crum, R. M., Warner, L. A., Nelson, C. B., Schulenberg, J., & Anthony, J. C. (1997). Lifetime co-occurrence of *DSM–III–R* alcohol abuse and dependence with other psychiatric disorders in the National Comorbidity Survey. *Archives of General Psychiatry, 54,* 313–321.

Kessler, R. C., McGonagle, K. A., Zhao, S., Nelson, C. B., Hughes, M., Eshleman, S., et al. (1994). Lifetime and 12-month prevalence of *DSM–III–R* psychiatric disorders in the United States: Results from the National Comorbidity Survey. *Archives of General Psychiatry, 51,* 8–19.

Kessler, R. C., Sonnega, A., Bromet, E., Hughes, M., & Nelson, C. B. (1995). Posttraumatic stress disorder in the National Comorbidity Survey. *Archives of General Psychiatry, 52,* 1048–1060.

Khantzian, E. J. (1985). The self-medication hypothesis of addictive disorders: Focus on heroin and cocaine dependence. *American Journal of Psychiatry, 142,* 1259–1264.

Khantzian, E. J. (1997). The self-medication hypothesis of substance use disorders: A reconsideration and recent applications. *Harvard Review of Psychiatry, 4,* 231–244.

Kilpatrick, D. G. (1990, August). *Violence as a precursor of women's substance abuse: The rest of the drugs–violence story*. Paper presented at a Topical Mini-Convention on Substance Abuse and Violence at the 98th Annual Convention of the American Psychological Association, Boston.

Kilpatrick, D. G., Acierno, R., Resnick, H. S., Saunders, B. E., & Best, C. L. (1997). A 2-year longitudinal analysis of the relationships between violent assault and substance use in women. *Journal of Consulting and Clinical Psychology, 65*, 834–847.

Kilpatrick, D. G., Acierno, R., Saunders, B., Resnick, H. S., Best, C. L., & Schnurr, P. P. (2000). Risk factors for adolescent substance abuse and dependence: Data from a national sample. *Journal of Consulting and Clinical Psychology, 68*, 19–30.

Kilpatrick, D., Resnick, H., Saunders, B., & Best, C. (1989). *The National Women's Study PTSD module*. Unpublished instrument, Medical University of South Carolina, Charleston.

Kilpatrick, D. G., Veronen, L. J., & Resick, P. A. (1979). Assessment of the aftermath of rape: Changing patterns of fear. *Journal of Behavioral Assessment, 1*, 133–148.

Kofoed, L., Friedman, M. J., & Peck, R. (1993). Alcoholism and drug abuse in patients with PTSD. *Psychiatric Quarterly, 64*, 151–171.

Kolb, L. D. (1985). The place of narcosynthesis in the treatment of chronic and delayed stress reactions of war. In S. M. Sonnenber, A. S. Blank, & J. A. Talbott (Eds.), *The trauma of war: Stress and recovery in Vietnam veterans* (pp. 211–236). Washington, DC: American Psychological Association.

Koltek, M., Wilkes, T. C. R., & Atkinson, M. (1998). The prevalence of posttraumatic stress disorder in an adolescent inpatient unit. *Canadian Journal of Psychiatry, 43*, 64–68.

Koob, G. F. (1999). Corticotrophin-releasing factor, norepinephrine, and stress. *Biological Psychiatry, 46*, 1167–1180.

Koopman, C., Classen, C., & Spiegel, D. (1994). Predictors of posttraumatic stress symptoms among survivors of the Oakland/Berkeley, Calif., firestorm. *American Journal of Psychiatry, 151*, 888–894.

Koss, M. P., & Gaines, J. A. (1993). The prediction of sexual aggression by alcohol use, athletic participation, and fraternity affiliation. *Journal of Interpersonal Violence, 8*, 94–108.

Koss, M. P., Gidycz, C., & Wisniewski, N. (1987). The scope of rape: Incidence and prevalence of sexual aggression and victimization in a national sample of higher education students. *Journal of Consulting and Clinical Psychology, 55*, 162–170.

Kosten, T. R., & Krystal, J. (1988). Biological mechanisms in posttraumatic stress disorder: Relevance for substance abuse. In M. Galanter (Ed.), *Recent developments in alcoholism* (Vol. 6, pp. 49–68). New York: Plenum.

Kotch, J. B., Browne, D. C., Dufort, V., & Winsor, J. (1999). Predicting child maltreatment in the first 4 years of life from characteristics assessed in the neonatal period. *Child Abuse & Neglect, 23*, 305–319.

Kounios, J., Litz, B., Kaloupek, D., Riggs, D., Knight, J., Weathers, F., et al. (1997). Electrophysiology of combat related PTSD. In R. Yehuda & A. C. McFarlane (Eds.), *Psychobiology of posttraumatic stress disorder* (Vol. 821, pp. 504–507). New York: New York Academy of Sciences.

Krinsley, K. E., Brief, D. J., Weathers, F. W., & Steinberg, H. R. (1994, November). *Problems associated with childhood trauma in substance abusers.* Paper presented at the annual meeting of the Association for Advancement of Behavior Therapy, San Diego, California.

Krinsley, K. E., Young, L. S., Weathers, F. W., Brief, D. J., & Kelley, J. M. (1992, November). *Behavioral correlates of childhood trauma in substance abusing men.* Paper presented at the Annual meeting of the Association for the Advancement of Behavior Therapy, Boston.

Kroenke, K., & Spitzer, R. L. (1998). Gender difference in the reporting of physical and somatoform symptoms. *Psychosomatic Medicine, 60,* 150–155.

Krystal, H. (1984). Psychoanalytic views on human emotional damages. In B. A. Van der Kolk (Ed.), *Posttraumatic stress disorder: Psychological and biological sequelae* (pp. 1–28). Washington, DC: American Psychiatric Press.

Kubany, E. S. (1998). Cognitive therapy for trauma-related guilt. In V. M. Follette, J. I. Ruzek, & F. R. Abueg (Eds.), *Cognitive–behavioral therapies for trauma* (pp. 124–161). New York: Guilford Press.

Kubany, E. S., Haynes, S. N., Abueg, F. R., Manke, F. P., Brennan, J. M., & Stahura, C. (1996). Development and validation of the Trauma-Related Guilt Inventory (TRGI). *Psychological Assessment, 8,* 428–444.

Kubany, E. S., Leisen, M. B., Kaplan, A. S., Watson, S. B., Haynes, S. N., Owens, J. A., & Burns, K. (2000). Development and preliminary validation of a brief broad-spectrum measure of trauma exposure: The Traumatic Life Events Questionnaire. *Psychological Assessment, 12,* 210–224.

Kulka, R. A., Schlenger, W. E., Fairbank, J. A., Hough, R. L., Jordan, B. K., Marmar, C. R., & Weiss, D. S. (1990). *Trauma and the Vietnam War generation: Report on findings from the National Vietnam Veterans Readjustment Study.* New York: Brunner/Mazel.

Kushner, M. G., Abrams, K., & Borchardt, C. (2000). The relationship between anxiety disorders and alcohol use disorders: A review of major perspectives and findings. *Clinical Psychology Review, 20,* 149–171.

LaCoursiere, R. B., Godfrey, K. E., & Ruby, L. M. (1980). Traumatic neurosis in the etiology of alcoholism: Vietnam and other trauma. *American Journal of Psychiatry, 137,* 966–968.

Lake, E. S. (1993). An exploration of the violent victim experiences of female offenders. *Violence and Victims, 8,* 41–51.

Lang, A. R., Patrick, C. J., & Stritzke, W. G. K. (1999). Alcohol and emotional response: A multidimensional–multilevel analysis. In K. E. Leonard & H. T. Blane (Eds.), *Psychological theories of drinking and alcoholism* (2nd ed., pp. 328–371). New York: Guilford Press.

Lang, P. J. (1979). A bio-informational theory of emotional imagery. *Psychophysiology*, *16*, 495–512.

Lang, P. J. (1995). The emotion probe: Studies of motivation and attention. *American Psychologist*, *5*, 372–385.

LeDoux, J. E. (1996). *The emotional brain*. New York: Simon & Schuster.

Lee, Y., & Davis, M. (1997). Role of the hippocampus, the bed of the nucleus of the stria terminalis, and the amygdala in the excitatory effect of corticotropin releasing hormone on the acoustic startle reflex. *Journal of Neuroscience*, *17*, 6434–6446.

Leigh, G., & Skinner, H. A. (1988). Drinking behavior and alcohol dependence: Physiological assessment. In D. M. Donovan & G. A. Marlatt (Eds.), *Assessment of addictive behaviors* (pp. 112–138). New York: Guilford Press.

Leonard, K. E., & Senchak, M. (1996). Prospective prediction of husband marital aggression within newlywed couples. *Journal of Abnormal Psychology*, *105*, 369–380.

Leonhard, C., Mulvey, K., Gastfriend, D. R., & Shwartz, M. (2000). The Addiction Severity Index: A field study of internal consistency and validity. *Journal of Substance Abuse Treatment*, *18*, 129–135.

Lerner, H. G. (1988). *Women in therapy*. Northvale, NJ: Jason Aronson.

Levitan, R. D., Blouin, A. G., Navarro, J. R., & Hill, J. (1991). Validity of the computerized DIS for diagnosing psychiatric inpatients. *Canadian Journal of Psychiatry*, *36*, 728–731.

Lewinsohn, P. M., Hops, H., Roberts, R. E., Seeley, J. R., & Andrews, J. A. (1993). Adolescent psychopathology: I. Prevalence and incidence of depression and other *DSM–III–R* disorders in high school students. *Journal of Abnormal Psychology*, *102*, 133–144.

Lilienfeld, D. E., & Stolley, P. D. (1994). *Foundations of epidemiology* (3rd ed.). New York: Oxford University Press.

Linehan, M. M., Schmidt, H., Dimeff, L. A., Craft, J. C., Kanter, J., & Comtois, K. A. (1999). Dialectical behavior therapy for patients with borderline personality disorder and drug dependence. *American Journal on Addictions*, *8*, 279–292.

Lipschitz, D. S., Winegar, R. K., Hartnick, E., Foote, B., & Southwick, S. M. (1999). Posttraumatic stress disorder in hospitalized adolescents: Psychiatric comorbidity and clinical correlates. *Journal of the American Academy of Child and Adolescent Psychiatry*, *38*, 385–392.

Lisak, D., Hopper, J., & Song, P. (1996). Factors in the cycle of violence: Gender rigidity and emotional constriction. *Journal of Traumatic Stress*, *7*, 507–523.

Lister, R. G., Gorenstein, C., Risher-Flowers, D., Weingartner, H. J., & Eckardt, M. J. (1991). Dissociation of the acute effects of alcohol on implicit and explicit memory processes. *Neuropsychologia*, *29*, 1205–1212.

Litz, B. T., Blake, D. D., Gerardi, R. G., & Keane, T. M. (1990). Decision making guidelines for the use of direct therapeutic exposure in the treatment of posttraumatic stress disorder. *The Behavior Therapist*, *13*, 91–93.

Litz, B. T., Orsillo, S. M., Friedman, M. J., Ehlich, P. J., & Batres, A. R. (1997). Posttraumatic stress disorder associated with peacekeeping duty in Somalia for U.S. military personnel. *American Journal of Psychiatry, 154,* 178–184.

Loftus, E. F., Garry, M., & Feldman, J. (1994). Forgetting sexual trauma: What does it mean when 38% forget? *Journal of Consulting and Clinical Psychology, 62,* 1177–1181.

Longabaugh, R., Wirtz, P. W., Zweban, A., & Stout, R. L. (1998). Network support for drinking, Alcoholics Anonymous, and long-term matching effects. *Addiction, 93,* 1313–1333.

Luntz, B. K., & Widom, C. S. (1994). Antisocial personality disorder in abused and neglected children grown up. *American Journal of Psychiatry, 151,* 670–674.

Machell, D. F. (1993). Combat posttraumatic stress disorder, alcoholism and the police officer. *Journal of Alcohol and Drug Education, 38,* 23–32.

Macleod, A. D. (1994). The reactivation of posttraumatic stress disorder later in life. *Australian and New Zealand Journal of Psychiatry, 28,* 625–634.

Maes, M., Delmeire, L. C. S., Janca, A., Creten, T., Mylle, J., Struyf, A., Pison, G., & Rousseeuw, P. J. (1998). The two-factorial symptom structure of posttraumatic stress disorder: Depression–avoidance and arousal–anxiety. *Psychiatry Research, 81,* 195–210.

Maeve, M. K. (2000). Speaking unavoidable truths: Understanding early childhood sexual and physical violence among women in prison. *Issues in Mental Health Nursing, 21,* 473–498.

Malgady, R. G., Rogler, L. H., & Tryon, W. W. (1992). Issues of validity in the Diagnostic Interview Schedule. *Journal of Psychiatric Research, 26,* 85–95.

Malinosky-Rummell, R., & Hansen, D. J. (1993). Long-term consequences of childhood physical abuse. *Psychological Bulletin, 114,* 68–79.

March, J. S., & Amaya-Jackson, L. (1993). Post-traumatic stress disorder in children and adolescents. *PTSD Research Quarterly, 4,* 1–7.

Marks, I., Lovell, K., Noshirvani, H., Livanou, M., & Thrasher, S. (1998). Treatment of posttraumatic stress disorder by exposure and/or cognitive restructuring: A controlled study. *Archives of General Psychiatry, 55,* 317–325.

Marlatt, G. A. (1996). Commentary on replications of Marlatt's taxonomy: Lest taxonomy become taxidermy: A comment on the Relapse Replication and Extension Project. *Addiction, 91*(Suppl.), S147–S153.

Marlatt, G. A., & Gordon, J. R. (Eds.). (1985). *Relapse prevention.* New York: Guilford Press.

Martin, J., Anderson, J., Romans, S., Mullen, P., & O'Shea, M. (1993). Asking about child sexual abuse: Methodological implications of a two stage survey. *Child Abuse & Neglect, 17,* 383–392.

Martin, S. S., Butzin, C. A., & Inciardi, J. A. (1995). Assessment of a multistage therapeutic community for drug-involved offenders. *Journal of Psychoactive Drugs, 27,* 109–116.

Maxfield, M. G., Weiler, B. L., & Widom, C. S. (2000). Comparing self-reports and official records of arrests. *Journal of Quantitative Criminology, 36*, 347–370.

Mazza, J. J., & Reynolds, W. M. (1999). Exposure to violence in young inner-city adolescents: Relationships with suicidal ideation, depression, and PTSD symptomatology. *Journal of Abnormal Child Psychology, 27*, 203–213.

McClellan, D. S., Farabee, D., & Crouch, B. M. (1997). Early victimization, drug use, and criminality. *Criminal Justice and Behavior, 24*, 455–476.

McCormick, R. A., & Smith, M. (1995). Aggression and hostility in substance abusers: The relationship to abuse patterns, coping style, and relapse triggers. *Addictive Behaviors, 20*, 555–562.

McCranie, E. W., & Hyer, L. A. (2000). Posttraumatic stress disorder symptoms in Korean conflict and World War II combat veterans seeking outpatient treatment. *Journal of Traumatic Stress, 13*, 427–439.

McDermott, P. S., Alterman, A. I., Brown, L., Zaballero, A., Snider, E. C., & McKay, J. R. (1996). Construct refinement and confirmation for the Addiction Severity Index. *Psychological Assessment, 8*, 182–189.

McEwen, B. S. (2000). The neurobiology of stress: From serendipity to clinical relevance. *Brain Research, 886*, 172–189.

McEwen, B. S., & Magarino, A. M. (1997). Stress effects on morphology and function of the hippocampus. In R. Yehuda & A. C. McFarlane (Eds.), *Psychobiology of posttraumatic stress disorder* (Vol. 821, pp. 271–284). New York: New York Academy of Sciences.

McFall, M. E., Fontana, A., Raskind, M. A., & Rosenheck, R. A. (1999). Analysis of violent behavior in Vietnam combat veteran psychiatric inpatients with posttraumatic stress disorder. *Journal of Traumatic Stress, 12*, 501–517.

McFall, M. E., Mackay, P. W., & Donovan, D. M. (1992). Combat-related posttraumatic stress disorder and severity of substance abuse in Vietnam veterans. *Journal of Studies on Alcohol, 53*, 357–363.

McFall, M., Smith, D., Roszell, D. K., Tarver, D. J., & Malas, K. L. (1990). Convergent validity of measures of PTSD in Vietnam combat veterans. *American Journal of Psychiatry, 147*, 645–648.

McGruder-Johnson, A. K., Davidson, E. S., Gleaves, D. H., Stock, W., & Finch, J. F. (2000). Interpersonal violence and posttraumatic symptomatology: The effects of ethnicity, gender, and exposure to violent events. *Journal of Interpersonal Violence, 15*, 205–221.

McLellan, A. T., Kushner, H., Metzger, D., Peters, R., Smith, I., Grissom, G., et al. (1992). The fifth edition of the Addiction Severity Index. *Journal of Substance Abuse Treatment, 9*, 199–213.

McMillen, J. C., North, C. S., & Smith, E. M. (2000). What parts of PTSD are normal: Intrusion, avoidance, or arousal? Data from the Northridge, California, earthquake. *Journal of Traumatic Stress, 13*, 57–75.

McNally, R. J. (1997). Implicit and explicit memory for trauma-related information in PTSD. In R. Yehuda & A. C. McFarlane (Eds.), *Psychobiology of posttraumatic stress disorder* (Vol. 821, pp. 219–224). New York: New York Academy of Sciences.

Meadows, E., & Foa, E. B. (1999). Cognitive–behavioral treatment of traumatized adults. In P. Saigh & D. Bremner (Eds.), *Posttraumatic stress disorder: A comprehensive text* (pp. 376–390). Boston: Allyn & Bacon.

Meichenbaum, D., & Cameron, R. (1983). Stress inoculation training: Toward a general paradigm for training coping skills. In D. Meichenbaum & M. E. Jaremko (Eds.), *Stress reduction and prevention* (pp. 115–157). New York: Plenum.

Meichenbaum, D. H., & Deffenbacher, J. L. (1988). Stress inoculation training. *The Counseling Psychologist, 16,* 69–90.

Meichenbaum, D., & Novaco, R. (1985). Stress inoculation: A preventative approach. *Issues in Mental Health Nursing, 7,* 419–435.

Meisler, A. W. (1996). Trauma, PTSD, and substance abuse. *PTSD Research Quarterly, 7,* 1–6.

Meisler, A. W. (1999). Group treatment of PTSD and comorbid alcohol abuse. In B. H. Young & D. D. Blake (Eds.), *Group treatments for post-traumatic stress disorder* (pp. 117–136). Philadelphia: Brunner/Mazel.

Mellman, T. A., Randolph, C. A., Brawman-Mintzer, O., & Flores, L. P. (1992). Phenomenology and course of psychiatric disorders associated with combat-related posttraumatic stress disorder. *American Journal of Psychiatry, 149,* 1568–1574.

Mendel, M. P. (1995). *The male survivor.* Thousand Oaks, CA: Sage.

Mercer, D., Carpenter, G., Daley, D., Patterson, C., & Volpicelli, J. (1994). *Addiction recovery manual* (Vol. 2). Philadelphia: University of Pennsylvania, Treatment Research Unit.

Merikangas, K. A., Stevens, D., & Fenton, B. (1996). Comorbidity of alcoholism and anxiety disorders. *Alcohol Health and Research World, 20,* 100–105.

Metzger, D. S., Navaline, H., & Woody, G. E. (2000). *The role of drug abuse treatment in the prevention: AIDS prevention and mental health.* New York: Kluwer Academic/Plenum.

Metzger, L. J., Orr, S. P., Lasko, N. B., Berry, N. J., & Pitman, R. K. (1997). Evidence for diminished P3 amplitudes in PTSD. In R. Yehuda & A. C. McFarlane (Eds.), *Psychobiology of posttraumatic stress disorder* (Vol. 821, pp. 499–501). New York: New York Academy of Sciences.

Miller, D., & Guidry, L. (2001). *Addictions and trauma recovery.* New York: Norton.

Miller, W. R., & Rollnick, S. (1992). *Motivational interviewing: Preparing people to change addictive behavior.* New York: Guilford Press.

Miller, W. R., Westerberg, V. S., & Waldron, H. B. (1995). Evaluating alcohol problems in adults and adolescents. In R. K. Hester & W. R. Miller (Eds.), *Handbook of alcoholism treatment approaches: Effective alternatives* (pp. 61–88). Needham Heights, MA: Simon & Schuster.

Miller, W. R., Zweben, A., DiClemente, C. C., & Rychtarik, R. G. (Eds.). (1995). *Motivational enhancement therapy manual* (Vol. 2). Rockville, MD: U.S. Department of Health and Human Services.

Millsaps, C. L., Azrin, R. L., & Mittenberg, W. (1994). Neuropsychological effects of chronic cannabis use on the memory and intelligence of adolescents. *Journal of Child and Adolescent Substance Abuse, 3,* 47–55.

Monti, P. M., Abrams, D. B., Kadden, R. M., & Cooney, N. L. (1989). *Treating alcohol dependence: A coping skills training guide.* New York: Guilford Press.

Monti, P. M., Rohsenow, D. R., Colby, S. M., & Abrams, D. B. (1995). Coping and social skills training. In R. K. Hester & W. R. Miller (Eds.), *Handbook of alcoholism treatment approaches: Effective alternatives* (pp. 221–241). Needham Heights, MA: Simon & Schuster.

Morgan, C. A. III, Grillon, C., Lubin, H., & Southwick, S. M. (1997). Startle deficits in women with sexual assault-related PTSD. In R. Yehuda & A. C. McFarlane (Eds.), *Psychobiology of posttraumatic stress disorder* (Vol. 821, pp. 486–490). New York: New York Academy of Sciences.

Morgan, C. A., Grillon, C., Southwick, S. M., Davis, M., & Charney, D. (1995). Fear-potentiated startle in posttraumatic stress disorder. *Biological Psychiatry, 36,* 378–385.

Morgan, C. A., Hill, S., Fox, P., Kingham, P., & Southwick, S. M. (1999). Anniversary reactions in Gulf War veterans: A follow-up inquiry 6 years after the war. *American Journal of Psychiatry, 156,* 1075–1079.

Morrissey, E. R., & Schuckit, M. A. (1978). Stressful life events and alcohol problems among women seen at a detoxification center. *Journal of Studies on Alcohol, 39,* 1559–1576.

Mowrer, O. A. (1960). *Learning theory and behavior.* New York: Wiley.

Murphy, R. T., Cameron, R. P., Sharp, L., & Ramirez, G. (1999). Motivating veterans to change PTSD symptoms and related behaviors. *National Center for PTSD Clinical Quarterly, 8,* 32–36.

Muss, D. (1991). *The trauma trap.* London: Doubleday.

Nace, E. P. (1988). Posttraumatic stress disorder and substance abuse: Clinical issues. In N. Galanter (Ed.), *Recent developments in alcoholism* (Vol. 6, pp. 9–26). New York: Plenum.

Najavits, L. M. (2000). Training clinicians in the *Seeking Safety* treatment for posttraumatic stress disorder and substance abuse. *Alcoholism Treatment Quarterly, 18,* 83–98.

Najavits, L. M. (2001). Early career award paper: Helping difficult patients. *Psychotherapy Research, 11,* 131–152.

Najavits, L. M. (2002a). Clinicians' views on treating posttraumatic stress disorder and substance use disorder. *Journal of Substance Abuse Treatment, 22,* 79–85.

Najavits, L. M. (2002b). *Seeking Safety: A treatment manual for PTSD and substance abuse.* New York: Guilford Press.

Najavits, L. M., Crits-Christoph, P., & Dierberger, A. E. (2000). Clinicians' impact on substance abuse treatment. *Substance Use and Misuse, 35,* 2161–2190.

Najavits, L. M., Dierberger, A. E., & Weiss, R. D. (1999, November). *PTSD/ substance abuse patients: Treatment utilization and satisfaction.* Poster presented at the 15th annual meeting of the International Society for Traumatic Stress Studies, Miami, FL.

Najavits, L. M., & Garber, J. (1989). *A cognitive–behavioral group therapy curriculum for inpatient depressed adolescents and adults.* Unpublished manuscript, Vanderbilt University.

Najavits, L. M., Gastfriend, D. R., Barber, J. P., Reif, S., Muenz, L. R., Blaine, J., et al. (1998). Cocaine dependence with and without PTSD among subjects in the National Institute on Drug Abuse Collaborative Cocaine Treatment Study. *American Journal of Psychiatry, 155,* 214–219.

Najavits, L. M., Schmitz, M., Gotthardt, S., & Weiss, R. D. (2002). *Seeking Safety plus Exposure Therapy-Revised: An outcome study in men with PTSD and substance dependence.* Manuscript submitted for publication.

Najavits, L. M., & Weiss, R. D. (1994). Variations in therapist effectiveness in the treatment of patients with substance use disorders: An empirical review. *Addiction, 89,* 679–688.

Najavits, L. M., Weiss, R. D., & Liese, B. S. (1996). Group cognitive–behavioral therapy for women with PTSD and substance use disorder. *Journal of Substance Abuse Treatment, 13,* 13–22.

Najavits, L. M., Weiss, R. D., Reif, S., Gastfriend, D. R., Siqueland, L., Barber, J. P., et al. (1998). The Addiction Severity Index as a screen for trauma and posttraumatic stress disorder. *Journal of Studies on Alcohol, 59,* 56–62.

Najavits, L. M., Weiss, R. D., & Shaw, S. R. (1997). The link between substance abuse and posttraumatic stress disorder in women. *American Journal on Addictions, 6,* 273–283.

Najavits, L. M., Weiss, R. D., & Shaw, S. R. (1999). A clinical profile of women with posttraumatic stress disorder and substance dependence. *Psychology of Addictive Behaviors, 13,* 98–104.

Najavits, L. M., Weiss, R., Shaw, S., & Dierberger, A. (2000). Psychotherapists' views of treatment manuals. *Professional Psychology: Research and Practice, 31,* 404–408.

Najavits, L. M., Weiss, R. D., Shaw, S. R., & Muenz, L. R. (1998). "Seeking Safety": Outcome of a new cognitive–behavioral psychotherapy for women with posttraumatic stress disorder and substance abuse. *Journal of Traumatic Stress, 11,* 437–456.

Nash, M. R., Hulsey, T. L., Sexton, M. C., Harralson, T. L., & Lambert, W. (1993). Long-term sequelae of childhood sexual abuse: Perceived family environment, psychopathology, and dissociation. *Journal of Consulting and Clinical Psychology, 61,* 276–283.

National Crime Victims Research and Treatment Center. (1989). *Victim reaction handout.* Unpublished document, National Crime Victims Research and Treatment Center, Department of Psychiatry and Behavioral Sciences, Medical University of South Carolina.

Nelson-Zlupko, L., Dore, M. M., Kauffman, E., & Kaltenbach, K. (1996). Women in recovery: Their perceptions of treatment effectiveness. *Journal of Substance Abuse Treatment, 13*, 51–59.

Nemeroff, C. B., Widerlov, E., Bissette, G., Walleus, H., Karlsson, I., Eklund, K., et al. (1984, December 14). Elevated concentrations of CSF cotricotropin-releasing factor-like immunoreactivity in depressed patients. *Science, 226*, 1342–1344.

Newcomb, M. D., & Bentler, P. M. (1988). Impact of adolescent drug use and social support on problems of young adults: A longitudinal study. *Journal of Abnormal Psychology, 97*, 64–75.

Nezu, A. M., & Carnevale, G. J. (1987). Interpersonal problem solving and coping reactions of Vietnam veterans with posttraumatic stress disorder. *Journal of Abnormal Psychology, 96*, 155–157.

Norris, F. H. (1990). Screening for traumatic stress: A scale for use in the general population. *Journal of Applied Social Psychology, 20*, 1704–1718.

Norris, F. H. (1992). Epidemiology of trauma: Frequency and impact of different potentially traumatic events on different demographic groups. *Journal of Consulting and Clinical Psychology, 60*, 409–418.

Norris, F. H., & Riad, J. K. (1997). Standardized self-report measures of civilian trauma and posttraumatic stress disorder. In J. P. Wilson & T. M. Keane (Eds.), *Assessing psychological trauma and PTSD* (pp. 7–42). New York: Guilford Press.

North, C. S., Nixon, S. J., Shariat, S., Mallonee, S., McMillen, J. C., Spitznagel, E. L., & Smith, E. M. (1999). Psychiatric disorders among survivors of the Oklahoma City bombing. *Journal of the American Medical Association, 282*, 755–762.

Novaco, R. W., & Chemtob, C. M. (1998). Anger and trauma: Conceptualization, assessment, and treatment. In V. M. Follette, J. I. Ruzek, & F. R. Abueg (Eds.), *Cognitive–behavioral therapies for trauma* (pp. 162–190). New York: Guilford Press.

Novick, R. W. (1975). *Anger control: The development and evaluation of an experimental treatment.* Lexington, MA: Heath.

Novick, R. W. (1977). Stress inoculation: A cognitive therapy for anger and its application to a case of depression. *Journal of Consulting and Clinical Psychology, 45*, 600–608.

Ochberg, F. (1996). The counting methods for ameliorating traumatic memories. *Journal of Traumatic Stress, 9*, 873–880.

O'Farrell, T. J., Maisto, S. A. (1987). The utility of self-report and biological measures of alcohol consumption in alcoholism treatment outcome studies. *Advances in Behavior Research and Therapy, 9*, 91–125.

Orr, S. P., & Kaloupek, D. G. (1997). Psychophysiological assessment of posttraumatic stress disorder. In J. P. Wilson & T. M. Keane (Eds.), *Assessing psychological trauma and PTSD* (pp. 69–97). New York: Guilford Press.

Orsillo, S. M., Roemer, L., Litz, B. T., Ehlich, P. J., & Friedman, M. J. (1998). Psychiatric symptomatology associated with contemporary peacekeeping: An examination of post-mission functioning among peacekeepers in Somalia. *Journal of Traumatic Stress, 11,* 611–625.

Otto, M. W., & Reilly-Harrington, N. A. (1999). The impact of treatment on anxiety sensitivity. In S. Taylor (Ed.), *Anxiety sensitivity: Theory, research, and treatment of the fear of anxiety* (pp. 321–336). Mahwah, NJ: Erlbaum.

Ouimette, P. C. (1997). Psychopathology and sexual aggression in nonincarcerated men. *Violence and Victims, 12,* 389–395.

Ouimette, P. C. (2000). [SUD–PTSD patients' abstinence rates and problems from substance use at follow-up]. Unpublished raw data.

Ouimette, P. C., Ahrens, C., Moos, R. H., & Finney, J. W. (1997). Posttraumatic stress disorder in substance abuse patients: Relationship to 1-year posttreatment outcomes. *Psychology of Addictive Behaviors, 11,* 34–47.

Ouimette, P. C., Ahrens, C., Moos, R. H., & Finney, J. W. (1998). During treatment changes in substance abuse patients with posttraumatic stress disorder: The influence of specific interventions and program environments. *Journal of Substance Abuse Treatment, 15,* 555–564.

Ouimette, P. C., Brown, P. J., & Najavits, L. M. (1998). Course and treatment of patients with both substance use and posttraumatic stress disorders. *Addictive Behaviors, 23,* 785–795.

Ouimette, P. C., Finney, J. W., & Moos, R. H. (1999). Two-year posttreatment functioning and coping of substance abuse patients with posttraumatic stress disorder. *Psychology of Addictive Behaviors, 13,* 105–114.

Ouimette, P. C., Humphreys, K., Moos, R. H., Finney, J. W., Cronkite, R., & Federman, B. (2001). Self-help group participation among substance use disorder patients with PTSD. *Journal of Substance Abuse Treatment, 20,* 25–32.

Ouimette, P. C., Kimerling, R., Shaw, J., & Moos, R. H. (2000). Physical and sexual abuse among women and men with substance use disorders. *Alcoholism Treatment Quarterly, 18,* 7–17.

Ouimette, P. C., Moos, R. H., & Finney, J. W. (2000). Two-year mental health service use and course of remission in patients with substance use and posttraumatic stress disorders. *Journal of Studies on Alcohol, 61,* 247–253.

Ouimette, P. C., Moos, R. H., & Finney, J. W. (in press). PTSD treatment and five-year remission among patients with substance use and posttraumatic stress disorders. *Journal of Consulting and Clinical Psychology.*

Ouimette, P. C., & Riggs, D. (1998). Testing a mediational model of sexually aggressive behavior in nonincarcerated perpetrators. *Violence and Victims, 13,* 117–130.

Ouimette, P. C., Wolfe, J., & Chrestman, K. R. (1996). Characteristics of posttraumatic stress disorder—Alcohol abuse comorbidity in women. *Journal of Substance Abuse, 8,* 335–346.

Owen, B., & Bloom, B. (1995). Profiling women prisoners: Findings from national surveys and a California sample. *Prison Journal, 75*, 165–186.

Parrish, S. K. (1994). Adolescent substance abuse: The challenge for clinicians. *Alcohol, 11*, 453–455.

Patrick, C. J., Berthot, B., & Moore, J. D. (1993). Effects of diazepam on startle reflex potentiation in human subjects [Summary]. *Psychophysiology, 130*, S49.

Pearlman, L. A., & Saakvitne, K. W. (1995). *Trauma and the therapist: Countertransference and vicarious traumatization in psychotherapy with incest survivors.* New York: Norton.

Penk, W. E., Peck, R. F., Robinowitz, R., Bell, W., & Little, D. (1988). Coping and defending styles among Vietnam combat veterans seeking treatment for post-traumatic stress disorder and substance use disorder. In M. Galanter (Ed.), *Recent developments in alcoholism* (pp. 69–88). New York: Plenum.

Perconte, S. T., & Griger, M. L. (1991). Comparison of successful, unsuccessful, and relapsed Vietnam veterans treated for posttraumatic stress disorder. *Journal of Nervous and Mental Disease, 179*, 558–562.

Perkonigg, A., Kessler, R. C., Storz, S., & Wittchen, H.-U. (2000). Traumatic events and post-traumatic stress disorder in the community: Prevalence, risk factors, and comorbidity. *Acta Psychiatrica Scandinavica, 101*, 46–59.

Peters, R. H., Strozier, A. L., Murrin, M. R., & Kearns, W. D. (1997). Treatment of substance-abusing jail inmates: Examination of gender differences. *Journal of Substance Abuse Treatment, 14*, 339–349.

Peterson, J. B., Finn, P. R., & Pihl, R. O. (1992). Cognitive dysfunction and the inherited predisposition to alcoholism. *Journal of Studies on Alcohol, 53*, 154–160.

Peterson, R. A., & Reiss, S. (1992). *Anxiety Sensitivity Index manual* (2nd ed.). Worthington, OH: International Diagnostic Systems.

Peugh, J., & Belenko, S. (1999). Substance-involved women inmates: Challenges to providing effective treatment. *Prison Journal, 79*, 23–45.

Pfefferbaum, B. (1997). Posttraumatic stress disorder in children: A review of the past 10 years. *Journal of the American Academy of Child and Adolescent Psychiatry, 36*, 1503–1511.

Picton, T. W. (1992). The P300 wave of the human event-related potential. *Journal of Clinical Neurophysiology, 9*, 456–479.

Piette, J. D., Baisden, K. L., & Moos, R. H. (1999). *Health services for VA substance abuse patients: Utilization for fiscal year 1998.* Palo Alto, CA: Program Evaluation and Resource Center.

Pihl, R. O., Peterson, J. B., & Finn, P. R. (1990). Inherited predisposition to alcoholism: Characteristics of sons of male alcoholics. *Journal of Abnormal Psychology, 99*, 291–301.

Pitman, R. K., Altman, B., Greenwald, E., Longpre, R. E., Macklin, M. L., Poire, R. E., & Steketee, G. S. (1991). Psychiatric complications during flooding therapy for posttraumatic stress disorder. *Journal of Clinical Psychiatry, 52,* 17–20.

Pohorecky, L. A. (1977). Biphasic action of ethanol. *Biobehavioral Research, 1,* 231–240.

Pollack, J. M. (1998). *Counseling women in prison.* Thousand Oaks, CA: Sage.

Pollock, V. E., Volavka, J., Goodwin, D. W., Mednick, S. A., Gabrielli, W. F., Knop, J., & Schulsinger, F. (1983). The EEG after alcohol administration in men at risk for alcoholism. *Archives of General Psychiatry, 40,* 857–861.

Powell, T. A., Holt, J. C., & Fondacaro, K. M. (1997). The prevalence of mental illness among inmates in a rural state. *Journal of Law and Human Behavior, 21,* 427–438.

Prendergast, M. L., Wellisch, J., & Falkin, G. P. (1995). Assessment of and services for substance-abusing women offenders in community and correctional settings. *Prison Journal, 75,* 240–255.

Prochaska, J. O., & DiClemente, C. C. (1986). Toward a comprehensive model of change. In W. R. Miller & N. Heather (Eds.), *Treating addictive behaviors: Processes of change* (pp. 3–27). New York: Plenum.

Proctor, S. P., Heeren, T., White, R. F., Wolfe, J., Borgos, M. S., Davis, J. D., et al. (1998). Health status of Persian Gulf War veterans: Self-reported symptoms, environmental exposures and the effect of stress. *International Journal of Epidemiology, 27,* 1000–1010.

Project MATCH Research Group. (1997). Matching alcoholism treatments to client heterogeneity: Project MATCH posttreatment drinking outcomes. *Journal of Studies on Alcohol, 58,* 7–29.

Rachman, S. J. (1991). A psychological approach to the study of comorbidity. *Clinical Psychology Review, 11,* 461–464.

Rasmusson, A. M., & Charney, D. S. (1997). Animal models of relevance to PTSD. In R. Yehuda & A. C. McFarlane (Eds.), *Psychobiology of posttraumatic stress disorder* (Vol. 821, pp. 332–351). New York: New York Academy of Sciences.

Rauch, S. L., & Shin, L. M. (1997). Functional neuroimaging studies in posttraumatic stress disorder. In R. Yehuda & A. C. McFarlane (Eds.), *Psychobiology of posttraumatic stress disorder* (Vol. 821, pp. 83–98). New York: New York Academy of Sciences.

Redmond, D. E. Jr. (1987). Studies of nucleus locu-caeruleus in monkeys and hypotheses for neuropsychopharmacology. In H. Y. Meltzer (Ed.), *Psychopharmacology: The third generation of progress* (pp. 867–875). New York: Raven Press.

Regier, D. A., Kaebler, C. T., Rae, D. S., Farmer, M. E., Knauper, B., Kessler, R. C., & Norquist, G. S. (1998). Limitations of diagnostic criteria and assessment instruments for mental disorders. *Archives of General Psychiatry, 55,* 109–115.

Reifman, A., & Windle, M. (1996). Vietnam combat exposure and recent drug use: A national study. *Journal of Traumatic Stress, 9,* 557–568.

Reilly, P. M., Clark, H. W., Shopshire, M. S., Lewis, E. W., & Sorensen, D. J. (1994). Anger management and temper control: Critical components of posttraumatic stress disorder and substance abuse treatment. *Journal of Psychoactive Drugs, 26,* 401–407.

Reinherz, H. Z., Giaconia, R. M., Lefkowitz, E. S., Pakiz, B., & Frost, A. K. (1993). Prevalence of psychiatric disorders in a community population of older adolescents. *Journal of the American Academy of Child and Adolescent Psychiatry, 32,* 369–377.

Resick, P. A., & Schnicke, M. K. (1993). *Cognitive processing therapy for rape victims: A treatment manual.* Newbury Park, CA: Sage.

Resnick, H. (1996). Psychometric review of National Women's Study Event History—PTSD Module. In B. H. Stamm (Ed.), *Measurement of stress, trauma, and adaptation* (pp. 214–217). Lutherville, MD: Sidran Press.

Resnick, H. S., Kilpatrick, D. G., Dansky, B. S., Saunders, B. E., & Best, C. L. (1993). Prevalence of civilian trauma and posttraumatic stress disorder in a representative national sample of women. *Journal of Consulting and Clinical Psychology, 61,* 984–991.

Resnick, H. S., Yehuda, R., & Acierno, R. (1997). Acute post rape cortisol, alcohol use, and PTSD symptom profile among recent rape victims. In R. Yehuda & A. C. McFarlane (Eds.), *Psychobiology of posttraumatic stress disorder* (Vol. 821, pp. 433–436). New York: New York Academy of Sciences.

Rice, C., Longabaugh, R., Beattie, M. C., & Noel, N. (1993). Age group differences in response to treatment for problematic alcohol use. *Addiction, 88,* 1369–1375.

Richards, D. A., Lovell, K., & Marks, I. M. (1994). Post-traumatic stress disorder: Evaluation of a behavioral treatment program. *Journal of Traumatic Stress, 7,* 669–680.

Richards, D. A., & Rose, J. S. (1991). Exposure therapy for post-traumatic stress disorder. Four case studies. *British Journal of Psychiatry, 158,* 836–840.

Richie, B. E. (2000, October). Keynote address presented at the National Institute of Justice's Research Conference on Violence Against Women and Family Violence, Washington, DC.

Richie, B. E., & Johnson, C. R. (1996). Abuse histories among newly incarcerated women in a New York City jail. *Journal of the American Medical Women's Association, 51,* 111–117.

Rivera, B., & Widom, C. S. (1990). Childhood victimization and violent offending. *Violence and Victims, 5,* 19–35.

Robins, L. N., Helzer, J. E., Cottler, L., & Golding, E. (1989). *NIMH Diagnostic Interview Schedule, Version III, Revised.* St. Louis, MO: Washington University.

Robins, L. N., Helzer, J. E., Croughan, J., & Ratcliff, K. S. (1981). National Institute of Mental Health Diagnostic Interview Schedule: Its history, characteristics, and validity. *Archives of General Psychiatry, 38,* 318–389.

Robins, L. N., & Regier, D. A. (Eds.). (1991). *Psychiatric disorders in America: The Epidemiologic Catchment Area Study.* New York: Free Press.

Roffman, R. A., & George, W. H. (1988). Cannabis abuse. In D. M. Donovan & G. A. Marlatt (Eds.), *Assessment of addictive behaviors* (pp. 325–363). New York: Guilford Press.

Roschke, J., Wagner, P., Mann, K., Fell, J., Grozinger, M., & Frank, C. (1996). Single trial analysis of event related potentials: A comparison between schizophrenics and depressives. *Biological Psychiatry, 40,* 844–852.

Rosen, C. S., Chow, H. C., Greenbaum, M. A., Finney, J. F., Moos, R. H., & Yesavage, J. A. (2000). *Use of best practices for posttraumatic stress disorder.* Manuscript submitted for publication.

Rossetti, Z. L., Longu, G., Mercuro, G., Hmaidan, Y., & Gessa, G. L. (1992). Biphasic effect of ethanol on noradrenaline release in the frontal cortex of awake rats. *Alcohol and Alcoholism, 27,* 477–480.

Roszell, D. K., McFall, M. E., & Malas, K. L. (1991). Frequency of symptoms and concurrent psychiatric disorder in Vietnam veterans with chronic PTSD. *Hospital and Community Psychiatry, 42,* 293–296.

Rothbaum, B. O., & Foa, E. B. (1993). Subtypes of post-traumatic stress disorder. In J. R. T. Davidson & E. B. Foa (Eds.), *Post-traumatic stress disorder: DSM–IV and beyond* (pp. 23–35). Washington, DC: American Psychiatric Press.

Rothbaum, B. O., Foa, E. B., Riggs, D. S., Murdock, T., & Walsh, W. (1992). A prospective examination of post-traumatic stress disorder in rape victims. *Journal of Traumatic Stress, 5,* 455–475.

Rubonis, A. V., Colby, S. M., Monti, P. M., Rohsenow, D. J., Gulliver, S. B., & Sirota, A. D. (1994). Alcohol cue reactivity and mood induction in male and female alcoholics. *Journal of Studies on Alcohol, 55,* 487–494.

Ruzek, J. I., Polusny, M. A., & Abueg, F. R. (1998). Assessment and treatment of concurrent posttraumatic stress disorder and substance abuse. In V. M. Follette, J. I. Ruzek, & F. R. Abueg (Eds.), *Cognitive behavioral therapies for trauma* (pp. 226–255). New York: Guilford Press.

Sable, M. R., Fieberg, J. R., Martin, S. L., & Kupper, L. L. (1999). Violent victimization experiences of pregnant prisoners. *American Journal of Orthopsychiatry, 69,* 392–397.

Saigh, P. A., Green, B. L., & Korol, M. (1996). The history and prevalence of posttraumatic stress disorder with special reference to children and adolescents. *Journal of School Psychology, 34,* 107–131.

Saigh, P. A., Yasik, A. E., Sack, W. H., & Koplewicz, H. S. (1999). Child–adolescent posttraumatic stress disorder: Prevalence, risk factors, and comorbidity. In P. A. Saigh & J. D. Bremner (Eds.), *Posttraumatic stress disorder: A comprehensive textbook* (pp. 18–43). Boston: Allyn & Bacon.

Saladin, M. E., Brady, K. T., Dansky, B. S., & Kilpatrick, D. G. (1995). Understanding comorbidity between PTSD and substance use disorders: Two preliminary investigations. *Addictive Behaviors, 20,* 643–655.

Saladin, M. E., Drobes, D. J., Coffey, S. F., Dansky, B. S., Brady, K. T., & Kilpatrick, D. G. (2001). *PTSD diagnosis and symptom severity as predictors of cue-elicited drug craving.* Manuscript submitted for publication.

Salloway, S., Southwick, S. M., & Sadowsky, M. (1990). Opiate withdrawal presenting as posttraumatic stress disorder. *Hospital and Community Psychiatry, 41,* 666–667.

Sananes, C. B., & Davis, M. (1992). N–methyl-D-aspartate lesions of the lateral and basolateral nuclei of the amygdaloid block fear-potentiated startle and shock sensitization of startle. *Behavioral Neuroscience, 106,* 72–80.

Sanders, J. F., McNeill, K. F., Rienzi, B. M., & DeLouth, T. B. (1997). The incarcerated female felon and substance abuse: Demographics, needs assessment, and program planning for a neglected population. *Journal of Addictions and Offender Counseling, 18,* 41–51.

Satel, S. L., Becker, B. R., & Dan, E. (1993). Reducing obstacles to affiliation with Alcoholics Anonymous among veterans with PTSD and alcoholism. *Hospital and Community Psychiatry, 44,* 1061–1065.

Saunders, J. B., Aasland, O. G., Babor, T. F., de la Fuente, J. R., & Grant, M. (1993). Development of the Alcohol Use Disorders Identification Test (AUDIT): WHO Collaborative Project on Early Detection of Persons With Harmful Alcohol Consumption II. *Addiction, 88,* 791–804.

Schaefer, M. R., Sobieraj, K., & Hollyfield, R. L. (1988). Prevalence of childhood physical abuse in adult male veteran alcoholics. *Child Abuse & Neglect, 12,* 141–149.

Schafer, J., & Brown, S. A. (1991). Marijuana and cocaine effect expectancies and drug use patterns. *Journal of Consulting and Clinical Psychology, 59,* 558–565.

Schiraldi, G. R. (2000). *The post-traumatic stress disorder sourcebook.* Los Angeles: Lowell House.

Schnitt, J. M., & Nocks, J. J. (1984). Alcoholism treatment of Vietnam veterans with posttraumatic stress disorder. *Journal of Substance Abuse Treatment, 1,* 179–189.

Schnurr, P. P., Friedman, M. J., & Rosenberg, S. D. (1993). Preliminary MMPI scores as predictors of combat-related PTSD symptoms. *American Journal of Psychiatry, 150,* 479–483.

Schulkin, J., Gold, P. W., & McEwen, B. S. (1998). Induction of corticotropin-releasing hormone gene expression by glucocorticoids: Implication for understanding the states of fear and anxiety and allostatic load. *Psychoneuroendocrinology, 23,* 219–243.

Schwab-Stone, M. E., Ayers, T. S., Kasprow, W., Voyce, C., Barone, C., Shriver, T., & Weissberg, R. P. (1995). No safe haven: A study of violence exposure in an urban community. *Journal of the American Academy of Child and Adolescent Psychiatry, 34,* 1343–1352.

Segal, B. M., & Stewart, J. C. (1996). Substance use and abuse in adolescence: An overview. *Child Psychiatry and Human Development, 26,* 193–210.

Seghorn, T. K., Prentky, R. A., & Boucher, R. J. (1987). Childhood sexual abuse in the lives of sexually aggressive offenders. *Journal of the American Academy of Child and Adolescent Psychiatry, 26,* 262–267.

Selzer, M. L. (1971). The Michigan Alcohol Screening Test: The quest for a new diagnostic screening instrument. *American Journal of Psychiatry, 127,* 1653–1658.

Seto, M. C., & Barbaree, H. E. (1995). The role of alcohol in sexual aggression. *Clinical Psychology Review, 15,* 545–566.

Shafik, E. N., Aiken, S. P., & McArdle, J. J. (1991). Regional catecholamine levels in brains of normal and ethanol-tolerant long-sleep and short-sleep mice. *Brain Research, 563,* 44–48.

Shalev, A. Y. (1997). Treatment failure in acute PTSD: Lessons learned about the complexity of the disorder. In R. Yehuda & A. C. McFarlane (Eds.), *Psychobiology of posttraumatic stress disorder* (Vol. 821, pp. 372–387). New York: New York Academy of Sciences.

Shalev, A. Y., Peri, T., Gelpin, E., Orr, S. P., & Pitman, R. K. (1997). Psychophysiologic assessment of mental imagery of stressful events in Israeli civilian posttraumatic stress disorder patients. *Comprehensive Psychiatry, 38,* 269–273.

Shalev, A. Y., & Rogel-Fuchs, Y. (1993). Psychophysiology of the posttraumatic stress disorder: From sulfur fumes to behavioral genetics. *Psychosomatic Medicine, 55,* 413–423.

Shapiro, F. (1995). *Eye movement desensitization and reprocessing: Basic principles, protocols, and procedures.* New York: Guilford Press.

Sharkansky, E. J., Brief, D. J., Peirce, J. M., Meehan, J. C., & Mannix, L. M. (1999). Substance abuse patients with posttraumatic stress disorder (PTSD): Identifying specific triggers of substance use and their associations with PTSD symptoms. *Psychology of Addictive Behaviors, 13,* 89–97.

Sheridan, C. L., Mulhern, M. A., & Martin, D. (1999). The role of social desirability, negative affectivity, and female reproductive symptoms in differences in reporting symptoms by men and women. *Psychological Reports, 85,* 54–62.

Shiffman, S. (1988). Behavioral assessment. In D. M. Donovan & G. A. Marlatt (Eds.), *Assessment of addictive behaviors* (pp. 139–188). New York: Guilford Press.

Shin, L. M., Kosslyn, S. M., McNally, R. J., Alpert, N. M., Thompson, W. L., Rauch, S. L., et al. (1997). Visual imagery and perception in posttraumatic stress disorder: A positron emission tomographic investigation. *Archives of General Psychiatry, 54,* 233–241.

Sierles, F. S., Chen, J., McFarland, R. E., & Taylor, M. A. (1983). Posttraumatic stress disorder and concurrent psychiatric illness: A preliminary report. *American Journal of Psychiatry, 140,* 1177–1179.

Skinner, H. A. (1982). The Drug Abuse Screening Test. *Addictive Behaviors, 7,* 363–371.

Skre, I., Onstad, S., Torgersen, S., & Kringlen, T. (1991). High interrater reliability for the Structured Clinical Interview for the *DSM–III–R:* Axis I. *Acta Psychiatrica Scandinavica, 84,* 167–173.

Sobell, L. C., & Sobell, M. B. (1992). Timeline follow-back: A technique for assessing self-reported alcohol consumption. In R. Z. Litten & J. P. Allen (Eds.), *Measuring alcohol consumption: Psychosocial and biochemical methods* (pp. 41–72). Totowa, NJ: Humana Press.

Sobell, L. C., & Sobell, M. B. (1995). *Timeline Followback users' manual.* Toronto, Ontario, Canada: Addiction Research Foundation.

Solomon, S. D., & Davidson, J. R. T. (1997). Trauma: Prevalence, impairment, service use, and cost. *Journal of Clinical Psychiatry, 58*(Suppl. 9), 5–11.

Solomon, S. D., Gerrity, E. T., & Muff, A. M. (1992). Efficacy of treatments for posttraumatic stress disorder. *Journal of the American Medical Association, 268,* 633–638.

Southwick, S. M., Bremner, J. D., Rasmusson, A., Morgan, C. A., Arnsten, A., & Charney, D. S. (1999). Role of norepinephrine in the pathophysiology and treatment of posttraumatic stress disorder. *Biological Psychiatry, 46,* 1192–1204.

Southwick, S. M., Krystal, J. H., Morgan, C. A., Johnson, D., Nagy, L. M., Nicolaou, A., et al. (1993). Abnormal noradrenergic function in posttraumatic stress disorder. *Archives of General Psychiatry, 50,* 266–274.

Speed, N., Engdahl, B., Schwartz, J., & Eberly, R. (1989). Posttraumatic stress disorder as a consequence of the POW experience. *Journal of Nervous and Mental Disease, 177,* 147–153.

Spiegel, D. (1997). Trauma, dissociation, and memory. In R. Yehuda & A. C. McFarlane (Eds.), *Psychobiology of posttraumatic stress disorder* (Vol. 821, pp. 225–237). New York: New York Academy of Sciences.

Spitzer, R. L., Williams, J. B., & Gibbon, M. (1987). *Structured Clinical Interview for DSM–III–R.* New York: Biometrics Research Department, New York State Psychiatric Institute.

Spitzer, R. L., Williams, J. B. W., Gibbon, M., & First, M. B. (1990). *User's guide for the Structured Clinical Interview for DSM–III–R.* Washington, DC: American Psychiatric Association.

Spitzer, R. L., Williams, J. B. W., Gibbon, M., & First, M. B. (1992). The Structured Clinical Interview for *DSM–III–R*, I: History, rationale, and description. *Archives of General Psychiatry, 49,* 624–629.

Spunt, B. J., Goldstein, P. J., Bellucci, P. A., & Miller, T. (1990). Race/ethnicity and gender differences in the drugs–violence relationship. *Journal of Psychoactive Drugs, 22,* 293–303.

Steadman, H. J., Mulvey, E. P., Monahan, J., Robbins, P. C., Appelbaum, P. S., Grisso, T., et al. (1998). Violence by people discharged from acute psychiatric inpatient facilities and by others in the same neighborhoods. *Archives of General Psychiatry, 55,* 393–401.

Steiner, H., Garcia, I. G., & Matthews, Z. (1997). Posttraumatic stress disorder in incarcerated juvenile delinquents. *Journal of the American Academy of Child and Adolescent Psychiatry, 36,* 357–365.

Stewart, S. H. (1996). Alcohol abuse in individuals exposed to trauma: A critical review. *Psychological Bulletin, 120*, 83–112.

Stewart, S. H. (1997). Trauma memory and alcohol abuse: Drinking to forget? In J. D. Read & D. S. Lindsay (Eds.), *Recollections of trauma: Scientific evidence and clinical practice* (pp. 461–467). New York: Plenum.

Stewart, S. H., Conrod, P. J., Pihl, R. O., & Dongier, M. (1999). Relationships between posttraumatic stress symptom dimensions and substance dependence in a community-recruited sample of substance-abusing women. *Psychology of Addictive Behaviors, 13*, 78–88.

Stewart, S. H., Conrod, P. J., Samoluk, S. B., Pihl, R. O., & Dongier, M. (2000). Posttraumatic stress disorder symptoms and situation-specific drinking in women substance abusers. *Alcoholism Treatment Quarterly, 18*, 31–47.

Stewart, S. H., & Israeli, A. L. (2002). Substance abuse and co-occurring psychiatric disorders in victims of intimate violence. In C. Wekerle & A.-M. Wall (Eds.), *The violence and addiction equation: Theoretical and clinical issues in substance abuse and relationship violence* (pp. 98–122). New York: Brunner/Routledge.

Stewart, S. H., Ouimette, P., & Brown, P. J. (in press). Gender and the co-morbidity of PTSD with substance use disorders. In R. Kimerling, P. C. Ouimette, & J. Wolfe (Eds.), *Gender and PTSD*. New York: Guilford.

Stewart, S. H., & Pihl, R. O. (1994). Effects of alcohol administration on psycho-physiological and subjective–emotional responses to aversive stimulation in anxiety-sensitive women. *Psychology of Addictive Behaviors, 8*, 29–42.

Stewart, S. H., Pihl, R. O., Conrod, P. J., & Dongier, M. (1998). Functional associations among trauma, PTSD, and substance-related disorders. *Addictive Behaviors, 23*, 797–812.

Stewart, S. H., Rioux, G. F., Connolly, J. F., Dunphy, S. C., & Teehan, M. D. (1996). The effects of oxazepam and lorazepam on implicit and explicit memory: Evidence for possible influences of time course. *Psychopharmacology, 128*, 139–149.

Stewart, S. H., Samoluk, S. B., Conrod, P. J., Pihl, R. O., & Dongier, M. (2000). Psychometric evaluation of the short form Inventory of Drinking Situations (IDS–42) in a community-recruited sample of substance-abusing women. *Journal of Substance Abuse, 11*, 305–321.

Stewart, S. H., Samoluk, S. B., & MacDonald, A. B. (1999). Anxiety sensitivity and substance use and abuse. In S. Taylor (Ed.), *Anxiety sensitivity: Theory, research, and treatment of the fear of anxiety* (pp. 287–319). Mahwah, NJ: Erlbaum.

Stine, S. M., & Kosten, T. R. (1995). Complications of chemical abuse and dependency. In M. J. Friedman, D. S. Charney, & A. Y. Deutch (Eds.), *Neurobiological and clinical consequences of stress: From normal adaptation to PTSD* (pp. 447–464). Philadelphia: Lippincott-Raven.

Stockwell, T., & Bolderston, H. (1987). Alcohol and phobias. *British Journal of Addiction, 82*, 971–979.

Stritzke, W. G., Patrick, C. J., & Lang, A. R. (1995). Alcohol and human emotion: A multidimensional analysis incorporating startle probe methodology. *Journal of Abnormal Psychology, 104,* 114–122.

Stuart, J. A., & Halverson, R. R. (1997). The psychological status of U.S. Army soldiers during recent military operations. *Military Medicine, 162,* 737–743.

Summers, M. N., Hyer, L. A., Boyd, S., & Boudewyns, P. A. (1996). Diagnosis of later-life PTSD among elder combat veterans. *Journal of Clinical Geropsychology, 2,* 103–115.

Sutherland, S. M., & Davidson, J. R. T. (1999). Pharmacological treatment of posttraumatic stress disorder. In P. Saigh & D. Bremner (Eds.), *Posttraumatic stress disorder: A comprehensive text* (pp. 327–353). Boston: Allyn & Bacon.

Sutker, P. B., Allain, A. N., & Winstead, D. K. (1993). Psychopathology and psychiatric diagnoses of World War II Pacific theater prisoner of war survivors and combat veterans. *American Journal of Psychiatry, 150,* 240–245.

Sutker, P. B., Uddo, M., Brailey, K., Allain, A. N., & Errera, P. (1994). Psychological symptoms and psychiatric diagnoses in Operation Desert Storm troops serving graves registration duty. *Journal of Traumatic Stress, 7,* 159–171.

Sutker, P. B., Uddo, M., Brailey, K., Vasterling, J. J., & Errera, P. (1994). Psychopathology in war-zone deployed and nondeployed Operation Desert Storm troops assigned graves registration duties. *Journal of Abnormal Psychology, 103,* 383–390.

Sutker, P. B., Winstead, D. K., Galina, Z. H., & Allain, A. N. (1990). Assessment of long-term psychosocial sequelae among POW survivors of the Korean conflict. *Journal of Personality Assessment, 54,* 170–180.

Swanson, J. W. (1993). Alcohol abuse, mental disorder, and violent behavior. *Alcohol Health and Research World, 17,* 123–132.

Tarrier, N., Pilgrim, H., Sommerfield, C., Faragher, B., Reynolds, M., Graham, E., & Barrowclough, C. (1999). A randomized trial of cognitive therapy and imaginal exposure in the treatment of chronic posttraumatic stress disorder. *Journal of Consulting and Clinical Psychology, 67,* 13–18.

Taylor, S., Koch, W. J., & McNally, R. J. (1992). How does anxiety sensitivity vary across the anxiety disorders? *Journal of Anxiety Disorders, 6,* 249–259.

Teplin, L. A. (1994). Psychiatric and substance abuse disorders among male urban jail detainees. *American Journal of Public Health, 84,* 290–293.

Teplin, L. A., Abram, K. M., & McClelland, G. M. (1996). Prevalence of psychiatric disorders among incarcerated women: I. Pretrial jail detainees. *Archives of General Psychiatry, 53,* 505–512.

Thevos, A. K., Johnston, A. L., Latham, P. K., Randall, C. L., & Malcolm, R. (1991). Symptoms of anxiety in inpatient alcoholics with and without DSM–III–R anxiety diagnoses. *Alcoholism: Clinical and Experimental Research, 15,* 102–105.

Tolin, D. F., & Foa, E. B. (1999). Treatment of a police officer with PTSD using prolonged exposure. *Behavior Therapy, 30,* 527–538.

Triffleman, E., Carroll, K., & Kellogg, S. (1999). Substance dependence posttraumatic stress disorder therapy: An integrated cognitive–behavioral approach. *Journal of Substance Abuse Treatment, 17,* 3–14.

Triffleman, E. G., Marmar, C. R., Delucchi, K. L., & Ronfeldt, H. (1995). Childhood trauma and posttraumatic stress disorder in substance abuse inpatients. *Journal of Nervous and Mental Disease, 183,* 172–176.

Trotter, C. (1992). *Double bind.* Minneapolis, MN: Hazelden Press.

True, W. R., & Pitman, R. (1999). Genetics and posttraumatic stress disorder. In P. A. Saigh & J. D. Bremner (Eds.), *Posttraumatic stress disorder: A comprehensive text* (pp. 144–159). Boston: Allyn & Bacon.

U.S. Department of Justice, Bureau of Justice Statistics. (1994). *Women in prison: Survey of state prison inmates, 1991* (Rep. No. NCJ 145321). Washington, DC: U.S. Government Printing Office.

U.S. Department of Justice, Bureau of Justice Statistics. (1999a). *Substance abuse and treatment, state and federal prisoners, 1997* (Rep. No. NCJ 172871). Washington, DC: U.S. Government Printing Office.

U.S. Department of Justice, Bureau of Justice Statistics. (1999b). *Women offenders* (Rep. No. NCJ 175688). Washington, DC: U.S. Government Printing Office.

U.S. Department of Justice, Bureau of Justice Statistics. (2000a, May). *Criminal victimization in United States, 1998 statistical tables: National Crime Victimization Survey* (NCJ No. 181585). Retrieved June 22, 2000, from http://www.ojp.usdoj.gov/bjs/abstract/cvusst.htm

U.S. Department of Justice, Bureau of Justice Statistics. (2000b). *Drug use, testing, and treatment in jails* (Rep. No. NCJ 179999). Washington, DC: U.S. Government Printing Office.

Van der Kolk, B. A. (1987). *Psychological trauma.* Washington, DC: American Psychiatric Press.

Veterans Health Administration. (1999). *VA clinical practice guideline for the management of persons with substance use disorders, Version 1.0.* Washington, DC: Author.

Veysey, B. M. (1998). Specific needs of women diagnosed with mental illnesses in U.S. jails. In B. Levin, A. K. Blanch, & A. Jennings (Eds.), *Women's mental health services: A public health perspective* (pp. 368–389). Thousand Oaks, CA: Sage.

Vuchinich, R. E., Tucker, J. A., & Harllee, L. M. (1988). Behavioral assessment. In D. M. Donovan & G. A. Marlatt (Eds.), *Assessment of addictive behaviors* (pp. 51–83). New York: Guilford Press.

Wang M.-C., & Chang, S.-H. (1999). Nonparametric estimation of a recurrent survival function. *Journal of the American Statistical Association, 94,* 146–153.

Warner, L. A., Kessler, R. C., Hughes, M., Anthony, J. C., & Nelson, C. B. (1995). Prevalence and correlates of drug use and dependence in the United States: Results from the National Comorbidity Survey. *Archives of General Psychiatry, 52,* 219–229.

Warshaw, M. G., Fierman, E., Pratt, L., Hunt, M., Yonkers, K. A., Massion, A. O., & Keller, M. B. (1993). Quality of life and dissociation in anxiety disorder patients with histories of trauma or PTSD. *American Journal of Psychiatry, 150,* 1512–1516.

Washton, A. M., Stone, N. S., & Hendrickson, E. C. (1988). Cocaine abuse. In D. M. Donovan & G. A. Marlatt (Eds.), *Assessment of addictive behaviors* (pp. 364–389). New York: Guilford Press.

Weathers, F. W., & Keane, T. M. (1999). Psychological assessment of traumatized adults. In P. A. Saigh & J. D. Bremner (Eds.), *Posttraumatic stress disorder: A comprehensive text* (pp. 219–247). Boston: Allyn & Bacon.

Weathers, F. W., & Litz, B. T. (1994). Psychometric properties of the clinician-administered PTSD scale, CAPS–1. *PTSD Research Quarterly, 5*(2), 2–6.

Weathers, F. W., Litz, B. T., Herman, D. S., Huska, J. A., & Keane, T. M. (1993, October). *The PTSD Checklist (PCL): Reliability, validity, and diagnostic utility.* Paper presented at the annual meeting of the International Society for Traumatic Stress Studies, San Antonio, TX.

Weeks, R., & Widom, C. S. (1998). Self-reports of early childhood victimization among incarcerated adult male felons. *Journal of Interpersonal Violence, 13,* 346–361.

Weiler, B. L., & Widom, C. S. (1996). Psychopathy and violent behavior in abused and neglected young adults. *Criminal Behaviour & Mental Health, 6,* 253–271.

Weinberg, N. Z., Rahdert, E., Colliver, J. D., & Glantz, M. D. (1998). Adolescent substance abuse: A review of the past 10 years. *Journal of the American Academy of Child and Adolescent Psychiatry, 37,* 252–261.

Weinshenker, D., Rust, N. C., Miller, N. S., & Palmiter, R. D. (2000). Ethanol-associated behaviors of mice lacking norepinephrine. *Journal of Neuroscience, 20,* 3157–3164.

Weisner, C., McLellan, A. T., & Hunkeler, E. M. (2000). Addiction Severity Index data from general membership and treatment samples of HMO members: One case of norming the ASI. *Journal of Substance Abuse Treatment, 19,* 103–109.

Weiss, D. S. (1997). Structured clinical interview techniques. In J. P. Wilson & T. M. Keane (Eds.), *Assessing psychological trauma and PTSD* (pp. 493–511). New York: Guilford Press.

Weiss, R. D., & Najavits, L. M. (1997). Overview of treatment modalities for dual diagnosis patients: Pharmacotherapy, psychotherapy, twelve-step programs. In H. R. Kranzler & B. J. Rounsaville (Eds.), *Dual diagnosis: Substance abuse and comorbid medical and psychiatric disorders* (pp. 87–105). New York: Marcel Dekker.

Welle, D., Falkin, G. P., & Jainchill, N. (1998). Current approaches to drug treatment for women offenders. *Journal of Substance Abuse Treatment, 15,* 151–163.

Wells, E. A., Catalano, R. F., Plotnick, R., Hawkins, J. D., & Brattesani, K. A. (1989). General versus drug-specific coping skills and posttreatment drug use among adults. *Psychology of Addictive Behaviors, 3,* 8–21.

Wexler, H. K., De Leon, G., Thomas, G., Kressel, D., & Peters, J. (1999). The Amity prison TC evaluation: Reincarceration outcomes. *Criminal Justice and Behavior, 26*, 147–167.

Widom, C. S. (1989, April 14). The cycle of violence. *Science, 244*, 160–166.

Widom, C. S., & Morris, S. (1997). Accuracy of adult recollections of childhood victimization: Part 2. Childhood sexual abuse. *Psychological Assessment, 9*, 34–46.

Widom, C. S., & Shepard, R. L. (1996). Accuracy of adult recollections of childhood victimization: Part 1. Childhood physical abuse. *Psychological Assessment, 8*, 412–421.

Williams, J. B. W., Gibbon, M., First, M. B., Spitzer, R. L., Davies, M., Borus, J., et al. (1992). The Structured Clinical Interview for *DSM–III–R*. *Archives of General Psychiatry, 49*, 630–636.

Williams, L. M. (1994). Recall of childhood trauma: A prospective study of women's memories of child sexual abuse. *Journal of Consulting and Clinical Psychology, 62*, 1167–1176.

Windle, M. (1994). Substance use, risky behaviors, and victimization among a US national adolescent sample. *Addiction, 89*, 175–182.

Winfield, I., George, L. K., Swartz, M., & Blazer, D. G. (1990). Sexual assault and psychiatric disorders among a community sample of women. *American Journal of Psychiatry, 147*, 335–341.

Wolfe, J., Erickson, D. J., Sharkansky, E. J., King, D. W., & King, L. A. (1999). Course and predictors of posttraumatic stress disorder among Gulf War veterans: A prospective analysis. *Journal of Consulting and Clinical Psychology, 67*, 520–528.

Wolfe, J., & Kimerling, R. (1997). Gender issues in the assessment of posttraumatic stress disorder. In J. P. Wilson & T. M. Keane (Eds.), *Assessing psychological trauma and PTSD* (pp. 192–238). New York: Guilford Press.

Worling, J. R. (1995). Sexual abuse histories of adolescent male sex offenders: Differences on the basis of the age and gender of their victims. *Journal of Abnormal Psychology, 104*, 610–613.

Yehuda, R. (1997a). Sensitization of the hypothalamic–pituitary–adrenal axis in posttraumatic stress disorder. In R. Yehuda & A. C. McFarlane (Eds.), *Psychobiology of posttraumatic stress disorder* (Vol. 821, pp. 219–224). New York: New York Academy of Sciences.

Yehuda, R. (1997b, March 14). Stress and glucocorticoids. *Science, 275*, 1662–1663.

Yehuda, R., Keefe, R. S. E., Harvey, P. D., & Levengood, R. A. (1995). Learning and memory in combat veterans with posttraumatic stress disorder. *American Journal of Psychiatry, 152*, 137–139.

Yehuda, R., & McFarlane, A. C. (1995). Conflict between current knowledge about posttraumatic stress disorder and its original conceptual basis. *American Journal of Psychiatry, 152*, 1705–1713.

Yehuda, R., Schmeidler, J., Wainberg, M., Binder-Brynes, K., & Duvdevani, T. (1998). Vulnerability to posttraumatic stress disorder in adult offspring of Holocaust survivors. *American Journal of Psychiatry, 155,* 1163–1171.

Zack, M., Toneatto, T., & MacLeod, C. M. (1999). Implicit activation of alcohol concepts by negative affective cues distinguishes between problem drinkers with high and low psychiatric distress. *Journal of Abnormal Psychology, 108,* 518–531.

Zeger, S. L., & Liang, K.-Y. (1986). Longitudinal data analysis for discrete and continuous outcomes. *Biometrics, 42,* 121–130.

Zlotnick, C. (1997). Posttraumatic stress disorder (PTSD), PTSD comorbidity, and childhood abuse among incarcerated women. *Journal of Nervous and Mental Disease, 185,* 761–763.

Zlotnick, C. (1999). Antisocial personality disorder, affect dysregulation and child abuse among incarcerated women. *Journal of Personality Disorders, 13,* 90–95.

Zlotnick, C., Najavits, L. M., & Rohsenow, D. J. (2002). *A cognitive–behavioral treatment for incarcerated women with substance use disorder and posttraumatic stress disorder: Findings from a pilot study.* Manuscript submitted for publication.

Zlotnick, C., Warshaw, M., Shea, T. M., Allsworth, J., Pearlstein, T., & Keller, M. B. (1999). Chronicity in posttraumatic stress disorder (PTSD) and predictors of course of comorbid PTSD in patients with anxiety disorders. *Journal of Traumatic Stress, 12,* 89–100.

Zweben, J. E., Clark, H. W., & Smith, D. E. (1994). Traumatic experiences and substance abuse: Mapping the territory. *Journal of Psychoactive Drugs, 26,* 327–344.

AUTHOR INDEX

Birnbaum, S. M., 63
Blake, D. D., 98, 109, 114, 118, 140, 176, 177, 178, 199
Blanchard, E. B., 35, 36, 62, 113, 117
Blank, A. S., 195
Blazer, D. G., 119
Bloom, B., 214, 216, 218, 219, 224
Blouin, A. G., 115
Bolderston, H., 35
Boldizar, J. P., 238
Bollerud, K., 165
Bollinger, A. R., 118
Boney-McCoy, S., 230
Borchardt, C., 30
Boscarino, J. A., 13, 26–27
Boucher, R. J., 80
Boudewyns, P. A., 98, 192, 194, 201
Boyd, S., 194
Brady, K. T., 4, 32, 38, 46, 52, 60, 93, 94, 99, 101, 104, 105, 108, 110, 111, 113, 119, 127, 128, 138, 152, 155, 165, 179, 185, 234, 236, 239, 242
Brailey, K., 196
Branchey, L., 194
Brawman-Mintzer, O., 34
Bremner, J. D., 39, 62, 63, 93, 102, 120, 173
Breslau, N., 10, 11, 12, 13–14, 14, 15, 21, 22n, 23, 24, 25, 27, 31, 33, 36, 37, 38, 43, 186, 200, 227, 231, 238
Brewin, C. R., 79
Brick, J., 117
Bride, B. E., 155
Brief, D. J., 40, 118, 128, 173, 200, 201
Briggs, F., 80
Brindis, C., 224
Brinson, T., 128, 145, 185
Brismar, B., 81
Bromet, E., 9, 34, 91, 118, 153, 173, 214, 229
Brown, C. H., 81
Brown, G., 109
Brown, P. J., 3, 4, 21, 38, 39, 45, 46, 49, 91, 92, 93, 94, 100, 103, 104, 106, 108, 109, 121, 123, 127, 128, 152, 171, 173, 174, 185, 186, 227, 236, 237, 239, 240, 241, 243
Brown, S. A., 39, 109

Browne, A., 216, 218, 219, 220, 224
Browne, D. C., 86
Browne, K. D., 86
Buccio-Notaro, P., 224
Buckley, T. C., 113
Buka, S. L., 229, 231, 233, 236, 237, 238, 239, 240, 241, 242
Burke, J. D., 228
Burke, K. C., 228
Bushman, B. J., 85
Butler, R. W., 59
Butzin, C. A., 210
Byrne, C. A., 83, 110

Caddell, J. M., 98, 129, 211, 213n
Cameron, R., 141
Cameron, R. P., 202
Campeau, S., 60
Capstick, C., 167
Carlson, E. B., 114
Carnevale, G. J., 103
Carpenter, G., 164
Carroll, K., 94, 128, 162, 163, 165, 240
Carroll, K. M., 52, 97, 135, 138, 155, 165, 187
Carver, C. S., 48, 177
Cashman, L., 113
Cauffman, E., 213, 214, 216
Centers for Disease Control and Prevention (CDC), 192, 229, 236, 238
Chaffin, M., 86
Chang, S.-H., 27
Charney, D. S., 34, 59, 65, 93, 120, 173
Chemtob, C. M., 202
Chen, J., 192
Chermack, S. T., 84, 85
Chesney-Lind, M., 218, 219, 221
Chilcoat, H. D., 12, 14, 15, 21, 22n, 23, 24, 25, 27, 31, 33, 36, 37, 38, 238
Chrestman, K. R., 104, 118, 197
Chu, J. A., 152, 155, 162
Clark, D. B., 231, 232, 233, 234, 236, 237, 239, 241
Clark, H. W., 94, 202
Clark, J. P., 79
Classen, C., 102
Clayson, Z., 224
Cloitre, M., 119
Clum, G. A., 98, 130, 133

Graham, J. M., 40
Grant, I., 35
Grant, M., 114
Gray, J. A., 61, 67
Greeley, J., 136
Green, B. L., 112, 227
Greene, S., 214, 216, 219, 221
Griffiths, R. R., 69
Griger, M. L., 92
Grillon, C., 59
Gross, D. M., 202
Grossman, H., 85
Grossman, L. S., 200
Groth, A. N., 80
Guidry, L., 165
Gurvits, T. V., 61
Gusman, F. D., 199

Halvorson, R. R., 196
Hamada, R. S., 202
Hamilton, C. E., 86
Haney, C., 214
Hankin, C. S., 197, 200, 206
Hankins, G. C., 80
Hansen, D. J., 81, 103, 174
Harllee, L. M., 121
Harralson, T. L., 77
Hart, S. D., 80
Hartnick, E., 232
Harvey, E. M., 51
Harvey, P. D., 61
Hawkins, R. M. F., 80
Heather, N., 136
Hegedus, A. M., 231
Helzer, J. E., 10, 12, 16, 115
Henderson, D. J., 216, 219, 220
Henderson, R. G., 124
Hendrickson, E. C., 117
Heney, J., 222
Herman, D. S., 109, 113
Herman, J. L., 151, 154, 155, 162, 164, 200
Herrmann, N., 194, 195
Hertzberg, M. A., 84
Hickling, E. J., 35, 36
Hien, D., 110, 167
Hijzen, T. H., 60
Hill, J., 115
Hill, S., 196
Hiller, M. L., 210, 221

Hillman, A., 117
Hoffman, K., 111
Hollenberg, J., 86
Hollyfield, R. L., 200
Holt, J. C., 210
Hopper, J., 81
Hops, H., 228
Horowitz, M. J., 142
Hotaling, G. T., 85
Houtzager, S. W., 60
Hughes, M., 9, 23, 34, 91, 118, 153, 173, 214, 227, 229
Hulsey, T. L., 77
Humphreys, K., 188
Hunkeler, E. M., 116
Hurley, D. L., 128, 145
Hurtado, A., 214
Huska, J. A., 109, 113
Huttunen, P., 64
Hwang, B. H., 64
Hyer, L. A., 98, 192, 194, 201

Imhof, J. E., 121
Inciardi, J. A., 210
Innis, R. B., 63
International Society for Traumatic Stress Studies (ISTSS), 100, 107
Iowa Persian Gulf Study Group, 196
Israeli, A. L., 30
Ito, J. R., 174

Jacob, F., 169
Jainchill, N., 214
Janca, A., 10, 119, 227
Janoff-Bulman, R., 153
Jaycox, L., 102, 113
Jenkins, E. J., 238
Jensen, C. F., 63
Johanson, C. E., 59, 70
Johnson, C. R., 214, 216
Johnson, D. R., 96
Johnson, E. M., 85
Johnson, R. A., 227
Johnston, A. L., 109
Johnston, L. D., 227, 238
Jones, W. J., 187
Jones-Alexander, J., 113
Joordens, R. J., 60

Molla, B., 224
Monti, P. M., 123, 135, 163, 174, 187
Moore, J. D., 59, 84
Moos, R. H., 4, 38, 46, 47, 49, 92, 93,
    95, 96, 100, 110, 122, 128, 172,
    174, 188, 198, 199, 204, 239, 240
Morgan, C. A. III, 59, 196
Morris, S., 79
Morrison, S., 79
Morrissey, C., 84
Morrissey, E. R., 35
Morse, E., 69
Morse, P. A., 136
Mowrer, O. A., 129
Mueller, T., 4, 46, 92, 100, 127, 128, 171
Muenz, L. R., 51, 52, 94, 98, 104, 110,
    138, 145, 147, 202, 223
Muff, A. M., 98, 155
Mulhern, M. A., 122
Mullen, P., 79
Mulvey, K., 116
Munsoo, K., 60
Muraoka, M. Y., 202
Murdock, T. B., 98, 129, 186
Murphy, R. T., 202
Murrin, M. R., 214
Muss, D., 155

Nace, E. P., 49
Najavits, L. M., 3, 4, 12, 34, 51, 52, 91,
    92, 93, 94, 97, 98, 101, 104, 108,
    110, 113, 116, 118, 119, 123,
    127, 128, 134, 135, 138, 139,
    143, 145, 147, 151, 152, 153,
    154, 155, 156, 157, 159n, 160,
    160n, 162, 163, 164, 166, 167,
    168, 169, 173, 178, 179, 186,
    202, 223, 227, 237, 239, 240
Nash, M. R., 77
National Crime Victims Research and
    Treatment Center, 136
Navaline, H., 136
Navarro, J. R., 115
Nelson, C. B., 9, 23, 34, 91, 118, 153,
    173, 186, 214, 227, 229
Nelson, R., 200
Nelson-Zlupko, L., 188
Nemeroff, C. B., 62
Newcomb, M. D., 227, 235, 239
Newman, C. F., 162

Newman, E., 84, 200
Nezu, A. M., 103
Nocks, J. J., 49, 102
Noel, N., 188
Norris, F. H., 112, 113, 114, 178, 179,
    200, 227
North, C. S., 11, 13, 26, 37
Noshirvani, H., 129, 155
Novaco, R. W., 140, 202
Novick, R. W., 134

Obert, J. L., 51
Ochberg, F., 155
O'Farrell, T. J., 118
Oliver, B., 60
O'Malley, P. M., 227
O'Malley, S. S., 59
Onstad, I., 115
Orr, S. P., 58, 60, 117
Orsillo, S. M., 196, 200
O'Shea, M., 79
Otilingam, Poorni, 91n
Otto, M. W., 41
Ouimette, P. C., 3, 4, 5, 38, 46, 47, 48,
    49, 82, 86, 92, 93, 94, 95, 96,
    103, 104, 110, 118, 119, 122,
    123, 127, 128, 172, 173, 174,
    185, 186, 188, 197, 198, 199,
    201, 204, 205, 227, 239, 240
Owen, B., 214, 216, 218, 219, 224

Padin-Rivera, E., 99, 165, 187, 199
Pakiz, B., 227
Pallmeyer, T. P., 117
Palmiter, R. D., 64
Parrish, S. K., 227, 235
Pashko, S., 194
Patrick, C. J., 59, 60, 61
Patterson, C., 164
Patterson, T. L., 35
Pearlman, L. A., 152
Peck, R., 94, 120, 152
Peck, R. F., 103
Peirce, J. M., 40, 128, 173, 201
Penk, W., 199
Penk, W. E., 103
Perconte, S. T., 92
Peri, T., 60

SUBJECT INDEX

Behavioral contracts, 122
Behavioral Therapies Development Program of National Institute on Drug Abuse, 147
Biological assessment methods, 116–118
Brain structures
and pathophysiology of PTSD, 61
See also Amygdala; Hippocampus; Prefrontal cortex
Breath-analysis tests, 117
Brief motivational coping skills intervention, 53, 55

CAPS (Clinician-Administered PTSD Scale), 109, 114, 140, 176–177
Case example of exposure-based treatment (C.W.), 142–143
Case study, composite (Frank), 74–77, 86–87
Causal relations underlying PTSD–SUD comorbidity, 29–30
Censoring, 23
Childhood sexual abuse, and alcohol problems, 41–42
Childhood trauma, 77
invisible cases of, 88
and PTSD, 73, 77
and substance abuse, 77
and violence, 78–83
Client appropriateness, in exposure therapy, 133–135
Client perceptions. *See* Patient perceptions
Clinical care, for veterans, 200–204
Clinical guidelines, for exposure-based therapy, 143–144
Clinical interviews, structured, 114–116
Clinical studies, potential for bias in, 10
Clinical Trials Network of National Institute on Drug Abuse, 168
Clinician-Administered PTSD Scale (CAPS), 109, 114, 140, 176–177
Cognitive avoidance, and PTSD–SUD relation, 48, 174–175
Cognitive–behavioral treatments (therapy) (CBT)
for PTSD, 97
and "Seeking Safety" treatment, 153, 162, 163–164

Collateral information, in assessment, 118
Combat veterans
and corticotropin releasing factor (CRF), 62
family members of, 42, 43
and military culture, 122
modified relapse prevention program for, 97
and patient perceptions, 39
and PTSD, 16, 192
and PTSD identification, 96
PTSD and SUD among, 92, 173
and PTSD–violence relationship, 83–84
studies of, 26–27
in temporality study, 34
See also Veterans; Vietnam War veterans
Combined SUD–PTSD treatment, 51–53, 97–98
Communication, in care for veterans, 203
Comorbidity, ix
Comorbidity, SUD–PTSD, xi, 3–4
and continuation of PTSD, 185–186
empirically based practice for, 108–110
exposure-based therapy for, 128–129
case example in (C.W.), 142–143
clinical guidelines for, 143–144
Concurrent Treatment of PTSD and Cocaine Dependence (CTPCD), 135–140
and exposure therapy for PTSD, 129–135
future directions for, 145–146
Substance Dependence PTSD Therapy (SDPT), 140–142
future directions in assessment and treatment of, 243–245
and gender, 173–174
implications of studies of, 100–101
among incarcerated women, 217
and alternatives to incarceration, 224
treatment for, 220–224
models of, 92–93
onset vs. maintenance of, 38
poor treatment outcome in, 127–128
prevalence of, 91–92

Korean War veterans, 193–195

Language, common, 123
Life-span perspective, xii
Life Stressor Checklist—Revised, 176
Locus ceoruleus noradrenergic (LC/NE)
      activity, 62
Longitudinal studies
      of adolescents, 239, 244
      data analytic strategies for, 27
      need for, 27
      on rape and assault, 35–36
      on temporality, 35

Male inmates, 210
Manual-based psychotherapy protocol, 99
Mean corpuscular volume (MCV), 117
Mediators, PTSD symptoms as, 41–42
Memory network model, 68–70, 71
Michigan Alcoholism Screening Test,
      102, 114
Military culture, and combat veterans,
      122
Motivational enhancement therapy, 164
Motivational factors, 47
Mourning, in "Seeking Safety" program,
      151
Murrah Federal Building bombing, Okla-
      homa City, 26, 37

Narcotics Anonymous, 203
National Comorbidity Survey, 34, 229
National Institute on Alcohol Abuse and
      Alcoholism, 135
National Institute on Drug Abuse, 135
      Behavioral Therapies Development
      Program of, 147
      Clinical Trials Network of, 168
National Institute on Drug Abuse Collab-
      orative Cocaine Treatment
      Study, 138
National Vietnam Veterans Readjust-
      ment Study, 191, 197
National Women's Study PTSD Module,
      114–115
Natural experiments, 11
      disaster as, 25–26

Naturalistic studies, 94
      of SUD–PTSD patients' treatment
      outcomes, 94–97
      National Survey of Adolescents,
      19–21
      National Women's Study, 19
      NCS, 14, 17–18
      on World Wide Web, 28
Neuroendocrine studies, 61–65
Neuropsychological and neuroimaging
      studies, 61
Numbing symptoms for PTSD, and levels
      of SUD symptoms, 33
Nurses, and SUD–PTSD veterans, 206

Oklahoma City bombing, 26, 37
Onset
      as first use vs. development of prob-
      lems, 17, 35
      patterns of in adolescents, 232–234
Options for Recovery (OFR), 224
Outcome assessment, 124
Outpatient men, in "Seeking Safety" pro-
      gram, 167–168
Outpatient mental health care, 110

Paradox of countertransference, 154–155
Patient handout, for "Seeking Safety"
      treatment, 157, 158–159
Patient perceptions
      of functional relations between
      PTSD and SUD, 38–39
      in assessment, 121
      of potential of depressant vs. stimu-
      lant drugs, 39
Patient-related barriers to treatment, 106,
      121
PE (therapy), 136
Peacekeeping missions, veterans of, 50,
      196
Physicians, primary care, and SUD–
      PTSD veterans, 206
Posttraumatic Stress Diagnostic Scale
      (PDS), 113
Posttraumatic stress disorder (PTSD), 3
      in adolescents with SUD, 231 (see
      also Adolescents)
      and alcohol abuse, 36, 41–42, 195
      assessment of

through psychophysiological
methods, 116–117
through self-report instruments,
113
through structured clinical interviews, 114–115
and substance abuse treatment
programs, 128
and withdrawal symptoms, 111–
112
and childhood trauma, 73
and comorbidity, xi
in composite case study (Frank),
75–76
and coping style, 103
as dependent on occurrence of traumatic event, 44
diagnostic criteria (symptom clusters) for, 3, 101–103
elevated startle response, 59
exposure therapy for, 129–135
guidelines for, 107–108
among incarcerated women, 213
prevalence of, 91–92
specific treatments for, 165
in SUD–PTSD study, 178–179
symptoms vs. general diagnosis of,
188
and violent behavior, 73, 77, 83–84
See also Comorbidity, SUD–PTSD;
at PTSD
Prefrontal cortex, 63, 70
and alcohol, 64, 67
and hippocampus, 65
Prevalence estimates 13–14
Primary care physicians, and SUD–PTSD
veterans, 206
Prison, women in. See Incarcerated
women
Prisoners of war, 43, 194
Process, and "Seeking Safety" treatment,
154
Prognoses, of comorbid SUD–PTSD,
101–105
and additional comorbidities, 104
Project MATCH, 135
Project WORTH (Women's Options for
Recovery, Treatment and
Health), 220–221
Prospective studies, 21–25, 27
Provider issues, in assessment, 123

Provider-related barriers to treatment,
105–106
Psychiatric disorders, among incarcerated
women, 213–215
Psychiatric distress
as PTSD indicator, 185
among PTSD patients, 179
and PTSD remission, 182
and PTSD–SUD combination, 48
as relapse predictor, 172
Psychiatric patients, and substance
abuse–violence relationship, 85
Psychological connectedness, patients'
perceptions of, 38–39
Psychological debriefing, 50
Psychological impairment, and PTSD–
SUD combination, 48
Psychophysiological assessment methods,
116–117
Psychophysiological studies, 59–61
Psychosocial functioning, and comorbid
SUD–PTSD (adolescents), 234–
235
Psychosocial models of functional associations between PTSD and SUD,
30–31, 53–55, 57–58
among adolescents, 236–237
and family studies, 42–44
gradient of effect, 31–33, 60
patient perceptions, 38–39
PTSD symptoms as mediators,
41–42
role of anxiety sensitivity, 41
situational specificity, 39–40
temporality, 33–38
treatment studies, 45–53
P300 abnormalities, 58–59
PTSD. See Posttraumatic stress disorder
PTSD checklist, 12
PTSD Checklist, 108–109, 113
PTSD outcome, studies assessing effect of
comorbid SUDs on, 172–173
PTSD remission, factors associated with,
181–183
PTSD Symptom Scale—Self-Report
(PSS—SR), 102, 108, 113
PTSD symptoms as mediators, 41–42

Quotation, in "Seeking Safety" session,
160

Racial group, and SUD–PTSD prevalence rates for incarcerated women, 214–215
Rape
    and alcohol, 86
    in family study, 43
    longitudinal study on, 35–36
    in NCS, 17–18
    PE therapy for, 136
Reconnection, in "Seeking Safety" program, 151
Recovery, as complex notion, 169
Referral
    for concurrent trauma/PTSD treatment, 109–110
    to self-help groups or family treatment, 110
Relapse
    higher risk for, 105
    minimizing of, 122–123
    and psychiatric distress, 172
    and treatment studies, 45, 46, 52
Relapse prevention
    for combat veterans, 97
    and coping strategies, 174
Relapse prevention treatment (RPT), 167
Relative risk, 21
Remission rates, and time since traumatic event, 186
Research
    epidemiological, 9–11 (see also Epidemiological studies of SUD–PTSD comorbidity)
    as hampered by schism between PTSD and SUD fields, 4
    on "Seeking Safety" treatment, 166–168
Research, future
    on adolescent SUD–PTSD comorbidity, 27, 237–240
    avenues recommended for, 244–245
    on different combinations of treatments, 55
    and epidemiological studies, 27
    family studies, 44
    for "Seeking Safety" treatment, 168–169
Revictimization
    and in vivo exposure, 132
    and women, 223
Revised DIS, 17

Role models, in "Seeking Safety" session, 161
Role play, in "Seeking Safety" session, 161
Running away, in mediating of childhood victimization and delinquency, 82

Safety, in "Seeking Safety" treatment, 148
SCID (Structured Clinical Interview for DSM—IV), 115
    PTSD module of, 115, 177
    SUD module of, 177
    Screening
    of adolescents, 241
    for PTSD, 124, 185
    of SUD patients, 108–109
        tests for, 102, 114
    of veterans, 205–206
SDPT (Substance Dependence PTSD Therapy), 99, 140–142, 165
"Seeking Safety" treatment, 51–52, 97–98, 147–155, 223
    areas omitted from, 155–156
    conducting of session in, 160–162
    development of, 162–163
    format of, 156–159
    future work on, 168–169
    for incarcerated women, 222–224
    vs. other treatments, 163–165
    patient selection for, 159–160
    and veterans, 202
Selection bias, 10
Self-help groups, 96, 100
    referral to, 110
    See also 12-step groups
Self-medication, 30, 57, 73
    in composite case study (Frank), 75
    for hyperarousal symptoms, 60–61
    and PTSD–SUD functional relation, 30, 35
    among Vietnam veterans, 103
Self-medication hypothesis or theory, 21, 23, 24, 25, 92, 243
    for adolescents, 237
    and criminality, 218–219
    and data on temporality, 37
    and intrusive memories, 68

ABOUT THE EDITORS

Paige Ouimette is associate professor of psychology at Washington State University (WSU) in Pullman. Prior to WSU, she was a research associate at the Center for Health Care Evaluation at the Veterans Affairs (VA) Palo Alto Health Care System and a consulting assistant professor of psychiatry and behavioral sciences at Stanford University School of Medicine. Dr. Ouimette received a BA from SUNY Binghamton and a PhD from SUNY Stony Brook, and she completed an internship/fellowship at the Boston VA Medical Center's National Center for Post-Traumatic Stress Disorder (PTSD). Her research interests are in evaluating treatment course and identifying effective practices for PTSD and substance use disorder comorbidity. She also is conducting research aimed at understanding etiologic processes in PTSD and comorbid conditions, including physical health problems. She recently completed a VA-funded Young Investigator Award to study the role of PTSD in the physical health of men and women. She teaches courses on psychopathology, assessment, and human sexuality. Dr. Ouimette maintains a clinical practice in Pullman.

Pamela J. Brown is a clinical psychologist in private practice in New Bedford, Massachusetts. Since 1994 she has been assistant professor at Brown University, affiliated with the Department of Psychiatry and Human Behavior. Dr. Brown received a BA from Bates College and a PhD in clinical psychology from Clark University. She completed her predoctoral internship at the Boston VA Medical Center and a two-year postdoctoral fellowship in addictive behaviors at Brown University's Center for Alcohol and Addiction Studies. Dr. Brown recently completed a FIRST Award funded by the National Institute on Alcohol Abuse and Alcoholism to study prospectively the course of substance use–PTSD comorbidity among men and women seeking addiction treatment. Her primary research interests include the course and treatment of substance use–PTSD comorbidity and concomitant gender issues in treatment.